Faulkner and the Black Litera

FAULKNER AND YOKN.

2013

Faulkner and the Black Literatures of the Americas

FAULKNER AND YOKNAPATAWPHA, 2013

EDITED BY
JAY WATSON
AND
JAMES G. THOMAS, JR.

UNIVERSITY PRESS OF MISSISSIPPI
JACKSON

www.upress.state.ms.us

The University Press of Mississippi is a member of the Association of American
University Presses.

Material from Lisa Hinrichsen's essay "Contemporary Black Writing and Southern Social Belonging:
Beyond the Faulknerian Shadow of Loss" appeared previously in her "Writing Past Trauma: Faulkner
and the Gothic," in *William Faulkner in Context*, ed. John T. Matthews (New York: Cambridge
University Press, 2015), 219–27. Reprinted with permission.

Material from Andrew B. Leiter's essay "Miscegenation and Progression: The First Americans of
Jean Toomer and William Faulkner" appeared previously in his *In the Shadow of the Black Beast:
African American Masculinity in the Harlem and Southern Renaissances* (Baton Rouge: Louisiana
State University Press, 2010) and has been substantially revised here.

The following poems by Jamaal May have been previously published and are reprinted here with the
permission of the author: "Ruin," *New Republic* 244, no. 19 (November 25, 2013): 55, and "They May
Come to Break Us," *The MacGuffin*, 23, no. 3 (Spring–Summer 2007): 22.

Material from Tim A. Ryan's essay "'Go to Jail about This Spoonful': Narcotic Determinism and
Human Agency in 'That Evening Sun' and 'A Spoonful Blues'" appeared in an earlier version in his
book *Yoknapatawpha Blues: Faulkner's Fiction and Southern Roots Music* (Baton Rouge: Louisiana
State University Press, 2015) and is reprinted with permission.

First printing 2016
∞
Library of Congress Cataloging-in-Publication Data

Names: Faulkner and Yoknapatawpha Conference (40th : 2013 : University of
Mississippi) | Watson, Jay, editor. | Thomas, James G., Jr., editor.
Title: Faulkner and the black literatures of the Americas : Faulkner and
Yoknapatawpha, 2013 / edited by Jay Watson, James G. Thomas.
Description: Jackson : University Press of Mississippi, 2016. | Series:
Faulkner and Yoknapatawpha | Papers presented at the fortieth Faulkner and
Yoknapatawpha Conference, sponsored by the University of Mississippi, held
from July 21–25, 2013. | Includes bibliographical references and index.
Identifiers: LCCN 2015042215 (print) | LCCN 2016001779 (ebook) | ISBN
9781496806345 (hardback) | ISBN 9781496806352 (epub single) | ISBN
9781496806369 (epub institutional) | ISBN 9781496806376 (pdf single) |
ISBN 9781496806383 (pdf institutional)
Subjects: LCSH: Faulkner, William, 1897–1962—Criticism and
interpretation—Congresses. | Yoknapatawpha County (Imaginary
place)—Congresses. | American literature—African American
authors—History and criticism—Congresses. | Caribbean literature
(English)—Black authors—History and criticism—Congresses. | Faulkner,
William, 1897–1962—Influence—Congresses. | African Americans in
literature—Congresses. | Race in literature—Congresses. | BISAC:
LITERARY CRITICISM / American / General. | LITERARY COLLECTIONS / American
/ General.
Classification: LCC PS3511.A86 Z78321137 2013 (print) | LCC PS3511.A86
(ebook) | DDC 813/.52—dc23
LC record available at http://lccn.loc.gov/2015042215

British Library Cataloging-in-Publication Data available

Contents

Introduction

Let's begin by turning the calendar back to 1945. In the midst of one of his more demoralizing stints in Hollywood, William Faulkner sits down at the typewriter to compose a letter of appreciation and encouragement to a younger writer and Mississippian whose latest publication is enjoying Book of the Month Club recognition and sales that put those of Faulkner's own books to shame. "Dear Richard Wright," the letter begins, "I have just read *Black Boy*. It needed to be said, and you said it well."[1] No effusiveness here, no hyperbole, just the even-tempered tone in which an established author offers affirmation to a fellow practitioner of the craft. Almost immediately, though, the tone shifts, to something more like that of a master addressing an apprentice, or perhaps a white southerner addressing a black southerner in the 1940s.

> You said it well, as well as it could have been said in this form. Because I think you said it much better in *Native Son*. I hope you will keep on saying it, but I hope you will say it as an artist, as in *Native Son*. (201)

Perhaps these are simply the words of a writer more temperamentally suited to fiction than to the somewhat more undisguised forms of self-revelation that characterize autobiography and memoir. Or perhaps they express the white southerner's discomfort when a black-authored story of African American anger and disillusionment is set close to home, in Mississippi, Arkansas, and Memphis, rather than in a reassuringly remote locale such as Chicago. Margaret Walker claims that Wright framed Faulkner's letter and placed it over his writing desk, but one suspects that this response to the qualified note of approval voiced by a figure who loomed large on his literary landscape must have been accompanied by ambivalence.[2]

Fast forward to 1953. Ralph Ellison is at the offices of his publisher in New York on the morning he is to receive the National Book Award for *Invisible Man*. As he sets the scene for his friend Albert Murray, in a letter reproduced in the *Trading Twelves* volume, he writes,

Saxe Commins told me to come place my coat in his office and meet Bill Faulkner. So I went in and there, amid several bags (suitcases, man suitcases!) was the great man. You've heard that crap about his beat-up clothes? Well, don't believe it. He's as neat as a pin. A fine cashmere sports jacket, tattersall vest, suede shoes and fine slacks, the correct tie and shirt collar rolling down! And I mean *down* down. Saxe says, "Bill, I want you to meet Ralph Ellison. He's one of our writers who's won the National Book Award."

"Glad to meet you, Mr. Ellison," Faulkner says.

"Well, Mr. Faulkner, this really completes the day for me," I said.[3]

Note the cordial, dignified exchange of "Misters" that complements the knowing salute to Faulkner's sartorial hipness. Ellison continues,

"You know," I said, "you have children all around now. You won't be proud of all of them, just the same they're around."

"Yes," Faulkner said, "I was surprised to learn how many people like the stuff."

"You shouldn't be at all surprised," I said. (45)

Despite Ellison's disclaimer that this was a "lame note" on which to conclude the conversation, the exchange speaks volumes. But this is far from the only note sounded on Faulkner in *Trading Twelves*. Of the Nobel Laureate's 1956 letter to *Life* magazine advocating a gradualist approach to desegregation, Ellison wrote Murray,

Faulkner has delusions of grandeur because he really believes that he invented these characteristics which he ascribes to Negroes in his fiction and now he thinks he can end this great historical action just as he ends a dramatic action in one of his novels with Joe Christmas dead and his balls cut off by a man not nearly as worthy as himself; Hightower musing, the Negroes scared, and everything just as it was except for the brooding, slightly overblown rhetoric of Faulkner's irony. Nuts! (117)

Murray's response was less measured. Replying to Ellison a month later, he wrote,

Sad, pitiful, and stupid thing for a writer like that to do. That underdog shit makes me puke. How can a son of a bitch sit up and fuckup morality like that? . . . Son of a bitch prefers a handful of anachronistic crackers to everything that really gives him a reason not only for being but for writing. I'm watching his ass but close forevermore. Imagine a fatass travelling all around the world selling humanity for the State Dept and then going back home pulling that kind of crap at the first sign of real progress. (125)

The graphic language, and the affective intensity it signals, are entirely to the point here. Beyond mere disappointment, there is a clear sense of betrayal at work as Murray and Ellison grapple with the public pronouncements of a writer whose art they obviously admire.

These encounters and exchanges begin—but can only begin—to capture the depth, range, and tonalities of the dialogue between the Faulkner oeuvre and the black literatures of the Americas. Unfolding primarily between and among authors, they do not yet put text in conversation with text. Transacted among contemporaries, they cannot reveal the complexities of Faulkner's relationship to his black literary ancestors, nor get at the meaning of his legacy for today's black artists, working a half-century after his death. Conducted exclusively among men, they cannot account for the lines of force running between Faulkner's work and that of the black women writers who published before, alongside, and after him. And as exclusively American affairs, they give us little insight into how writers of color from the Caribbean and other regions of the hemisphere have responded to Faulkner's writings, and he to theirs. The essays collected in this volume attempt to extend the discussion in all of these important directions. They also aim to take the conversation beyond the admittedly compelling but also limiting question of influence—who read whom, whose works draw from whose—to explore the confluences between Faulkner's writings and black writing in the Americas: the common questions framed in these bodies of work, the responses to common problems, precursors, and events.

Faulkner didn't make it easy for the critic seeking to trace these connections. Throughout his career, he was remarkably reticent about the black writers and intellectuals who shaped his outlook and sensibility. Combing his published letters, interviews, and public statements for acknowledgments of his debts to, affinities with, or interest in black authors, one finds precious little to go on. In addition to his 1945 letter to Wright, Faulkner wrote two letters to the poet, editor, and critic William Stanley Braithwaite in February 1927, asking for advice about recovering unpaid royalties from the Four Seas Company, publisher of *The Marble Faun* (*Selected Letters*, 35–36). It's by no means certain, however, that Faulkner was even aware that Braithwaite, a leading literary tastemaker who had published Faulkner in a poetry anthology of 1925, was African American. Faulkner's 1956 telegram to W. E. B. Du Bois declining an invitation to debate the issue of racial integration was published in the *New York Times* and widely reprinted in the black press (398). Nor are the four volumes of Faulkner's interviews, class conferences, and other conversations any more forthcoming. Again the figure singled out for most attention is Richard Wright, though with the same reservations voiced in the letter of 1945. In a 1955 interview, Faulkner alludes to "others" on the black literary scene "that don't have the talent" of Wright or Ralph Ellison, but he never names these lesser writers.[4] This is the extent of Faulkner's public assessment of black literary achievement in the Americas.

Yet when we turn to his fiction, we see abundant evidence of a much wider, deeper, and more sustained engagement with black literary predecessors and cohorts. Certainly, *Native Son* loomed large in Faulkner's imagination from the moment of its publication in 1940. Almost immediately afterward, we start to encounter a series of Faulkner characters that represent creative approximations (if not outright appropriations) of the Bigger Thomas figure: African Americans who are incarcerated for the murder (or suspected murder) of whites and who go on to mount disturbing racial performances from the space of the jail cell. The list begins with Rider, from the 1940 story "Pantaloon in Black" (later revised for *Go Down, Moses*), continues with Butch Beauchamp of "Go Down, Moses" (like Bigger, a resident of the Chicago area when he commits homicide) and with Butch's grandfather Lucas Beauchamp in 1948's *Intruder in the Dust*, and arguably culminates in 1951 with *Requiem for a Nun*'s Nancy Mannigoe, who like Bigger ends the life of an elite white daughter in the girl's own bedroom, the very citadel of white domestic space, and later engages in gripping jailhouse conversations with the girl's mother and the attorney for the defense.

But Faulkner didn't have to wait until 1940 to awaken to the creative power and literary uses of black writing. His explorations of the mixed-race figure and the passing narrative in characters like Joe Christmas from *Light in August* and Charles and Valery Bon from *Absalom, Absalom!* owe a clear debt not only to Mark Twain's *Pudd'nhead Wilson* and other white-authored passing and tragic mulatto tales but to a black tradition as well that includes Frances E. W. Harper, Pauline Hopkins, Charles Chesnutt, and—in the period of Faulkner's own emergence as a novelist—Jean Toomer's *Cane* (1923), James Weldon Johnson's reissue of *The Autobiography of an Ex-Colored Man* (1927), and Nella Larsen's *Passing* (1929). It seems most unlikely that Faulkner would have been unaware of Toomer's work when they shared a publisher (Horace Liveright) and when both placed poems in the *Double-Dealer* during the 1920s. Indeed, another Faulkner effort in the passing genre, the 1934 story "Elly," shares even stronger thematic affinities with Toomer's "Bona and Paul," included in *Cane*.

Another intriguing literary debt across the color line surfaces unexpectedly, and no doubt unintentionally, in a letter of encouragement that Faulkner wrote to Eudora Welty in 1943. "Dear Welty," the letter begins,

You are doing fine. You are doing all right. I read THE GILDED SIX BITS, a friend loaned me THE ROBBER BRIDEGROOM, I have just bought the collection named GREEN something, haven't read it yet, expect nothing from it because I expect from you [*sic*].[5]

In what is clearly an honest mistake that doubles as an intertextual, interracial Freudian slip, Faulkner here confuses *Eudora* Welty with *Zora* Neale Hurston, whose story "The Gilded Six-Bits" appeared in the same August 1933 issue of *Story* magazine as Faulkner's "Artist at Home." Once alerted to this involuntary confession of familiarity with Hurston's tale, we need only turn back to "Pantaloon in Black" for undeniable evidence that Faulkner not only remembered "The Gilded Six-Bits" years after its publication but actively harvested the story for material. Compare Faulkner's account of the weekly Saturday ritual between Rider and Mannie, in which "the first hour would not have passed noon when he would mount the steps and knock . . . and enter and ring the bright cascade of silver dollars onto the scrubbed table in the kitchen where his dinner simmered on the stove,"[6] with Hurston's narrative of the love play between Missie May and her husband, Joe: "There came the ring of singing metal on wood. Nine times. . . . [Missie May] knew that it was her husband throwing silver dollars in the door for her to pick up and pile beside her plate at dinner. It was this way every Saturday afternoon."[7] This black source material, however, went unacknowledged. And this in turn suggests that for Faulkner, the phenomenon that Harold Bloom terms the "anxiety of influence"—the "strong" author's relation to a formidably problematic, problematically formidable precursor figure—bore an explicit racial dimension: that in Jim Crow America, the white writer may have felt that acknowledging the existence of black precursors would put his literary credentials and perhaps even his racial status at risk.[8] Elsewhere so candid about the writer's mandate to steal ideas from anyone and everyone, even his own mother,[9] and so unrepentant in listing his victims, Faulkner draws the line at crediting the contributions of his black brothers and sisters, foremothers and forefathers, to his fictional oeuvre as a literary world they made together.

For her part, Hurston seems to have been as silent about Faulkner as he was about her. There is no mention of Faulkner, for instance, in Carla Kaplan's eight-hundred-page edition of Hurston's letters. Fortunately, however, other black writers from the United States and elsewhere in the hemisphere have been more forthright in addressing the Faulkner legacy. Several have made Faulkner the explicit focus of essays, lectures, and other critical writings: Richard Wright in his 1950 essay, "L'Homme du Sud" (The man of the South); James Baldwin in "Faulkner and

Desegregation" (1956); Langston Hughes in a *Chicago Defender* article from the same year; Ellison in numerous essays, perhaps most notably in "Twentieth-Century Fiction and the Black Mask of Humanity" (1953); Sterling Brown in his 1957 lecture "The Negro in Faulkner's Novels"; Alice Walker in her 1970 essay "The Black Writer and the Southern Experience"; and Murray and Margaret Walker in keynote lectures at Faulkner and Yoknapatawpha.[10] In a 1983 essay, Guyanese author Wilson Harris analyzed the "cross-cultural mind" he discerned in, of all places, *Intruder in the Dust* (a novel pilloried by some for its overinvestments in political, regional, and ethnic forms of "homogeneity"), and Martinican Édouard Glissant devoted an entire book, 1999's *Faulkner, Mississippi*, to the novelist's life, work, and vision.[11]

To these figures we can add a large chorus of writers who have shared their opinions, judgments, and feelings about the Mississippian in published interviews, in accents ranging from deep appreciation to skepticism, disappointment, and anger. In this collective reckoning, superlatives often abound. "The supreme American novelist since the Civil War," said Ellison.[12] Chester Himes agreed: "Among American writers, Faulkner comes first. . . . He was, to me, the greatest writer in the world until he died."[13] A "genius," said Margaret Walker, one of the "great, great writers."[14] Trinidadian intellectual C. L. R. James pronounced Faulkner and Wright the greatest American writers of the twentieth century,[15] and Glissant goes even farther, declaring Faulkner "the greatest writer of this century (despite Proust and despite Joyce, or because of them)."[16] Wright singled out Faulkner's "purity of . . . artistic intention" as especially significant.[17] Toni Morrison praised his "refusal-to-look-away approach," an especially fierce commitment of the artistic gaze to difficult, uncomfortable subject matter.[18] Ellison commended his "willingness to become the other," a negative capability that was "not a racial matter" but one of "sensibility" and "talent."[19] This particular talent led a number of midcentury African American writers to declare Faulkner's art of black characterization unparalleled among white American writers, if not unmatched in all US writing. "Faulkner got some of the most admirable Negroes there ever was," Murray told an interviewer.[20]

Some younger writers, however, sounded a more cautious note. Baldwin observed in 1961 that "Faulkner . . . can really get . . . the truth of what the black-white relationship is in the South, and . . . what a dark force it is in the Southern personality" but added that "it is one thing for Faulkner to deal with the Negro in his imagination, where he can control him; and quite another thing to deal with him in life, where he can't control him. In life, obviously, the Negro, the uncontrollable Negro,

simply is determined to overthrow everything in which Faulkner imagines he believes."[21] Ishmael Reed was less moderate in his response,
telling an interviewer that he preferred his own white characters to
Faulkner's black ones.[22] For some of these writers, the relationship to
Faulkner evokes an anxiety of influence not so unlike Faulkner's own with
respect to Hurston, Wright, Toomer, Johnson, and others but crossing the
color line in the opposite direction. "You can't get by Faulkner," Murray
notes somewhat ruefully. "You've got to come through Faulkner. You've
got to do something so that if you're in a jam session with Faulkner he
would say, 'Hey, that was a good solo.'"[23] Ellison sounds a similar note: "I
can remember reading things by Faulkner long before he was generally
acclaimed, and just wishing I could have written those things."[24] Morrison
tilts over into frustration with readers and critics who would place her
work in the long shadow of Faulkner and other strong precursors: "I am
not *like* James Joyce; I am not *like* Thomas Hardy; I am not *like* Faulkner.
I am not *like* in that sense. I do not have objections to being compared
to such extraordinarily gifted and facile writers, but it does leave me sort
of hanging there when I know what my effort is to be *like* something that
has probably only been fully expressed perhaps in music."[25]

Several of Morrison's contemporaries have described writing back
against Faulkner's black characters. Though Ellison praised the Dilsey
Gibson character as "one of the greatest figures in American fiction,"[26]
Ernest J. Gaines has described the voice of his unforgettable Jane Pittman as what might have emerged had Faulkner allowed Dilsey to speak
from her own kitchen rather than so largely confining her to the Compson kitchen, a space that places significant constraints on her ability
to speak freely and copiously.[27] Gloria Naylor also found Dilsey problematic. Acknowledging that Faulkner's portrayal of the character was
grounded in his love for Caroline Barr, Naylor nonetheless deplored "the
whole social process that turned [Barr] into a Dilsey," diminishing her in
the process.[28] Naylor countered with her character of Mattie Michael in
The Women of Brewster Place. Mattie, Naylor claims with some pride,
has "been given the things Faulkner never gave his Dilsey. She's been
given a sexuality, she's been given a sort of ulterior motive for mothering,
and it's selfishness on her part."[29]

For poet Yusef Komunyakaa, the troubling Faulknerian figure was
Tobe of "A Rose for Emily," the African American manservant who
assists Emily Grierson in concealing the murder of Homer Barron and
then vanishes from Jefferson after Emily's death. To Komunyakaa, "It
seems as if it were impossible for Faulkner to give [Tobe] a voice."[30] The
poet's response was to develop an assignment for his creative writing
classes in which students were asked to "write a monologue in Tobe's

voice, with what he would have said, living and coming to that house as a servant, as a cook, as an individual, shocked—what he would have said."[31] Eventually, Komunyakaa took up the assignment himself, and the result was his arresting poem, "Tobe's Blues." In the sexually charged environment of post-Reconstruction Mississippi, Tobe and Emily would "walk miles around / each other in that old house. / No, I can't say her lavender // never stole my breath, / that we never placed a hand / over each other's mouth," in gestures that at once signal complicitous silence and hint at reciprocal, unspeakable desire.[32] "I'm in these woods," Tobe declares at poem's end, "because I have a tongue," a voice capable of uttering unpalatable truths about the subversive and often violent intimacies linking black men, white women, and white men in the post-Reconstruction social order.[33]

Two additional elements of the Faulkner legacy have proven particularly useful and stimulating for his black successors. First, the invention of Yoknapatawpha County, the tight focus on native materials as a keystone and gateway to larger insights, offered a valuable lesson in how to use the local as a means of accessing the universal. Gwendolyn Brooks admitted to an interviewer, "I can't write about America inclusively. But that's all right—I'm not sorry. You know, William Faulkner felt that if he just stayed with Yoknapatawpha County he was all right, and that in just concentrating on that single area—and that single multiplicity!—of life, that would be 'general' enough for his purposes."[34] Murray borrows Faulkner's favorite trope for Yoknapatawpha to make a related point: "We should develop a sensibility which encompasses what the experience of man is at this stage of the game in the twentieth century. . . . And you do that by looking right at that little postage stamp of a world that Faulkner talks about and trying to do the best that you can."[35] Novelist Caryl Phillips, who hails from the Caribbean island of St. Kitts, uses Faulkner's example to clarify how, as "a product of diaspora,"[36] his own experiences of mobility and change offered him a different set of literary resources:

> When I began to write, one of the writers I admired the most was Faulkner. I used to think lucky sod; he's got his little square of Mississippi that is forever home. He has his maps and things. . . . But I don't really feel that so much anymore because of the amount of traveling that I do and maybe because I suspect my literary influences and people I consider to be my peers have changed, and a lot of those people don't have a sense of home.[37]

Clarence Major cites the Faulkner oeuvre to make a similar observation about his own fiction: "I don't have a particular place that I identify with like Faulkner or Paule Marshall. We always moved a lot. I don't have that rootedness that some people have. I used to think that was a disadvantage, but now I think it's an asset because it gives me more flexibility, and it gives me a chance to start over again in a fresh way with new ideas."[38] But perhaps the ultimate tribute to Yoknapatawpha County as an example and inspiration for black writers is to be found in the work of Randall Kenan, who mined his own little postage stamp of native North Carolina soil to create the fictional community of Tims Creek, a recurring setting for his fictions.

A second vital contribution Faulkner has made to the black literary tradition is the example of *As I Lay Dying*, which among his novels seems to have had an inordinate influence on later African American writers. The same Gloria Naylor who expressed such reservations about Dilsey Gibson in *The Sound and the Fury* credits *As I Lay Dying* and its prismatic use of multiple interior monologues with getting her "over the hump" in the composition of her acclaimed 1988 novel *Mama Day*.[39] The narrative technique of *As I Lay Dying* also informs Gaines's 1983 novel *A Gathering of Old Men*, which employs multiple character-narrators to unfold the story of an interracial killing on a Louisiana plantation. More recently, Suzan-Lori Parks borrows irreverently and hilariously from the Bundren family's ordeal to recount the death of and subsequent burial odyssey for a black family matriarch in the 2003 novel *Getting Mother's Body*. And Mississippi native Jesmyn Ward channels elements of Bundren family structure and dynamics, including the death of a mother and the unplanned pregnancy of a teenage daughter, in *Salvage the Bones* (2011), her National Book Award–winning novel of the African American Batiste family. Such rich and often unexpected crosscurrents between Faulkner's oeuvre and that black canon surface throughout the seventeen essays in this collection.

We open, however, not with a critical analysis of such crossracial intertextuality but with another memorable example of it. "African American Poetic Responses to Faulkner" brings together five young writers, Chiyuma Elliott, Rachel Eliza Griffiths, Derrick Harriell, Randall Horton, and Jamaal May, in a chapbook of poems that employs an invigorating range of tonalities and moods to engage directly with Faulkner's writings, characters, and verbal art, as well as with his historical example as a race-haunted white southerner who struggled, often unsuccessfully, with the changing racial landscape of twentieth-century America.

In "The Street Ran through Cities: Faulkner and the Early African American Migration Narrative," James Smethurst traces the impact of a key fictional genre of black modernism in the early and mature work of William Faulkner. Introduced to black literary culture in part through his participation in the New Orleans literary and artistic scene that revolved around the *Double-Dealer* in the 1920s, Faulkner went on to create racially marked characters such as Joe Christmas and Valery Bon who exhibit "the permanently unsatisfied, restless, rootless existence" associated with the literary protagonists of migration narrative, a condition "that finds resolution only in death." All in all, concludes Smethurst, "it is in Faulkner's work, with the possible exception of Gertrude Stein's 'Melanctha,' that one sees the clearest adaptation of the characters and cultural geography of the early black Jim Crow migration narrative by a non-African American modernist writer."

Continuing the exploration of Faulkner's "relationship to black cultural expressive and creative traditions," Thadious M. Davis zeroes in on the "sometimes flawed but often pitch-perfect reproduction" of black "voice soundings in his writing." "Lingering in the Black: Faulkner's Illegible Modernist Sound Melding" traces these soundings to three important sets of sources: the vernacular storytelling of Faulkner's "black other mother," Caroline Barr; the culture of literary modernism, which offered "one access route to 'the new'" through "the under-explored yet heard difference of minority voices, particularly black southern voices"; and the specific sonic legacy of James Weldon Johnson, a writer Faulkner "not only . . . read but also . . . emulated," as evidenced by the direct line of "visible, audible, and significant influence" running from the verse-sermons of Johnson's 1927 volume *God's Trombones* to Reverend Shegog's Easter sermon in *The Sound and the Fury*.

George Hutchinson turns from specific questions of influence to examine the "institutional affiliations" and personal networks that link Faulkner's career with "the development of modern African American fiction." "Tracking Faulkner in the Paths of Black Modernism" credits the formative role of the Greenwich Village cultural scene for young writers like Faulkner and Toomer; the support of publishers like Boni & Liveright and Harcourt, Brace for Faulkner and for Harlem Renaissance authors; the impact of Sherwood Anderson and H. L. Mencken as literary patrons and guides; the emergence of publications like *Jet*, *Negro Digest*, and *Ebony* that made white authors more aware of "an educated black readership" forming its own judgments about their work; and World War II–era civil rights activism with simultaneously opening up paths for black modernist writers and for their white Mississippi contemporary.

Andrew B. Leiter cites the influence of Jean Toomer's work on Faulkner in order to challenge "the traditional critical paradigm in Faulkner studies that treats miscegenation as a threat to 'whiteness.'" "Miscegenation and Progression: The First Americans of Jean Toomer and William Faulkner" argues instead that "Toomer's vision of progressive racial evolution culminating in a multiracial, original American," a vision emergent in *Cane* and other poetic efforts from the early 1920s, contributed significantly to Faulkner's "interest in transformational racial identity from the 1930s to the civil rights years," an interest that culminates in *Go Down, Moses*, which like *Cane* "presents a culture and population already thoroughly hybrid and so advanced in amalgamation as to render white and black obsolete were it not for the ongoing racial violence," detailed in stories like Toomer's "Blood-Burning Moon" and Faulkner's "Pantaloon in Black."

Tim A. Ryan widens the purview of the literary to address a different sort of contemporaneity at work between Faulkner and the black cultural expression of his era. "'Go to Jail about This Spoonful': Narcotic Determinism and Human Agency in 'That Evening Sun' and 'A Spoonful Blues'" uncovers provocative affinities between Faulkner's mature fiction and the oeuvre of Mississippi Delta bluesman Charley Patton, who recorded the bulk of his work in the Faulknerian *annus mirabilis* of 1929–1930. Noting that both artists "used revolutionary formal techniques to describe, explore, and imagine . . . Mississippi in the early decades of the twentieth century," Ryan then zeroes in on the "productive dialogue" between Patton's 1929 recording "A Spoonful Blues" and Faulkner's 1931 story "That Evening Sun," both of which explore "the fabled prevalence of cocaine use in black communities." Each artist, argues Ryan, "asserts the essential dignity and agency of black Americans in the face of language and social systems that existed to suppress and dehumanize them."

Dotty Dye turns to the call and response between Faulkner and Jamaica-born Harlem Renaissance writer Claude McKay. "Narrative Leaps to Universal Appeal in McKay's *Banjo* and Faulkner's *A Fable*" ascribes to each writer "an international consciousness that operates in an oppositional manner against . . . 'native' roots" to shape "approaches to race, gender, class, and nationalism." In Faulkner's case, "the interrogation of identity begins with the local and the oppressive weight of history on the individual" before reaching "toward the elsewhere . . . to engage with issues endemic to the South." For the expatriate and nomad McKay, global travel fostered a cosmopolitan political awareness but also a literary sensibility in which the role of home became increasingly central to his aesthetic. The two novelists illustrate how a transnational literary perspective places the native and the foreign, "home" and "elsewhere," in a generative dialectic.

Two decades before Faulkner and Du Bois found themselves on opposite sides of the desegregation debate, their views on the significance

of another pivotal historical struggle exhibited some suggestive conver-
gences. In "Reconstructions: Faulkner and Du Bois on the Civil War,"
T. Austin Graham places Faulkner's 1938 anthology novel, *The Unvanquished*, alongside Du Bois's magisterial *Black Reconstruction* (1935).
Written "during a moment of unprecedented scholarly disagreement
about the war's stakes," *The Unvanquished* "actively invites contentious
reading" as a text that "considers various historical approaches to the
Civil War rather than chooses one" and "suggests the overwhelming
importance of race to the conflict even as it tries to overlook it." On one
hand, the novel's sometimes "rosy . . . view of race and labor" and its
depictions of "broadminded slaveholders and unbounded slaves" would
not be out of place in period studies like Avery Craven's *The Repressible
Conflict* (1939). On the other hand, the portrait of the Sartoris slave
Loosh "as a figure of liberation and black agency" aligns Faulkner's narrative with Du Bois's monumental work, which swam against the tide
of 1930s historiography in "put[ting] race at the center of the Civil War
and . . . argu[ing] for the absolute justice of the conflict." In its ultimately unresolved stance toward the historical problems and questions
that troubled Du Bois, Faulkner's novel, suggests Graham, "captures not
the past but rather the ongoing struggle of Americans to understand,
interpret, and shape that past" in the turbulent decade of the 1930s.

In "'The President Has Asked Me': Faulkner, Ellison, and Public
Intellectualism," Joseph Fruscione documents how one of midcentury
America's greatest writers and thinkers "mobilized intellectualism, aesthetics, and racial politics to navigate Faulkner's influence and broader
issues of intellectual celebrity" and to "refin[e] his intellectual brand" in
the post–*Invisible Man* period. Ellison's correspondence with Faulkner
about the Eisenhower-era People-to-People Program "joined yet distinguished" the two novelists, "while also helping Ellison feel that he was
entering the upper echelon of American literary culture" in his interactions with the Nobel Laureate. A number of published and unpublished
essays from the 1950s and 1960s presented Faulkner as "a literary-racial
touchstone and intellectual springboard" and fashioned "an important
Twain-Faulkner-Ellison literary lineage" that implicitly "elevated" the
latter's "critical standing." In this way Ellison constructed "a nuanced
association with Faulkner in which he located himself within literary
tradition yet sought to enhance his professional ethos."

Ben Robbins turns to the relationship between Faulkner and another
important midcentury figure in "Dangerous Quests: Transgressive
Sexualities in William Faulkner's 'The Wild Palms' and James Baldwin's
Another Country." Observing that Faulkner haunts Baldwin's essays "as
a split self—alternately progressive and backward, forward-thinking and

restrictively traditional, his voice vacillating between the private realm of literature and the public realm as self-appointed spokesman for the national consciousness," Robbins focuses on one particular product of that private realm, the 1939 novel *If I Forget Thee, Jerusalem*, which in some important respects anticipates Baldwin's 1962 novel, *Another Country*. Both novels explore, and link, sex and art as "productive and dangerous acts of transgression that critique the way power polices the boundaries of social division."

John Wharton Lowe examines the many affinities between the Faulkner oeuvre and that of one of the South's most important contemporary authors. "From Yoknapatawpha County to St. Raphael Parish: Faulknerian Influence on the Works of Ernest J. Gaines" begins by noting the powerful geographical and intertextual imagination at work in the two writers: each created a bounded fictional domain that served as the principal setting for numerous works (Faulkner's county of Yoknapatawpha and Gaines's Louisiana parish of St. Raphael), each used recurring characters across multiple fictions, and "each writer's assembled *books* speak in a kind of dialogue with each other" that integrates and amplifies the impact of the overall body of work. By his own generous admission, Gaines learned much from Faulkner, but just as important, according to Lowe, are the "things to avoid" that Gaines found in Faulkner. Where the latter too often portrays African Americans in narrow terms of victimization or sheer endurance, Gaines went beyond those limitations to present black figures who achieve a full human standing acknowledged by the larger community.

Two essays turn to the literature of the black Caribbean to place Faulkner's work in comparative context. Jenna Sciuto's "'For Fear of a Scandal': Sexual Policing and the Preservation of Colonial Relations in William Faulkner and Marie Vieux-Chauvet" explores the cultures of sexual surveillance and control that link Faulkner's Mississippi and the Haiti of novelist Marie Vieux-Chauvet. Sciuto finds such sexual policing to be typical of "periods of historical transition in which adherence to colonial ideologies begins to break down." The late 1930s and early 1940s proved to be just such a transitional era for Faulkner's South and Vieux-Chauvet's Haiti, as evidenced by *Go Down, Moses*, where characters such as Ike McCaslin in "Delta Autumn" participate in "the sexual policing of the color line" in their condemnations of interracial relationships involving their kinsmen, and by Vieux-Chauvet's 1968 novel *Love*, set in 1939 in a Haitian village where colonial legacies resurface in the obsessive social oversight and discipline of interracial and same-sex relationships. Sharron Eve Sarthou finds in the work of a contemporary Haitian American writer an important critique of Faulkner's racialized imagination of the Caribbean. "In the Book of the Dead, the Narrator Is the Self: Edwidge Danticat's *The Dew Breaker* as a Response to Faulkner's Haiti in *Absalom, Absalom!*" argues that Faulkner's 1936 novel presents Haiti as "an infantilized and demonized land," a trope that has been "historically used to marginalize Haitians and rationalize US paternalism in Haiti." Countering this long history of oppressive representations, Danticat's 2007 novel focuses not on the "blurring of racial lines" that makes Haitian figures like Charles and Eulalia Bon so fascinating to Faulkner and his white narrators but on subtler forms of ethical hybridity and transnational entanglement that make her Haitian and Haitian American characters complex and compelling. These characters are all in various ways implicated in Haiti's difficult history, but they also "prosper in the US, claim a historically situated culture," and exhibit a complex understanding of "their own responsibilities to the past, the present, and maybe even the future, and often speak two or more languages."

Lisa Hinrichsen's "Contemporary Black Writing and Southern Social Belonging: Beyond the Faulknerian Shadow of Loss" explores how African American writers like Randall Kenan have negotiated the notorious gothicism of Faulkner's fiction. Faulkner helped shape an influential image of the US South as "a gothic region saturated in loss and haunted by a history that sets it apart from the progressive temporality of the nation-at-large." Gothic's habit of "historically stress[ing] the black body's deviance," however, has made the genre problematic for black writers. Kenan's response to this problem, in his short fiction and especially his 1989 novel, *A Visitation of Spirits*, has been to double down on the gothic penchant for "queering reality through . . . defamiliarization and the fantastic" with a "queer appropriation" that reorients the genre around alternate forms of racial and sexual identity and experience. Drawing on the Faulkner legacy (especially in *As I Lay Dying*) to experiment with forms of "posthumous narration, queer knowledge, and magical thinking," *A Visitation* directs these textual strategies toward "black queer subjectivity instead of melancholic white loss," issuing an explicit challenge to southern Lost Cause-ism and its debilitating "sense . . . that progressive history is impossible."

Placing Faulkner's work alongside that of contemporary fiction writer Edward P. Jones, Matthew Dischinger focuses on a defining technology of economic and racial power in the antebellum US South: the plantation ledger. "'It Was Enough That the Name Was Written': Ledger Narratives in Edward P. Jones's *The Known World* and William Faulkner's *Go Down, Moses*" contrasts Faulkner's account of the McCaslin family ledgers, which works to "reif[y]" their "authority," with Jones's 2003 novel, which "deploys varied forms of recording" (census reports, political pamphlets, scholarly history) alongside the plantation ledger "to form an archival pastiche that throws the historical objectivity of any one of them into question." This revisionary interrogation of a key Faulknerian motif and the official history it purports to frame permits in turn a circling back to *Go Down, Moses*, with a renewed appreciation for its progressive representations of black agency.

In "Morrison's Return to Faulkner: *A Mercy* and *Absalom, Absalom!*," Doreen Fowler argues that "Faulkner's great strength is to show the way whites use language to socially exclude people of color," whereas "Morrison's is her ability to channel the interiority of the marginalized, the ones she calls the forgotten ones." To flesh out this contrast, Fowler turns to a pair of novels that examine "the drive of a lower-class white man to become a powerful planter-patriarch," Faulkner's *Absalom, Absalom!* and Morrison's 2008 novel, *A Mercy*. Where Faulkner uses the privileged white character-narrators of *Absalom* to dramatize how strategies of linguistic obfuscation work to exclude even as they register African American personhood, Morrison creates a more socially and racially diverse group of narrators in *A Mercy*, drawing on white, black, Native, free, and enslaved speakers to "represence the missing [racial] signified." In this way and others, Morrison "returns to Faulkner's novel to reclaim . . . racial meanings that have been disguised or covered over" by the dominant regime.

In "Natasha Trethewey's Joe Christmas and the Reconstruction of Mississippi Nativity," Ted Atkinson focuses on the Mississippi poet laureate's "provocative reimagining" of *Light in August* and its racially ambiguous protagonist in her poem "Miscegenation." Trethewey follows, and in her own biracial nativity reproduces, the strange career of Joe Christmas in demonstrating how childhood identity becomes complexly entangled with and within the institutions, laws, and imperatives of the racialized state in Jim Crow regimes like twentieth-century Mississippi. By rejecting the "tragic role that Faulkner wrote for his doomed literary creation," however, Trethewey effects "a bold redefinition of native status" that also "complicates the meaning of belonging as well, exploring a form of identification that accounts for the pain of exclusion and the desire for different emotional investments."

At the turn of the millennium, Glissant offered the bold prediction that "Faulkner's oeuvre will be made complete when it is revisited and made vital by African Americans," a goal that "will be achieved by a radically 'other' reading."[40] Individually and collectively, the essays and creative works gathered here, and the impressive cast of US and Caribbean literary artists represented therein, reveal that the revisionary work

Glissant describes has been long underway in the Americas. They return us to Faulkner with new insight not only into the magnitude and impact of his achievement but also—just as meaningfully—into its limits.

Jay Watson
The University of Mississippi
Oxford, MS

NOTES

1. Joseph Blotner, ed., *Selected Letters of William Faulkner* (New York: Random House, 1977), 201. Subsequent references to this edition will be cited parenthetically in the text.

2. Margaret Walker, *Richard Wright, Daemonic Genius: A Portrait of the Man, a Critical Look at His Work* (New York: Warner Books, 1988), 49. Wright was not the only prominent African American writer to exhibit a quasi-totemic attitude toward material artifacts associated with Faulkner. Ralph Ellison included a photograph of Faulkner and Andre Malraux among his "household gods," and Albert Murray called the attention of more than one interviewer to the pride of place he assigned his Faulkner first editions in his personal library. See Arnold Rampersad, *Ralph Ellison: A Biography* (New York: Knopf, 2007), 500, and Gene Seymour, "Talking with Albert Murray: A Hero and the Blues," in *Conversations with Albert Murray*, ed. Roberta S. Maguire (Jackson: University Press of Mississippi, 1997), 55.

3. Albert Murray and John F. Callahan, eds., *Trading Twelves: The Selected Letters of Ralph Ellison and Albert Murray* (New York: Modern Library, 2000), 44. Subsequent references to this edition will be cited parenthetically in the text.

4. James B. Meriwether and Michael Millgate, eds., *Lion in the Garden: Interviews with William Faulkner, 1926–1962* (1968; repr. Lincoln: University of Nebraska Press, 1980), 185.

5. Quoted in Suzanne Marrs, *Eudora Welty: A Biography* (San Diego, CA: Harcourt, 2005), 98.

6. William Faulkner, *Go Down, Moses*, rev. ed. (1942; repr. New York: Vintage International, 1991), 134.

7. Zora Neale Hurston, *The Complete Stories* (New York: HarperCollins, 1995), 87.

8. Harold Bloom, *The Anxiety of Influence: A Theory of Poetry* (New York: Oxford University Press, 1973). See also Harold Bloom, *A Map of Misreading* (1975; repr. New York: Oxford University Press, 2003), 63–81.

9. Meriwether and Millgate, *Lion in the Garden*, 239.

10. Richard Wright, "L'Homme Du Sud," in *Richard Wright: Books and Writers*, by Michel Fabre (Jackson: University Press of Mississippi, 1990), 199–200; James Baldwin, "Faulkner and Desegregation," in *Collected Essays* (New York: Library of America, 1998), 209–14; Langston Hughes, "Concerning a Great Mississippi Writer and the Southern Negro," in *Langston Hughes and the Chicago Defender: Essays on Race, Politics, and Culture, 1942–62*, ed. Christopher C. De Santis (Urbana: University of Illinois Press, 1995), 91–92; Ralph Ellison, "Twentieth-Century Fiction and the Black Mask of Humanity," in *Shadow and Act* (1964; repr. New York: Signet, 1966), 42–60 (see esp. 58–59); Clare Whitfield, "Faulkner's Negroes Traced by Brown," *Vassar Chronicle* 14, no.

20 (March 16, 1957), 3; Alice Walker, "The Black Writer and the Southern Experience," in *In Search of Our Mothers' Gardens: Womanist Prose* (New York: Harcourt, Brace Jovanovich, 1983), 15–21 (see esp. 19–20); Albert Murray, "Me and Old Uncle Billy and the American Mythosphere," in *Faulkner at 100: Retrospect and Prospect, Faulkner and Yoknapatawpha, 1997*, ed. Donald M. Kartiganer and Ann J. Abadie (Jackson: University Press of Mississippi, 2000), 238–49; and Margaret Walker, "Faulkner and Race," in *The Maker and the Myth: Faulkner and Yoknapatawpha, 1977*, ed. Evans Harrington and Ann J. Abadie (Jackson: University Press of Mississippi, 1978), 105–21. See also Albert Murray, *South to a Very Old Place*, rev. ed. (1971; repr. New York: Vintage, 1991).

11. Wilson Harris, "Reflections on *Intruder in the Dust* in a Cross-Cultural Complex," in *The Womb of Space: The Cross-Cultural Imagination* (Westport, CT: Greenwood, 1983), 12; Édouard Glissant, *Faulkner, Mississippi*, trans. Barbara Lewis and Thomas C. Spear (New York: Farrar, Straus and Giroux, 1999).

12. Ellison quoted in Rampersad, *Ralph Ellison*, 314.

13. Michel Fabre, "Chester Himes Direct," in *Conversations with Chester Himes*, ed. Michel Fabre and Robert E. Skinner (Jackson: University Press of Mississippi, 1995), 137.

14. Ruth Campbell, "Interview with Margaret Walker," in *Conversations with Margaret Walker*, ed. Maryemma Graham (Jackson: University Press of Mississippi, 2002), 97.

15. As cited in Walker, *Richard Wright*, 49.

16. Glissant, *Faulkner, Mississippi*, 35.

17. Wright, "L'Homme," 199.

18. Toni Morrison, "Faulkner and Women," in *Faulkner and Women: Faulkner and Yoknapatawpha, 1985*, ed. Doreen Fowler and Ann J. Abadie (Jackson: University Press of Mississippi, 1986), 297.

19. Ralph Ellison, "A Dialogue with His Audience," in *Conversations with Ralph Ellison*, ed. Maryemma Graham and Amritjit Singh (Jackson: University Press of Mississippi, 1995), 137.

20. Joe Wood, "The Soloist: Albert Murray's Blues People," in Maguire, *Conversations with Albert Murray*, 106.

21. Studs Terkel, "An Interview with James Baldwin," in *Conversations with James Baldwin*, ed. Fred L. Stanley and Louis H. Pratt (Jackson: University Press of Mississippi, 1989), 7.

22. Joseph Henry, "A MELUS Interview: Ishmael Reed," in *Conversations with Ishmael Reed*, ed. Bruce Dick and Amritjit Singh (Jackson: University Press of Mississippi, 1995), 208.

23. John Seigenthaler, "An Interview with Albert Murray, Author of *The Spyglass Tree*," in Maguire, *Conversations with Albert Murray*, 60.

24. "What's Wrong with the American Novel," in Graham and Singh, *Conversations with Ralph Ellison*, 60.

25. Nellie McKay, "An Interview with Toni Morrison," in *Conversations with Toni Morrison*, ed. Danille Taylor-Guthrie (Jackson: University Press of Mississippi, 1994), 152.

26. David L. Carson, "Ralph Ellison: Twenty Years After," in Graham and Singh, *Conversations with Ralph Ellison*, 204.

27. John Lowe, "An Interview with Ernest Gaines," in Lowe, ed., *Conversations with Ernest Gaines* (Jackson: University Press of Mississippi, 1995), 313.

28. Virginia Fowler, "A Conversation with Gloria Naylor," in *Conversations with Gloria Naylor*, ed. Maxine Lavon Montgomery (Jackson: University Press of Mississippi, 2004), 129.

29. Ibid., 134.

30. Kristin Naca, "Hotbeds and Crossing over Poetic Traditions," in *Conversations with Yusef Komunyakaa*, ed. Shirley A. James Hanshaw (Jackson: University Press of Mississippi, 2010), 29.

31. Ibid.

32. Yusef Kounyakaa, "Tobe's Blues," in *Taboo: The Wishbone Trilogy, Part One* (New York: Farrar, Straus and Giroux, 2006), 52.

33. Ibid., 54.

34. George Stavros, "An Interview with Gwendolyn Brooks," in *Conversations with Gwendolyn Brooks*, ed. Gloria Wade Gayles (Jackson: University Press of Mississippi, 2003), 48.

35. Seigenthaler, "An Interview with Albert Murray," 61.

36. Jenny Sharpe, "Of This Time, of That Place: A Conversation with Caryl Phillips," in *Conversations with Caryl Phillips*, ed. Renée T. Schatteman (Jackson: University Press of Mississippi, 2009), 30.

37. Ibid., 38.

38. Nancy Bunge, "'What You Know Gets Expanded,'" in *Conversations with Clarence Major*, ed. Nancy Bunge (Jackson: University Press of Mississippi, 2002), 117.

39. Fowler, "A Conversation with Gloria Naylor," 133.

40. Glissant, *Faulkner, Mississippi*, 55.

Note on the Conference

The fortieth Faulkner and Yoknapatawpha Conference sponsored by the University of Mississippi in Oxford took place July 21–25, 2013, with more than two hundred of the author's admirers in attendance. Seventeen presentations on the theme "Faulkner and the Black Literatures of the Americas" are collected as essays in this volume. Brief mention is made here of other conference activities.

The program began on Sunday with a reception at the University Museum for the photographic exhibition *Portraits as Landscapes, Landscapes as Portraits: Yoknapatawpha County in the 1960s*, by Alain Desvergnes, who taught photography at the university in the early 1960s and captured the physical and social landscape of the area in a stunning series of black and white photographs, many of which were collected in the 1990 volume *Yoknapatawpha: The Land of William Faulkner*. Following the reception, Kenneth Warren presented his keynote address, "On Faulkner and the Liberal Imagination," and a special conference session was devoted to remembering the life and evaluating the work of noted Faulkner scholar and conference stalwart Noel E. Polk. Following a buffet supper at Rowan Oak that evening, George "Pat" Patterson, mayor of Oxford, and Morris Stocks, provost of the University of Mississippi, welcomed participants, and Ted Atkinson, vice president of the William Faulkner Society, introduced winners of the 2013 John W. Hunt Scholarships. These scholarships, awarded to graduate students pursuing research on William Faulkner, are funded by the Faulkner Society and the *Faulkner Journal* in memory of John W. Hunt, Faulkner scholar and emeritus professor of literature at Lehigh University. James G. Thomas, Jr., associate director of the Center for the Study of Southern Culture, presented the 2013 Eudora Welty Awards in Creative Writing. Lee Schmidt from St. Andrew's Episcopal School in Ridgeland won first place, $500, for her story "Rebecca." Samantha Gibson from Petal High School won second place, $250, for her poem *Sadderday*. Honorable mention for fiction went to Pace Ward from DeSoto Central High School in Southaven for "A Letter Concerning the Sixteenth Slash," and honorable mention for poetry went to Keyoshia Scott from South Delta

High School in Rolling Fork for *Absence of Color*. The late Frances Patterson of Tupelo, a longtime member of the Center Advisory Committee, established and endowed the awards, which are selected through a competition held in high schools throughout Mississippi. A special writers' panel rounded out the evening. The panel, moderated by University of Mississippi faculty members Chiyuma Elliott and Derrick Harriell, included poetry readings by Rachel Eliza Griffiths, Randall Horton, and Jamaal May. An exclusive poetry chapbook, featuring the work of these five African American poets responding to Faulkner's literary, cultural, and historical legacy, was compiled for conference registrants.

Monday's program began with Charles A. Peek and Terrell L. Tebbetts leading the first "Teaching Faulkner" session, "'Done Been Abolished': Faulkner's Racial Agenda(s)," and a panel titled "If We Must Write: Du Bois, McKay, Ellison, Faulkner" followed, with Erin Kay Penner, Dotty Dye, and Joseph Fruscione presenting their work. That afternoon Chad Jewett, John Wharton Lowe, and Cheryl Lester each presented short papers on the topic of "William Faulkner, African American Writing, and the 'New Literary Souths.'" The day's program also included sessions during which Seth Berner, a book dealer from Portland, Maine, presented "Collecting Faulkner's Most Splendid Failure: *The Sound and the Fury*"; Thadious M. Davis presented her keynote address, "Lingering in the Black: Faulkner's Illegible Modernist Sound Melding"; and Peter Lurie, Ben Robbins, and Melanie Masterson each presented papers on the topic of "Mobile Identities in and after Faulkner: Modernity, Transgression, and Liberation in Faulkner's Black Literary Heirs." The day's activities ended with Colby Kullman, Vickie M. Cook, and Wil Cook hosting Faulkner on the Fringe, an open-mike evening at Southside Gallery on the Oxford Square.

Tuesday's program included the second "Teaching Faulkner" session, "Stories of African Americans: 'Dry September,' 'That Evening Sun,' 'Red Leaves,' 'Centaur in Brass,'" led by James B. Carothers, Theresa M. Towner, and Brian McDonald. A panel, "Revisioning Miscegenation and Trauma in Faulkner and the African American South," included papers by Andrew Leiter, Ted Atkinson, and Lisa Hinrichsen and was followed by a panel, "Faulkner and Contemporary Haitian Women Writers," which included papers by Jenna Sciuto, Sharron Eve Sarthou, and Carrie Helms Tippen. That afternoon James Smethurst presented his lecture, "The Street Ran through Cities: Faulkner and the Early African American Migration Narrative," followed by Tim A. Ryan presenting "'Go to Jail about This Spoonful': Narcotic Determinism and Human Agency in 'That Evening Sun' and the Delta Blues." Following Ryan's lecture there was an afternoon party at Tyler Place, hosted by Colby Kullman and his neighbors Harold and Dinah Clark.

Wednesday's program began with a panel on "Du Bois and Faulkner" that included scholarly papers by Rebecca B. Clark, T. Austin Graham, and Joanna Davis-McElligatt. The following panel, "Genre, Pedagogy, Labor: Deepening the Conversation," included paper presentations by Jacob Agner, Amritjit Singh, and Sasha Morrell. The last panel session of the morning consisted of papers on Faulkner and Toni Morrison by Meredith Kelling, Doreen Fowler, and Maia Butler. George Hutchinson presented a lecture, "Tracking Faulkner in the Paths of Black Modernism," that afternoon, and concurrent panels that included papers by Matthew Dischinger, Dai Xiaoli, Randall Wilhelm, Stephanie Tsank, and Eurie Dahn brought the conference presentations to a close. A late afternoon walk through Bailey Woods ended at Rowan Oak, where the annual picnic on the grounds concluded the day's events.

Guided tours of North Mississippi, including Oxford and Lafayette County, New Albany and Ripley, and the Delta took place on Thursday, and the conference ended with a party at Off Square Books.

Three exhibitions were available throughout the conference. The Department of Archives and Special Collections of the University's John Davis Williams Library exhibited William Faulkner portraits, film posters, and other materials related to his life and work. The University Museum hosted the exhibition of photography by Alain Desvergnes, and the University Press of Mississippi exhibited Faulkner books published by university presses throughout the United States.

The conference planners are grateful to all the individuals and organizations that support the Faulkner and Yoknapatawpha Conference annually. In addition to those mentioned above, we wish to thank Square Books, Southside Gallery, the City of Oxford, and the Oxford Convention and Visitors Bureau.

Faulkner and the Black Literatures of the Americas

African American Poetic Responses to Faulkner

Chiyuma Elliott, Rachel Eliza Griffiths, Derrick Harriell, Randall Horton, Jamaal May

William Faulkner is an important (and polarizing) figure in African American letters. In *Think Black*, Haki Madhubuti declares, "We must destroy Faulkner, dick, jane, and other perpetrators of evil."[1] In *Playing in the Dark*, Toni Morrison writes, "I am in awe of the authority of Faulkner's Benjy."[2] Few other American writers inspire such an impassioned range of creative response.

Previous scholarship has focused on Faulkner's influence in fiction. This collection of poems considers instead what Faulkner means to contemporary African American poetry. The project was part of the "Faulkner and the Black Literatures of the Americas" conference at the University of Mississippi, where three of the contributors (Rachel Eliza Griffiths, Jamaal May, and Randall Horton) read and discussed their poems.

The conference and collection are part of a larger conversation about race, poetry, and literary legacies. A central theme of that conversation is the politics of influence. Specifically, what is at stake when African American artists declare a meaningful connection with a canonical dead white male author who is often lauded for his insights about race and African American culture? One perspective (succinctly articulated by Madhubuti) is that Faulkner is both a symbol and perpetrator of the exclusion of African Americans and needs to be violently erased from the black literary landscape; merely to evoke Faulkner is to perpetuate evil.

The potential danger of a relationship with Faulkner is also explored in "My Friend Mary Stone from Oxford, Mississippi," by the late Lucille Clifton, which begins, "We know we ought to be enemies."[3] Though the speaker is explicitly talking about her improbable relationship with Mary Stone, the poem is, at least in part, a direct address to Faulkner.

Or rather, to "Mr. Faulkner," whose 1950 Nobel Prize acceptance speech the poem directly quotes. The honorific (Mr.) suggests both the high formal status of the addressee and also perhaps his distance (particularly if we read it as a racial marker of white privilege in the Jim Crow era). The speaker styles her hair to evoke "the warrior women of Dahomey" and is thus different from Mary Stone. And yet, according to the poem, there's something important about transcending these differences, however exhausting and "awe full" that work is; "we know we have to try it," says the speaker. At the end of the poem, the friends' bodies are depicted as part of the same landscape: "red as the clay hills and blacker than loam." And Mr. Faulkner, too, is linked to that place, and to the important connections being forged there.

At the time Faulkner received the Nobel Prize in Literature, only one African American author had been awarded a major mainstream American literary prize (Gwendolyn Brooks's *Annie Allen* had won a Pulitzer earlier in 1950). America's brutal history of racial oppression meant that Paul Laurence Dunbar was the only black poet regularly in print before the publishing boom of the Harlem Renaissance/New Negro movement in the 1920s. As both Clifton and Madhubuti make plain, African American poets writing (or not writing) about Faulkner are often writing against and about this troubled literary backdrop.

At this moment, the relationship of African American authors to the American literary mainstream is changing in some dramatic ways, which makes a collection about poetic responses to Faulkner particularly exciting. Two events stand out. The 2011 *Penguin Anthology of Twentieth-Century American Poetry*, edited by Rita Dove, touched off a debate about its simultaneous inclusion of rarely lauded writers of color and exclusion of noted white poets (such as Sylvia Plath and Allen Ginsberg).[4] Also, for the first time, a spate of black poets was awarded the nation's most prestigious literary prizes, including Pulitzers, National Book Awards, and commendations from the Library of Congress.

Shortly after Mississippi native Natasha Trethewey became the US Poet Laureate in 2012, Thomas Sayers Ellis read his poem "All Their Stanzas Look Alike," about the literary establishment's marginalization of black writers, to an enthusiastic crowd at a Cave Canem reading in Pittsburgh:

> All their artist colonies
>   All their core faculties
> All their stanzas look alike
>   All their Selected Collecteds
> All their Oxford Nortons

All their Academy Societies
All their Oprah Vendlers
All their stanzas look alike

But this time, Ellis's litany broke down before its written ending (which evokes Rita Dove, talks about exceptions, and maintains that "Exceptional or not, / One is not enough"). With the audience yelling the refrain in unison, Ellis reached the line "All their Poet Laureates." But instead of finishing the poem as written, he instead grabbed his head, leaned back, and exclaimed "Oooohhh!" There was a long pause, during which the audience cheered. Then, after briefly resuming the poem, Ellis abruptly broke off and said, "Now why Natasha had to go and do that!" Black writers are collectively rethinking our relationship to the American literary canon, and Ellis's reading both celebrated and dramatized this fact. The long-established narrative of African American literary exclusion is breaking down, and poets are self-consciously writing (and revising) in this moment of fracture.

Part of the work that each poem in this chapbook does is to define the terms of engagement with Faulkner and to make some sort of statement about the reason (or reasons) that connection matters. No two answers look alike. Faulkner was a voracious borrower, drawing on everything from plantation account books to popular blues lyrics to overheard speech. The poets in this volume are equally eclectic in drawing on his life and work. In some of the poems, Faulkner's words are implicitly recast, as in Derrick Harriell's "All the Dead Pilots," which uses a Faulknerian epigraph about "lean young men who once swaggered" as prologue and counterpoint to an alternative story set in 1995 about "a neighbor- / hood of angry Nikes and Jheri curls." Other poems hijack and reconfigure a short story's narrative threads, as in Chiyuma Elliott's "For Emily," which uses Faulkner to link racism, romantic love, and fatherhood. Still other work turns on exploration of Faulknerian characters, such as Rachel Eliza Griffiths's "Bundren Elegy," which repeats the word "dying" like a mantra as it asks and answers impossibly difficult and abstract questions: "The grammar of nails? They go down in wood. The fiction of dying / soars like a flame." In Randall Horton's "Southern Dialect," the speaker suggests that, despite the use of detached formal terms like "tonal beauty," writers who linger in "delta" speech are ultimately captives of its "juju spell," albeit happy ones: "i could sit for days in her cool / dialect swaying like tea leaves." In Jamaal May's "They May Come to Break Us" (set in Vicksburg, Mississippi, in 1877), the epigraph from Faulkner's "Mistral" casts the speaker's vigilant lookout for the arrival of a lynching party as a kind of defiance: "*You must either watch a fire or burn up in it."* When we initially proposed the chapbook to fellow writers, it quickly became clear that most poets either already had written, or were itching to write, a Faulkner poem. The range of this response is what we hope we've adequately captured.

Thanks are due to the poets who shared their work with us. We also want to acknowledge Jay Watson, without whose support and encouragement neither the original chapbook nor the conference panel and reading would have come to pass. This project was financially supported by the Faulkner and Yoknapatawpha Conference, as well as by several departments and programs at the University of Mississippi: African American Studies, the MFA Program, and the Department of English. We are grateful for the opportunity to share some beautiful and provocative new poetry and grateful to participate in an extraordinarily interesting conversation about Faulkner and the Black Literatures of the Americas.

Chiyuma Elliott
Derrick Harriell

CHIYUMA ELLIOTT
Self-Portrait in Aposematic Colors

Self-portrait as your mother, the centipede.
As venom. With gazing ball, with rear-view mirror,
self-portrait in every reflective surface. Self-portrait
losing water through the skin. As your mother.
Writing all the ways she thought to kill you
deep in the woods. Self-portrait as the cabin.
You dropping a glass, unable to breathe. Self-portrait
opening the vein—like ripping out a hem.
Self-portrait casually holding you under.

Self-portrait as the road through the woods. Each rut
and detour. Because I remember everything
about your hands, how small they were. One of them
still grazes my cheekbone when I sleep.
Self-portrait as my mother, who only tried
to kill herself. Self-portrait on a dead leaf,
in aposematic colors: viper yellow, noxious red.
Saying *M-my m-mother is a fish*. Self-portrait.
Saying *I sh-shall n-n-not want*.

CHIYUMA ELLIOTT
Entourage

The candle gutters, the candle faints,
Bill dreams her body; slopes
into that whip-charm, forgets to breathe.

Next morning, northing birds whip
over Pascagoula. Trees ripple. Each leaf
one word of a prophecy, but disarranged.

Nothing makes sense. Except the curve
of her breasts under June linen. Or
her bare knees. Or the dry grass. Bill,

we, too, stupidly place things
in brown bags, they over-ripen.
We find waking unwieldy. How slovenly,

our use of the moon! How slack,
our use of tides! Too, our every song
ends with someone's eyes.

CHIYUMA ELLIOTT
For Emily

How to explain it? Why you have to get up
so early in the morning, take a car ride
to the big town for school, away from
your friends. Emily, you saw a black lady
for the first time, and your daddy
was holding your hand. He watched
her gentle meet your curious halfway
across the sidewalk, then saw her eyes
go wary-tired when she looked him.
He did what he could. Quit wearing
baseball caps in town. Made you
into a tiny white neon sign
that flashed *I am not the enemy.*

Darling. I'd have called you Rose.
You'd have been black like me, and
none of this would have happened.

CHIYUMA ELLIOTT
Joe Christmas's New Suit

1

Once upon a time a calf was worth a watch
and a new suit.
But even if you owned the calf,
there were rules about selling.
And when rules were broken
(like old china plates
against scrubbed wood floorboards)
the sound was terrible, but it didn't echo.
You could keep on wanting,
and nothing would change.

2

Which one would you be?
He thinks, riffling his thumb over the book's edge
as if there were a second half to shuffle.

Says, *Not Joe.*

3
Nothing is wasted.

RACHEL ELIZA GRIFFITHS
After Absalom

*As a reader you have been forced to hunt for a drop of black blood
that means everything and nothing.*
—Toni Morrison

And what am I hunting in these groves, the words swilling through my consciousness, moon-sunken, shrunken spiders, fly-in-milk. And who am I hunting in these stalls, a bit in my mouth, my hair wild as blades, tilting flames &

syllables, shining the tongue like a lamp in the grotto of the voicebox, *bury that*. Because I am looking the way you wanted, always wanted, not to look away at this. And I gather the limbs you've strewn, alphabet-shaped, incantatory, unrelenting as sunlight beneath mud. Because there are hints everywhere, the shadow of a blackcat dream, the dream of shadows shackled to whipping posts & wagon wheels, the gallop of tincture, the snout of pigment, illiterate pigmeat, the ivory jewels of feet shaped like coals. American majestic. American terror. It's the same diamond. So shameless the summer undressing spring's delicate throat with a kiss. Some of us land without a sound, turning back to watch the clouds fall over like a woman. O, motherless devil burning the fields. The sweet blood of flight slick as cane. The blue blood air wings forget. Because you know what we hunt, what we must know as we look into any face, shucking spirit from pulp. It slips between the thumbs, only to be dust. The things blood cannot do for us. Dusk-dyed flight edging the field with wails. It's good enough for the blackbirds. One drop.

RACHEL ELIZA GRIFFITHS
Requiem, Yoknapatawpha County

Scythe these words to bones, roots.
The dead return like a wildfire, a hive of ghosts.
Apocryphal fields. Crows, eagles, buzzards.
What the slow water of memory remembers
like a face. Unknown in contour, a map.
The fields plowed by sparse vernacular, the fields
gouged by blood, the fields turning on their sides
to show the bruises we make early in the morning
through the stalls of stars at night.
Pass through blood, pass it under the pines,
let it grow as high as oaks, let the long clouds
squeeze it down, a veil frosting our shoulders,
the crowns of our speech. Carve these kings
& daughters to tongue. Raze every justice, cruel
as a gray rose. Where Moses went down, where
the railroad flung its black-lipped sutures, where
the spotted horses were seen, flailing like men
in love, tilling their lives in God's spit.
The dead twisting like a terror in stories
when we open the book. Bones reaching
for their relatives, aching for how blood pours
volume over volume.

RACHEL ELIZA GRIFFITHS
Her White Children Bless Her

The dirt holds this, the words inside of stone, the flesh
of the law, the way it was, is, & may always never please never always
be. I'm looking for you, come across it. I need imagery, your lines
are fruit, tribes, whiskeys. You're inside this seed. Sarcophagus of the
    anti-pastoral
America, a scribe. Lucid horseman. The matter of a man is
every man's weight. The spines of your words rear, flash their eyes,
bare gin teeth, four-legged, flogged with rain, cheek. Words thunderous,
    hooves.
Days ago I thought about the last horse throwing you into air
& that you don't fall, you don't ever land, injured, & waiting
for the black gloves or the sanitarium where they will take
you closer. I thought about the body pulsing between your thighs,
the leather, the animal stars you struck as air ripped you up like the music
of oaks in rain. And whatever your face might have seen in the dark,
it was like that. It was what I can't always see from the half-slave quarters
of my world. I'm mostly free. And when I remember the stones I wish I was
    the kind
of rain that could pull a man's tongue out of his own destiny.
I wish I could bless the meaning of whiteness, which often
is defined as absence. Some say black & white are both
stains where all colors melt in the jury of bloodlines. The god
stone was marbled with both. And I'm not sure what Callie Barr Clark's
laughter would sound like in the trees, wide & beloved. Everywhere I read,
an unseen voice, like a moon behind night, like a window half-opened
in a woman's mouth, like the way I can't always bear to look at history
but look anyway, saying nothing, everywhere an unseen voice
kindly repeats, *"almost like family, almost . . ."*

RACHEL ELIZA GRIFFITHS
Bundren Elegy

1

Who has washed her face? Poured with the shadow of dying,
    a woman trembles in a box. Her life chafes like the light
    of wingless pain. This is the journey winter forgets, jerking
        in spring with dying.

2

The world braced as paper. A horse kneeling, dying
in the love it obeyed. Trampled like a ghost in spring.

Will kindling burn in a fire of rain? Is it dying?
Their faces are white coal, magnolia, Bundren, stripped to scent.

Their eyes & buzzards are the same. Black with dying.
Pilgrims of elegy crawling to Jefferson, a cross of water
floods spring with dying.

Who has kissed Dewey Dell with poor ripening? Who unmade
a mother's eyes? Mouthless, biting, her husband begrudging nothing?

What hunger saddled Jewel's horse to buck in spring with dying?

3

The grammar of nails? They go down in wood. The fiction of dying
soars like a flame. They carried her impatiently like fire, spared
their dying everything but air. You are a country of fictions, bones,
& work music, *you*. The women were all singing in the still body.
A promise sanded like wood. Nothing moved. The opal fish splayed open
in a boy's grief, unnameably dying in spring. Will her body burn in the fire of
God?
Is paradise dying or rebirth? Their lives blossom like smudges of blood,
stripped
to faith. Sewn into the earth like a seam of wildflowers in spring with dying.

DERRICK HARRIELL
Black Music

money too easy to earn
I tell him after
he tells me his woman
called off the whole goddamn thing.
We swallow pints
he tells me there ain't a bitter bullet
in his bones, or in the revolver
beneath the rented tuxedo.

He tells me all this shit
is about money, about the lot
he'll cast, the power of positive thinking
laws of attraction. *Some is born*
for one thing. And the fellow that is born
a tadpole, when he tries to be
a salmon all he is going to be
is a sucker he says while shooting
a Beam. We laugh at the bright
cummerbunds and bow ties
we almost strapped to our waists
and necks, pull cigarettes from
our ears, blow smoke out
our asses.

DERRICK HARRIELL
Dry September

The dark world seemed to lie stricken beneath
the cold moon and lidless stars

—*William Faulkner*

When you can't flood
your stomach with spirit
you turn to matinees.
And when the doctor
X's out lovemaking
you convince the old
you that the new
you is more evolved.
But deep down
you are niggerlovers
and with housemates the color
of coffee, all you can do
cry until September.

DERRICK HARRIELL
All the Dead Pilots

the lean young men who once swaggered

—*William Faulkner*

In the pictures, the snapshots hurriedly made,
I gaze, no, I'm crouching on a stoop, on a porch
in the middle of a typhoon of a neighbor-
hood of angry Nikes and Jheri curls
that only shake when the rent's due or the baby
need new shoes.

They're all dead
once upon a time, these pilots
drove chariots and Mustangs through galaxies and black-
holes now in someone's head
and the patchwork from the dirt only makes for dark
rainbows. The rainbows are dead too
but in 1995 hovered project castles
like a halo. And when Tyrone said
"All I have to do is be Black
and die" we watched the omen
float above our domes, baffled
by its clarity.

DERRICK HARRIELL
Uncle Willy

while he just used dope, we saw a lot of him

—*William Faulkner*

Jabbed needle leans out the bend
of a used arm, an attached lover that ain't learned
how to unlove. Remember they said I
was hooked, latched on the smack
half my body banging from a Memphis hospital
liver. Remember all the women
who poured bible verses along my feet,
who dreamed me naked in the pulpit.

DERRICK HARRIELL
That Will Be Fine

Then it began to get dark
and they started to shoot.
Just a couple minutes before
Uncle Rodney saved the barbecue
with a lady who looked like Beyonce.
And she wouldn't quit rubbing
his bald head. And I wondered
if she had a little girl or niece
to play cans with. And every time
I was about to ask, Uncle Rodney
would say boy
go grab me a beer. Sometimes
he would say boy
give this to her. And each time
I got tired of running
he'd reach in his wallet
put a dollar behind my ear.

DERRICK HARRIELL
A Courtship

There was a wise man of ours who said once
how a woman's fancy is like a butterfly

—*William Faulkner*

That's exactly what Uncle Red said,
that my parents met at a June festival,
that my father couldn't keep his head
or contain the fire ablaze his afro. The disco ball
had dropped at the center of the merry-go-round
the mistletoe blew and spewed a lover's root.
The gods' plan had worked this time. *Aint Too Proud*
To Beg, my mother's Hot Pants blues
baby if you want me, show me.
So the young boy rolled a tank top
'til it revealed a cotton field. 'Til the mercy
thumped like Gaia's runway gallop.

RANDALL HORTON
A Red Clay Vision

slashes through my eyes quick sunlight,
& a logician's puzzle tells me i am not

seeing what i am seeing. this vision i keep
waking up to among the trees, dead static

in my ear, a blue gray sky over the archaic
carriage house, a shadow floating, hung

alongside rain clouds ready to unleash
the image: a little girl this time. pleated

into the yellow. against which horizon she
openly lies sprawled. on the green grass

with the horizon parallel, inside the girl,
screaming up at high noon & beyond

is a ventriloquist's voice stuck. *h-e-l-p m-e*
echoes the valley, a mute scream it is,

crepe-myrtle trees sing soft this brittle night,
every branch tip whistling erasure

over the mountaintop, the ardent wind says
in my dream: the dead are alive, too—

RANDALL HORTON
Southern Dialect

from down south the woman
growing up delta could not

possibly know her dixie accent
indicated tonal beauty,

produced a slow drawl of vowels
longer than idyllic nights, like

she wasn't country but a nation
unique & identical to nothing,

i could sit for days in her cool
dialect swaying like tea leaves.

how ya doing whispered often,
the mason jar in her icebox

voice so sweet, the sound rattling
summer eternity, syllables

warming my earhole, a juju spell—
can taste language on my tongue.

RANDALL HORTON
Peetie Wheatstraw Play William Faulkner a Tune Coursey of Legba

there is no such thing as an Anglo-Saxon heritage and an African heritage
—William Faulkner

DEAR MR. WHEATSTRAW:

bye & bye secular music will enter yr earhole
     concise but then louder & louder

the catalogue ordered guitar love it like a novel woman
     yr baby the sweet devil honey chile gone come

cop a seat in earleene's clapboard covered jook
     where you at is a sacred place for living

strum them eyelids keep 'em closed & 'member
     the hard work savagery loving of the tongue

lick it again yr lips & swallow along with gin the good time
     rock to the buzzard lope the slow drag

the itch you gotta scratch sometimes but don't
    look cause there is an orisha beside you now

on blind faith beyond what you can conceive
    sacrifice the musical instrument & pluck

of what you got nobody knows the chosen hands
    playing until they surrender to legba his brim

pulled low over the sloped forehead cane propped
    he will pull yr fingertips clipping each nail

the baptism of blood trickling don't look
    his guitar is fading gone he is gone now play.

JAMAAL MAY
Ruin

Ruin means the barn is on fire
or the house is in flames
or the soil is as fertile
as ash

or the belly swells with unwanted
limbs and yet another belly
to fill with this week's
wages.

Ruination means the barn is full
of livestock when it collapses
and the fertile are ash
in soil

or the unwanted swell in numbers
until the shelter is fat
like the belly
of a hog.

Fire means clean in the way
clean means erasure

in that peculiar
way erasure

means an ugly kind of dead, the face
a scorched topography, ruined
into an unrecognizable
relief.

JAMAAL MAY
They May Come to Break Us
Vicksburg, Mississippi, 1877

You must either watch a fire or burn up in it.
                    —*Narrator in Faulkner's "Mistral"*

Outside sheets twist
this way and that.

Fields are smoke,
smoke is air.

We wait for fingers to be bent
knuckle to knuckle,

the porch overrun
with rope and rifle

but the hounds don't show.
I minister to my wilting husband,

he sings like there's nothing outside
but road, salt marsh, and fields

of wildflowers growing
farther than we can walk.

Torches may come like fox paws
to steal away what we plant,

but with our bodies bound
by the skin, my arc to his curve,

we are stalks that will bend
and bend and bend . . .

NOTES

1. Don L. Lee (Haki Madhubuti), *Think Black* (Detroit: Broadside Press, 1967), 6.

2. Toni Morrison, *Playing in the Dark: Whiteness and the Literary Imagination* (New York: Vintage, 1992), 4.

3. Lucille Clifton, *The Collected Poems of Lucille Clifton 1965–2010* (Rochester, NY: BOA, 2012), 15.

4. Rita Dove, ed., *The Penguin Anthology of Twentieth-Century American Poetry* (New York: Penguin, 2011).

The Street Ran through Cities:
Faulkner and the Early African American
Migration Narrative

JAMES SMETHURST

While the peripatetic, rootless, and often mixed-race characters of such novels as Pauline Hopkins's *Contending Forces*, Paul Laurence Dunbar's *The Sport of the Gods*, James Weldon Johnson's *The Autobiography of an Ex-Colored Man*, Jean Toomer's *Cane*, and Nella Larsen's *Quicksand* anticipate the protagonists of much modernist US fiction (and poetry), it is in Faulkner's work, with the possible exception of Gertrude Stein's short story, "Melanctha," that one sees the clearest adaptation of the characters and cultural geography of the early black Jim Crow migration narrative by a non-African American modernist writer. This should not surprise us. The peculiar social, political, and cultural location of African Americans in the South (where 90 percent of black people still lived at the beginning of the twentieth century) made the modern subject par excellence. It is worth recalling the intense violence with which the Jim Crow system of segregation and black disenfranchisement was installed and maintained, the sheer weirdness of it, and the deep sense of despair and betrayal that attended it for African American artists and intellectuals (and black people generally). We know, and indeed Faulkner reminds us, of the violent aspect of the Jim Crow regime. Still, it is hard to grasp the virulence and sheer destructiveness of the white race riots and mob violence (such as the Wilmington, North Carolina, riot of 1898 that helped install Jim Crow and the riots of the Red Summer of 1919 that helped maintain it). Similarly, we are likely to be freshly shocked when presented not only with the insane and multilayered violence of lynching's racial terror, a violence that could erupt from the slightest public display of black self-expression or demonstration of ambition, but also with its communal nature, as white participants often brought their whole families, had photographs taken, collected grisly souvenirs from the mutilated body of the victim, had postcards made of the event, and so on. Our shock, though, is but a distant reflection of the shock and disorientation that black people felt in that early moment of Jim Crow.

As to the legal, social, political, and cultural weirdness of Jim Crow, one has only to look at the infamous *Plessy v. Ferguson* Supreme Court decision of 1896 essentially legitimating segregation and the somewhat less famous, but also extraordinarily important *Williams v. Mississippi* ruling of 1898, which declared the various devices by which black voters were disenfranchised to be constitutional. The Fourteenth and the Fifteenth Amendments were not repealed. They continued to exist alongside the new Jim Crow laws that were obviously in conflict with them and that were now legitimated by the Supreme Court. In short, African Americans were faced with a situation in which the laws of the land declared on one hand that they were political and cultural citizens with rights that could not be abridged and on the other that in the region where the vast majority of black people lived, their citizenship was constrained in virtually every arena that could be imagined. This insanely contradictory system was maintained not only by law but also by madly intense and often communal violence on the part of lunatics who often professed to "love" black people even as they publically burned, hanged, castrated, and butchered them with impunity. It was also not lost on African Americans that this system was not some atavistic holdover from slavery but a new system that arose precisely as the rapidly urbanizing United States became the world's preeminent industrial power and an eminent international power with overseas colonies in Asia, the Pacific, and the Caribbean. In other words, Jim Crow and the new racism were constitutive features of US modernity.

For the generation of W. E. B. Du Bois, Paul Laurence Dunbar, Pauline Hopkins, and James Weldon Johnson—the first generation of black artists to grow up after Emancipation during the period of Reconstruction, with its promise of full black political, legal, economic, educational, and cultural citizenship—to come of artistic and intellectual age as this wildly contradictory Jim Crow regime was taking command was disheartening and disillusioning in the extreme. It resulted in various expressions and formulations of African American dualism reflecting this weird reality, such as Du Bois's "double-consciousness" and "the veil," Dunbar's "mask," and the early Jim Crow migration narrative.

However, Jim Crow was a key constitutive element of modernity throughout the United States, not just in the South. The cities of the United States were transformed in novel ways, spatially as much as culturally and politically. The advent of the black ghetto was a new phenomenon of the twentieth century without any real precedent in the United States. This development had a number of important consequences for

African American expressive culture specifically and for US culture generally. "Blackness" became a territory that urban white Americans could
easily visit for various purposes, including primitivist sexual and cultural
fantasies. For African Americans, the new ghetto in the North was both
"home" (and even a site where one might imagine true black self-determination or how a black nation might look) and a sort of prison that was
difficult (and often physically very dangerous) to leave except as some
sort of servant or to travel to another ghetto or to the Jim Crow regime
of the South with its attendant risks and restrictions. Furthermore, there
was a pronounced sense among many black artists and intellectuals that
the city, particularly in the urban North, was a site where older forms of
African American sociality, cultural values, racial solidarity and identity,
and "roots" became attenuated or melted into air under the press of the
dynamic, yet cold and impersonal, modern US industrial-commercial
society.

The journey between the South and North had been a central feature
of African American letters long before the Jim Crow era. The key nineteenth-century genre that featured this journey was the autobiographical
fugitive slave narrative—to which one could add fiction structured on
the slave narrative, such as William Wells Brown's *Clotel*. The master
narrative of this journey North, especially in Frederick Douglass's 1845
Narrative of the Life of Frederick Douglass, An American Slave, is one of
individual self-development (often closely tied to literacy), demonstrating the black potential for genuine citizenship in an ideal, nonracial-
ized (at least so far as citizenship is concerned) United States. Perhaps
paradoxically, that individual self-creation, both actual and potential, is
linked to the elevation of African Americans as a group.

Almost necessarily, this individual self-development tied to group
elevation also generally entails a flight from the southern folk and their
culture. One might add that the genre introduced the North-South
axis to literature by white Americans, with a significant impact on such
crucial mid- and late-nineteenth-century US works as Harriet Beecher
Stowe's *Uncle Tom's Cabin* and Mark Twain's *The Adventures of Huckleberry Finn* (which becomes a sort of bitterly humorous slave narrative as
Huck and Jim float deeper and deeper into the South when their efforts
to reach "free" territory go askew).

Subsequently, the "immersion narrative," in which the alienated and
rootless black subject of the urban North travels into the Black Belt of
the South to reengage with the folk, became an established trope in
African American literature by the turn of the century.[1] The best-known
literary forerunner of this reverse migration narrative is Frances E. W.
Harper's 1892 novel *Iola Leroy*.[2] At the end of the novel, the extremely

light-skinned protagonist, Iola Leroy, along with her brother Harry and various other African Americans with formal educations and professional skills, returns to the South, where they live and work with and among the folk for the elevation of the race and the preservation of black citizenship in the face of segregationist attacks. In doing this, Iola rejects both the half-freedom of living as a Negro in the North (which is shown to confront its own virulent brand of discrimination) and the self-hating and family-denying opportunism of passing for white in either the North or the South. This is a sort of counternarrative to the one told by Douglass. In Douglass's narratives, there is a journey toward individual selfhood and away from the folk. In Harper's novel, there is a journey toward a communal identity in which individual self-interest is sacrificed for a larger good linked with the southern black folk and the southern soil. While there is still a sense of the intellectual-professional as the leader who uplifts the folk, the novel also promotes the concept that the southern folk and its culture is the locus of African American identity and that life in the North is alienating in the extreme, both practically and psychologically.

Both the ascent northward to freedom and the immersion narrative seen in Douglass's autobiographies and Harper's *Iola Leroy* make their way into the early Jim Crow black migration narratives, but without the sort of resolution seen in the earlier genres. A recurring motif of the Jim Crow–era migration narrative is the individual or family who leaves the folk in the South only to be destroyed in the North. Perhaps the most developed early example of this motif can be found in Paul Laurence Dunbar's naturalist novel of 1902, *The Sport of the Gods*.[3] Dunbar's novel starts in the South, where a wealthy white landowner, Maurice Oakley, becomes convinced that his hitherto loyal servant Berry Hamilton has robbed him. In a perfunctory trial, Hamilton is condemned to a long term in prison. Unable to bear the shame and scorn caused by Berry's imprisonment, the Hamiltons move to New York City, resulting in their moral, spiritual, and physical corruption in a "black bohemia" of clubs, dance halls, gambling joints, vaudeville theaters, hotels, and boarding houses that attend black life in the urban North.

Berry's son, Joe, immediately falls into a milieu of con artists, drunks, sleazy show business people, white bohemians on the make, and white voyeurs. Chief among these is the black and possibly gay grifter-bohemian-dandy (the dandy was a recognizable gay literary type at that time), "Sadness" Williams. Williams, too, is a migrant to the city, driven there by Jim Crow and racial terror, who now wanders the black bohemian byways of New York's Tenderloin district. Upon his arrival, Sadness was initiated into the interface of crime and popular culture (and deviant sexuality) that is black bohemia through his victimization by a con artist. In turn, he participates in a similar initiation of Joe.

In short order, Joe Hamilton is lured to his ruin and then jailed for the demented murder of his girlfriend, Hattie, a black vaudeville actress on a career slide. His sister, Kitty, becomes a jaded and prematurely aging showgirl. Berry's wife, Fannie, with the support of Kitty, bigamously marries an abusive drunk. This compendium of urban degeneration is what Berry finds when he is released from prison and comes North. As in *Iola Leroy*, we see a journey to the North that is very different from that of Douglass, a journey into a kind of new slavery to mass culture; the evils of urban modernity; and racism, northern-style. After the sudden death of Fannie's second husband, Berry and Fannie reunite after a fashion and return South to their former hometown. But unlike Iola and her family's move to the South, it is a sort of living death, not a restoration.

While *Sport of the Gods*, along with Pauline Hopkins's *Contending Forces* (1900), helped to establish the Jim Crow migration narrative, it is in James Weldon Johnson's *Autobiography of an Ex-Colored Man*, first published anonymously in 1912 and reprinted under Johnson's name during the Harlem Renaissance in 1927, that the mature migration novel takes shape.[4] As in *Sport of the Gods*, the protagonist, here unnamed, moves back and forth between North and South without truly coming to rest. He is a very light-skinned "Negro," born in the South to a former slave and her former owner, raised in the North by his mother, and financially underwritten by his largely absent father. He is unaware that he is a "Negro" until an incident at his school makes him aware of it. He now knows what he is by the standards of the United States, but he has no idea what that means. Much of the rest of the novel could be described as various and sometimes contradictory tutorials in the meaning of being a "Negro."

First, the ex-colored man attempts to solve his crisis by going South to attend the historically black Atlanta University. This plan is altered when he is robbed of his tuition money, leading him to Jacksonville, Florida, where he enters and is educated about the black skilled working class and middle class. He is initiated into and educated about the joys and limitations of southern black middle-class life as circumscribed by the new Jim Crow regime. Restless and ambitious, he abandons a possible union with a black schoolteacher and leaves for the metropolis of New York City.

As with the Hamiltons in *The Sport of the Gods*, there the ex-colored man is instructed in the chaos, possibility, and boundary-blurring of black bohemia, a world of drinking, gambling, and ragtime that brings together black artists and criminals and white artistic and sexual voyeurs.

He becomes both a skilled gambler and a ragtime pianist. On the path of destruction that consumed the Hamiltons, he is rescued by one of the voyeurs in black bohemia, a rich European man of indeterminate nationality and sexuality. This man hires the narrator to provide musical entertainment at his social gatherings of members of an upscale but often unconventional intelligentsia (including recognizably gay and lesbian figures), first in New York, then in Europe. Europe is both culturally and socially overwhelming but ultimately unsatisfying. The narrator returns to the South and receives yet another lesson in blackness by studying the sacred and secular music, oratory, and other cultural forms of the black folk with the idea of creating a modern "high" black art that will truly express the African American people. After the shock of recognition of the power of the folk music and religion—a shock frequently described by black artists and intellectuals of that era—he witnesses a lynching in which a man is burned alive. One might call this the final lesson, as he is traumatized not only by the insane violence and cruelty but also by the fact that he as a "Negro" could be treated with such demented and vicious contempt. He recoils from this meaning of "Negro," and by extension from himself, and flees back to New York. As a sort of angry and alienated "practical joke on society," he avoids any mention of his racial ancestry, letting others make their own assumptions about his identity, which, apparently, in every case is judged white. Eventually, he falls in love with a white woman. Though he reveals that he is a "Negro," she marries him. Nonetheless, the fact that he is "colored" remains otherwise unspoken, even to his children. As he prospers in business, he abandons his musical ambitions, which were rooted in his pursuit of what it meant to be a Negro. While financially successful, the narrator "cannot repress the thought that, after all, I have chosen the lesser part, that I have sold my birthright for a mess of pottage."[5] The course of study, then, is still incomplete—or at least his lessons, yo-yoing between North and South, have brought no final definition or stable identity in which he can rest easy.

This sense of gothic melancholy pervades many of the migration narratives of the Harlem Renaissance and in fact takes on a new intensity there. By gothic, I refer to the circular or cyclical nightmare logic of the gothic-horror genre, in which the protagonist never truly escapes and the antagonist never truly dies but is constantly revived or reborn so that the drama-terror is repeated endlessly. The black subject is caught in an impossible existential bind in the United States. As in *Sport of the Gods* and *Autobiography*, the old home of the South, with its connection to nature and to a line of cultural transmission seen reaching directly to Africa, is either practically or spiritually untenable. The sense of the urban ghetto as simultaneously new home, refuge, trap, and exile, of black metropolis as destroyer of black culture and racial values, a view pioneered by Dunbar, Johnson, and Hopkins, and further developed by such Harlem Renaissance authors as Toomer, Rudolph Fisher, Nella Larsen, and Claude McKay, was immensely strengthened by the continued growth and hypersegregation of African American populations in the urban centers of the United States during the Great Migration. In short, for the black (often mixed-race) literary protagonist, the Jim Crow South is unbearable, but so is the northern city, resulting in a permanently unsatisfied, restless, rootless existence that finds resolution only in death—or, occasionally, in departure from North America altogether.

The initial black migration narratives are forerunners of a modernist sensibility in US and European fiction, not only by writers of the Harlem Renaissance, but also by white writers. The protagonists of the early migration narratives, in their yo-yoing between North and South, black and white, citizen and some other, less classifiable status, private space and public space, are radically divided intellectually. The sort of radical alienation from any sort of cultural roots or identity and the fragmentation of the self into often warring parts often rendered spatially—motifs that will come to be associated with artistic modernism—are here writ large and early.

For many white US modernists, including William Faulkner, one important aspect of white modernist adoption and adaptation of black expressive culture is a consequent anxiety over whether one's culture, one's writing, or even one's self is "white" enough, even as one ventriloquizes black voices and bodies as a way of asserting an "American" vanguard identity. What is interesting is that this anxiety (or even anguish) and impersonation are not generally linked to the visible biological traits associated with "race" but instead to language, expressive culture, movement, clothing styles, and sexual desire in ways that promise greater freedom from the constraints of "American civilization" but at the same time compromise the stability of the "white" subject much as Jim Crow compromised the stability of the "Negro" subject.

Before moving on to a discussion of the black migration novel and specific novels and stories of William Faulkner, it is worth saying a few things about the ways and forms in which the migration novel might have been transmitted and made accessible to Faulkner. To put it simply, what evidence do we have that he was familiar with the genre? We know from the books in his library and from his correspondence with Richard Wright that he knew and was enthusiastic about some of the most important black narratives in the migration tradition of the 1940s and 1950s: Wright's *Native Son* and *Black Boy*, Ralph Ellison's *Invisible Man*, and

James Baldwin's *Go Tell It on the Mountain*.[6] And certainly he was very familiar with the literary North-South axis of the slave narrative, if only as transmuted by Twain's *Huckleberry Finn*. But what about the black migration narratives of the early Jim Crow and modernist eras, from about 1900 to 1932?

One key circuit of transmission was the bohemian nexus of the French Quarter and the *Double-Dealer* magazine that was so important to Faulkner's development in the middle 1920s. John Shelton Reed argues that Jim Crow made the sort of physical interaction of black and white artists and intellectuals that characterized bohemia in New York and Chicago extremely difficult in New Orleans. He notes, however, that African Americans and their culture(s) in the complicated racial environment of New Orleans had a significant impact on the white intelligentsia through white bohemian interaction with black servants and observation of black street life.[7] However, Reed underestimates the interest in black writers and artists generally, and in what became known as the Harlem Renaissance in particular, among at least some key members of the Dixie bohemia that he studies. As he remarks, the journalist and fiction writer Lyle Saxon was significant in promoting the career of key Harlem Renaissance artist Richmond Barthe in the 1920s. Reed represents this relationship as "an individual act of kindness," but it is also very possible to see it as a New Orleans version of the interracial gay network that connected Harlem Renaissance artists to the "mainstream" culture industries.[8]

Moreover, the *Double-Dealer*'s founding editor, John McClure (with whom Faulkner spent considerable time), showed a pronounced interest in black literature. Books by black authors were reviewed from the journal's earliest issues. While generally cautious about directly challenging Jim Crow, the *Double-Dealer* exhibited a significant evolution in racial attitudes from its first issues to its last, as illustrated by McClure's change in standard usage from the lower-cased "negro" to the capitalized "Negro." McClure, following the arguments of Du Bois, Johnson, and other black cultural critics, declared the spirituals and blues to be the greatest body of "folk" poetry created in the United States, providing a model that might inspire and empower future black writers.[9] Like Langston Hughes and other emerging African American writers, McClure eventually saw Toomer's *Cane* as the realization of that folk promise in a very favorable review in the January 1924 issue of the *Double-Dealer*.[10] Toomer was famously reluctant to be pigeonholed in the racial binary of Negro and white, but both black and white modernists understood his generically complex novel, his early sketches that first found publication in the *Double-Dealer*, and indeed, Toomer himself to be "Negro." While McClure proclaimed Toomer to be the first black writer to produce this new "Negro" writing, an extremely favorable *Double-Dealer* review of Langston Hughes's 1926 collection, *The Weary Blues*, in the May 1926 issue, not only pushed hard against the ideology of literary Jim Crow but also showed a knowledge of other Harlem Renaissance poets, including McKay and Countee Cullen, as well as Dunbar.[11]

The African American literary figure with whom Faulkner had the most documented interaction as a young writer is William Stanley Braithwaite, a poet, editor, and critic whose yearly *Anthology of American Magazine Verse* and poetry column in the *Boston Evening Transcript* made him, along with *Poetry* magazine editor Harriet Monroe, one of the key promoters of the New Poetry in the United States. Braithwaite included one of Faulkner's early poems in his 1925 anthology, and it was to Braithwaite that Faulkner turned for advice about a Boston publisher who was slow in paying Faulkner royalties.[12] Though it was well known in Boston and in the US poetry world generally that Braithwaite was black, it is unclear whether Faulkner was aware of this. However, it is clear that Faulkner encountered the work of James Weldon Johnson through Braithwaite's anthologies: Johnson's "The Creation" (the first of the poems that would be collected in the 1927 volume, *God's Trombones*) appeared in the 1920 *Anthology of American Magazine Verse*, one of the relatively few books from the 1920s found in Faulkner's library after his death.[13] Also, the fact that the artist William Spratling and Faulkner would create *Sherwood Anderson and Other Famous Creoles: A Gallery of Contemporary New Orleans* (1926) as an adaptation of and sort of homage to Miguel Covarrubias's *The Prince of Wales and Other Famous Americans* suggests that Spratling, who much admired Covarrubias's caricatures, and Faulkner would have some consciousness of the emerging Harlem Renaissance through Covarrubias's work in *Vanity Fair* and elsewhere, work in which the Harlem scene and artistic personalities featured prominently.

As Eric J. Sundquist has noted, Toomer's *Cane* is the key Jim Crow migration narrative that Faulkner was almost certain to have read early in his career—though it strikes me that he was also likely to have looked at the 1927 reprinting of *The Autobiography of an Ex-Colored Man* that was published under James Weldon Johnson's name.[14] Like other modernists of various stripes and identities, Toomer takes up what he sees as the problem of modern isolation, fragmentation, and warring selves (racial, gendered, sexual, economic, intellectual, natural, and spiritual) within a formally fragmented narrative that challenges or completely jettisons traditional notions of generic conventions, narration, unity of plot, and even a stable protagonist. However, the trajectory of this fragmented novel also follows the yo-yoing pattern of the Jim Crow migration narrative, moving from South to North to South without any clear resolution in the concluding "Kabnis" section. The most one may claim is that there is a possibility (but no more than a possibility) of some satisfactory closure in *Cane*.

Faulkner's deepest-held views on race remain murky. He was capable of praising such radical black writing as Richard Wright's *Native Son* and denouncing the murder of Emmett Till while making deeply racist statements in public and private. Certainly, black African American characters (as opposed to mixed-race or possibly mixed-race characters, such as Charles Bon and Charles Etienne de St. Valery Bon in *Absalom, Absalom!* and Joe Christmas in *Light in August*), like women for the most part, appear as forces of nature more than human beings. Still, whatever his precise beliefs on racial equality, Faulkner proposes that original sins marked out the trajectory of the United States: the commodification of the land (as it was bought or seized from Native peoples) and the commodification of people in chattel slavery, setting the United States in general and the South in particular on a tragic course, with the journey of Byron and Lena in *Light in August* possibly offering a countervailing glimmer of hope.

Interestingly, one of the very few times that Faulkner attempts to render the consciousness of a dark-skinned African American on the page is in one of his early New Orleans sketches, "New Orleans." The sketch, published in the *Double-Dealer*, presents the thoughts of a black longshoreman—perhaps betraying the influence of Faulkner's mentor in his move from poetry to fiction, Sherwood Anderson, who had a deep fascination with black stevedores on the New Orleans docks—along with those of a gallery of, apparently, white people. These thoughts are a Toomeresque mixture of spirituals, stylized black vernacular English, and what might be seen as high poetic passages. As in the Jim Crow migration narratives (certainly as in *Cane*), there is a sense of the city as a place of alienation from nature and from roots: "These cities are not my cities, but this dark is my dark, with all the old passions and fears and sorrows that my people have breathed into it."[15] While one can see in this a sort of primitivism not unlike that of Sherwood Anderson's *Dark Laughter*, the cultural mélange of the longshoreman's thoughts, again much like and no doubt influenced by *Cane*, betrays a radically divided and alienated consciousness rather any simple "natural" being.

Such internal division on the part of dark-skinned black characters is rarely, if ever, displayed directly in Faulkner's subsequent fiction. However, bearing in mind Dunbar's notion of "the mask" and other figurations of African American dualism, we can perhaps intuit such divided consciousnesses that might impel black subjects into movement (albeit movement that is unlikely to arrive at any satisfactory destination or resolution) in certain black characters from Faulkner's early fiction. One example might be Caspey Strother, a young black veteran of World War I in Faulkner's *Flags in the Dust* (written in 1927), who returns to the Sartoris plantation denouncing the Jim Crow system and declaring his unwillingness to tolerate it any longer.[16] Strother is violently forced to abandon his new beliefs, at least openly, by old Bayard Satoris. As Thadious M. Davis points out, Faulkner here shows an awareness of a new African American spirit, or at least a new, more militant presentation of the African American spirit, one consonant with the New Negro Renaissance.[17] In addition, Faulkner at least implicitly projects a consciousness for which life in the Jim Crow South is unbearable even if Strother ultimately exhibits outward acceptance. One can imagine Strother taking to the road, to Chicago, Detroit, Cleveland, or even New York—though Faulkner does not let the reader see so neat a resolution.

Still, it is in Faulkner's early mixed-race or possibly mixed-race characters that the North-South, urban-rural, individual-collective yo-yoing of the Jim Crow migration novel is most clearly seen. Again, mixed-race protagonists were a hallmark of much African American migration fiction, such as Johnson's *Autobiography*, Toomer's *Cane* (especially in the final "Kabnis" section), Larsen's *Quicksand*, McKay's *Home to Harlem*, and even in its own way Harper's *Iola Leroy*. Though Faulkner's *Light in August* (1932) features several journeys, the story of the possibly mixed-race Joe Christmas is quite literally a black migration narrative. The novel is unlike the usual black narrative with a "passing" element, however, in that neither Christmas nor the reader is absolutely sure he is a "Negro," since the tales of his parentage are told by variously self-interested and/or mad characters, none of whom could be said to be reliable or possess reliable information. Nonetheless, *Light in August* delineates the familiar black migration protagonist's gothic yo-yoing between North (including the newly formed ghettos of the urban North) and South, without any sort of rest or resolution until Christmas's shooting and castration by vigilante Percy Grimm. It does not matter where he is; all the roads that Christmas travels become the same street running between North and South, with no real possibility of rest, rootedness, or closure except in death:

> From that night the thousand streets ran as one street, with imperceptible corners and changes of scene, broken by intervals of begged and stolen rides, on trains and trucks, and on country wagons with he at twenty and twentyfive

and thirty sitting on the seat with his still, hard face and the clothes (even when soiled and worn) of a city man and the driver of the wagon not knowing who or what the passenger was and not daring to ask. The street ran into Oklahoma and Missouri and as far south as Mexico and then back north to Chicago and Detroit and then back south again and at last to Mississippi. . . . And always, sooner or later, the street ran through cities, through an identical and well-nigh interchangeable section of cities without remembered names, where beneath the dark and equivocal and symbolical archways of midnight he bedded with the women and paid them when he had the money, and when he did not have it he bedded anyway and then told them that he was a negro.[18]

Similarly, Christmas yo-yos between black and white, feeling black while living with white people and white while living with black people, a violation not only of Jim Crow but of his own sense of order:

Sometimes he would remember how he had once tricked or teased white men into calling him a negro in order to fight them, to beat them or be beaten; now he fought the negro who called him white. He was in the north now, in Chicago and then Detroit. He lived with negroes, shunning white people. He ate with them, slept with them, belligerent, unpredictable, uncommunicative. He now lived as man and wife with a woman who resembled an ebony carving. At night he would lie in bed beside her, sleepless, beginning to breathe deep and hard. He would do it deliberately, feeling, even watching, his white chest arch deeper and deeper within his ribcage, trying to breathe into himself the dark odor, the dark and inscrutable thinking and being of negroes, with each suspiration trying to expel from himself the white blood and the white thinking and being. And all the while his nostrils at the odor which he was trying to make his own would whiten and tauten, his whole being writhe and strain with physical outrage and spiritual denial. (225–26)

One might say, as some observers such as James A. Snead have, that Lucas Burch resembles or is a weird double of Christmas.[19] Certainly both are on a sort of endless, restless, cyclical, unsatisfying journey that will only end with death. But they are quite different, if intertwined. Burch is the embodiment of the corruption caused by the sin of the commodification of the land and nature, as seen in US literature from as far back as James Fenimore Cooper to modernist fictions like *The Great Gatsby*, whose closing scene invokes the rupture that takes place after the Dutch sailors (who are, after all, on a commercial mission) are first awed by the green breast of Long Island, or *Light in August*, which opens with images of the dilapidated logging equipment left behind as the loggers moved on in search of new forests to cut (5–6). Burch

refuses to fulfill his obligations to Lena and their son and seals his fate
when he jumps on a train to escape, leaving Byron happily to take that
place on another sort of journey. Christmas, as the name suggests, bears
the Burden (pun intended) of the sin of the commodification of people
and the deep corruption of and anxiety about identity that attended that
commodification in a nation where a universalist notion of inalienable
human rights was enshrined in the document that literally constituted
the United States and defined the legal, political, and philosophical
nature of being American. As in the African American migration novel,
Christmas's perpetual journeying between North and South, city and
country, black and white reveals not potential or self-development but a
crisis of the individual (and nation):

> He thought that it was loneliness which he was trying to escape and not him-
> self. But the street ran on: catlike, one place was the same as another to him.
> But in none of them could he be quiet. But the street ran on in its moods and
> phases, always empty: he might have seen himself as in numberless avatars, in
> silence, doomed with motion, driven by the courage of flagged and spurred
> despair; by the despair of courage whose opportunities had to be flagged and
> spurred. (226)

Interestingly, Gail Hightower's existential crisis is closely bound up
with that of Christmas despite little direct interaction between the two
characters. One might say that Hightower, too, is haunted by a crisis
of whiteness and its inevitable proximity to and permeability by blackness, though unlike Christmas, Hightower goes nowhere physically
after settling in Jefferson. After all, he is a minister who essentially loses
his congregation and, apparently, his wife through his obsessive reconstruction (and whitening) of his grandfather as a heroic Confederate
martyr—when in fact the grandfather was killed by an angry farmer for
stealing chickens, an activity racialized and stereotyped as black in the
minstrel and "coon" literary and performance genres. The townspeople
of Jefferson, too, are deeply troubled and even outraged by Hightower's
inability to act sufficiently "white" or at least to maintain what they see
as sufficient social distance between himself and his black cook. It is only
at the end, through his delivery of Lena Grove's child and his attempt to
aid Christmas, that Hightower is finally able to resolve the modernist-era
racial anxiety encoded in or even masquerading as a Lost Cause version
of history. While Hightower's death is not as certain as that of Christmas,
it seems likely that this resolution, too, comes only as he dies.

One might make many of the same points about *Absalom, Absalom!*
It is not Charles Bon but his son Charles Etienne de St. Valery Bon who

most resembles the black migration protagonist (and Joe Christmas) as an apparently white (and somewhat sexually ambiguous) man traveling from one interchangeable town or city to another with his dark-skinned black wife, in "intervals . . . of furious and incomprehensible and apparently reasonless moving, progression,"

> the man apparently hunting out situations in order to flaunt and fling the ape-like body of his charcoal companion in the faces of any and all who would retaliate: the negro stevedores and deckhands on steamboats or in city honky-tonks who thought he was a white man and believed it only the more strongly when he denied it; the white men who, when he said he was a negro, believed that he lied in order to save his skin, or worse: from sheer besotment of sexual perversion; in either case the result the same: the man with body and limbs almost as light and delicate as a girl's giving the first blow, usually unarmed and heedless of the numbers opposed to him, with that same fury and implacability and physical imperviousness to pain and punishment, neither cursing nor panting, but laughing.[20]

Joe Christmas's (and Charles Etienne de St. Valery Bon's) endless street raises a problem long treated by African American authors and raised, too, by white US modernists influenced by fin de siècle African American literature: once the phenomenon of "passing" is brought up either as an actuality or a possibility, the boundaries of "black" and "white" are destabilized for white people because one can never really be certain about one's own "whiteness," much less anyone else's. Another problem anticipates Jacques Derrida's theoretical notion that opposing terms in a binary pair, particularly "presence" and "absence," inevitably exist in each other as a sort of negative trace that takes on a positive existence even as it strangely effaces or "occults" itself.[21] This is particularly true of the privileged term *white*, which excludes or represses all that is not "white" and assigns it to "Negro" or "black." As such, one might see a racial crisis that directly or more obliquely draws on the black migration narrative not only with respect to mixed-race "Negro" characters such as Christmas and Bon, but also with respect to "white" characters, such as Gail Hightower and Quentin Compson (a sexually troubled and ambivalent man who also finds himself yo-yoing between South and North before his suicide), whose crises are encoded in the obsessive historical narrative defense of personal and family "whiteness." Of course, long before Derrida or even Toni Morrison's *Playing in the Dark*, Ralph Ellison famously, and hilariously, represented the presence of this sort of trace in the metaphysics of race in the United States in the Liberty Paint episode of *Invisible Man*. There, it is revealed that a few drops of

black are necessary to produce "Optic White" paint—with "Optic" serving as a reminder that, according to the "one-drop" racial logic of the
United States, the paint is in fact "black," even if it appears "white."[22]
The episode evokes the same endless regress of uncertainty over racial
presence and absence (and sexual presence and absence) presented in
the prologue of the novel, where the preacher in a hallucinatory sermon
asserts, "Black will make you . . . or black will un-make you"—an anxious
prospect that suffuses much modernist literature in the United States,
nowhere more than in the novels of William Faulkner.[23]

NOTES

1. Robert Stepto, *From Behind the Veil: A Study of Afro-American Narrative* (Urbana: University of Illinois Press, 1991), 70–74.

2. Frances E. W. Harper, *Iola Leroy, or, Shadows Uplifted* (Boston: Beacon Press, 1987).

3. Paul Laurence Dunbar, *The Sport of the Gods*, in *The Sport of the Gods and Other Essential Writings*, ed. Shelley Fisher Fishkin and David Bradley (New York: Modern Library, 2005), 293–433.

4. James Weldon Johnson, *The Autobiography of an Ex-Colored Man*, in *Three Negro Classics* (New York: Avon, 1965), 391–511.

5. Ibid., 511.

6. Frederick R. Karl, *William Faulkner: American Writer* (New York: Weidenfeld & Nicolson, 1989), 728.

7. John Shelton Reed, *Dixie Bohemia: A French Quarter Circle in the 1920s* (Baton Rouge: Louisiana State University Press, 2012), 59–67.

8. Ibid., 60.

9. John McClure, "*Negro Folk Rhymes* by Thomas Talley," *Double-Dealer* (August 1922): 107.

10. John McClure, "*Cane* by Jean Toomer," *Double-Dealer* (January 1924): 26.

11. Joseph Hilton Smith, "*The Weary Blues* by Langston Hughes," *Double-Dealer* (May 1926): 358.

12. Karl, *William Faulkner*, 287.

13. Joseph Blotner, *William Faulkner's Library: A Catalogue* (Charlottesville: University Press of Virginia, 1964), 15.

14. Eric J. Sundquist, "Faulkner, Race, and the Forms of American Fiction," in *Faulkner and Race: Faulkner and Yoknapatawpha, 1986*, ed. Doreen Fowler and Ann J. Abadie (Jackson: University Press of Mississippi, 1987), 14–17.

15. Carvel Collins, ed., *William Faulkner: New Orleans Sketches* (New York: Random House, 1967), 9.

16. William Faulkner, *Flags in the Dust*, in *Novels 1926–1929*, ed. Joseph Blotner and Noel Polk (New York: Library of America, 2006), 541–875.

17. Thadious M. Davis, *Faulkner's "Negro": Art and the Southern Context* (Baton Rouge: Louisiana State University Press, 1983), 67.

18. William Faulkner, *Light in August*, rev. ed. (1932; New York: Vintage International, 1990), 223–24. Subsequent references to this edition will appear parenthetically in the text.

19. James A. Snead, *"Light in August* and the Rhetorics of Racial Division," in *Faulkner and Race: Faulkner and Yoknapatawpha, 1986,* ed. Doreen Fowler and Ann J. Abadie (Jackson: University Press of Mississippi, 1987), 164–65.

20. William Faulkner, *Absalom, Absalom!* (1936; New York: Random House, 1986), 167.

21. Jacques Derrida, *Of Grammatology*, trans. Gayatri Chakravorty Spivak (Baltimore: Johns Hopkins University Press, 1976), 47.

22. Ralph Ellison, *Invisible Man* (1952; New York: Random House, 1989), 199–202.

23. Ibid., 10; emphasis in quotation removed.

Lingering in the Black: Faulkner's Illegible Modernist Sound Melding

Thadious M. Davis

Adele, the British pop singer, enabled me to think both about the title of this essay and also about the process by which unique talents emerge out of a confluence of cultural and crosscultural models and patterns. Her signature "Rolling in the Deep," released at the end of 2010, is a testament to her powerful voice and consummate talent, yet at the same time it is also a tribute to countless African American soul singers whose music and style permeated and influenced Adele's rendering and presentation. While she does not imitate, she does have distinct models and stylistic influences that come from outside of Britain and across racial lines, and their soundings in the background provide an extra measure of hearing pleasure. Described as a breakthrough performance in a "bluesy gospel mode," "Rolling in the Deep," along with Adele's particular crosscultural positioning in a breakout moment with a mature, distinctive sound that resonated with untold histories of blues women and multiple traditions of music, occasioned my thinking about William Faulkner and his relationship to black cultural expressive and creative traditions at the start of his career.[1] The confident, authoritative sound of "Rolling in the Deep" reminded me of the confidence Faulkner displayed in making his move from poetry to fiction in the 1920s, or perhaps more accurately, widening his sphere into the realm of fiction, since he would continue to write poetry during this period. In addition, I was reminded of his confident critical assessment of the major American poets at the same moment he was expanding his range of writing and of his studied acquisition of new sounds that went beyond the lyric.[2] To put it in terms that I will return to shortly, the presumption of knowledge about, the assumption of authority over, is dramatically freeing and enabling, bringing with it an undeniable authenticity within that specific area. We hear it in twenty-two-year-old Adele's voice and its technically flawless reproduction in the recording, and we hear it too in the sounds of the

36

fiction Faulkner began to create in the 1920s—in sometimes flawed but often pitch-perfect reproduction of voice soundings in his writing.

Like Adele, Faulkner's voice is marked by specific underpinnings, of which some are identifiable immediately while some are muffled, perhaps intentionally. Black soundings are at once both apparent and muted in Faulkner's work. The different auditory registers seem to emerge in his early writings and from several influential sources. First, the modernist soundings becoming in the 1920s so central to the aesthetics and artistry of recognized and prize-winning writers were primarily derived from an effort to find and locate the new, and to do so often specifically within the contexts of the underexplored yet heard difference of minority voices, particularly black southern voices. Second, several personal exposures to black soundings in Faulkner's Mississippi upbringing opened him to the possibilities suggested by modernist aesthetics. The music of black musicians that Faulkner heard as a youth in Oxford made an indelible mark on his aesthetics. But in addition to black music, Faulkner also heard the stories told to him by Caroline Barr and his black caretakers when he was a boy. According to Judith Sensibar's research, as a child Faulkner often accompanied Caroline Barr into the black residential areas around Oxford, where he was exposed to social experiences—religious (Sunday church) and secular (Saturday entertainments)—of rural black people. Their stories and their voices, according to Faulkner's own accounts, later resurfaced in his writing. Third, a key figure in forwarding Faulkner's synthesizing the "new" of modernism's exploration of minority voices as art with the soundings of black music and black storytellers from his Mississippi experiences was James Weldon Johnson, a poet, songwriter, novelist, and critic. As I will show, James Weldon Johnson was not only a writer Faulkner read but also a writer Faulkner emulated. Johnson's attention to sound and to the ways in which the sounds of black life and culture could be rendered in literary art entered into Faulkner's practice and remain audible in his black soundings. Johnson's writing, creative and critical, can be heard echoing in Faulkner's fiction through the 1920s and beyond.

At the beginning of his writing career, when Faulkner still conceived of himself as a poet in the vein of Verlaine and Swinburne, the mechanical reproduction of sound was one of the major modern technological innovations. A cursory view of Faulkner's early drawings and writing reveals that he was a product of the modern US jazz era, which was formed out of the music and sound produced by black instrumentalists and singers whose soundings were also being reproduced by the advancements in recording technology. Records, along with radio, made accessible to a wide population the music and voices previously off limits to some segments of society. Recordings of black music became central to modernity, as Alexander Weheliye explains through his usage of the term *phonography* to signify not only the linkage between black cultural production and sound technologies but also the centrality of those processes in twentieth-century global culture.[3]

Here I would like to explore two points of entry into a more diverse modern artistic world for Faulkner. Both bear on blackness and its relation to American modernism, especially white American modernism, despite Hegel and others having placed blacks outside of history. Both relate to the sounds of James Weldon Johnson that are apparent in Faulkner's work, and both address the choice of authorial affiliation that Faulkner made early on in his writing career.

One is the world of modern music punctuated by black music ushered into Faulkner's youthful life in the 1910s and anchored initially in the black contemporary rags, blues, and jazz played by the black traveling bands of composer W. C. Handy for dances at the University of Mississippi. Based in Memphis, Handy led the Knights of Pythias Band in playing popular dance music and his own compositions throughout the surrounding areas until 1919, when he moved to New York's Tin Pan Alley and began having his compositions recorded by the great black musicians of the time, including James P. Johnson, who made an early piano roll of Handy's music including his tribute to the University of Mississippi, "Ole Miss Blues."[4] We know from Faulkner's first biographer, Joseph Blotner, that in the fall of 1915, Faulkner attended dances in the ballroom of Gordon Hall, where jazz was the popular music and where Handy's band frequently appeared and played his syncopated "Memphis Blues" and "St. Louis Blues."[5] Faulkner's friend Ben Wasson remembers Faulkner's being so excited at the sound of what was possibly Handy's orchestra that he insisted they listen to the music from outside of Gordon Hall where a formal dance was taking place.[6]

Years later, "St. Louis Blues" would remain a Faulkner favorite, so much so that during a visit to New York and a tour of its nightlife, including Harlem's, Faulkner would request only "St. Louis Blues" at every venue.[7] And by 1930, he had incorporated the first line of Handy's blues into the title of his story, "That Evening Sun Go Down," also tentatively titled, with an unmistakable blues twist, "Never Done No Weeping When You Wanted to Laugh," and ultimately titled simply "That Evening Sun." These three titles all suggest Handy's own description of the blues scale—"the expression of the emotional life of the race"—and of playing between what he called "the breaks."[8] Importantly, the recordings of Handy's music and that of other musicians, both black and white, enabled Faulkner to listen over and over again to them while he wrote.

He wore out three recordings of George Gershwin's "Rhapsody in Blue," for example, one after another, while working on *Sanctuary*.[9]

Despite the acculturation of black music as new or American music in the 1920s, it is worth remembering the politics of sound and the relationship between race and power articulated especially in the blues produced out of the Mississippi Delta. Clyde Woods emphasizes the music as "an important component of orature," a way of speaking directly to the conditions of black life within racist structures. Yet in the blues especially, according to Woods, there is "the continuation of numerous African vocal, instrumental and composition traditions" that also include "the continuity of the role of performers as educators. . . . Language and music also intersect with performance styles. . . . The complex of language, music and performance must be understood as a whole."[10] In a sense, the music as expressive culture is inextricable from language and performance and from the articulation of identity and with it heritage and history.

Faulkner's early fiction finds its voice to educate readers on the reality of emotions, most often loss and grief, and in the inequity of power dynamics in the performance of blues even when the articulation suggests sacred music, as in "The Longshoreman" (first published in the January–February 1925 issue of the *Double-Dealer*), where strains of "Swing Low, Sweet Chariot" and "All God's Chillen Got Wings" echo throughout the lament of a black dockworker who sings, "White man gives me clo'se and shoes, but dat dont make no pavement love my feets. These cities are not my cities, but this dark is my dark, with all the old passions and fears and sorrows that my people have breathed into it. Let this blood sing: did I make this blood?"[11] Shifting between the performance of the black longshoreman and a white perspective on his experience, the uneven dialect of the monologue is a blues attempting to encompass the black man's existence, in which "white folks says, and nigger does" within a specific urban life experience. The blues lament is sung in racial terms: "wash me whiter'n sno-o-w!"[12] *Snow* is elongated to emulate song. The effect is reminiscent of Louis Armstrong's recording of "Black and Blue," used by Ralph Ellison in *Invisible Man* to mark the ironic side of racial identification.

Whether portraying unnamed women servants making brief appearances or haunted white men wandering lost, Faulkner represents these characters as soundings with a common base in what is constituted as a contrapuntal black presence, embodied in sad, knowing song that can be labeled "sound travels." What "The Longshoreman" gestures toward is the undertone of black sound echoing beneath any personal lament in particular or any societal critique in general. The guise of language is necessarily then always bifurcated in this sense in Faulkner's fiction, as is an implicit dependence on monologue, interior or narrated.

In an earlier essay, I have already pointed to the place of music, and black music in particular, in Faulkner's imaginative life, including his drawings and his fiction.[13] To the structures of feeling and types of representation there, I would now add that Faulkner's epistemology of sound in his fiction emerges at least in part out of his attention to black expressive culture—music, yes, but stories, poetry, and sermons as well. I would be remiss, however, if I did not reiterate here the well-observed ways in which black new music provided a way for whites to reconnect with their own premodern or affective pasts by recasting both whites themselves and black others in public performances of race. James Weldon Johnson observed in his 1933 autobiography, *Along This Way*, "I have been amazed and amused watching white people dancing to a Negro band in a Harlem cabaret; attempting to throw off crusts and layers of inhibitions laid on by sophisticated civilization; striving to yield [to the] feel and experience of abandon; seeking to recapture a taste of primitive joy in life and living; trying to work their way back into the jungle which was the original Garden of Eden; in a word, doing their best to pass for colored."[14] Johnson iterates one of the standard ways of thinking about the documented appeal of black music, black sound, and black life more generally for white Americans and in particular for the artistic avant-garde and modernists among them determined to come out from under whatever Victorian constraints remained.[15] "Passing for colored" or what was imagined to be "colored" in the public imagina-tion, as Johnson put it, is an echoing of imagined subjectivities, a sound-ing that vibrates within the containment of fixed perceptions of raced bodies.

I would like to pose Johnson's observation alongside remarks by Con-rad Aiken, the poet whose 1916 volume *Turns and Movies, and Other Tales in Verse* Faulkner reviewed and whose poetry he admired. In 1939 Aiken published an *Atlantic Monthly* essay on Faulkner in which he names himself among "the most passionate of Mr. Faulkner's admir-ers" and compares Faulkner's style to that of one of the most famous jazz bands of the 1920s: "The exuberant and tropic luxuriance of sound which Jim Europe's jazz band used to exhale, like a jungle of rank creep-ers and ferocious blooms taking shape before one's eyes,—magnificently and endlessly intervolved, glisteningly and ophidianly in motion, coil sliding over coil, and leaf and flower forever magically interchanging,— was scarcely more bewildering, in its sheer inexhaustible fecundity, than Mr. Faulkner's style."[16] Aiken points to sound—and the specific sound of Jim Europe, the legendary black jazz maestro—in order to describe

Faulkner's style. Although written in the 1930s, his description is yet another way of contextualizing not only stylistic relations between the new music and modernist writing but also the legibility of perceptual soundings from black life central to so much of that writing, especially Faulkner's own. In his prose, from the New Orleans sketches through *Soldiers' Pay, Sartoris, Sanctuary*, and *The Sound and the Fury* and liminally beyond, Faulkner uses music generated within black sites or bodies to propagate sound as affect or emotion in other sites.

The second entry into Faulkner's turn to fiction and American modernism that I take up here is the New Orleans avant-garde concentrated around the little magazine named the *Double-Dealer: A National Magazine from the South*, which between 1921 and 1926 published Ezra Pound, H. D., Ernest Hemingway, Jean Toomer, Djuna Barnes, Thornton Wilder, Carl Van Vechten, Hart Crane, and Maxwell Bodenheim, as well as a contingent of southern Agrarians and Fugitives (Donald Davidson, John Crowe Ransom, Allen Tate, and Robert Penn Warren). This period is fairly well covered in Faulkner studies, but I will tease out several aspects that I think may have been less discussed because of the important focus on the relationship between Faulkner and Sherwood Anderson in New Orleans. These have to do with the ways in which Faulkner's understanding of American modernist writing began to shift and expand but also to absorb the potential for black dialect. I suggest that this difference can be charted in *Soldiers' Pay*, with its later chapters in particular demonstrating a changed and charged sensibility that is much more sympathetic to and evocative of the American modernist writing that Faulkner experienced during his time in New Orleans, when his contemporaries were experimenting with using the sound, substance, and subject of black life in Louisiana to propel themselves and their work into the thick of American modernism, just as the *Double-Dealer* showcased its active participation in both a southern artistic enterprise and a national avant-garde modernism.

Predictably, the sketches Faulkner published in the *Double-Dealer*, as well as in the *Times-Picayune*, are legible in their attention to the sounds of an urban world of diverse people. The titles and content reference not only the music of Handy, jazz, and blues but also traditional black work songs; secular folk songs; and black sacred music, sorrow songs, and spirituals. However, they also display a dependence on reproducing the sound of voices, especially by creating black vocalities and dialect. Significantly, Faulkner's literary circle in New Orleans included writers who explored folk culture in their work and experimented with using minority voices. One was Lyle Saxon, whose short stories in the 1920s focused on black dialect and whose 1937 novel *Children of Strangers* treated the mixed-raced people in the Cane River plantation area of Louisiana, a subject Ernest Gaines would later explore in his fiction. A second was Hamilton Basso, whose early work featured both blacks and immigrants. (He was the son of Italian Americans in New Orleans.) A third was Oliver La Farge, whose 1929 novel *Laughing Boy* deployed Native American life and lore and incorporated his anthropological work on the Navajo. These three young men, perhaps even more so than Anderson because they were Faulkner's peers, were influential in their vision of what constituted the "new" in American writing. Even William Spratling, primarily a visual artist who would turn his attention to Mexico, to the Indians around Taxco, and to silversmithing, wrote a piece for *Scribner's* in 1928 on the Creole people of Isle Brevelle, in the Cane River area of Natchitoches, Louisiana.

These artists were bohemian and, for the times, somewhat iconoclastic in social and sexual mores.[17] As French Quarter residents and active with the *Double-Dealer*, they were part of the push toward an American modernism that for them meant the turn to minorities: their voices, their folklore, and their lives. While they appropriated what they could of black and other minority people for their art, they were not racial progressives. In appropriating black materials and locating blacks as touchstones for difference in their writing, they participated in controlling and limiting the artistic representation of blacks in public discursive spheres. In this endeavor, they exhibited the same hegemonic assumptions about black difference as a "natural state" that Aldon Nielson has identified as typical of many white writers during the period, assumptions that led to literary representations of blacks as "the most radically *other*" and that in effect perpetuated the exercise of power over blacks.[18]

Sherwood Anderson's interest in the sound of black voices, evident in his championing of Gertrude Stein's modernist *Melanctha: Each One as She May* (included in her *Three Lives* [1909]) and manifested in his own *Dark Laughter* (1925), should not be glossed over too quickly here. Clearly that interest was not lost on Faulkner, who in this phase of his apprenticeship availed himself of all the advice and models in his New Orleans milieu.[19] Faulkner's story "Sunset" (first published in the *Times-Picayune* on May 24, 1925), for example, relies heavily on an attempt to recreate black voice and also to translate it into an unresponsive white culture. "Sunset" traces the tragic fate of a black man from the Louisiana countryside who decides to return to Africa but whose expressed desire is ridiculed and misunderstood. His words—"But cap'n . . . I jest wants to go to Af'ica. I kin pay my way"—function as audible noise, not as actual speech.[20] When he is tricked into believing that a boat has set him ashore in Africa, he kills a cow thinking it is a lion. That mistake leads to his bloody confrontation, rendered from his perspective and voice, with those he presumes to be Africans and cannibals. The newspaper story, "Black Desperado Slain," that prefaces the narrative concludes, "No reason has been ascertained for the black's running amuck, though it is believed he was insane."[21] The news account dramatizes the words in standard English that can be heard as speech communicating a message, as opposed to the speaking voice of the protagonist, whose dialect is not heard as speech. The structure foreshadows "Pantaloon in Black," and the unnamed tragic figure is an embryonic Rider. By 1942 and the publication of *Go Down, Moses*, Faulkner had surpassed his legible influences because by then, in addition to mimicry of sound, he had developed his potential for hearing. By the 1940s, too, his more finely tuned ear made it possible at once to blend mimicked sounds and to distinguish among them.

In the mid-1920s, however, Anderson's *Dark Laughter* and its style of incorporating black voice in mimicry still held sway with Faulkner. *Dark Laughter* is one of the books from the 1920s found in Faulkner's personal library.[22] Both *Dark Laughter* and *The Green Pastures: A Fable*, Marc Connelly's 1929 book, also in Faulkner's library, utilize the sounds and voices of blacks. Anderson's text deploys sound as a way of underscoring and counterpointing what is missing in modern life. Connelly's play is an adaptation of Roark Bradford's *Ol' Man Adam and His Chillun*, a 1928 collection of biblical folktales told from the perspective of southern African Americans. Bradford, a white Tennessean and a University of California, Berkeley, graduate, worked as a journalist in New Orleans during Faulkner's stay in the 1920s. As the night editor of the *Times-Picayune*, he was most likely responsible for the publication of Faulkner's newspaper sketches. Like *Dark Laughter*, *Ol' Man Adam and His Chillun* stemmed from listening to the voices of blacks in and around New Orleans. Bradford's text ventriloquized the voices of blacks in all of the tales.

Following Bradford, Connelly's Pulitzer Prize–winning play delved into the stories and tales that gave shape to systems of belief and sustenance for African Americans. Connelly's work became a blockbuster Broadway show and in 1936 a major motion picture, produced during the same period in which Faulkner was a scriptwriter in Hollywood, where he became acquainted with Connelly and socialized with him. Texts such as *Ol' Man Adam and His Chillun* and *The Green Pastures* play upon the dialectal difference in order to make something new for popular aesthetic consumption. They also reinforce black sounding as modernist discourse for Faulkner, and Connelly's success may have planted the idea of transforming *Sanctuary* into the play *Requiem for a Nun*.

That white modernists were turning from traditionally white subjects and mining blackness did not go unnoticed by black writers in this
period. The poet Countee Cullen, in his foreword to *Caroling Dusk: An
Anthology of Verse by Negro Poets* (1927), does not hesitate to proclaim
"that the day of dialect as far as Negro poets are concerned is in the
decline. . . . In a day when artificiality is so vigorously condemned, the
Negro poet would be foolish indeed to turn to dialect. The majority of
present-day poems in dialect are the efforts of white poets."[23] Like James
Weldon Johnson, who would critique dialect at length in the same year,
Cullen notes how the way in which black sound had taken hold in the
creative imagination of prominent white writers as strictly modern. What
is at stake in the white view/black view of dialect is control of and authority over representation, meaning, and authenticity precisely because of
the way in which sound had taken hold of the creative imagination as a
strictly modern phenomenon.

Michael North has explained the ways in which dialect had become
an innovative and experimental tool for key modernist poets such as
Eliot and Pound, but he notes that "it is less often acknowledged just
how far . . . racial cross-identification went or how widespread it was.
Writers as far from Harlem as T. S. Eliot and Gertrude Stein reimagined themselves as black, spoke in a black voice, and used that voice to
transform the literature of their time."[24] A part of his thesis is that "dialect became a prototype of the most radical representational strategies
of English language modernism."[25] He posits that "linguistic mimicry
and racial masquerade were not just shallow fads but strategies without
which modernism could not have arisen."[26] While it is a very large claim,
North supports it with his observations of the visible and widespread use
of dialect and language mimicry functioning within what is considered
to be high modernism. He puts a positive spin on crossracial mimicry
in dialect by speculating that the practice functioned to break down the
privileging of Standard English.

More recent interrogations add the perspective of the American
racial landscape as informing the practice of dialect usage and place
more pressure on considerations of modernism. From that vantage
point, Houston A. Baker Jr., Aldon Nielson, Laura Winkiel, and others
read a simultaneous, alternative modernism that incorporates a counter-
modernism formulated by people of color.[27] That alternative modernity
"interrupts a singular modernity with a particularly disjunctive cultural
crossing."[28]

I point to this development in modernist studies because in a sense
it may be effective in thinking about how, like the "disjunctive cultural
crossing" developed to mark an interjection into an existing dominant

narrative, Faulkner's black soundings intersect with high modernist discourse to forward a way not merely of seeing modern life but also of hearing it. Faulkner's canon may even exemplify North's claim "that the modern covets the primitive—perhaps even created it."[29] In Faulkner's case, I would add that he also creates himself in precisely the vein of the so-labeled "primitive." His various guises and self-fabrications, along with his fictive representations of himself, suggest his participation in creating specific identities reverberating off "the primitive."

Judith Sensibar in *Faulkner and Love* shows how Faulkner crossed the divide between black and white in Oxford when as a child he walked with Caroline Barr to visit her daughters and relatives. Sensibar's interviews with surviving Barr kin indicate the complexity of exposures Faulkner had to the voices of Mississippi blacks during his formative years; for example, his visits to Molly Barr's juke joint.[30] While these scenes from Faulkner's childhood are significant, I would not want to overemphasize them, although they may convey the possibility of a less conventional relationship to racial mores in Mississippi. However, I do believe that these formative early experiences are part of a confluence of accumulated real and vicarious experiences that results in an emphasis on black soundings in Faulkner's writing. The confluence suggests the increased significance of sound as a modern medium and the ways in which specific black sounds came together from both Faulkner's childhood and young manhood and vicariously from his readings of James Weldon Johnson in particular but also of Jean Toomer, whose "Storm Ending," "Harvest Song," and "Nora" were published in the *Double-Dealer* in 1922, the year before the publication of his experimental *Cane*. The conjoining of these various experiential threads enables an identification both of difference and with difference.

In the matter of identification with difference, for example, Hortense Spillers's theorizing of the law of the mother for black men intersects with Judith Sensibar's analysis of the centrality of Mammy Callie Barr as one of Faulkner's two mothers, a black one and a white one.[31] Spillers contends that cultural inheritance is understood as a legitimate procedure in fatherhood but not motherhood, yet given the legal and cultural erasures of fathers under slavery, "the African-American woman, the *mother*, the daughter, becomes historically the powerful and shadowy evocation of a cultural synthesis long evaporated—the law of the Mother."[32] Following this line of reasoning, Spillers concludes, "It is the heritage of the *mother* that the African-American male must regain as an aspect of his own personhood—the 'power' of 'yes' to the 'female' within."[33] Although Spillers links this phenomenon specifically to black American males, or as she puts it, "the *only* American community of males which has had the specific occasion to learn *who* the female is within itself," her very framing recalls the situation of the white southern male alienated from the father and raised from infancy by a black other mother who, to use Spillers's analogy, "breaks in upon the imagination with a forcefulness that marks both a denial and an 'illegitimacy.'"[34]

In other words, the approach that Spillers takes for the study of African American maleness and subjectivity may also be applicable to the condition of surrogacy linking the white male with the black mother surrogate, in keeping with Sensibar's thinking about Faulkner and the maternal. Not only did "Faulkner's white racial consciousness spring from his doubly mothered childhood," but also, according to Sensibar, white southern "cultural conventions prevented him from ever fully acknowledging" the black woman Callie Barr as mother and "often required that she be demeaned."[35] The question of legitimacy and illegitimacy is also bound up in the issue of authenticity and authority. What happens if, following the condition of having a black second or other mother, a white male crossidentifies as black in some aspects of his subjectivity and identity? What happens if that white male specifically resorts to the soundings of black life to voice and articulate aspects of being associated not merely with the female, but with the black female? On an emotive level, the result could be shame and grief. On another register, the result might well be an auditory capacity to hear at unexpected frequencies and to reproduce sounds heard surreptitiously from across the racial divide.

When reading Faulkner's representations of himself in *Mosquitoes* as "a little kind of black man," we perhaps should include in the mental imaging an envelope of sound as well as of skin.[36] John Duvall, Dorothy Stringer, and other Faulkner critics have already explored the relationship between Faulkner's representation of the artist and blackness in *Mosquitoes* and *Sanctuary*, though primarily in terms of appearance and racialized traits or conceptions of blacks that are essentialized and projected onto blackness or black materiality.[37] Most often, the idea of blackness goes quickly to the matter of skin and coloring and behavioral patterns whether actual or assumed, as in *Sanctuary*, with its references to Popeye as "that black man,"[38] but an added layer of what constitutes the representation of blackness is sonic: sound, voice, the difference that is auditory, that is a heard distinction, a separation and a point of identification. In the envelope of sound as opposed to skin, there is a disengagement from actual or real black people, but there is an investment in and a need for both the cover and the comfort of sound, voice. The shift, as in the move to the mechanical production of the voices of blacks, does not require a body, only a kind of essentialized rendering of traits and with those a compilation of abstract possibilities, open and available for being filled in by the reader or the audience.

Recall that in the last chapter of *Soldiers' Pay*, a white boy overwhelmed by grief experiences his familiar surrounding as "strange," but his house is "where he ate and slept . . . where darkness was kind and sweet," and where, "wanting his mother" who was not there, he "found himself running suddenly through the hall toward a voice raised in comforting, crooning song."[39] It is a voice, not a person; it is sound diffracted. The sound is projected into the affective space of grief and loss, and only then do we discover what the voice represents: "a friend mountainous in blue calico, her elephantine thighs undulating, gracious as the wake of a ferry." The scene ends with the boy's weeping while being rocked and held "against her balloon-like breast" (299). The passing through grief into weeping necessitates coming into the sound offered by the initially disembodied voice and its "crooning song" (298). The boy's hearing sensitivity allows him to translate the crooning into a sound of comfort. This nameless cook is first voice and then body, but her identity is withheld; her subjectivity is filtered through the boy's longing for comfort. Allowed to sing and to speak ("She broke off her mellow, passionless song, exclaiming: 'Bless yo' heart, honey, what is it?'" [298]), she functions only outside of herself as the sounding of comfort. She remains constituted in the realm of lyric as expressive of emotion and affect.

It is not surprising, then, that in an essay-fragment that is not as widely known as his two essays introducing *The Sound and the Fury*, but that in a sense may actually reveal more about the process of his early fiction writing, Faulkner explains how he came to write *Sartoris*: "So I got me some people, some I invented, others I created out of the tales that I learned of nigger cooks and stable boys (of all ages between one armed Joby . . . 18, who taught me to write my name in red ink on the linen duster he wore for some reason we both have forgotten, to . . . old Louvinia who remarked when the stars 'fell' and who called my grandfather and my father by their Christian names until she died)."[40] Faulkner makes clear that the verb "created" in relation to the heard stories has to be modified: "Created I say, because they are partly composed from what they were in actual life and partly from what they should have been and were not."[41] What they should have been is as unclear as what they were not. The only hint is that the use of the n-word along with the named work categories of the servants points toward racial divisions under the segregationist regime in the South and to the racial subservience, inequality, and denial of opportunity that resulted for black men and women. The very physicality of sound he connects to tales emanating from blacks. In a melding of black sonics with storytelling, Faulkner later writes in *Absalom, Absalom!* an echo of the words from his essay: "creating between them, out of the rag-tag and bob-ends of old tales and talking, people who perhaps had never existed at all anywhere."[42] His methodology of sound thus travels through time to place Joby and Louvinia's soundings in white bodies.

That Rosa and Judith, Quentin and Shreve in *Absalom, Absalom!* hear "some stories" in the kind of telling and hearing that Faulkner recalls participating in when he himself got some stories from black cooks and stable boys suggests a completed cycle of sound that occurs over time. His admission stands out not only because of the language he uses to name the race of the cooks and stable boys but also because this acknowledgment of his appropriation of black tales and voices to foment his imagination, which then "invented" some people and "created" others out of the tales he had heard, is not once found elsewhere. Nowhere else, in fact, does Faulkner identify a Joby or Louvinia, named as the youngest and the oldest of those from whom he "learned" tales. Neither of those names appears in *My Brother Bill*, the memoir that John Faulkner wrote following William's death, which identifies a number of black caretakers and residents of the Hollow: not only "Mammy Callie" (Caroline Barr) but also Nancy Snowball, a laundress and cook; Mary, a cook and the mother of Durwur, a playmate of the Faulkner boys; and Mink and Jerry Hayes, Mallory, and Dooley—but no Joby or Lovinia.[43] Yet William's recollection of those voices telling stories remains not merely a part of his auditory sense but also a part of his process for constructing meaning accessed by years of sounding. His signature orality in *Absalom, Absalom!* can be read or heard, then, as a melding of black voices reverberating and tuned now crossracially in white speaking bodies.

Faulkner did not just have remembered and recreated black tales to infuse into his fiction; he also had the literary production of James Weldon Johnson. In 1922, Johnson published the first edition of *The Book of American Negro Poetry* with a preface, completed the year before, in which he laid out his understanding of the criteria for aesthetic achievement in poetry by African Americans. In particular, Johnson attended to music as a gateway to poetry in his preface. He specifically names the spirituals—which he also refers to as "slave songs" and the "greatest body of folk songs" America has produced—and ragtime, which he states is "the one artistic production by which America is known the world over."[44] In one sense, he expands the work on spirituals and black music that W. E. B. Du Bois initiated in *The Souls of Black Folk* (1903). Johnson, however, pushes his conclusions beyond music and into the area of prose achievements. Despite being leery of the ability of dialect to express a full range of emotions, he considers the Uncle Remus tales, reclaimed from the white Joel Chandler Harris's adaptations, some of the most important contributions that African Americans made to American and world culture. His valuation resonates with the contemporaneous use of black sound and appropriation of black dialect in high modernist writing; Eliot and Pound, for example, drew heavily upon the language of Uncle Remus to express their rebellion against the strictures of the literary establishment in England, and as North concludes, their use of dialect was "the private double of the modernist poetry they were jointly creating and publishing."[45]

Johnson was especially concerned about the transcription of black voice, and he understood the implications of conceding black sound to white practitioners. His own songs and poetry and his novel, *The Autobiography of an Ex-Colored Man*, particularly after its 1927 republication, placed raced voices prominently in the public sphere and along with those voices the ways in which racial identity was made, constructed, and created by the culture and the ways in which soundings, whether in music or poetry, might be an avenue for black uplift. In other words, Johnson made accessible in his work the reality that soundings made by blacks could influence and subvert both the cultural hegemony and the racial hierarchy. Although he incorporated images of lynching and violence against blacks and utilized them to dramatize issues of dominance and control, Johnson forwarded the transmission of creative black voice to demonstrate the social contributions and aesthetic achievements of blacks. His body of work from the 1910s and 1920s figures in the background of Faulkner's early fiction.

It is, however, Johnson's *God's Trombones: Seven Negro Sermons in Verse* that seems to be the most visible, audible, and significant influence on the black soundings in Faulkner's fiction. Writing in 1927, Johnson begins his preface to *God's Trombones* with an important statement: "A good deal has been written on the folk creations of the American Negro: his music, sacred and secular; his plantation tales, and his dances; but that there are folk sermons, as well, is a fact that has passed unnoticed."[46] In a revealing look at the "old-time preacher" as "a man of positive genius" (4), Johnson describes how one such minister, "after reading a rather cryptic passage[,] took off his spectacles, closed the Bible with a bang and . . . said, 'Brothers and sisters, this morning—I intend to explain the unexplainable—find out the undefinable—ponder over the imponderable—and unscrew the inscrutable'" (4–5). Johnson points particularly to the fact that the Negro preacher "was above all an orator, and in good measure an actor. He knew the secret of oratory, that at bottom it is a progression of rhythmic words more than it is anything else" (5).

He was, according to Johnson, "a master of all the modes of eloquence. He often possessed a voice that was a marvelous instrument, a voice he could modulate from a sepulchral whisper to a crashing thunder clap. His discourse was generally kept at a high pitch of fervency, but occasionally he dropped into colloquialisms and, less often, into humor. . . . His imagination was bold and unfettered. He had the power to sweep his hearers before him; and so himself was often swept away. At such times his language was not prose but poetry" (5).

Johnson's description of the "old-time" black preacher strikes a chord with what we hear of Reverend Shegog in Faulkner's 1929 novel *The Sound and the Fury*. Johnson emphasizes voice—its power and amplitude and its close relation to the trombone, to musical instrumentality. The example he provides of one such preacher in action, in performance of his sermon, is especially relevant:

> He was a dark-brown man, handsome in his gigantic proportions. He appeared to be a bit self-conscious, perhaps impressed by the presence of the "distinguished visitor" on the platform, and started in to preach a formal sermon from a formal text. The congregation sat apathetic and dozing. He sensed that he was losing his audience and his opportunity. Suddenly he closed the Bible, stepped out from behind the pulpit and began to preach. He started intoning the old folk-sermon that begins with the creation of the world and ends with Judgment Day. He was at once a changed man, free, at ease and masterful. The change in the congregation was instantaneous. An electric current ran through the crowd. It was in a moment alive and quivering; and all the while the preacher held it in the palm of his hand. He was wonderful in the way he employed his conscious and unconscious art. He strode the pulpit up and down in what was actually a very rhythmic dance, and he brought into play the full gamut of his wonderful voice, a voice—what shall I say?—not of an organ or a trumpet, but rather of a trombone, the instrument possessing above all others the power to express the wide and varied range of emotions encompassed by the human voice—and with greater amplitude. He intoned, he moaned, he pleaded—he blared, he crashed, he thundered. (6–7)

Recall the visiting preacher in the fourth section of *The Sound and the Fury*. He is "insignificant" and "countrified" in comparison to the regular minister's "imposing bulk."[47] The physicality of Johnson's minister is reversed in Faulkner's text, but Shegog's transformation follows the pattern Johnson describes:

> They began to watch him as they would a man on a tight rope. They even forgot his insignificant appearance in the virtuosity with which he ran and posed

and swooped upon the cold inflectionless wire of his voice, so that at last, when
with a sort of swooping glide he came to rest again beside the reading desk
with one arm resting upon it at shoulder height and his monkey body as reft
of all motion as a mummy or an emptied vessel, the congregation sighed as if
waked from a collective dream and moved a little in its seats. (366)

Here, as in Johnson, the quality or timbre of sound, its acoustical properties, and its resonant properties make the voice musical and appealing,
yet powerful in its ability to modulate pitch, loudness, and frequency.

Faulkner's representation of Reverend Shegog's transformation, along
with the subject and sound of his sermon, mimics at least four of Johnson's sermons from *God's Trombones*: "Go Down Death—A Funeral
Sermon," "The Crucifixion," "Let My People Go," and "The Judgment
Day." The four poems also underlie the affective core of later Faulkner
texts, including the elegiac *Go Down, Moses* (1942). "Go Down Death—
A Funeral Sermon" for Sister Caroline, delivered to comfort a family
dealing with a mother's death, suggests the everlasting life to which Shegog alludes when he says, "I sees de resurrection en de light; sees de
meek Jesus sayin Dey kilt Me dat ye shall live again; I died dat dem whut
sees en believes shall never die" (370). Johnson's verse sermon appeared
in H. L. Mencken's widely circulated *American Mercury* magazine in
1927, the same year it was published in *God's Trombones*. It begins with
the exhortation, "Weep not, weep not, / She is not dead; / She's resting in the bosom of Jesus. / Heart-broken husband—weep no more; /
Grief-stricken son—weep no more" (27). That message evolves into a
personification of Death, summoned by God to take Sister Caroline to
rest "on the loving breast of Jesus," who "took his own hand and wiped
away her tears" (30). The image calls to mind the tears of Dilsey and the
members of her church who wept upon hearing the healing words of
Reverend Shegog.

"The Crucifixion" personalizes Jesus in a manner similar to Shegog's
sermon: "Jesus, my gentle Jesus, / Walking in the dark of the Garden—
/. . . / Saying to the three disciples: / Sorrow is in my soul— / Even unto
death" (39). Throughout the poem, Jesus is at once the speaking subject
and the crucified object rendered by the preacher's voice: "I see my
Jesus go. / I see him, stumble beneath the load, / I see my drooping Jesus
sink. . . . / They crucified my Jesus" (41). The interjection of Mary, his
mother, "Weeping Mary, / Sees her poor little Jesus on the cross" (42),
resonates with the progression of Shegog's sermon and moves toward
the sacrifice that she makes of "her sweet, baby Jesus" (41) ultimately to
redeem the sinners of the world.

"Let My People Go" and "The Judgment Day" both issue a call for freeing human beings and refer to a form of redemption. From God's calling to Moses and speaking in "a voice of thunder" (46) to instruct Moses, "Let My People Go" emphasizes the transformative power of speech and sound. It concludes with the command: "Listen!—Listen! / All you sons of Pharaoh / Who do you think can hold God's people / When the Lord God himself has said, / Let my people go?" (52). In "The Judgment Day," an active God calls on Gabriel to "blow his silver trumpet" and "wake the living nations" (53). That sound marks the beginning for the great day of deliverance when a voice will be heard, "crying, crying: Time shall be no more! / And the sun will go out like a candle in the wind. / The moon will turn to dripping blood, / . . . And the earth shall melt away and be dissolved" (56). The sermon rains down destruction but promises that "God will blot out time, / And start the wheel of eternity" (56). The transformation brought about by the sound in the sermon's message calls attention to the power of the voice itself as much as of the message.

The Sound and the Fury uses the sound of Reverend Shegog's voice as a figuration of the transformations of identity and the fluidity of subjectivity represented in Johnson's text and apparent in much of Faulkner's fiction. Faulkner allows the concept of the instability of subjectivity to unfold as a vocal transformation, as a sound transmitted in different registers to indicate the multiplicity of human being. It is sound that marks the metamorphosis, not physical appearance. The materiality of the voice changes its quality, its range, and its strength.[48] The description of Shegog's voice initially links him to a verbal whiteness: "When the visitor rose to speak he sounded like a white man. His voice was level and cold" (366). Given the "cold inflectionless wire of his voice," Reverend Shegog is not expected to move the congregation as a black preacher would. That expectation rests upon the function of black preachers in delivering sermons and not disappointing the congregation: "They did not mark just when his intonation, his pronunciation, became negroid [*sic*], they just sat swaying a little in their seats as the voice took them into itself" (368). The play of voice—the modulation of tone, the control over the physical characteristics of sound—is what Shegog and behind him Faulkner have mastered.

In the sermon, Faulkner directs his attention to sound from two different areas: first, to black speaking voices, dialect, folk vernacular, and "negroid" inflection and intonation; and second, to musical instrumentation, the sound of jazz music, and the syncopated rhythmic soundings of black music in marching bands and recordings. Both signify a decentering of the subject. Notice that "the voice died in sonorous echoes between the walls. It was different as day and dark from his former tone, with a sad, timbrous quality like an alto horn" (367). The insertion of a reference to an alto horn introduces the secular into the sacred; the sound associated with the "new" music is here used to convey the sound of the transformative "new" preaching voice. The music of the alto horn—as it were, a movement away from Johnson's trombone—is a "new" language that is "sinking into their hearts and speaking there again when it had ceased in fading and cumulate echoes" (367). The sound vibrates affectively and carries in its language the power to speak to the emotions and feelings. While in Faulkner's earlier fiction sound and language were separated, in *The Sound and the Fury* they come together to allow for the sound itself to resonate with multiple possible meanings that anticipate potential deconstructive readings of the sermon. More than a melding of the sacred and the profane, the sermon is an exploration of voice and the power of voice, voice projected in sound and heard on different registers: its transformational power, its impact, its societal function, its ability to collapse the space always already existing between human beings, and its capacity to permeate the seemingly fixed boundaries conscripting or confining the material body to a seemingly known and limited entity.

Written in dialect, Faulkner's sermon defies Johnson's discussion of why the use of dialect was inappropriate for the sermons of *God's Trombones*. Faulkner flaunts the command he has over the very choice of sound, and in the process he distances himself from Johnson's text and formulation. Or so he thinks—but not quite. We know the appeal of dialect as white modernist sound, but we also know Johnson's seven sermons in verse. Faulkner chooses the way of successful white writers of his generation, including the coterie from his New Orleans sojourn, and while utilizing and appropriating Johnson's model of the black preacher and the black sermon, for the distinctive value added a counternarrative to his modern story of a white family's deterioration, he rejects overt identification with the black writer as well as the latter's eschewing of black dialect.

This method or way of using black sound to effect feeling, to bring about affective possibilities that could move an audience of hearers, continues through much of Faulkner's fiction. It is influenced by Johnson's critical and creative work, but not in the choice of how dialect or vernacular speech should be rendered or represented. This lingering in the black is Faulkner's tendency to rely upon the soundings—real or imagined—of black voice, music, and words to open spaces within his texts in which he could meld meaning and form. Although he uses dialect for Shegog's sermon to race himself as white author, what Faulkner gets right in his representation of the sermon and its reception is the

collectivity of ritual, the performativity of identity, and the value of the
oral and the auditory, for both the preacher as black man and the congregation as black people. Extemporizing from Johnson's critical explanation in the preface to *God's Trombones* and from his poetic sermons,
Faulkner understands the work of the sermon in terms elucidated by
Dolan Hubbard: "To the extent that the sermon, as well as other modes
of black American expressive culture, enables the preacher and the people to articulate the self, it challenges the dominant culture's ordering
of reality (history)."[49] As is the case in his critical examinations of black
sermons, Hubbard focuses on the intersectional formations between the
minister and the congregation, especially the fact that a black preacher
"must struggle to win his voice and . . . an audience that will assent to his
testimony. From an epistemological perspective, the preacher's recovery of the community's voice dictates that he must bind the present to
the past while he projects a benevolent cosmology and teleology. Thus,
the people see themselves as an extension of history, as both actors and
reactors."[50]

This process speaks to the way in which Faulkner deals with the sound
and the hearing, the dual representing of the preacher's sermon and its
reception by the congregation, in *The Sound and the Fury*. The sound
of the human voice is conjoined not only with the flows of consciousness
but also with its ability to be transmitted or projected into (or ultimately
recorded in) places where the material body itself is absent.

Consider, for example, that no matter the affection that Faulkner held
for those blacks who, like Caroline Barr, attended to him and his needs,
they still functioned in segregated spheres, a white one and a black
one, despite the crossings that occurred when blacks had to attend to
whites in their most intimate spaces or when a white child like the young
Faulkner could be admitted to intimate black spaces. I want to include
this reminder as a relational idea to the concept of *haunting*, in which
the invisible black or blackness lingers and remains fixed. In chapter 19,
one of the three endings to *Light in August*, for example, we immediately apprehend sight, the castrated body of Joe Christmas, but lynching
itself is not new or unexpected, given the focus on Percy Grimm and his
obsession with killing Joe Christmas.[51] On the other hand, we notice that
voice sears into memory, that it is sound that can permeate all barriers.
The siren at the end is sound replicating black voice and standing in for
Joe Christmas's unheard or silenced scream: "the scream of the siren
mounted toward its unbearable crescendo, passing out of the realm of
hearing" (465). Faulkner places Joe's silence into the text, but the siren
fills in voice. The mechanical siren is a way of reincorporating the race
and voice of blacks martyred, killed, or lynched back into a disturbing

haunting of the white community. That haunting is magnified in the second ending of *Light in August* (chapter 20), in which Gail Hightower remembers and hears the voice of Cinthy, his black nurse. She was one of the phantoms (474) with "the mask of a black tragedy between scenes" (476), who "talked" and told young Hightower the stories of his grandfather and her husband Pomp that haunted the boy's future. It is her voice and way of telling "with musing and savage sorrow and pride" that kept the ghosts alive (477). It is the sound of Cinthy's voice that, while unidentified, forms and haunts Hightower's hearing in the concluding sentence of the chapter: "It seems to him that he still hears them: the wild bugles and the clashing sabres and the dying thunder of hooves" (493).

Recall, too, that there is a haunting of voice and black sound at the end of *Absalom, Absalom!*, where Faulkner consciously chooses to have the haunting presence of sound lingering over the conclusion of the text. He colors that conclusion to be specifically related to the black Bon progeny, Jim Bond: "one nigger Sutpen left" (302). Ultimately, at least according to Shreve, all inhabitants of the North American continent in generations to come will also be related to Jim Bond: "You cant catch him and you dont even always see him. . . . But you've got him there still. You still hear him at night sometimes." Sound is blackened and haunting but transmitted by a white voice. The sonic haunting is palpable and even pitch perfect for coming to terms not so much with meaning but with hearing itself, which ultimately amplifies Faulkner's lingering so self-consciously in the black.

NOTES

1. Barry Walters, "Rolling in the Deep" by Adele (song review), *Rolling Stone*, December 9, 2010, http://www.rollingstone.com/music/songreviews/rolling-in-the-deep-20101215.

2. See Faulkner's review of Conrad Aiken's *Turns and Movies and Other Tales in Verse*, in *William Faulkner: Early Prose and Poetry*, ed. Carvel Collins (Boston: Little, Brown, 1962), 74–75.

3. See Alexander Weheliye, *Phonographies: Grooves in Sonic Afro-Modernity* (Durham, NC: Duke University Press, 2005), 3–8.

4. See Eileen Southern, *The Music of Black Americans: A History* (1971; New York: W. W. Norton, 1997); W. C. Handy, *Father of the Blues: An Autobiography* (New York: Macmillan, 1941); Abbe Niles, "Critical Text," in *A Treasury of the Blues*, ed. W. C. Handy (New York: Charles Boni, 1926); and Scott E. Brown, *A Case of Mistaken Identity: The Life and Music of James P. Johnson* (New Brunswick, NJ: Scarecrow Press, 1984). See also James P. Johnson's piano roll of Handy's "Ole Miss Blues," also referred to as "Ole Miss Rag."

5. See Joseph Blotner, *Faulkner: A Biography* (New York: Random House, 1974), 1:174–75. Blotner's research into Faulkner's young manhood revealed not only the dances at the university, but also the in-home dance parties on Sallie Murry's porch with music from a player piano pumped by Chess Carothers and at Estelle and Dorothy Oldham's house with live music from Lucius Pegues's three-piece band (1:174).

6. Ben Wasson, *Count No Count: Flashbacks to Faulkner* (Jackson: University Press of Mississippi, 1983), 36–37.

7. Nathan Irvin Huggins, *Harlem Renaissance*, rev. ed. (1971; New York: Oxford University Press, 2007), 100.

8. W. C. Handy, "The Heart of the Blues" (1940), in *Readings in Black American Music*, ed. Eileen Southern (New York: W. W. Norton, 1971), 203.

9. Blotner, *Faulkner*, 1:754.

10. Clyde Woods, *Development Arrested: Race, Power, and the Blues in the Mississippi Delta* (New York: Verso Books, 1998), 34–35.

11. William Faulkner, "The Longshoreman," in *New Orleans Sketches*, ed. Carvel Collins (1958; repr., Jackson: University Press of Mississippi, 2002), 9.

12. Ibid.

13. See Thadious M. Davis, "From Jazz Syncopation to Blues Elegy: Faulkner's Development of Black Characterization," in *Faulkner and Race: Faulkner and Yoknapatawpha, 1986*, ed. Doreen Fowler and Ann J. Abadie (Jackson: University Press of Mississippi, 1987), 70–92. This essay provides a major reading of music and representation in Faulkner's fiction from early sketches through *Go Down, Moses*.

14. James Weldon Johnson, *Along This Way: The Autobiography of James Weldon Johnson* (New York: Viking Press, 1933), 328.

15. See W. Fitzhugh Brundage, ed., *Beyond Blackface: African Americans and the Creation of American Popular Culture, 1890–1930* (Chapel Hill: University of North Carolina Press, 2011); and John Minton, *78 Blues: Folksongs and Phonographs in the American South* (Jackson: University Press of Mississippi, 2008).

16. Conrad Aiken, "William Faulkner: The Novel as Form" (1939), in *William Faulkner: Three Decades of Criticism*, ed. Frederick J. Hoffman and Olga W. Vickery (New York: Harcourt, Brace & World, 1960), 135.

17. See Gary Richards, "The Artful and Crafty Ones of the French Quarter: Male Homosexuality and Faulkner's Early Prose Writings," in *Faulkner's Sexualities: Faulkner and Yoknapatawpha, 2007*, ed. Annette Trefzer and Ann J. Abadie (Jackson: University Press of Mississippi, 2010), 21–37; and John Shelton Reed, *Dixie Bohemia: A French Quarter Circle in the 1920s* (Baton Rouge: Louisiana State University Press, 2012).

18. See Aldon Lynn Nielsen, *Reading Race: White American Poets and the Racial Discourse in the Twentieth Century* (Athens: University of Georgia Press, 1988), 4.

19. For an analysis of the similar stylistic uses of black life, music, sound, and language in Anderson's *Dark Laughter* and Faulkner's first novel, *Soldiers' Pay*, see Thadious M. Davis, "Novel Beginnings" in her *Faulkner's "Negro": Art and the Southern Context* (Baton Rouge: Louisiana State University Press, 1983), 32–64. See also Judith L. Sensibar's account of the Faulkner-Anderson relationship in *Faulkner and Love: The Women Who Shaped His Art* (New Haven, CT: Yale University Press, 2009), 441–55.

20. William Faulkner, "Sunset," in *New Orleans Sketches*, ed. Carvel Collins (1958; repr., Jackson: University Press of Mississippi, 2002), 77.

21. Ibid., 76.

22. See Joseph Blotner, *William Faulkner's Library: A Catalogue* (Charlottesville: University Press of Virginia, 1964), 15.

23. Countee Cullen, foreword to *Caroling Dusk: An Anthology of Verse by Negro Poets*, ed. Countee Cullen (New York: Harper & Brothers, 1927), xiv.

24. Michael North, preface to his *The Dialect of Modernism: Race, Language, and Twentieth-Century Literature* (New York: Oxford University Press, 1994), n.p.

25. Ibid.

26. Ibid.

27. For example, see Laura Winkiel, *Modernism, Race, and Manifestoes* (Cambridge: Cambridge University Press, 2008), 184–85. See also Aldon Lynn Nielson, "The Future of Allusion: The Color of Modernity," in *Geomodernisms: Race, Modernism, Modernity*, ed. Laura Doyle and Laura Winkiel (Bloomington: Indiana University Press, 2005), 30; and Houston A. Baker Jr., *Modernism and the Harlem Renaissance* (Chicago: University of Chicago Press, 1987).

28. See Winkiel, *Modernism*, 184–85.

29. North, preface, *Dialect of Modernism*, n.p.

30. See Sensibar, *Faulkner and Love*, 57–63.

31. Ibid., 100–10.

32. Hortense J. Spillers, "Mama's Baby, Papa's Maybe: An American Grammar Book," *Diacritics* 17, no. 2 (Summer 1987): 80.

33. Ibid.

34. Ibid.

35. Sensibar, *Faulkner and Love*, 102.

36. William Faulkner, *Mosquitoes, Novels 1926–1929*, ed. Joseph Blotner and Noel Polk (New York: Library of America, 2006), 371.

37. John N. Duvall, "Faulkner's Black Sexuality," in *Faulkner's Sexualities: Faulkner and Yoknapatawpha, 2007*, ed. Annette Trefzer and Ann J. Abadie (Jackson: University Press of Mississippi, 2010), 131–47; and Dorothy Stringer, *Not Even Past: Race, Historical Trauma, and Subjectivity in Faulkner, Larsen, and Van Vechten* (New York: Fordham University Press, 2009), 22–43.

38. William Faulkner, *Sanctuary*, rev. ed. (1931; New York: Vintage International, 1993), 42.

39. William Faulkner, *Soldiers' Pay* (1926; repr. New York: Liveright, 1954), 298. Subsequent references to this edition will appear parenthetically in the text.

40. Joseph Blotner, "William Faulkner's Essay on the Composition of *Sartoris*," *Yale Library Gazette* 47 (January 1973): 123.

41. Ibid.

42. William Faulkner, *Absalom, Absalom!*, rev. ed. (1936; New York: Vintage International, 1990), 243. Subsequent references to this edition will be cited parenthetically in the text.

43. See John Faulkner, *My Brother Bill: An Affectionate Reminiscence* (New York: Trident Press, 1963), 15, 35, 40–47.

44. James Weldon Johnson, preface, *The Book of American Negro Poetry*, ed. James Weldon Johnson, rev. ed. (New York: Harcourt Brace Jovanovich, 1959), 10, 11.

45. North, *Dialect of Modernism*, 77.

46. James Weldon Johnson, preface to *God's Trombones: Seven Negro Sermons in Verse* (New York: Viking Press, 1927), 1. Subsequent references to this edition will be cited parenthetically in the text. For renewed attention to Johnson's significance as a critic, see Gerald Early, introduction, *My Soul's High Song: The Collected Writings of Countee Cullen, Voice of the Harlem Renaissance*, ed. Gerald Early (New York: Doubleday, 1991), 33–36, 70; Brent Edwards, "The Seemingly Eclipsed Window of Form: James Weldon Johnson's Prefaces," in *The Jazz Cadence of American Culture*, ed. Robert G. O'Meally (New York: Columbia University Press, 1998), 580–601; and Noelle Morrissette, *James Weldon Johnson's Modern Soundscapes* (Iowa City: University of Iowa Press, 2013), 116–49.

47. William Faulkner, *The Sound and the Fury* (1929; New York: Vintage, 1954), 365. Subsequent references to this edition will be cited parenthetically in the text.

48. I have pointed out that Faulkner treats Reverend Shegog's voice as an "aesthetic object" that "connects folk artist and audience in the creation of an emotionally satisfying, aesthetic experience" as much as in a religious one. See Davis, *Faulkner's "Negro,"* 115.

49. Dolan Hubbard, *The Sermon and the African American Literary Imagination* (Columbia: University of Missouri Press, 1994), 5.

50. Ibid.

51. William Faulkner, *Light in August*, rev. ed. (1932; New York: Vintage International, 1990), 464–65. Subsequent references to this edition will be cited parenthetically in the text.

Tracking Faulkner in the Paths of
Black Modernism

George Hutchinson

Let me begin by explaining my title. This essay is not chiefly about William Faulkner's influence on black writers, nor vice versa, but rather about the paths of black modernism that were also the paths opened for Faulkner. Ancillary to that, it is about how the development of black modernism created a new environment for his work, for his work's reception, and ultimately for his literary imagination.

Faulkner's career tracks the development of modern African American fiction and has close institutional affiliations with it. The interest in New Negro fiction in the 1920s and 1930s, coincident with Faulkner's emergence, connected with that in regionalism, particularly southern regionalism, and in theories of cultural pluralism. Faulkner's own regionalist loyalty, which is part and parcel of his critique of white southern culture, developed out of many of the same intellectual crosscurrents that gave rise to interest in African American writing. Du Bois's *The Souls of Black Folk*, for example, was commissioned by Alexander McClurg in Chicago in part because of McClurg's interest in writing about the South.[1] But if interest in literature about the South helped nourish interest in African American literature, the converse was also true. Writers like Julia Peterkin and DuBose Heyward gained prominence in the mid-twenties based on novels focusing on black southern characters, like *Scarlet Sister Mary*, which Zora Neale Hurston and Sterling Brown considered a model for literary uses of black vernacular speech. Roark Bradford, Faulkner's good friend during his New Orleans days, found success with the novel *Ol' Man Adam and His Chillun* (1928), which was later adapted into the smash-hit Broadway play *Green Pastures*, considered at the time a breakthrough for African Americans on the stage, despite the script's stereotypical elements. Critics noted that the success of the play depended on the skill of the actors, particularly Richard B. Harrison as "De Lawd," and on the Hall Johnson Choir's performance of spirituals. As southern fiction developed in the early twentieth century, it did so in tandem with the development of African American literary and performance traditions and interest in African American literary subjects.

In the Harlem Renaissance era proper, the closest cousin to *The Souls of Black Folk* is Jean Toomer's *Cane*, published by Boni & Liveright in 1923 with a foreword by Toomer's friend Waldo Frank. Sherwood Anderson, a more famous figure than Frank but for whom Frank had also been inspirational, wanted to write the foreword to *Cane*, but Toomer stuck with Frank out of loyalty and a sense that Frank understood him better than Anderson, whom Toomer accused of "limiting" him "to Negro."[2] Toomer insisted that his book was not "Negro literature" or solely about the black South; he sought, rather, like his character Kabnis, to "become the face of the South."[3] Frank wrote in his foreword, with Toomer's approval, that *Cane* was not just *about* the South; it *was* the South. Its first lines, an epigraph by Toomer himself, read:

Oracular.
Redolent of fermenting syrup,
Purple of the dusk,
Deep-rooted cane.[4]

Toomer claimed an oracular authenticity to his literary utterance comparable to Faulkner's oracular ambition, which is one source of Faulkner's stylistic radicalism.

There's a scene out of Faulkner's writing life that I find particularly riveting, when his daughter walked into his study and found him lying on his back on the floor. Startled, she began to speak to him and he told her sharply to go away, he was working. He was conjuring characters, as if in a trance. This trancelike creative mode accounts for the exhaustion and emotional dislocation that followed the completion of each of his novels, often accompanied by binge drinking.[5] It might even have something to do with his singular, absorptive literary style.

Faulkner spent the autumn of 1921 in Greenwich Village and worked in the Doubleday bookstore attached to Lord & Taylor (where he came to know Elizabeth Prall, soon to be Sherwood Anderson's wife). At this time, Toomer moved to Sparta, Georgia, to become acting principal at an industrial training school. There he caught the inspiration for *Cane*. His imagination had been prepared for the experience by Anderson's work and by Waldo Frank, whom he had met in Greenwich Village in August 1920 and with whom he soon developed an intense relationship, each addressing the other as "Brother."

The importance of Greenwich Village for Toomer and Faulkner bears some investigation. Both lived there only briefly and before either achieved a literary voice. Yet both made important connections there, and the ambience of the Village set their imaginations on fire, reorienting their artistic aspirations. Faulkner called it "a place with a few unimportant boundaries but no limitations where young people of any age go to seek dreams."[6] While there, Faulkner published an essay touting Eugene O'Neill's use of the "earthy strength" of the American language—like an American Synge.[7] About the same time, Jean Toomer wrote an adulatory essay on "Negro psychology" in O'Neill's play *The Emperor Jones*, which premiered in Greenwich Village in November 1920.[8] What Blotner wrote of the Village's effect on Faulkner could be said with equal justice about Toomer: "He found himself removed from the familiar environment and set down amid an alien culture. In this new world he could also absorb unfamiliar attitudes and discern different currents, which could help him to reassess what was best about his own world—to see not only its weaknesses but its strengths as they really were when seen from the outside rather than as they had been described by custom and codified by tradition at home."[9] It was precisely such a new perspective and reassessment that accounts for the electric impact of *Cane* on the Negro Renaissance.

Cane was also the first book about the South published by Boni & Liveright, a new firm led by a New York Jew and Faulkner's first trade publisher.[10] This is especially significant because the firm identified with the daring and modern: T. S. Eliot's *The Waste Land*, Lytton Strachey's *Napoleon*, Dreiser, and the early Hemingway. Shortly after *Cane*, it published Waldo Frank's *Holiday*, a modernist novel set in the South and focused on the intersection between racial terror and interracial sexuality. And in 1925 came Sherwood Anderson's *Dark Laughter*, another book set largely in the South and focusing in part on white-black issues, written during the very time Anderson befriended Faulkner in New Orleans.

Faulkner's relationship with Sherwood Anderson turned Faulkner from poetry to fiction and from a derivative Anglophile and Francophile literary imagination to a self-consciously "American" one.[11] Anderson's influence on Jean Toomer is likewise difficult to underestimate—in Toomer's search for literary inspiration in a rural Georgia town; in his turn to "lyric fiction"; and in his settling on a composite cycle of stories, sketches, and poems as opposed to novelistic form. Anderson learned of Toomer through the editor John McClure and sent Toomer a letter predicting that his work would be of major importance.[12] Toomer replied, "Just before I went down to Georgia I read *Winesburg, Ohio*. And while there, living in a cabin whose floorboards permitted the soil to come up between them, listening to the old folk melodies that Negro women sang at sun-down, The Triumph of the Egg came to me. The beauty, and the full sense of life that these books contain are natural elements, like the rain and sunshine, of my own sprouting."[13] Toomer's *Cane* nourished Anderson's interest in African Americans, which in turn affected Faulkner's own sense of the fictional resources of Oxford, Mississippi.

Faulkner may have been aware of Toomer by way of his friendship with Anderson and McClure in New Orleans, shortly after Toomer was corresponding with Anderson and Anderson offered to introduce *Cane*. McClure published three Toomer poems in the *Double-Dealer*, including "Harvest Song" in the December 1922 issue—the same issue in which Faulkner's poem "Portrait" first appeared.[14] It was a "little review" eagerly followed by both authors and in which Faulkner would continue to place work into the mid-1920s. I should add that McClure felt forced to turn down Toomer's sketches "Fern" and "Karintha" as "too powerful" for his southern white readers.[15] Toomer responded fervently to McClure's admiration and encouragement, sending him another batch of manuscripts and his assurance that he understood McClure's difficulties: "I too feel, in a very sincere way, that the Double Dealer cannot afford to hazard its existence for any single contributor."[16]

Toomer's friend Gorham Munson called "Fern" "too Andersonian,"[17] and it bears the impress of Anderson's approach to lyric prose—structuring a sketch or story poetically through repetition, refrain, musical cadences, and patterned imagery more than plot and suffusing the whole with unrequited longing in which the erotic blends into the spiritual and vice versa. Both Toomer and Faulkner, under Anderson's spell, experimented with multigeneric writing, mixing prose sketches with lyric experiments.[18] Toomer's uses of the gothic in early sections of *Cane* often seem to anticipate Faulkner, particularly "Blood-Burning Moon," featuring the theme of the skeleton hand of the past haunting the present and leading to violence as people resist changes and as racial relations shift. Moving from poetry to prose, Faulkner also experimented with the "lyric prose" advocated by Anderson and Frank and which has so much to do with the style of *Cane*.

While Waldo Frank delivered *Cane* to Boni & Liveright, Anderson hooked Faulkner up with the same firm, which published *Soldiers' Pay* in February 1926 and *Mosquitoes* in April 1927. When Boni & Liveright turned down *Flags in the Dust*, Faulkner found a different publisher—Harcourt, Brace. Like Liveright, this was one of the chief publishers of the Harlem Renaissance, also closely linked to the NAACP because its vice president, Joel Spingarn, was at the time the president of that organization. Books by and about African Americans were one of its specialties.[19]

Faulkner's themes and motifs have much in common with Toomer's—in part, perhaps, because of *Cane*'s influence on Sherwood Anderson's *Dark Laughter*—but there are far stronger echoes between Toomer and Faulkner than between Toomer and the midwesterner Anderson, to whom Negroes were more exotic. It is like a resemblance between cousins across the color line. What Toomer and Faulkner emphasize that is notably missing in Anderson's work is the presence of the past and the haunted landscape, both related to the legacy of slavery—and also major motifs of *The Souls of Black Folk*. What Toomer described as the "skeleton stone walls" of a "pre-war cotton factory" in the story "Blood-Burning Moon,"[20] the lynchings and entanglements of bloodlines, the transformation of the southern economy and the dissolving connection between the people and the land, anticipate major motifs of Faulkner's fiction. However Faulkner came onto this path, my point is that he was entering territory already present in such texts as *The Souls of Black Folk* and *Cane*.

Notably, however, Faulkner's attitudes to race and so-called miscegenation contrasted strongly with Toomer's (and other black authors'). Sherwood Anderson said that Faulkner told him in the early 1920s that race mixing led to sterility: he spoke of "the cross between the jack and the mare that produced the mule and . . . that, as between the white man and the Negro woman, it was just the same."[21] This was a common belief at the time, particularly in the white South (where one would think it would be contradicted by overwhelming evidence), and Faulkner's fiction before the 1940s expresses a dread of miscegenation, which comes across as, at best, tragic. This contrast is particularly intriguing because there is so much of a structural parallel, plotwise, between Faulkner's fictions of racial crossing prior to the 1940s and those of his African American cohort, who counters the white ideology around race mixing with stories that focus instead on the tragedy due to that ideology while understanding interracial rape and sexual relationships as common facts of southern life. The focus on the tragedy as well as brutality of white ideology becomes a theme for Faulkner himself from the mid-1930s on—after, say, Langston Hughes's *The Ways of White Folks* (1934), which included the story "Father and Son," about a white plantation owner who refuses to acknowledge his black son, the son's refusal to act like a "nigger," and his ultimate murder of the father. In fact, *The Ways of White Folks* bears many points of comparison and contrast with Faulkner's ethical dilemmas of the 1930s and 1940s.

Faulkner was slow in picking up on paths opened by African American fiction because of how opaque black consciousness was to him and his apparent resistance to taking black authors seriously before the advent of Richard Wright. He could only follow the trail through the shadows of blackness in his own exquisitely sensitive yet always self-definitively white consciousness. Thadious Davis has put it well: the early Faulkner, she writes, "is obsessed not with the Negro as a rounded character or as part of the world of humankind, but with the Negro as an idea which impinges upon the white man's internal world of thought and feeling, and upon the artist's own imaginative world."[22] She adds that Faulkner's achievement emerged "out of the . . . milieu of New Orleans and out of Sherwood Anderson's tutelage and example."[23]

The relationship of blackness to Faulkner's oracular function is singularly revealed in his second novel, *Mosquitoes*:

> "I got to talking to a funny man. A little kind of black man—"
>
> "A nigger?"
>
> "No, no. He was a white man, except he was awful sunburned and kind of shabby dressed—no necktie and hat. Say, he said some funny things to me. . . . He said he was a liar by profession. . . . I think he was crazy. Not dangerous: just crazy."
>
> . . . .
>
> "I remember [his name] because he was such a funny kind of man. . . . Oh yes, I remember—Faulkner, that was it."
>
> "Faulkner?" The niece pondered in her turn. "Never heard of him," she said at last, with finality.[24]

Lothar Hönnighausen has used this passage in speaking of Faulkner's various masks and their relation to his personal idiosyncrasies in the world he inhabited.[25] Indeed, we all know that Faulkner was a "funny" kind of white southerner, often regarded as a traitor to his own people. He published "That Evening Sun" in H. L. Mencken's *American Mercury*, infamous in the South for Mencken's excoriations of the region. Thadious Davis has written of Faulkner's indebtedness to "Mencken's essay 'The Sahara of the Bozart,' a formidable attack on the South . . . which helped to goad the region into artistic endeavors in the early twenties."[26] Fred Hobson has argued that Mencken "played perhaps *the* central role in the first phase" of the southern renaissance; it was nearly of equal importance to the Negro Renaissance.[27]

As various critics have pointed out, going back at least to Sterling A. Brown in the mid-1950s, Faulkner's use and depiction of black characters shifts beginning with the stories in *Go Down, Moses*,[28] and the denial by white southerners of kinship across racial lines draws particular attention as a betrayal of humanity, one they are too cowardly to confront. So-called miscegenation is no longer a "tragedy," although it is too much for even so idealized a character as Ike McCaslin to deal with. His attempts to keep himself pure by renouncing property are inadequate, and his inadequacy is nowhere more evident than when confronted by an unnamed black woman and her child by Roth Edmonds. (Edmonds seems to have truly loved her and yet lacks the courage to marry her, which would be impossible in the South in any case.) Ike advises the woman to go find a man of her own race in the North. "Go back North. Marry: a man in your own race. That's the only salvation for you—for a while yet, maybe a long while yet. We will have to wait."[29] The most tortured moment in *Go Down, Moses* (the only book for which Faulkner took a title from black expressive tradition) comes when Ike, who has been built up as the conscience of the white South, simply breaks down in the face of this female descendant of the black and white lines of his family and the heritage of incest. "Old man," she replies, "have you lived so long and forgotten so much that you dont remember anything you ever knew or felt or even heard about love?"[30] What makes the moment particularly critical is that it occurs in the very camp, in the last of the deep woods, that Ike considers his refuge from contagion. Yet here his own white shame and guilt come dramatically to light as he pushes the woman out of his sight.

A quasi-parallel moment occurs in *Absalom, Absalom!* of 1936, but here, where the horror of interracial mixing exceeds that of incest in the mind of the white center of consciousness, one finds a suggestion that such mixing leads to idiocy and decadence, whereas *Go Down, Moses* makes no such prophecy and leaves the future wide open for the mixed-race child, if taken out of the South. Indeed, while Ike is child-less and the "white" side of Carothers McCaslin's descendants heads for extinction in the male line, the "black" descendants survive. Ike says of the woman's child, "It's a boy, I reckon. They usually are."[31] Mother and child, moreover, serve as moral judgment on the white father who refuses to acknowledge them, even though we are given to believe he loved the mother and seems to be going through a moral crisis, an intense misanthropy and self-hatred, connected with the specter of German fascism and its American parallels.

What accounts for the increasing centrality and complexity of Faulkner's black characters in the 1940s—that is, their increasing humanity? I think there are three chief factors: (1) the death of Caroline Barr and his sudden awareness of her separate life and family; (2) his reading of African American literature; and (3) World War II, which struck him as a fundamental challenge to racial tyranny in the United States.

Joseph Blotner has pointed out that "Pantaloon in Black," finished in early 1940, "showed a very different perception of the inner lives of black people from that in the portrayal of Caspey and Simon Strother a dozen years earlier in *Sartoris*."[32] In this story, the white deputy at the end misinterprets all of the black protagonist Rider's actions because he cannot perceive them as motivated by grief over the death of his wife. Blotner notes that Caroline Barr, to whom Faulkner would dedicate *Go Down, Moses*, died in January of 1940. Some of the phrasing of his eulogy for Barr bears comparison to that applied to Mollie Beauchamp in "The Fire and the Hearth."[33] The Faulkners took her to her cabin after she suffered a stroke, and her many children and grandchildren came to hold vigil until she died.[34] Faulkner seemed suddenly aware of how much of her life was outside his ken. His sermon for her funeral speaks eloquently and humbly of her importance to his life, yet with an awareness that this was not all her life meant in the larger scheme of things. The shock of this recognition infuses his fiction after 1940. Blotner informs us that even toward the end of his life, Faulkner "would talk of the difficulty of understanding Negroes' thoughts and feelings, compelled as they had been to develop patterns of concealment from white people."[35] Yet not all Negroes were so concealing of their thoughts and feelings. The year 1940 was also when *Native Son* appeared and became a literary sensation, one that Faulkner read and admired. It is difficult to read *Go Down, Moses*—especially the final story of the same title—hard upon *Native Son* and not feel the effect of Wright's novel. Samuel Beauchamp (Mollie's grandson) is a Bigger Thomas figure of the zoot-suit generation. Mollie's insistence upon the return of his body and on staging a public funeral procession through the courthouse square, as well as upon a newspaper story of his life and death, are acts of witness.

After the 1920s there was a growing awareness, throughout American literary culture, of African American writers and readership. One finds it in the work of another Mississippi writer, Eudora Welty, most powerfully in her story "Powerhouse," inspired by a performance of Fats Waller in her hometown. Welty had first heard and seen Waller in New York. Intriguingly, in a letter Faulkner wrote her in April 1943 to congratulate her on her work, he wrote, "You are doing all right. I read THE GILDED SIX BITS, a friend loaned me THE ROBBER BRIDEGROOM, I have just bought the collection named GREEN something, haven't read it yet, expect nothing from it because I expect from you."[36] "The Gilded Six-Bits" (1933) is actually a story by Zora Neale Hurston, a climactic theme of which is whites' gross miscomprehension of black people and obliviousness to their grief (much as in "Pantaloon in Black"). This fascinating misidentification might be interpreted in a number of ways, but it signals Faulkner's awareness of black writing about the South. His awareness of an educated black readership, similarly, is encoded in the portrayal of black characters throughout *Go Down, Moses*; *Intruder in the Dust*; and *Requiem for a Nun*. Indeed, one might call a number of these characters excellent "readers" of white character in a way far more complex than one finds in Faulkner's earlier fiction. The characters come in a greater variety; the stories convey more of a sense of the whites being watched and judged and manipulated by the black characters. The black characters withhold speech from the whites even as they claim agency and in various ways seek to manipulate or defeat the whites who subordinate, dominate, or oppose them.

The success of *Native Son* probably has something to do with this change in Faulkner's portrayal of black characters, but so does the legacy of the Harlem Renaissance. Entrenched narratives about that movement's "failure" have obscured a lot of what might shed light on Faulkner's development, because those narratives read the movement only in relation to the development of African American literature. Yet New Negro writing and criticism reverberated through American literary culture in the 1930s and 1940s, even as the Harlem Renaissance was relegated to the dustbin—in part because it had established a new threshold of achievement and a variety of conflicting aesthetic and political practices and critical standards. And it got white writers thinking about black writers and black audiences. (This is not to insist that Faulkner was personally impressed by the literary achievements of the Renaissance.)

Faulkner wrote Wright after reading *Black Boy* in the fall of 1945:

I have just read *Black Boy*. . . . You said it well, as well as it could have been said in this form. Because I think you said it much better in *Native Son*. I hope you will keep on saying it, but I hope you will say it as an artist, as in *Native Son*. I think you will agree that the good lasting stuff comes out of one individual's imagination and sensitivity to and comprehension of the suffering of Everyman, Anyman, not out of the memory of his own grief.[37]

Later, on a visit to Japan in the mid-1950s, when asked his opinion of black writers, Faulkner replied, "There was one that had a great deal of talent, named Richard Wright. He wrote one good book and then he went astray, he got too concerned in the difference between the Negro man and the white man and he stopped being a writer and became a Negro."[38] This quotation (later reprinted in *Jet* magazine) indicates the extent of Faulkner's—and, of course, most white authors'—presumption of literary authority at the time.

Yet it is fair to say that before 1923, very few white writers in America wrote with any concern about, or even awareness of, black readers or writers. By the 1940s, no serious white writer dealing with black characters wrote without an awareness of *Native Son*. And the new magazine

Negro Digest aggressively recruited white authors to address its readers. It had a regular feature called "If I Were a Negro," to which Eleanor Roosevelt and many others contributed over the years and which was continued in *Ebony* after *Negro Digest* retired (to be reborn as *Negro World* and then renamed *Black World* during the black power movement). Under such auspices, Faulkner's problematic "If I Were a Negro" statement appeared in 1956.[39] What is significant here is not only what it tells us about his racial politics at the time but also the way in which his thoughts on race, while always central to Faulkner's ethical universe, became increasingly insistent and responsive to awareness of a black audience.

Alfred Kazin, prompted by *Intruder in the Dust*, wrote in his journal in September 1948 about what he called Faulkner's *"sounding* of all our immense possibilities for good and evil." He singled out the novelist's evocation of "the relationship of the oppressor and the oppressed, seen from the point of view of the oppressor himself. . . . It is the awareness, the Southern writer's, of the *relationship* between master and servant, between guilt and history, and the fact that this relationship is seen from above [that] is all the more significant to his own possession of the complexity of his experience."[40] In contrast, Kazin believed, "The Jewish writer thinks of himself as the oppressed, the alienated, the man things are done to. . . . The oppressor-class writer is often the greater, because he has not lost his dignity by abjection, and has even *added* to it by understanding of his guilt. The oppressed has the consciousness of his ethical superiority; the oppressor of his central place in the human domain."[41]

A black Cornell graduate student named Chloe Ardellia Wofford made a curiously related point in a 1955 master's thesis on Faulkner and Virginia Woolf. Here the young woman known today as Toni Morrison contends that Faulkner's ethical vision is greater than Woolf's because, rather than seeing alienation as a state imposed on a person or as inevitable, Faulkner sees it "as a matter of choice on the part of the individual and as a sin." He thus provided "a means for its transcendence in love."[42] This insight may tell us even more about what is central for Toni Morrison than about what is central to William Faulkner, and I do not bring it up as evidence of Faulkner's influence on Morrison. In 1955, the theme of alienation was pervasive in contemporary literature, but it had a particular purchase in African American writing. Think of Richard Wright, Ralph Ellison, and James Baldwin. Morrison's thesis concerning Faulkner's work—in relationship with the feminist Woolf's—can be interpreted as a meditation on the situation of the black woman writer, and perhaps particularly so when the American literary canon was exclusively white and almost exclusively male.

Morrison's insight remains significant in its own right. In Faulkner's later fiction particularly, the form that self-imposed isolation takes is the white man's, or white boy's, denial of his connection with black people, and especially the denial of family relations across the color line—a main point, as well, of Langston Hughes's "Father and Son" of the 1930s. But to return to Morrison's thesis, "Those capable of restoring the order needed," she writes, "are the Negroes, like Dilsey, who 'endured,' but it is only those who have incurred the guilt who have the right to expiate it."[43] This emphasis on "endurance" has since been criticized, but Sterling Brown also prized the quality of "endurance" in some of Faulkner's black characters—not surprisingly, as it was also one of Brown's own values, a form of endurance he found inherent in the blues and the spirituals.[44] It is related to Morrison's and Brown's notions of the relationship of African Americans to time itself.

Faulkner believes, Morrison concludes, that "the reconciliation of man to his condition is at hand when he learns to live outside of self within time. When one is detached he opposes nature for he refuses to take his place in the 'system of things.'"[45] "Man," Faulkner believes in Morrison's estimation, "has a responsibility to time and must endure it."[46] If the crime of incest correlates with a repudiation of the outer world, so does opposition to time. White people's opposition to nature, their destruction of the environment, and their opposition to people of color are connected to a misguided attempt to suspend, conquer, or ignore time—by which I think Morrison means temporalities of the natural world; this misguided ambition dominates Thomas Sutpen, and in a different way, Quentin Compson—and even, ultimately, Isaac McCaslin. No one can expiate the guilt of the Compsons (or Sutpen) except those who incurred it, which they do not because of "pride and self-isolation." Faulkner said the premise of *Intruder in the Dust* was that "the white people in the south, before the North or the government or anyone else, owe and must pay a responsibility to the Negro."[47] Gavin Stevens makes this point for Faulkner in the novel itself.

The war years, Joseph Blotner has written, brought a new soul-searching to his earlier anguish over the sins of the past. In a 1943 letter to his stepson, Malcolm Franklin, Faulkner wrote of some African American pilots who

finally got congress to allow them to learn how to risk their lives in the air. They are in Africa now, under their own negro lt. colonel, did well at Pantelleria, on the same day a mob of white men and white policemen killed 20 negroes in Detroit. . . .

A change will come out of this war. If it doesn't, if the politicians and the
people who run this country are not forced to make good the shibboleth they
glibly talk about freedom, liberty, human rights, then you young men who
live through it will have wasted your precious time, and those who dont live
through it will have died in vain.[48]

In a 1957 lecture, Sterling A. Brown noticed the shift in Faulkner's
novels of the 1940s, specifically *Go Down, Moses* and *Intruder in the
Dust*, in which Faulkner "tries to understand the Negro's mind and
situation."[49] Brown was particularly struck by the character of Lucas
Beauchamp, through whom Faulkner struggles to get at the interiority
of a black character as never before. This shift in Faulkner's imagination coincides with a broader awakening in the years leading up to the
civil rights movement, a shift signaled not only by the integration of the
armed forces and A. Philip Randolph's March on Washington Movement, but also by the sensation caused by Wright's *Black Boy* and such
novels as Lillian Smith's *Strange Fruit*. Burning critiques of American
racism crop up in the literature of World War II, and desegregation
comes to seem inevitable, not only in left-wing publications but even in
such a politically conservative novel as James Gould Cozzens's *Guard of
Honor*, which won the Pulitzer Prize in 1949.

However, the seeming inevitability of desegregation could also become
an excuse for forestalling it. Morrison identified in Faulkner's work the
assertion that the reconciliation of man to his condition depended on
a surrender of self to live "within time." This emphasis forms an ironic
counterpoint to Faulkner's appalling counsel to civil rights movement
leaders to "go slow," which I understand to derive in part from his belief
that white southerners themselves must genuinely repent and end segregation rather than being forced to do so by "outlanders."[50] Faulkner's
statement confirms Morrison's point that he believed no one except the
Compsons (or Sutpen) can expiate their sins. The white South could not
exorcise its demons except through its own awakening to the enormity
of its crimes. A change imposed from "outside" would drive white southerners into a murderously reactionary position—exactly the opposite of
a surrender of self to live within time. When confronted with a conflict
in temporalities between what one might call "white time" and "black,"
one finds the conversion of white people, their guilt, their duty to "the
Negro" and themselves, the important thing. This puts the need of white
southerners to exorcise their demons ahead of the need of black southerners to be free. On whose time does freedom come? Here Faulkner
could have learned a thing or two from Martin Luther King Jr.

Let's return now to Toni Morrison's 1955 master's thesis, in which she wrote that "those capable of restoring the order needed are the Negroes." This takes us to Martin Luther King Jr.'s charge that southern liberals like Faulkner suffered from a "tragic misconception of time."[51] Faulkner was a year dead and his counsel to "go slow" was several years old by the time King wrote his "Letter from Birmingham Jail" in 1963, but King's letter might just as well have been written to the author of *Intruder in the Dust* as to Birmingham's liberal men of the cloth. In fact, what could possibly force the awakening of white people to the nature of their condition if not black people's own seizing of the day? Even in Faulkner's own case, the "New," "Newer," and "Newest" Negroes had been the crucial factor in the changing landscape of his imagination and the literary landscape in which his work was received. Faulkner's awakening came only in relationship to the black otherness that continually forced him, an oracle of the white South obsessed with the nature of time, who prized above all the hard work of writing honestly at the edge of one's own moral awareness, into new territory.

NOTES

1. George Hutchinson, *The Harlem Renaissance in Black and White* (Cambridge, MA: Harvard University Press, 1996), 345.

2. Jean Toomer to Waldo Frank, early January 1923, in Jean Toomer, *Cane: An Authoritative Text, Backgrounds, Criticism*, 2nd ed., ed. Rudolph P. Byrd and Henry Louis Gates Jr. (New York: W. W. Norton, 2011), 164.

3. Toomer, *Cane: An Authoritative Text*, 81.

4. Jean Toomer, *Cane* (New York: Boni & Liveright, 1923), n.p. The epigraph has unaccountably been omitted from the Norton Critical Edition of *Cane* edited by Byrd and Gates.

5. Joseph Blotner, *Faulkner: A Biography* (Jackson: University Press of Mississippi, 2005), 397–98, 225–26.

6. William Faulkner, *The Town*, rev. ed. (1957; New York: Vintage, 1961), 350.

7. See William Faulkner, "American Drama: Eugene O'Neill," in *Essays, Speeches, and Public Letters*, ed. James B. Meriwether (New York: Modern Library, 2004), 314–16. Originally published in the *Mississippian*, the student newspaper at the University of Mississippi, on February 3, 1922, 5.

8. Jean Toomer, "Negro Psychology in *The Emperor Jones*," in *Selected Essays and Literary Criticism*, ed. Robert B. Jones (Knoxville: University of Tennessee Press, 1996), 6.

9. Blotner, *Faulkner*, 107.

10. I discuss the connection of Boni & Liveright with the Harlem Renaissance in *Harlem Renaissance in Black and White*, 367–72.

11. See particularly Thadious M. Davis, *Faulkner's "Negro": Art and the Southern Context* (Baton Rouge: Louisiana State University Press, 1983), 38–45.

12. Cynthia Earl Kerman and Richard Eldridge, *The Lives of Jean Toomer: A Hunger for Wholeness* (Baton Rouge: Louisiana State University Press, 1987), 93.

13. Jean Toomer to Sherwood Anderson, December 18, 1922, in *A Jean Toomer Reader: Selected Unpublished Writings*, ed. Frederik L. Rusch (New York: Oxford University Press, 1993), 17.

14. Blotner, *Faulkner*, 113.

15. Quoted in Kerman and Eldridge, *Lives of Jean Toomer*, 92.

16. Jean Toomer to John McClure, July 22, 1922, in Rusch, ed. *Jean Toomer Reader*, 13.

17. Quoted in Kerman and Eldridge, *Lives of Jean Toomer*, 93.

18. A number of scholars have discussed the relationship between Anderson and Toomer, most extensively Mark Whalan in *Race, Manhood, and Modernism in America: The Short Story Cycles of Sherwood Anderson and Jean Toomer* (Knoxville: University of Tennessee Press, 2007). See also Charles Scruggs, "The Reluctant Witness: What Jean Toomer Remembered from *Winesburg, Ohio*," *Studies in American Fiction* 28 (2000): 77–100; Darwin T. Turner, "An Intersection of Paths: Correspondence between Jean Toomer and Sherwood Anderson," *CLA Journal* 17 (1974): 455–67; and Mark Helbling, "Sherwood Anderson and Jean Toomer," *Negro American Literature Forum* 9 (1975): 35–39.

19. I discuss Harcourt, Brace's connections with the Harlem Renaissance in *Harlem Renaissance*, 372–78.

20. Toomer, *Cane: An Authoritative Edition*, 31.

21. Sherwood Anderson, *Sherwood Anderson's Memoirs* (New York: Harcourt, Brace, 1942), 474.

22. Davis, *Faulkner's "Negro,"* 64.

23. Ibid.

24. William Faulkner, *Mosquitoes, Novels 1926–1929*, ed. Joseph Blotner and Noel Polk (New York: Library of America, 2006), 371–72.

25. Lothar Hönnighausen, *Faulkner: Masks and Metaphors* (Jackson: University Press of Mississippi, 1997), 22.

26. Davis, *Faulkner's "Negro,"* 10–11. Fred C. Hobson Jr's *Serpent in Eden: H. L. Mencken and the South* (Chapel Hill: University of North Carolina Press, 1974) details the effect of Mencken's work on the rise of southern literature. On Mencken's importance for the Harlem Renaissance, see esp. Charles Scrugg's *The Sage in Harlem: H. L. Mencken and the Black Writers of the 1920s* (Baltimore: Johns Hopkins University Press, 1984).

27. Fred Hobson, "'This Hellawful South': Mencken and the Late Confederacy," in *Critical Essays on H. L. Mencken*, ed. Douglas C. Stenerson (Boston: G. K. Hall, 1987), 122. See also my discussion of Mencken and the *American Mercury* in *The Harlem Renaissance in Black and White*, 313–41.

28. Cecile Gerletz, "S. Brown Considers Faulkner's Negroes," *Vassar Miscellany News*, March 13, 1957.

29. William Faulkner, *Go Down, Moses*, rev. ed. (1942; New York: Vintage International, 1990), 346.

30. Ibid.

31. Ibid., 345.

32. Blotner, *Faulkner*, 415.

33. Blotner writes that Mollie Beauchamp's portrayal in "The Fire and the Hearth" "was drawn directly from Mammy Callie, and her closeness to Edmonds was not unlike that of Mammy Callie to William Faulkner" (414). See esp. the description of Mollie Beauchamp's relationship with Roth Edmonds and Faulkner's description of Caroline Barr's role in his own life: *Go Down, Moses*, 113–14; and Faulkner, "Funeral Sermon for Mammy Caroline Barr," in *Essays, Speeches, and Public Letters*, ed. James B. Meriwether (New York: Modern Library, 2004), 119.

34. Blotner, *Faulkner*, 413.

35. Ibid., 414–5.

36. William Faulkner to Eudora Welty, April 27, 1943, Eudora Welty Collection, Mississippi Department of Archives and History, Jackson, quoted in Suzanne Marrs, *Eudora Welty: A Biography* (New York: Harcourt, 2005), 98.

37. William Faulkner to Richard Wright, probably September 11, 1945, *Selected Letters of William Faulkner*, ed. Joseph Blotner (New York: Random House, 1977), 201.

38. James B. Meriwether and Michael Millgate, eds., *Lion in the Garden: Interviews with William Faulkner, 1926–1962* (1968; repr., Lincoln: University of Nebraska Press, 1980), 185. Faulkner's comments were reprinted in *Esquire* and *Jet* in December 1958.

39. William Faulkner, "A Letter to the Leaders of the Negro Race," in *Essays, Speeches, and Public Letters*, 107–12; originally published as "If I Were a Negro," *Ebony*, September 1956, 70–73. The piece was solicited by the editor of *Ebony*.

40. Alfred Kazin, *Alfred Kazin's Journals*, ed. Richard M. Cook (New Haven, CT: Yale University Press, 2011), 120–21.

41. Ibid., 121.

42. Chloe Ardellia Wofford, "Virginia Woolf's and William Faulkner's Treatment of the Alienated" (master's thesis, Cornell University, 1955), 3.

43. Ibid., 35.

44. Gerletz, "S. Brown," 2.

45. Wofford, "Virginia Woolf's," 35.

46. Ibid., 34.

47. Quoted in Blotner, *Faulkner*, 491, from a letter to Harold Ober.

48. William Faulkner to Malcolm A. Franklin, July 4, 1943, in *Selected Letters of William Faulkner*, 175–76.

49. Gerletz, "S. Brown," 2. Lee Jenkins also emphasizes a major shift in Faulkner's depiction of black characters beginning with *Go Down, Moses* and further advanced in *Intruder in the Dust*. See Lee Jenkins, *Faulkner and Black-White Relations: A Psychoanalytic Approach* (New York: Columbia University Press, 1981), 226–37, 261.

50. Faulkner, "A Letter to the Leaders of the Negro Race," 108. See also, for example, "Letter to a Northern Editor," in *Essays, Speeches, and Public Letters*, 86–91, originally published as "A Letter to the North" in *Life*, March 5, 1956, 51–52.

51. Martin Luther King Jr., "Letter from Birmingham Jail," in his *Why We Can't Wait* (New York: New American Library, 1964), 86.

Miscegenation and Progression:
The First Americans of Jean Toomer and
William Faulkner

Andrew B. Leiter

Scholars have documented William Faulkner's extensive influence on any number of African American authors from Richard Wright to Toni Morrison. This valuable work and its delineation of the manner in which black writers engage, expand, and revise Faulkner's racial vision, unfortunately, have not been matched by a corresponding critical effort to understand how Faulkner's art might have been shaped by African American writing. Eric J. Sundquist, Philip Weinstein, Margaret Bauer, and Martyn Bone, among others, have demonstrated how reading Faulkner in conjunction with his African American contemporaries can enhance our understanding of his art, yet rarely do critics posit black literary influence on Faulkner.[1] My essay analyzes aspects of miscegenation in Faulkner's work relative to African American antecedents, contends that Jean Toomer's work contributed to Faulkner's treatment of the subject, and argues for at least a partial realignment of the traditional critical paradigm in Faulkner studies that treats miscegenation as a threat to "whiteness." Specifically, Toomer's vision of progressive racial evolution culminating in a multiracial, original American helps us frame Sam Fathers as Faulkner's first American (or "the Man") who represents not simply the end of an era but rather an originary model for an evolving mixed-race nation.

Although I find *Go Down, Moses* (1942) to be the Faulkner novel most at ease with miscegenation, his fiction and interviews contain various pseudoevolutionary passages and comments that address racial amalgamation and suggest his interest in transformational racial identity from the 1930s through the civil rights era.[2] In *Light in August* (1932), the half-crazed abolitionist Calvin Burden conceives of the secessionist South as a miscegenated population in which even whites evince the physical stain of slavery: "Damn, lowbuilt black folks: lowbuilt because of the weight of the wrath of God, black because of the sin of human bondage staining their blood and flesh. . . . But we done freed them now, both black and white alike. They'll bleach out now. In a hundred years they will be white folks again. Then maybe we'll let them come back into America."[3] At the conclusion of *Absalom, Absalom!* (1936), Shreve McCannon comments whimsically on the Sutpen family tragedy:

> I think that in time the Jim Bonds are going to conquer the western hemi-sphere. Of course it wont quite be in our time and of course as they spread toward the poles they will bleach out again like the rabbits and the birds do, so they wont show up so sharp against the snow. But it will still be Jim Bond; and so in a few thousand years, I who regard you will also have sprung from the loins of African kings.[4]

Neither Burden's ranting nor Shreve's flippancy represents a Faulkne-rian voiceover, but they share a sense that an amalgamated homogeneity offers a curative of sorts to the racial conflict in their respective novels. In this, they prefigure sentiments Faulkner expressed during the civil rights era.

In Faulkner's notorious 1956 interview about desegregation with Rus-sell Warren Howe of the London *Sunday Times*, Faulkner stated that "in the long view, the Negro race will vanish in three hundred years by intermarriage. It has happened to every racial minority everywhere, and it will happen here."[5] He made similar comments several days later in an interview with the *Tex and Jinx* radio show and again in a public address in Virginia in 1958: "I would say though in five hundred years he [the Negro] would have vanished, and I imagine then anyone that wants to join the DAR will have to prove that she's got somewhere a strain of Negro blood."[6] Some common threads are readily identifiable in both the fictional and personal examples: the statements evince no alarm over the prospect of widespread amalgamation and instead identify homo-geneity as a solution to racial conflict; the anticipated time spans for full amalgamation—one hundred to a thousand years—resonate with Faulkner's gradualist approach to integration; and whiteness remains intact as the normative racial marker, having absorbed and eliminated blackness. It is safe to say that privileging whiteness and the centuries involved take some of the radical sheen off casual assertions about the amalgamation of American society. Published during the World War II era—arguably Faulkner's most democratically inclusive period—*Go Down, Moses*, however, offers an exception to the prioritization of white-ness and gradualism in its preference for a progressive amalgamation that can best be understood within the context of Faulkner's African American contemporaries.[7]

African American authors of the early twentieth century offered alternative visions of racial mixing that rejected demagogic assertions of miscegenation as the deterioration of "whiteness" and instead embraced notions of a mixed-race society as an imminent and progressive development for humanity. Numerous works on racial passing and mulatto fiction imply as much, while other authors offered overt considerations of the direction of racial mixing in America. Charles W. Chesnutt frequently described the United States as a biological melting pot in essays and speeches such as "Age of Problems" (1906), in which he contends that "every student of Darwin knows that all progress in nature comes through departure in types. History shows us that the most virile and progressive races have always been mixed races. . . . Taking our nation in the raw, and finding in its present population the ingredients of our future race, ours is a mixed race already—combined of every variety of mankind under the sun."[8] Similarly, we might turn to George Schuyler's comic novel *Black No More* (1931). A hilariously irreverent novel, *Black No More* portrays the full amalgamation of American society through the invention of a whitening machine that turns out to be largely superfluous when a genealogical study reveals the vast extent of racial mixing that has already occurred throughout American history. Such visions of an amalgamated nation do not rely on a distant and blanketing whiteness to subsume blackness but emphasize rather the extent to which a genuinely mixed-race population already exists. A member of that mixed-race population, Jean Toomer was arguably the most consistent proponent of mixed-race America as the site of a biological and spiritual evolutionary process culminating in a new man, and his work offers enlightening possibilities for understanding some of the origins of Faulkner's racial concepts.

The ideas in this essay are an extension of ideas left untapped in a previous book chapter in which I discuss Joe Christmas and *Light in August* relative to Schuyler's *Black No More*. In that work, I assess the likelihood of Faulkner's familiarity with various contemporaneous African American authors, and I contend that Faulkner would have known Toomer's avant-garde masterpiece *Cane* (1923) based on publishing connections and their shared friendship with Sherwood Anderson. Furthermore, I argue that *Cane* influenced Faulkner's development of Christmas's violent racial interstitiality, but of necessity I left undeveloped what I believe is Toomer's fairly widespread influence on Faulkner's art.[9] In *Faulkner and Love*, Judith Sensibar has drawn on the Toomer-Anderson-Faulkner connection to argue that "some of the best writing in Faulkner's *Soldiers' Pay* was inspired by *Cane*," and I believe that other short stories and sketches composed in the 1920s bear stylistic and thematic similarities to *Cane*.[10] "Nympholepsy," for example, is a sexually charged, surrealistic, pastoral piece reminiscent of *Cane* in its content as well as its poetic prose style. Likewise, the fragmented, semisurreal style of "Peter" and its emphasis on the sexuality of African American life resonates with *Cane*. Faulkner's "Elly" (1934) and the torturous relationship between the racially ambiguous Paul de Montigny and Elly may also owe something to the strained relationship between the titular characters of Toomer's short story "Bona and Paul."

Go Down, Moses, however, offers extensive thematic resonance with Toomer's interest in an evolving racial population emerging from an American history of materialism and ongoing modernization. As a mixed-race individual capable of passing in white society, Toomer's interest in racial amalgamation stemmed from a very personal impetus and was reflected in a lifelong search for a satisfying sense of identity and spirituality. His affiliation with both white modernist circles and Harlem Renaissance writers, his identification as a Negro author upon the publication of *Cane* with Boni & Liveright, his rejection of an exclusively Negro identity, and various other aspects of his life have led to extensive scholarly debate about Toomer's racial identity and its relevance for understanding *Cane* and its place in the canon. The critical debates notwithstanding, Toomer was largely consistent in his own identification as racially composite, leading Rudolph P. Byrd and Henry Louis Gates Jr. to describe him as "a pioneering theorist of hybridity."[11] In letters to editors and publishers, statements defending his marriage to Margery Latimer, essays, and autobiographies, Toomer rejected the prescriptive racial categories of black and white to embrace a mixed-race identity: "In my body were many bloods, some dark blood, all blended in the fire of six or more generations. I was, then, either a new type of man or the very oldest."[12] Toomer's sense of his blended racial identity was a microcosm of his vision of broader American society outlined in detail in his sociological essay "Race Problems and Modern Society" (1929). In it Toomer contends that race has little relevance as a biological concept and is far more a matter of socialization. Much historical racial tension, he writes, should be attributed to economics in the United States, where "the 'acquisitive urge' for land, natural resources, and cheap labor variously gave rise to the problems of the whites and Indians, the whites and the negroes, the whites and the Asiatics, the old stock and the immigrants."[13] Within this historical continuum of greed, the racial intermixture at a biological level has been so extensive that a new "American type" is emerging, although "the consciousness of most so-called Americans lags far behind the organic process."[14]

Readers of *Go Down, Moses* will recognize Faulkner's kindred interest in the "acquisitive urge" relative to the natural and human depredations—including racial mixture—that structure *Go Down, Moses* as voiced so despairingly by the elderly Isaac McCaslin at the end of "Delta Autumn":

> This Delta. *This land which man has deswamped and denuded and derivered in two generations so that white men can own plantations and commute every night to Memphis and black men own plantations and ride in jim crow cars to Chicago to live in millionaires' mansions on Lakeshore Drive, where white men rent farms and live like niggers and niggers crop on shares and live like animals, where cotton is planted and grows man-tall in the very cracks of the sidewalks, and usury and mortgage and bankruptcy and measureless wealth, Chinese and African and Aryan and Jew, all breed and spawn together until no man has time to say which one is which nor cares. . . .* No wonder the ruined woods I used to know dont cry for retribution! he thought: The people who have destroyed it will accomplish its revenge.[15]

Isaac's despair is precipitated by his confrontation with his distant kins-woman, the light-skinned African American paramour of Roth Edmonds who has borne Roth's child. Isaac balks at the miscegenation: *"Maybe in a thousand or two thousand years in America,* he thought. *But not now! Not now!* He cried, not loud, in a voice of amazement, pity, and outrage: 'You're a nigger!'"* (344). Isaac's failure to transcend the racial barriers on an intellectual or emotional level at this moment reflects the inefficacy of his effort to remove himself from the historical continuum of racial responsibility through material renunciation. The refusal of a plantation, the delivery of an inheritance to African American cousins, the crass money offered to an abandoned woman and child—these provide no substitute for human decency across racial lines. In the face of continued intergenerational miscegenation, Isaac's "consciousness," to borrow Toomer's words, "lags far behind the organic process." *Go Down, Moses*, however, offers an alternative racial vision running counter to the standard limitations of the white South and indeed elucidating Isaac's failings. In Faulkner's oeuvre, Sam Fathers represents the notable exception to the pattern of mixed-race characters through whom Faulkner explores the widely espoused segregation-era notions of social and biological incompatibility between different races. Amidst the swirl of racial conflict and concomitant psychological turmoil of *Go Down, Moses*, Sam Fathers exists as a representative "whole" man, not in spite of his mixed-race ancestry but because of it. It is here in the depictions of racially composite "first men" where the most intriguing connections lie between Toomer and Faulkner.

Inspired by the southern folk music he encountered while a substitute principal in Sparta, Georgia, in 1921, Toomer famously described *Cane* as a "swan song" for "the folk-spirit [that] was walking in to die on the modern desert."[16] A montage of prose sketches, poems, songs, short stories, and experimental drama, *Cane* highlights—often painfully— African American cultural transition to modernity. Toomer believed this cultural transformation was part of a holistic physical and spiritual transformation, as he explained in a letter to Waldo Frank in 1923: "The Negro is in solution, in the process of solution. As an entity, the race is loosing [*sic*] its body and its soul, is approaching a common soul."[17] *Cane* suggests that inherent strife and psychological discomfiture accompany the metamorphosis into a postracial entity, and the work is rich with Toomer's disappearing folk sounds at times juxtaposed to and at times complementary to his other thematic staples: a fecund southern land- scape, a sterile and often surreal urbanscape, alienated individuals (most of them mulatto), sexually objectified women who in turn undermine and problematize their objectification, segregation, a persistent failure of language, and racial violence.

In terms of racial divisions, both *Cane* and *Go Down, Moses* explore the most graphic instance of racial subordination during the segregation era in lynching stories (Toomer's "Blood-Burning Moon" and Faulkner's "Pantaloon in Black"), while sexual depredations and other brutalities further highlight the unbalanced binary of a divided black and white South. The worlds of *Cane* and *Go Down, Moses*, however, are not struc- tured along these binaries, nor do we witness a white world threatened by blackness or miscegenation. Rather, Faulkner and Toomer present a culture and population already thoroughly hybrid and so advanced in amalgamation as to render white and black obsolete were it not for the ongoing racial violence intended to maintain the racial hierarchy being constantly eroded by unstable racial identities. The first two sec- tions of *Cane* feature numerous multiracial characters such as Becky's sons, Fernie Mae Rosen of black and Jewish ancestry, the nearly white Esther, and the racially indeterminate Paul, among others. The wide- spread amalgamation apparent in these sections becomes a predominant concern of the "Kabnis" section, where most of the major characters, including Ralph Kabnis, Lewis, Fred Halsey, and Carrie K., have mixed ancestry,[18] and portraits of Halsey's family highlight a pattern of racial mixing permeating the southern population. His great-grandfather's "portrait is that of an English gentleman who has retained much of his culture," while his great-grandmother's reveals a "Negro strain" and a group portrait depicts the subsequent generations: "It includes himself some thirty years ago when his face was an olive white, and his hair luxuriant and dark and wavy. The father is a rich brown. The mother, practically white. Of the children, the girl, quite young, is like Fred; the two brothers, darker" (85). The biological transformation, Toomer suggests, is widespread and well advanced.

Despite featuring more presumably white characters than *Cane*, Faulkner's *Go Down, Moses* represents an equally hybrid world. Whether or not we accept Richard Godden and Noel Polk's skepticism about Isaac's interpretation of the old plantation ledgers and his conclusion that his grandfather committed incest with his slave daughter, Tomey's Turl is identified early as a "white half-McCaslin" (6) who is widely accepted by subsequent generations to have been the son of the ruthless patriarch Lucius Quintus Carothers McCaslin.[19] These African American descendants are more numerous than the white descendants and include most prominently Turl; Lucas Beauchamp; Samuel Worsham Beauchamp; and the light-skinned, unnamed female whose child by Roth Edmonds reunites the "black" and "white" lines of the family. Additionally, Faulkner offers Boon Hogganbeck of European and Indian ancestry and Sam Fathers of Indian, African, and European ancestry as representatives of a vanishing race, "what of blood they left behind them running now in another race and for a while even in bondage" (159).

Even the ostensibly white characters of *Go Down, Moses* contribute to the sense of amalgamation in the novel, and ambiguities pertaining to Isaac's ancestry have led Polk to suggest that Isaac may have black ancestors.[20] The text is far from definitive on this point, but the miscegenation is so widespread in the novel that it encourages such speculative reading. Regardless of their presumed biological "whiteness," various white characters of the novel have an explicitly multiracial familial identity. Zach Edmonds and Lucas, for example, "in age . . . could have been brothers, almost twins too" (46) and "had lived until they were both grown almost as brothers lived" (54). Their sons, Carothers Edmonds and Henry Beauchamp, are "foster-brother[s]" (107), and to Carothers, Mollie Beauchamp is "the negro woman who had been the only mother he ever knew" (97). Likewise, the white Miss Worsham says of Mollie, "We grew up together as sisters would" (357). We might dismiss these relationships as examples of idealized paternalist nostalgia reflecting Faulkner's feelings for Caroline Barr, his mammy, to whom he dedicated the novel. The interracial familial relationships in the novel, however, seem too deeply ensconced, ultimately, in painful racial awareness to suggest nostalgia. Rather, I think Faulkner intends to stress the extensive hybrid racial realities of southern identity, and this seems particularly true when we note that Sam Fathers not only serves as a father figure to Isaac but actually transmits something to him of Sam's "vanished and forgotten people" in almost biological fashion (175). When Isaac kills his first deer under Sam's tutelage, the mentor ritualistically dips his hands in the deer's blood and places them on Isaac's face: "They were the white boy, marked forever, and the old dark man sired on both sides by savage kings, who had marked him, whose bloody hands had merely formally consecrated him . . . joining him and the man forever, so that the man would continue to live past the boy's seventy years and then eighty years" (159). Clearly an initiation moment, the bloody hands on the head also suggest the delivery of a newborn, and the ritual establishes Isaac as Sam's posterity.

Within these hybrid worlds that Toomer and Faulkner present, we might identify some details that suggest intertextual borrowing on Faulkner's part. The respective lynching victims, Tom Burwell and Rider, are both targeted for justifiably killing white men in scenes that similarly describe near decapitations. Boon Hogganbeck's penchant for fighting both Indians and whites, depending on his racially alienated mood, might be traced back not only to earlier Faulkner characters in *Absalom, Absalom!* and *Light in August*, but even farther to Becky's violent mixed-race sons. I am more interested, however, in the less easily identifiable but more fascinating intersections I see in the shared import of these envisioned hybrid worlds. George Hutchinson reads *Cane* as an effort "to provoke a new 'racial' consciousness that would displace the dualistic racial consciousness of 'white' and 'black' Americans," and he contends that in the "Kabnis" section, "Toomer achieves the most concentrated and complex articulation of his theme. He dramatizes the tortured 'dusk-before-dawn' of a new kind of ethnic subject, the possibility of whose existence was disallowed by both 'white' and 'black' definitions of 'racial' subjectivity."[21] While not all critics agree with Hutchinson's assessment, the content of "Kabnis," Toomer's own statements, and *Cane*'s relationship to his long poem "Blue Meridian" (already in progress in the early twenties) suggest that *Cane* exists in a continuum of Toomer texts evincing an interest in racial transformation. Details of Toomer's vision in this regard resonate with *Go Down, Moses* and help us understand the underlying promise of hybridity in Faulkner's work.

Two passages, in particular, from the "Kabnis" section of *Cane*, are worth highlighting as they anticipate Toomer's fully postracial vision in "Blue Meridian" and elucidate Faulkner's treatment of Sam Fathers. The first passage conjoins the "pain and beauty of the South" by conflating the southern racial mix with the natural world: "White faces, pain-pollen, settle downward through a cane-sweet mist and touch the ovaries of yellow flowers. Cotton-bolls bloom, droop. Black roots twist in a parched red soil beneath a blazing sky. Magnolias, fragrant, a trifle futile, lovely, far-off" (105). The highly sexualized imagery speaks to the individualized

acts of miscegenation as well as the broader procreant urge that contributes to an amalgamated population emerging at the expense—as I
read "parched red soil"—of the American Indian. The second passage
is the well-known birth song at dawn that follows Kabnis's emergence
from "the Hole," a richly multivalent name for Halsey's basement that
serves not only as a womb metaphor but also to convey the way the space
houses and entombs Father John, the prophetic remnant of slavery. As
sunlight encircles Carrie K. and Father John, the last lines of *Cane* suggest a new era: "Outside, the sun arises from its cradle in the tree-tops
of the forest. Shadows of pines are dreams the sun shakes from its eyes.
The sun arises. Gold-glowing child, it steps into the sky and sends a
birth-song slanting down gray dust streets and sleepy windows of the
southern town" (115). The promise of new beginnings is ambiguous and
unrealized within the context of the work, but in *Cane*'s hybrid world, so
marred by disunion and strife, this conclusion suggests ascension beyond
the individual and racial divisions. In doing so, *Cane* posits mixed-race
identity as the site for American progress, an idea Toomer was concur-
rently exploring in his long poem "Blue Meridian."

Toomer began "Blue Meridian" in the early 1920s before he began
work on *Cane*, and the poem, originally titled "The First American,"
developed over the years, with a section published as "Brown River,
Smile" in *Pagany* (1932) before the entire poem appeared in the last
volume of the American Caravan Series, *The New Caravan* (1936).
Faulkner was familiar with the series, having published "Ad Astra" in
American Caravan IV (1931), but whether he read the last installment
I cannot say for sure. The similar content of *Go Down, Moses* and "Blue
Meridian" suggests that he might have done so and, at the very least,
demonstrates a shared trajectory in the two writers' treatment of mixed-
race America. Accurately described by Bernard Bell as "the poetic zenith
of Toomer's quest for identity," "Blue Meridian" brings to poetic fruition
Toomer's dream of a postracial America.[22] Toomer posits the passing of
the "old peoples"—red, white, and black—and the emergence of the
"new American," "new people," or "blue man," as Toomer variously
describes the newly evolved human entity.[23] Each of the "old peoples"
had its unique role, with the Europeans modernizing and mechanizing
the nation, the Africans laboring and grieving, and the Indians offering
spiritual renewal with their disappearance. Extensive correlations might
be drawn between similarly racialized roles in *Go Down, Moses*, but
the sacrificial Indian figure warrants particular attention relative to Sam
Fathers. "Blue Meridian" offers a fuller treatment of the "parched red
soil" metaphor:

The great red race was here.
In a land of flaming earth and torrent-rains,

. . . .

But pueblo, priest, and Shalakos
Sank into the sacred earth
To fertilize the seven regions of America,

and ultimately the Indian serves

To resurrect—
To project into this conscious world
An example of the organic.[24]

Indians, in this formulation, no longer exist as an ethnic group; however, their biological and spiritual essence contributes to the new American. This contribution relies so heavily on the connection between Indian and natural world that the biological transition is not genetically based but rather achieved by the transmission of organic energy through decomposition and a return to earth. A similar transmission, which itself represents the spiritual lesson of unity, or the "organic" as Toomer terms it, is central to my assessment of Sam Fathers and Faulkner's consideration of amalgamated America in *Go Down, Moses*.

To what extent, then, did Faulkner share Toomer's sense of progressive racial amalgamation and express it in what many readers contend is Faulkner's most sophisticated engagement of racial issues? I disagree with Arthur F. Kinney's assessment of *Go Down, Moses* that "from the first, Faulkner sees the conflict of racial bloods as a fatal battleground."[25] Isaac McCaslin views racial mixing as the tragic manifestation of southern rapaciousness and greed that it is, but his resultant horror of exogamy should not cloud for the reader Faulkner's emphasis on the strength of exogamous progeny nor the text's refusal to prioritize white blood or its purity. For example, looking at Lucas's "impenetrable face with its definite strain of white blood, the same blood which ran in his own veins" (68–69), Roth Edmonds thinks, *"I am not only looking at a face older than mine and which has seen and winnowed more, but at a man most of whose blood was pure ten thousand years when my own anonymous beginnings became mixed enough to produce me"* (69). Disinherited because of his black ancestry and seeking ways to navigate his subject position in a white world, Lucas adheres, as Thadious M. Davis argues, to a "perspective of masculine power" grounded in his relationship to old Carothers McCaslin, his grandfather.[26] As problematic as this masculine emphasis is in many ways, Lucas embodies this aspect of the South to its fullest in Roth's mind:

> *He's more like old Carothers than all the rest of us put together, including old Carothers. He is both heir and prototype simultaneously of all the geography and climate and biology which sired old Carothers and all the rest of us and our kind, myriad, countless, faceless, even nameless now except himself who fathered himself, intact and complete, contemptuous, as old Carothers must have been, of all blood black white yellow or red, including his own.* (114–15)

The suggestion is that Lucas, with his hybrid racial identity, embodies the entirety of a ruthless and acquisitive South. This might be read pejoratively in terms of a mixed-race individual exhibiting negative characteristics, but I think it more significant that the mixed-race individual oxymoronically represents the purest and prototypical form.

As such, Lucas exhibits a hybrid strength that emerges at various points in the novel to contradict the notion that blood-mixing entails deterioration. Isaac's fyce—the tiny dog that first brings Old Ben to bay—is a mongrel possessing courage of the highest degree, entirely disproportionate to its size. Likewise, Lion, *"the* dog" (208) with the size, strength, courage, and ferocity to engage Old Ben, is "part mastiff, something of Airedale and something of a dozen other strains probably" (209). Read in this context, the mixed-blood Sam Fathers, so closely associated with Old Ben and Lion, represents something similar as Faulkner's purest man. The opening paragraph of "The Bear" asserts as much: "Only Sam and Old Ben and the mongrel Lion were taintless and incorruptible" (183). The son of a quadroon slave woman and the Chickasaw chief Ikkemotubbe (known also as Du Homme, "the man," or Doom), Sam does not inherit the chieftainship or ancestral lands. Rather, he endures servitude without servility. To describe Sam as "taintless" suggests not only that he is uncorrupted by slavery but also, if we accept Isaac's premise that Ikkemotubbe betrayed the land by presuming to own it, that Sam's very disinheritance may shelter him from just such a betrayal. In short, Sam can be read as untainted by either owning or being owned, and yet, in a novel so invested in notions of blood, "taintless" must also simultaneously reject concerns of biological corruption through racial mixing.

Sam's death, so closely associated with those of Lion and Old Ben, is generally understood to be emblematic of the disappearing wilderness, and since at least R. W. B. Lewis's inclusion of "The Bear" in his classic *The American Adam*, the wilderness has been associated in various ways with the Edenic myth. To understand Sam as "the man" in a pre- and postlapsarian context requires us to think in terms of his ending and his origin. Sam's unusual patronymic, Had Two Fathers, is shortened to Fathers, a transition that suggests he is both product and progenitor. Like Lucas, Sam is both "heir and prototype," but one who offers a spiritual antithesis to Lucas's materialism that is most fully realized when Isaac visits Sam's grave. This scene both encapsulates the sense of unity in life that Sam represents and resembles Toomer's emphasis on dusk and dawn, birth, and the Native American body as fertilizer for a new American spirituality. Although it sounds odd to discuss Sam's gravesite as a birth song, this association represents the culmination of a thematic trajectory Faulkner has already emphasized in "The Old People," the conclusion of which features McCaslin Edmonds and Isaac discussing Isaac and Sam's visit to a spirit grove where they sighted a magnificent buck. McCaslin conjoins sexual desire and death in his description of "all the blood hot and strong for living, pleasuring, that has soaked back into" the earth, before he associates death with rebirth: "And the earth dont want to just keep things, hoard them; it wants to use them again. Look at the seed, the acorns, at what happens even to carrion when you try to bury it: it refuses too, seethes and struggles too until it reaches light and air again, hunting the sun still" (179). McCaslin's description of this organic life cycle, tinged as it is with a spiritual dimension relative to Sam's mentorship, evolves into a multifaceted concept of transformation in the wake of Sam's death, the ever-receding wilderness, and Isaac's reading of the ledgers.

Comparable to the suggestive promise of a new beginning that *Cane* offers when Kabnis emerges from the tomb-like and vaginal "Hole," Isaac's visit to Sam's burial site conflates death and birth in deference to a spiritual vision of unity and origination that extends from Sam's multiracial identity. All visible evidence of Sam's grave has disappeared "in that place where dissolution itself was a seething turmoil of ejaculation tumescence conception and birth, and death did not even exist" (312). The transition of organic energy from Sam's body to other organisms, here coded in terms of human procreation, quickly moves from the biological dimension to a more spiritual one:

> He had not stopped, he had only paused, quitting the knoll which was no abode of the dead because there was no death, not Lion and not Sam: not held fast in earth but free in earth and not in earth but of earth, myriad yet undiffused of every myriad part, leaf and twig and particle, air and sun and rain and dew and night, acorn oak and leaf and acorn again, dark and dawn and dark and dawn again in their immutable progression and, being myriad, one. (313)

As poignantly beautiful an expression of human integration with the natural world as this is, the text urges us to think similarly in terms of human relationships. By specifically describing Sam as "of earth," Faulkner associates him with Adam as the first man from whom all others descend and the most fundamental symbol in the Judeo-Christian tradition for the unity of mankind or the myriad in the one. Likewise, the sexualized descriptors ("ejaculation tumescence conception and birth") for the transition of Sam's mixed-race body evoke the numerous acts of human procreation that constitute the hybrid racial world of *Go Down, Moses* and illustrate the human failings at the social level to transcend the limitations of binary absolutes never existent at the biological level.

Ultimately, then, I see in Sam Fathers a profound echo of Toomer's assessment of himself as "either a new type of man or the very oldest," and I see comparable hybrid worlds in Faulkner's and Toomer's work that delineate the distance between the social and biological realities regarding race in America. Within those depictions they exhibit—exuberantly in Toomer's case and surprisingly in Faulkner's—a distinct comfort with an amalgamated America. The correlations are not exhaustive, as Faulkner does not match Toomer's optimistically oracular assumption of human transformation into the new man. For Faulkner, the promise and the model of human unity exist in the mixed-race man, but humanity—being what it is—may have to wait, as Isaac so painfully claims, "two thousand years" for the social to catch up with the biological.

NOTES

This essay was supported by a Lycoming College Sabbatical Leave.

1. Eric J. Sundquist, "Faulkner, Race, and the Forms of American Fiction," in *Faulkner and Race: Faulkner and Yoknapatawpha, 1986,* ed. Doreen Fowler and Ann J. Abadie (Jackson: University Press of Mississippi, 1987), 1–34; Philip M. Weinstein, "Postmodern Intimations: Musing on Invisibility; William Faulkner, Richard Wright, and Ralph Ellison," in *Faulkner and Postmodernism: Faulkner and Yoknapatawpha, 1999,* ed. John N. Duvall and Ann J. Abadie (Jackson: University Press of Mississippi, 2002), 19–38; Margaret Donovan Bauer, *William Faulkner's Legacy: "What Shadow, What Stain, What Mark"* (Gainesville: University Press of Florida, 2005); Martyn Bone, "Intertextual Geographies of Migration and Biracial Identity: *Light in August* and Nella Larsen's *Quicksand,*" in *Faulkner and Formalism: Returns of the Text: Faulkner and Yoknapatawpha, 2008,* ed. Annette Trefzer and Ann J. Abadie (Jackson: University Press of Mississippi, 2012), 144–62.

2. For an extensive assessment of Faulkner's engagement with evolutionary thought, see Michael Wainwright, *Darwin and Faulkner's Novels: Evolution and Southern Fiction* (Basingstoke, UK: Palgrave Macmillan, 2008).

3. William Faulkner, *Light in August*, rev. ed. (1932; New York: Vintage International, 1990), 247–48.

4. William Faulkner, *Absalom, Absalom!*, rev. ed. (1936; New York: Vintage International, 1990), 302.

5. James B. Meriwether and Michael Millgate, eds., *Lion in the Garden: Interviews with William Faulkner* (1968; repr., Lincoln: University of Nebraska Press, 1980), 258.

6. See Joseph Blotner, *Faulkner: A Biography* (New York: Random House, 1974), 2: 1592; and Frederick L. Gwynn and Joseph L. Blotner, eds., *Faulkner in the University* (Charlottesville: University of Virginia Press, 1995), 215.

7. I have in mind Faulkner's fiction and nonfiction from the period that questions class, regional, religious, ethnic, and racial divisions in light of the war effort. Specifically, short stories such as "The Tall Men" (1941) and "Shall Not Perish" (1943) elide class and regional distinctions in celebration of patriotic duty and sacrifice, and in a letter written to his stepson, Malcolm A. Franklin, on the Fourth of July, 1943, Faulkner discusses the death of Robert Haas Jr. (son of the Random House vice president) and praises the sacrifice of Jewish Americans during the war before noting, "I just hope I dont run into some hundred percent American Legionnaire until I feel better." (William Faulkner, in *Selected Letters of William Faulkner*, ed. Joseph Blotner [New York: Random House, 1977], 175.) Faulkner then decries police violence against African Americans in Detroit as particularly reprehensible in light of African American military service in the war despite America's atrocious racial record. He concludes, "A change will come out of this war. If it doesn't, if the politicians and the people who run this country are not forced to make good the shibboleth they glibly talk about freedom, liberty, human rights, then you young men who live through it will have wasted your precious time, and those who dont live through it will have died in vain" (176).

8. Joseph R. McElrath Jr., Robert C. Leitz III, and Jesse S. Crisler, eds., *Charles W. Chesnutt: Essays and Speeches* (Stanford, CA: Stanford University Press, 1999), 248. For similar assertions, see Chesnutt's "The Future American: A Complete Race-Amalgamation Likely to Occur" (131–35) and "Race Prejudice: Its Causes and Cures" (233).

9. See Andrew B. Leiter, *In the Shadow of the Black Beast: African American Masculinity in the Harlem and Southern Renaissance* (Baton Rouge: Louisiana State University Press, 2010), 88–133.

10. Judith Sensibar, *Faulkner and Love: The Women Who Shaped His Art* (New Haven, CT: Yale University Press, 2009), 446.

11. Rudolf P. Byrd and Henry Louis Gates Jr., "'Song of the Son': The Emergence and Passing of Jean Toomer," in *Cane: Authoritative Text, Contexts, Criticism*, ed. Byrd and Gates (New York: Norton, 2011), xxxviii.

12. Jean Toomer, *The Wayward and the Seeking: A Collection of Writings by Jean Toomer*, ed. Darwin T. Turner (Washington, DC: Howard University Press, 1980), 93.

13. Jean Toomer, "Race Problems in [*sic*] Modern Society," in *The Uncollected Works of American Author Jean Toomer 1894–1967*, ed. John Chandler Griffin (Lewiston, NY: Edwin Mellen, 2003), 159.

14. Ibid., 163.

15. William Faulkner, *Go Down, Moses*, rev. ed. (1942; New York: Vintage International, 1990), 347. Subsequent references to this edition will appear parenthetically in the text.

16. Toomer, *Wayward*, 123.

17. Toomer, *Cane: Authoritative Text*, 166.

18. Ibid., 106. Subsequent references to this edition of the novel will appear parenthetically in the text.

19. Richard Godden and Noel Polk, "Reading the Ledgers," *Mississippi Quarterly* 55 (Summer 2002): 301–59.

20. Noel Polk, *Faulkner and Welty and the Southern Literary Tradition* (Jackson: University Press of Mississippi, 2008), 79.

21. George Hutchinson, "Jean Toomer and American Racial Discourse," in *Interracialism: Black-White Intermarriage in American History, Literature, and Law*, ed. Werner Sollors (Oxford: Oxford University Press, 2000), 376.

22. Bernard W. Bell, "Jean Toomer's 'Blue Meridian': The Poet as Prophet of a New Order of Man," in *Jean Toomer: A Critical Evaluation*, ed. Therman B. O'Daniel (Washington, DC: Howard University Press, 1988), 344.

23. Jean Toomer, "Blue Meridian," in *The New Caravan*, ed. Alfred Kreymborg, Lewis Mumford, and Paul Rosenfeld (New York: Norton, 1936), 635, 633, 637, 651.

24. Ibid., 636, 651.

25. Arthur F. Kinney, introduction to *Critical Essays on William Faulkner: The McCaslin Family*, ed. Arthur F. Kinney (Boston: G. K. Hall, 1990), 12.

26. Thadious M. Davis, *Games of Property: Law, Race, Gender, and Faulkner's "Go Down, Moses"* (Durham, NC: Duke University Press, 2003), 156.

"Go to Jail about This Spoonful": Narcotic Determinism and Human Agency in "That Evening Sun" and "A Spoonful Blues"

TIM A. RYAN

The blues tradition not only constitutes one of the central foundations of modern African American literature—influencing such authors as Langston Hughes, Zora Neale Hurston, Amiri Baraka, and August Wilson—but is also a palpable presence in Yoknapatawpha County. This is hardly surprising, given that Faulkner's emergence as a novelist was directly contemporaneous with both the development of recording technology and the rise of popular music as a commercial form. The author's initial wave of novels and stories—from *Soldiers' Pay* through "That Evening Sun" to *Light in August*—appeared during the first golden era of blues, jazz, country, folk, and gospel records. The blues, in particular, illuminates Faulkner's fiction, just as the Yoknapatawpha novels and tales shed light on the meanings of the blues.

The *blues* is a broad, flexible, and imprecise term that refers to a diverse spectrum of music. As Elijah Wald jokingly observes, "The rule seems to be that if a black person played it before 1950, and it is not classifiable as jazz, classical, or gospel, then it must be blues."[1] In fact, *blues* is such an expansive category that it involves folk songs made by and for black people in largely southern, rural communities at one end of the continuum and urban, mainstream, and—often—white adaptations of African American musical traditions at the other. Exponents of the genre thus include not only Robert Johnson and Charley Patton, or Bessie Smith and Ma Rainey, but also W. C. Handy's Orchestra of Memphis, Marion Harris, Bobby Bland, Eric Clapton, and the White Stripes.[2]

The music of rural Mississippi had very little to do with the national blues craze of the 1910s and early 1920s. For the majority of Americans in the early decades of the twentieth century, the blues meant Handy's sheet music compositions, orchestral numbers by dance bands, and performances by such white singers as Bee Palmer, Gilda Gray,

Morton Harvey, and Margaret Young. It is no wonder that Faulkner once observed that African American "music and poetry have passed to the white man, and what the white man has done with them is not Negro any more but something else."[3]

In fact, there was no commercial American recording of a black artist singing the blues until 1920. Mamie Smith's revolutionary "Crazy Blues" paved the way for a series of records by African American vocalists—mostly female and usually backed by full jazz bands—which commonly owed as much to pop and Tin Pan Alley as to the black musical traditions of the rural South. The most prominent member of this urban, classic, or vaudeville blues scene was Bessie Smith, whose powerful voice earned her the title Empress of the Blues.[4]

In contrast, the southern folk blues was a marginal local phenomenon until the mid-1920s and, even when it finally appeared on commercial records, remained a music consumed largely by black listeners. In the spring of 1926—just a few weeks after the publication of Faulkner's debut novel—Blind Lemon Jefferson's first blues record "shocked the music world" with its presentation of what Ted Gioia calls "the raw, unfiltered blues of rural America."[5] Jefferson's songs presented a dramatic alternative to the polished productions of the urban singers. There was no piano, no trumpet, no clarinet, just the singer accompanying his sparse lyric by strumming his guitar "in real southern style," as one advertisement put it,[6] but the record was an unexpected hit in black communities, inspiring music companies to recruit other guitar-toting purveyors of down-home songs.

If Jefferson hailed from Texas, and Georgia could boast such singer-songwriters as Blind Willie McTell and Blind Blake, it is now clear that Mississippi was the Mecca of the country blues in this era. The northern hill country—the blues center closest to Faulkner's Oxford—was home to such major figures as Fred McDowell and Sid Hemphill, although its denizens made very few recordings until after World War II.[7] During Faulkner's flowering as a writer in the late 1920s and early 1930s, the landmark records of the Mississippi blues primarily came from artists associated with the Delta, including Son House, Skip James, and Mississippi John Hurt. Among the region's impressive roster, William Barlow singles out one particular singer as "the heart and soul of the early Delta blues tradition": Charley Patton, the man who recorded such imperishable numbers as "High Water Everywhere," "Moon Going Down," and "A Spoonful Blues."[8]

Patton and the Mississippi Delta blues enjoyed only a brief golden age of recording. When the Great Depression all but demolished the American music industry, record companies abandoned the rural blues as rapidly as they had embraced it just a few years previously.[9] Patton continued to perform in and around his native Sunflower County, but after waxing forty-two songs between June 1929 and the summer of 1930, he did not set foot in a studio for more than three years while his remaining record releases suffered radically declining sales before tailing off altogether in early 1932. Patton participated in only one more recording session, just a few months before his death in 1934.

Although music histories today emphasize the importance of the southern country blues, the records of Patton and his peers remained largely unknown outside of black communities until after World War II. In 1940, Langston Hughes claimed that Handy's "St. Louis Blues" was "sung more than any other song on the air waves, is known in Shanghai and Buenos Aires, Paris and Berlin—in fact, is heard so often in Europe that a great many Europeans think it must be the American National Anthem."[10] In contrast, the down-home Mississippi blues languished in obscurity, and most of Patton's records were out of print by the mid-1930s.

The blues revival of the 1950s finally brought rural black music squarely into the American mainstream. Enterprising aficionados painstakingly transferred blues songs from scratched, warped, and battered 78 rpm records. LP reissues made the works of the prewar country blues singers available for the first time in decades. Some long-forgotten Mississippi musicians—including House, James, Hurt, and McDowell—even enjoyed a brief renaissance, making new records and performing for appreciative crowds at folk festivals, finally receiving the acclaim many of them had truly earned decades earlier.

The most renowned example of the radically changing fortunes of the Mississippi blues is the case of Robert Johnson. Scoring only a single, minor local hit record in his lifetime and dying in 1938 at the tender age of twenty-seven, Johnson easily could have been forgotten forever. The postwar blues revival, however, lionized him as the King of the Delta Blues Singers, and in 1990, a CD box set of his recordings unexpectedly achieved platinum sales. In 2012, even the president of the United States consented to sing one of Johnson's songs at a White House event.[11] If only a few thousand people heard Johnson and his records during his lifetime, his music now thrills millions across the world.

We like to think of Faulkner as one of those rare white people who treasured the blues, and in particular, the Mississippi country blues, long before the world at large belatedly caught on to the music's greatness. After all, he was born and raised close to both the northern hill country and the Delta, and his fiction includes several appearances by black musicians. Joseph Blotner's biography even includes a photograph of the author as a young man posing with a guitar.[12] It is tempting to assume that Faulkner belongs in the company of such individuals as John and Alan Lomax, the famous father-and-son team who made field recordings of southern folk music,[13] or H. C. Speir, the Jackson-based purveyor of blues records who was also a talent broker for the black musicians of the region.[14] In our imaginations, Faulkner is much closer to such figures than, say, to Keith Dockery, whose husband's plantation had nurtured such talents as Patton and House but who confessed in later years that "we never heard these people sing. . . . I wish we had realized that these people were so important."[15]

The historical record confirms Faulkner's broad exposure to African American vernacular music. His black caretaker, Mammy Callie Barr, may have taken him to a local juke joint when he was a child, and as a young man he danced to Handy's orchestra at local functions, regularly visited a roadside honky-tonk during excursions into the Delta with his lawyer friend, Phil Stone, and once sat outside an African American church with a girlfriend, thrilling to the sound of the congregation's singing.[16] The author even listened to Bessie Smith records on an old windup Victrola at Rowan Oak.[17] At the time of his death, Faulkner's library included a copy of *Been Here and Gone*, Frederic Ramsey's 1960 book about black folkways and African American music.[18] Most strikingly, in 1956 *Ebony* magazine's Moneta Sleet photographed Faulkner's encounter with legendary jazz singer Billie Holiday—a meeting that the singer's biographer suggests came about at the author's request.[19] David Krause goes so far as to claim that Faulkner "listened compulsively to the music of the Afro-American experience."[20]

Certainly, black music appears with some frequency in Faulkner's fiction before 1932, if rarely afterwards. In their invaluable studies—presented at previous Faulkner and Yoknapatawpha conferences—Thadious Davis and Adam Gussow assess the author's knowledge of the blues and portrayals of African American music in his work, from the appearance of Handy's band in *Soldiers' Pay*[21] to the description of a black street musician in *Flags in the Dust*.[22] Erich Nunn draws attention to the subtle ways in which both black and white popular music are central to the design of *Sanctuary*.[23] Several critics—including Charles Peek, Carol Gartner, and Ken Bennett—have examined blues elements in "That Evening Sun," a story that famously takes its title from the opening lines of Handy's "St. Louis Blues."[24] H. R. Stoneback, meanwhile, suggests that the characters and situations of "Pantaloon in Black" derive from another Handy song, "Easy Rider."[25] Finally, Jane Isbell Haynes identifies provocative parallels between the traditional blues ballad "Stagolee" and the brief scene in *The Hamlet* in which V. K. Ratliff imagines Flem Snopes defeating the Devil.[26]

Given the immensity of Faulkner's canon, however, some have questioned whether a handful of brief references to the blues in just a few novels and stories really amounts to very much. One prominent music critic has even expressed surprise at "the scarcity of blues description" in Faulkner's work.[27] Gussow judiciously suggests that "Faulkner's place in the literary blues tradition is . . . closer to the margins than the center."[28]

It is true that there were significant limits to the author's knowledge of vernacular and African American music. Karl Zender's characterization of Faulkner having a "profound antipathy toward American popular culture"[29] may stretch a point, but the writer's dislike of amplified or recorded music was sufficiently known to the proprietors of Oxford restaurants that they needed no prompting to unplug jukeboxes or turn off radios whenever Faulkner entered their premises.[30] Zender notes, furthermore, that the author's later fiction includes regular diatribes against phonographs, radios, and amplified sound in general, such as the vivid descriptions in both *Intruder in the Dust* and *Requiem for a Nun* of the cacophony of recorded music in Jefferson's town square.[31]

Those critics who laud the author's appreciation of the blues and celebrate its significance to his fiction are no less correct than those who question the extent of Faulkner's knowledge of black music and wonder why there is so little popular music in the Yoknapatawpha novels and stories. The truth is that Faulkner understood both much more and much less than about the blues than we do. Like anyone who came of age in the early twentieth century, Faulkner was aware of the blues as a popular phenomenon. Furthermore, as a Mississippian, the writer was directly familiar with the blues as a regional folk form. If, however, Faulkner was attentive to local black singers and relished mainstream pop adaptations of the blues, it is unlikely that he ever heard—or even heard of—the particular Mississippi musicians or blues records that we consider canonical today.

Just as our only access to Faulkner's imaginative world is via his published works, our only way of engaging with the songs of prewar blues musicians is through their recordings. If live performance was and is central to the blues, the history of the music nonetheless goes hand in hand with the evolution of recording technology. Had it not been for the invention of the phonograph, the major Mississippi bluesmakers would be forgotten today, save in the dim memories of a few elderly members of black communities. After all, virtually nothing is known about the generation of blues pioneers who lived immediately prior to the age of recording.[32] Just as the creation of writing saved Homer's epic poems from oblivion, so did the invention of sound recording preserve the artistry of such singers as Charley Patton.

Even though Faulkner may have owned copies of both Gershwin's "Rhapsody in Blue" and Bessie Smith's urban blues,[33] there is no evidence that he ever purchased a single record of the Mississippi country blues. Furthermore, Faulkner largely seems to have valued the blues he heard locally as what he took to be a reassuringly pure and enduring African American folk tradition, not for what we now consider it to be: one of black America's primary contributions to the modernist arts and popular culture. If Krause is correct that the author sometimes listened intently to the music of the African American experience, Faulkner was probably no more aware than the owners of Dockery Plantation of the historical and artistic importance of particular singers on southern farms.

Even if the evidence suggests that Faulkner—like most other white people of his time—was unfamiliar with the canonical artists and records of the country blues, it is provocative that Patton's major phase as a recording artist exactly matches Faulkner's most prolific and remarkable period as a writer of fiction. The Delta bluesman made and released his first recordings in 1929, the same year as the publication of *Sartoris* heralded the beginning of the Yoknapatawpha chronicle. Even the titles of Patton's releases and Faulkner's publications in the late 1920s and early 1930s echo each other. In October 1929, one could listen to Patton's latest record, "Screamin' and Hollerin' the Blues," while reading Faulkner's new novel, *The Sound and the Fury*. The author's next book, *As I Lay Dying*, arrived in stores in October 1930, at the very same time as Patton's "Jesus Is a Dying-Bed Maker." Finally, one of Patton's last great records, "Moon Going Down," appeared at the beginning of 1931, shortly before the publication of Faulkner's "That Evening Sun Go Down"—as it was then called—in H. L. Mencken's *American Mercury*.

If Faulkner probably knew nothing about what we now consider the canonical texts of the country blues, and for that matter, if Patton was unlikely to have been an admirer of the Yoknapatawpha fiction, the parallels between the works of these two artists are nonetheless myriad. It is more than just provocative happenstance that they produced fiction and songs with similar titles. Both used revolutionary formal techniques to describe, explore, and imagine the same world: Mississippi in the early decades of the twentieth century. Patton's "Tom Rushen Blues" (1929) is the comic tale of a shrewd African American bootlegger's interactions with the white power structure, which is to say that it closely resembles the "Fire and the Hearth" section of *Go Down, Moses*. Faulkner's story of a character caught up in the chaos of the 1927 Mississippi flood, "Old

Man," echoes "High Water Everywhere," Patton's song about the same event. Jason Compson's argument with Uncle Job about the boll weevil in *The Sound and the Fury* is curiously reminiscent of the lyrics of Patton's "Mississippi Bo Weavil [*sic*] Blues." Where the white man in Faulkner's novel likens the black man to the agricultural pest, the African American singer gleefully assumes the voice of the troublesome insect. In terms of content, setting, and theme, Faulkner's fiction habitually has at least as much in common with Patton's lyrics—and those of the blues more broadly—as with the writings of such black literary contemporaries as Jean Toomer, Nella Larsen, Claude McKay, and later, Ralph Ellison.

The relevance of the blues to Faulkner's work, then, transcends the author's knowledge of the genre or its explicit appearances in his novels and stories. The scant evidence regarding Faulkner's demonstrable familiarity with the music is less illuminating than the many provocative correspondences between the lyrics of canonical blues records and the Yoknapatawpha fiction. Take, for example, the parallels between Horace Benbow's obsession with shrimp in *Sanctuary* and Robert Johnson's somber anthem about impotence, "Dead Shrimp Blues." Or consider the similarities between Mink Snopes's experiences at Parchman Farm Penitentiary in *The Mansion* and Bukka White's 1940 series of songs about the notorious prison. Although the major Mississippi blues singers and Faulkner presumably never met, scholars today can put their works into productive dialogue in order to understand each of them in new ways.

A case in point is the relationship between Patton's "A Spoonful Blues" (1929) and Faulkner's "That Evening Sun." Both texts allude to the fabled prevalence of cocaine use in black communities, and both present addicts as mindless and violent automatons. Furthermore, while story and song alike use narcotic abuse to frame their tales of dehumanization, each simultaneously asserts the essential dignity and agency of black Americans in the face of language and social systems that existed to suppress and to dehumanize them.

"A Spoonful Blues" is rooted in paradox and contradiction. For one thing, it does not even mention cocaine, even though virtually all blues critics now agree that the drug is its primary subject.[34] In addition, aside from its brief spoken introduction—"I'm about to go to jail about this spoonful"[35]—the song never includes the eponymous word *spoonful* either, and although it is one of the most remarkable achievements of prewar Delta music, it is technically not a blues at all, most likely deriving from a novelty vaudeville rag. What is more, "A Spoonful Blues" is an infectiously catchy, even comic, song but concerns such dour topics as addiction, incarceration, domestic violence, madness, and death. As Patton's biographers note, "In its flippant thematic treatment of its subject and the diatonic character of its melody," it could not be farther "from conventional black music."[36]

The song's lyrics are not just unusual; they are also sometimes close to impenetrable. The poor sound quality of the existing recordings—copied from aged and worn 78s in the absence of surviving studio masters—and Patton's notoriously incomprehensible diction present serious obstacles to any listener. Even Son House—one of Patton's colleagues and contemporaries—complained about the incoherence of his vocals, observing, "You could sit at Charley's feet and not understand a word he sang."[37] While numerous passages in Patton's oeuvre remain open to question despite the painstaking efforts of scholarly transcribers, there is a relatively clear consensus regarding the lyrics of "A Spoonful Blues."[38]

I'm about to go to jail about this spoonful
1   In all a spoon, oh, that spoon . . .
    Women goin' crazy every day in their life 'bout a . . .
2   It's all I want in this creation is a . . .
    I go home, *wanna fight* 'bout a . . .
3   Doctors dying *way in Hot Springs* jus' 'bout a . . .
    These women going crazy every day in their life 'bout a . . .
4   "Would you kill a man, babe?" *"Yes I will,"* jus' 'bout a . . .
    Ah, babe, I'm a fool about my . . .
5   *Don't take me long* to get my . . .
    Hey, baby, you know I need my . . .
6   It's mens on Parchman *done lifetime* jus' 'bout a . . .
    Hey, baby, *you know I ain't long* about my . . .
7   All I want, *baby, in this creation* is a . . .
    I go to bed, get up, and wanna fight 'bout a . . .
8   *"Looky here, baby, would you slap me?"* "Yes I will," jus' 'bout a . . .
    Say, baby, *you know I'm a fool a*-bout my . . .
9   "Would you kill a man?" *"Yes, I would, you know I'll kill,"* jus' 'bout a . . .
    Most every man *that you see is* fool 'bout his . . .
10 *You know, baby, I need* that ol' . . .
    Hey, baby, *I wanna hit the jug about* 'bout a . . .
11 *"Baby, you gon' quit me?"* "Yeah, hon'," jus' 'bout a . . .
    It's all I want, *baby,* in this creation is a . . .
12 *Looky here, baby, I'm leavin' town* jus' 'bout a . . .
    Hey, baby, *you know I need* that ol' . . .
13 *Don't make me mad, baby,* 'cause I want my . . .
    Hey, baby, I'm a fool 'bout that . . .

14 *Looky here, honey,* I need that . . .
    Most every man livin' 'thout a . . .
15 Some of these men *I know they are* 'thout a . . .
    Hey, baby, *I'm sneakin' 'round here* and they ain't got me a . . .
16 Oh, that spoon . . .
    Hey, baby, you know I need my . . .

If the lyrics of "A Spoonful Blues" depict a world in which cocaine turns people into mindless and heartless brutes, the recording itself is a thrilling tour de force of musical creativity and technical mastery. Charlie Jackson had already recorded a version of the song in 1925, titled "All I Want Is a Spoonful,"[39] but while there is nothing original about the material, Patton's performance is one of the most creative accomplishments of his career. The bluesman adopts multiple voices and glides between sung and spoken lines as he plays the roles of numerous characters, all of them driven by a single overriding compulsion: they will do anything for just a single "spoonful" of narcotic pleasure—fight, abandon their loved ones, go to jail, abuse their partners, lose their minds, even commit murder. Although the song is about dehumanization and the absence of free will, the performance is a joyous celebration of human ingenuity and agency. One man and his guitar create a soundscape that, as John Fahey notes, "sounds like there are 20 or 30 people on it."[40]

In short, "A Spoonful Blues" flaunts the tension between its implacable, soulless, and machinelike protagonists and the artistry and inventiveness of its human performer. This tension is most vividly embodied in the way in which the performance seems to privilege an inanimate object over a human voice: although Patton does not sing the word *spoonful,* he uses a bottleneck slide effect at the end of each line so that his guitar appears to be "saying" that word. The musical instrument's apparent power to appropriate human speech is, of course, just an illusion: it is only the artist's skill that permits the guitar any such semblance of agency.

In an era in which blues and country songs habitually addressed narcotics overtly,[41] the absence of the word *cocaine* in Patton's lyric suggests that the song concerns larger issues than drug addiction. Fahey argues that, if "the spoonful" specifically refers to a quantity of cocaine, it also broadly "represents all those things which can drive a person to do things he would not otherwise consider."[42] More precisely, the spoonful represents all those things that a person might say to account for or justify his most irresponsible actions. On one hand, the song marvels at the fact that the smallest amount of cocaine—or desire, or anger, or whatever else—can cause people to perpetrate horrifying acts. On the other hand, the song's litany of crimes is so endless and so circular that the recurrent refrain that they are all simply attributable to "that spoonful" becomes absurd. One might equally say, "I was only obeying orders" or "The Devil made me do it." Ultimately, "A Spoonful Blues" is less about people who have lost control because of addiction and more about the ways people rationalize and excuse their most inhuman acts as loss of control.

In other words, "A Spoonful Blues" is a song about determinism that interrogates the very principles of determinism. The lyrics present people who claim to be the hapless pawns of biological drives and social forces, but the virtuosity of the performance asserts the power of human agency over environmental conditioning. This record about individual potency in the face of a dehumanizing universe has particular resonance coming from a black man who lived in Mississippi during the era of segregation and repression. Indeed, "A Spoonful Blues" locates Patton in a tradition of African American writers—including Paul Laurence Dunbar and Richard Wright—whose fictions flirt with naturalism while simultaneously complicating its insistence that all human activity results from heredity and/or environment. Naturalist dogma could not adequately speak to black artists who aspired to transcend the factors that had traditionally limited their destinies.[43]

"That Evening Sun" has more in common with "A Spoonful Blues" than just an allusion to cocaine use among southern black populations. Like Patton's recording, Faulkner's story suggests the power of cocaine to degrade black humanity. However, just as the singer's dazzling performance dismantles the rhetoric of determinism that the song invokes, so does "That Evening Sun" highlight the absurdity of the discourses that the tale's white characters mobilize to rationalize their culture's racial hierarchy and to justify their most inhuman acts.

The single reference to cocaine in "That Evening Sun" encapsulates the white community's distorted and dismissive view of Nancy, the black employee of the Compson family. When Nancy publicly accuses the banker, Stovall, of failing to pay her for sexual services, and he responds by violently assaulting her, it is she, not the brutish white man, who is taken to jail for causing a disturbance.[44] Following Nancy's subsequent attempt to hang herself in her prison cell, the Jefferson jailer provides a dubious explanation of the character's erratic behavior: "He said that it was cocaine and not whisky, because no nigger would try to commit suicide unless he was full of cocaine, because a nigger full of cocaine wasn't a nigger any longer."[45]

This flippant and offensive rationalization is no more persuasive an account of Nancy's actions than the declaration by one of Patton's characters that "I'm about to go to jail about this spoonful." As Philip Momberger notes, "The jailer is blind to Nancy's anguished humanity because he has reduced her to a categorical abstraction."[46] Faulkner's story vividly shows how such blindness is endemic amongst the white people of Jefferson. Even Quentin—at least as a child—appears to accept the jailer's assumptions. His initial explanation of the cause of Nancy's habitual tardiness and oversleeping is superseded by the jailer's claims: "we thought it was whisky *until* that day they arrested her again."[47] Several critics have observed, however, that beyond the jailer's blithe assertions, the narrative offers no firm evidence that Nancy ever uses narcotics.[48] Both Laurel Bollinger and Paula Sunderman explain the jailer's crude evaluation of Nancy as a transparent attempt to frame the black woman's disruptive behavior within the conventional rhetorical frameworks of Jim Crow society.[49]

The scene is not important just because of how the jailer seeks to control the meanings of Nancy's actions by reducing her to a stereotype; its function is also to underline—and even satirize—the sheer irrationality and inhumanity of the white community's ideologies. The jailer's characterization of Nancy is not just racist and reductive; it is also illogical and incoherent. The inherent contradictions of the convoluted discourse that he employs to dehumanize her are so overt, in fact, that the ultimate effect is to emphasize, not to diminish, Nancy's subjectivity and agency, even though the jailer is blind to this fact. Faulkner explored the same issue in "Pantaloon in Black"—the 1940 short story that eventually became part of *Go Down, Moses*—the protagonist of which, a black lumber worker named Rider, may be inspired, as Stoneback suggests, by another Handy blues composition. Just as the white characters in "That Evening Sun" are oblivious to the sources of Nancy's anger and pain, the complacent sheriff's deputy in "Pantaloon in Black" fails to grasp that it is Rider's grief for a deceased wife that accounts for his erratic and, ultimately, violent behavior. The painfully misguided conclusion that the purblind deputy draws from his encounter with Rider is that "them damn niggers . . . aint human."[50]

In "That Evening Sun," the jailer's explanation of Nancy implies that the black woman possesses neither the sense of self nor the agency necessary to commit suicide. It is inconceivable to the jailer that Nancy could enact the kind of honorable suicide performed by such classical avatars as Seneca, Marc Anthony, and Lucretia. A brooding, hypersensitive, and unhappy white intellectual—like Quentin Compson in *The Sound and the Fury*—might well kill himself, but not an uneducated black washerwoman. Sunderman paraphrases the jailer's words as follows: "I know niggers and they are too cowardly to commit suicide. I know they get drunk but whiskey won't make them commit suicide—only something stronger like cocaine will."[51] In other words, the jailer can account for Nancy's suicide attempt only by substituting one reductive stereotype for another: it was not the act of a "nigger" but that of a deranged "cocaine fiend." As the jailer sees it, Nancy did not choose suicide; the cocaine chose for her: it reduced her to a mindless and self-destructive beast, and thus her attempt to hang herself was not an action rooted in human thought or emotion. From the jailer's perspective, Nancy is, as Patton's song has it, just a fool about a spoonful.

The irony is that although the jailer aims to reduce Nancy to a negative stereotype, his rhetoric subtly humanizes her—just as Patton's idiosyncratic performance of his song is the opposite of the inhuman behavior and robotic rationalizations of its characters. Within the scheme of Faulkner's story, the point of the jailer's convoluted explanation of Nancy is precisely that it is entirely paradoxical in its implications. "That Evening Sun" is reminiscent not only of "A Spoonful Blues" but also of Greil Marcus's discussion of the scene in *The Godfather* film in which the Mafia dons decide to sell heroin exclusively to black people. "They're animals anyway," one of the crime bosses asserts, "so let them lose their souls."[52] As Marcus notes, "The Mafia may have missed the contradiction in that line, but Francis [Ford] Coppola certainly did not; neither did the black men and women in the theaters."[53] Nor should anyone miss the contradictory nature of the jailer's statement in Faulkner's story. If it really is the case that cocaine is responsible for transforming Nancy into a maniacal beast, it follows that she was rational—certainly as rational as any white person—before she took the narcotic.

Furthermore, while young Jason Compson spends much of the story relentlessly labeling each and every black person employed by his family a "nigger,"[54] the torturous nature of the jailer's explanation of Nancy ultimately achieves the opposite. Even as he uses "nigger" three times in one sentence, the jailer inadvertently liberates Nancy from that repulsive racial epithet and all its associations. A passage in Faulkner's subsequent novel, *Light in August*, echoes the jailer's heavy-handed rhetoric, including three uses of "nigger" in a single sentence. The townsperson who narrates the arrest of Joe Christmas speaks of one of the captors having "already hit the nigger a couple of times in the face, and the nigger acting like a nigger for the first time and taking it, not saying anything."[55] Instead of cementing Joe's racial status, the hyperbolic repetition of "nigger" only emphasizes the constructed and ambiguous nature of his identity, as well as the violence—both physical and discursive—required to reduce him to the position of "other."

The jailer's frenetic repetition of "nigger" in "That Evening Sun" similarly exposes the flimsy rationalizations and thunderous disjunctions of racist discourse. Paralleling the deputy's evaluation of Rider in "Pantaloon in Black," when the jailer claims that Nancy "wasn't a nigger any longer" after taking cocaine, he means to say that the narcotic rendered her less than human. In terms of the social and rhetorical logic of Jim Crow, however, this construction of Nancy carries an alternative implication to which the jailer is apparently oblivious: that cocaine turned a woman of color Caucasian. If she "wasn't a nigger any longer"—if she was "other than" instead of explicitly "less than"—then the jailer's imprecise designation allows for the possibility of Nancy being "more than a nigger," which is to say, in terms of the culture's racial ideologies, of her being white or, at least, equal to white people. Although segregationist culture was rooted in the notion, as expressed in Aesop's famous fable, that the Ethiopian cannot be washed white,[56] the jailer's words actually suggest that racial categories are arbitrary and mutable cultural constructions.

What is more, the jailer's rhetorical short circuit—in which Nancy is reduced to the level of an animal while simultaneously being elevated to the social status of whiteness—logically implies a relationship between "subhuman" and "Caucasian." If Nancy's behavior suggests that she "wasn't a nigger any longer," then she must possess the very qualities the jailer associates exclusively with white people that make them capable of suicide, whether courage, despair, or defiance. Simultaneously—and paradoxically—if Nancy's frenzied actions indicate that she is not "a nigger any longer," the necessary implication is that to not be a "nigger"— to be white—is to be prone to manic, irrational, and violent behavior. Despite the jailer's evident assumptions about black people, his convoluted rhetoric actually implies that Nancy has no less humanity, no less dignity, and no less agency than any white person, but also that the mindless fury of a cocaine fiend embodies the very essence of "whiteness"—and that to be white is thus to be less than fully human.[57]

In sum, the jailer's single reported line of dialogue in "That Evening Sun" encapsulates the story's corrosive critique of the inhuman absurdity of the prevailing system of race relations and the torturous forms of discourse required to rationalize and perpetuate that system. In her naked and vulnerable humanity, Nancy is sharply distinct from the story's white characters. Beneath a fragile veneer of gentility and their claims of racial superiority, the white people of Jefferson reveal themselves to be just as irrational, as illogical, and as mindlessly destructive as the compulsive addicts in "Spoonful." They are little more than automatons who are conditioned to respond—if in some cases reluctantly—to the crisis of a person of color with passivity, indifference, or even outright cruelty. Like the characters in the blues lyric, the white people of Yoknapatawpha try to hide behind a rhetoric that supposedly justifies their abnegation of human responsibility. White power in Faulkner's story is every bit as dehumanizing as white powder in Patton's song.

It is no wonder, then, that after the jailer saves Nancy from hanging, he beats and whips her.[58] By attempting suicide, which the jailer sees as a white prerogative, Nancy has traduced Jefferson's racial etiquette. In a world in which white people assume that they have mastery over the lives and destinies of black people—and in which whites have the authority to dispense disciplinary violence to people of color—Nancy's self-destructive act suggests that she does not "know her place." The jailer's rhetoric alone appears to be insufficient to restore Nancy to her conventional position in the racial hierarchy, so he also employs coercive violence to reduce her to a stereotypical abstraction—a "nigger"—again.

Nancy appears to embrace both the subject position and the rationalization now provided her—that, as a black person, she has no moral responsibility or agency. Throughout the remainder of the story, her consistent response to her dire situation is, "I aint nothing but a nigger. . . . It aint none of my fault."[59] Like the jailer's convoluted rationalizations, and like the absurdly endless disavowals of responsibility in "A Spoonful Blues," however, Nancy's earlier bold actions—whether exposing Stovall's use of black prostitutes or attempting suicide—undermine this claim. In light of Patton's masterful ventriloquization of the voices of passive addicts in "A Spoonful Blues," one cannot help but wonder about the fierce humanity behind the blankly passive mask that Nancy adopts in the latter half of "That Evening Sun."

At the very least, if the white people of Jefferson only confine, repress, abuse, and discard Nancy—in both deed and word—the story's ambivalent ending avoids any imposition of narrative closure upon her. Critics cannot agree whether Nancy survives her night of trauma or dies at the hands of her former lover, if she is a passive victim of circumstance or the active singer of her own tragic blues.[60] Where the jailer, Stovall, young Jason Compson, and the white community at large seek to suppress Nancy through physical violence and/or repressive language, Quentin's narrative and Faulkner's tale grant her the open destiny of an unfinished story. If there is a continual tension in Faulkner's canon between a white author's growing realization that his knowledge of black subjectivities is inherently limited and an increasing tendency to present people of color as so unknowable that they are "disembodied from the reality of ordinary human life,"[61] the ending of "That Evening Sun" at least refuses to reduce Nancy to a literary stereotype or a rhetorical construction. Unlike the white people whom they describe, author and narrator alike—whatever the limitations of their racial perspectives—relinquish their power to define Nancy through discourse. Neither Quentin nor Faulkner will assert their authority as white men to tell us exactly who Nancy is or what finally becomes of her.

Although Faulkner derived the title of "That Evening Sun" from his beloved "St. Louis Blues," in thematic terms it shares at least as much in common with Patton's "A Spoonful Blues," a recording with which the author almost certainly was unfamiliar. If neither the storyteller nor the singer-songwriter was aware of the accomplishments of the other, and if they stood on either side of the racial chasm that divided the South in the era of Jim Crow, the ways in which both artists interrogate the notion of determinism through their portrayals of cocaine addiction reveal surprisingly close kinship between them. Despite the hierarchies and divisions that separated them during their lifetimes, there is regular and meaningful contact between Faulkner and Patton whenever we think about their creative works as an intertextual dialogue about Mississippi, the South, and America in the modern age.

NOTES

This essay draws upon material in Tim A. Ryan, *Yoknapatawpha Blues: Faulkner's Fiction and Southern Roots Music* (Baton Rouge: Louisiana State University Press, 2015).

1. Elijah Wald, *Escaping the Delta: Robert Johnson and the Invention of the Blues* (New York: Amistad Press, 2005), 5.

2. Regarding the diversity of blues music, see ibid., 4.

3. William Faulkner, "Interview with Russell Howe," in *Lion in the Garden: Interviews with William Faulkner 1926–1962*, ed. James B. Meriwether and Michael Millgate (New York: Random House, 1968), 264.

4. For discussions of the music variously termed *classic, urban,* or *vaudeville* blues, see William Barlow, *"Looking Up at Down": The Emergence of Blues Culture* (Philadelphia: Temple University Press, 1989), 113–52; Francis Davis, *The History of the Blues* (New York: Hyperion, 1995), 80–86; Paul Oliver, *The Story of the Blues* (Boston: Northeastern University Press, 1997), 66–80; and Wald, *Escaping the Delta,* 21–26.

5. Ted Gioia, *Delta Blues: The Life and Times of the Mississippi Masters Who Revolutionized American Music* (New York: Norton, 2008), 42.

6. *Chicago Defender,* April 3, 1926, 7, col. 5.

7. My thanks to Ann J. Abadie for reminding me of the importance of the North Mississippi blues. Hemphill (b. 1876) made no commercial recordings during his lifetime, although Alan Lomax captured him on tape for the Library of Congress in 1942, and McDowell (b. 1904) did not make any records until 1959. See Alan Lomax, *The Land Where the Blues Began* (New York: Dell, 1995), 314–57.

8. Barlow, *"Looking Up at Down,"* 33.

9. See Gioia, *Delta Blues*, 74; Barlow, *"Looking Up at Down,"* 115; and Guido van Rijn, *Roosevelt's Blues: African American Blues and Gospel Songs on FDR* (Jackson: University Press of Mississippi, 1997), 26.

10. Langston Hughes, "Songs Called the Blues," *Phylon* 2, no. 2 (1941): 145.

11. President Obama performed a chorus of "Sweet Home Chicago" at a Black History Month celebration of the blues at the White House in February 2012, accompanied by such luminaries as Buddy Guy, B. B. King, and Mick Jagger. See Mary Bruce, "Obama Brings It Home: Sings 'Sweet Home Chicago' with B. B. King," *ABC News*, http://abcnews.go.com/blogs/politics/2012/02/obama-brings-it-home-sings-sweet-home-chicago-with-b-b-king (accessed September 26, 2012).

12. Joseph Blotner, *Faulkner: A Biography* (New York: Random House, 1974), 151.

13. See John Lomax, *Adventures of a Ballad Hunter* (New York: Macmillan, 1947), and A. Lomax, *The Land Where the Blues Began*.

14. For discussion of H. C. Speir, see Gioia, *Delta Blues*, 51–59; Stephen Calt and Gayle Dean Wardlow, *King of the Delta Blues: The Life and Music of Charlie Patton* (Newton, NJ: Rock Chapel Press, 1988), 11–17, 176–89, 213–19; and Gayle Dean Wardlow, *Chasin' That Devil Music: Searching for the Blues* (San Francisco: Miller Freeman, 1998), 125–49.

15. Quoted in Robert Palmer, *Deep Blues* (New York: Penguin, 1982), 55.

16. For discussions of Faulkner's encounters with blues music, see Thadious M. Davis, "From Jazz Syncopation to Blues Elegy: Faulkner's Development of Black Characterization," in *Faulkner and Race: Faulkner and Yoknapatawpha, 1986*, ed. Doreen Fowler and Ann J. Abadie (Jackson: University Press of Mississippi, 1987), 70–92; Adam Gussow, "Plaintive Reiterations and Meaningless Strains: Faulkner's Blues Understandings," in *Faulkner's Inheritance: Faulkner and Yoknapatawpha, 2005*, ed. Joseph R. Urgo and Ann J. Abadie (Jackson: University Press of Mississippi, 2007), 58–64; Blotner, *Faulkner: A Biography*, 155, 175; Judith L. Sensibar, *Faulkner and Love: The Women Who Shaped His Art* (New Haven, CT: Yale University Press, 2009), 22, 57–61; and Joel Williamson, *William Faulkner and Southern History* (New York: Oxford University Press, 1993), 173, 187, 201.

17. See Jane Isbell Haynes, "A Note on Faulkner and the Stagolee/Faust Legends," *Mississippi Quarterly* 64, nos. 3–4 (Summer–Fall 2011): 441.

18. Joseph Blotner, *William Faulkner's Library: A Catalogue* (Charlottesville: University Press of Virginia, 1964), 48.

19. Donald Clarke, *Wishing on the Moon: The Life and Times of Billie Holiday* (London: Penguin, 1995), 456–57. For discussion of the frequent mislabeling of Holiday as a blues singer, see ibid., 51, 66, 69, 137, 445.

20. David Krause, "Faulkner's Blues," *Studies in the Novel* 17, no. 1 (Spring 1985): 80.

21. William Faulkner, *Soldiers' Pay, Novels 1926–1929* (New York: Library of America, 2006), 156–59.

22. William Faulkner, *Flags in the Dust, Novels 1926–1929* (New York: Library of America, 2006), 638–39.

23. Erich Nunn, "'Dont Play No Blues': Race, Music, and Mourning in Faulkner's *Sanctuary*," *Faulkner Journal* 24, no. 2 (Spring 2009): 77–98.

24. Charles A. Peek, "'That Evening Sun(g)': Blues Inscribing Black Space in White Stories," *Southern Quarterly* 42, no. 3 (Spring 2004): 130–50; Carol B. Gartner, "Faulkner in Context: Seeing 'That Evening Sun' through the Blues," *Southern Quarterly* 34, no. 2 (Winter 1996): 50–58; Ken Bennett, "The Language of the Blues in Faulkner's 'That Evening Sun,'" *Mississippi Quarterly* 38, no. 3 (Summer 1985): 339–42.

25. H. R. Stoneback, "Faulkner's Blues: 'Pantaloon in Black,'" *Modern Fiction Studies* 21, no. 2 (Summer 1975): 241–45.

26. Haynes, "A Note on Faulkner," 349.

27. David Evans, quoted in Gussow, "Plaintive Reiterations," 54.

28. Ibid., 53.

29. Karl F. Zender, *The Crossing of the Ways: William Faulkner, the South, and the Modern World* (New Brunswick, NJ: Rutgers University Press, 1989), 22.

30. Blotner, *Faulkner: A Biography*, 1220, 1698, 1713; Zender, *Crossing of the Ways*, 20–23.

31. See William Faulkner, *Intruder in the Dust*, rev. ed. (1948; New York: Vintage International, 1991), 231–32; and William Faulkner, *Requiem for a Nun*, in *Novels 1942–1954*, ed. Joseph Blotner and Noel Polk (1951; New York: Library of America, 1994), 637.

32. The historical record provides only sketchy references to such enigmatic figures as Henry Sloan and Ben Maree. See Gioia, *Delta Blues*, 112; Calt and Wardlow, *King of the Delta Blues*, 56–57, 97, 104; and David Evans, *Big Road Blues: Tradition & Creativity in the Folk Blues* (New York: Da Capo, 1987), 175, 178.

33. Blotner, *Faulkner: A Biography*, 754, 1054; Haynes, "A Note on Faulkner," 441.

34. For discussions of "A Spoonful Blues" as a song about cocaine, see Calt and Wardlow, 95, 209; John Fahey, "Charley Reconsidered, Thirty-Five Years On," liner notes, *Screamin' and Hollerin' the Blues: The Worlds of Charley Patton*, Revenant No. 212, 2001, compact disc; and Dick Spottswood, "Going Away to a World Unknown: Song Notes and Transcriptions," in *Screamin' and Hollerin'*, 57.

35. Charley Patton, "A Spoonful Blues," in *Screamin' and Hollerin'*.

36. Calt and Wardlow, *King of the Delta Blues*, 95.

37. Quoted in Jeff Todd Titon, *Early Downhome Blues: A Musical and Cultural Analysis* (Urbana: University of Illinois Press, 1977), 52. For other discussions of the difficulty of understanding Patton's lyrics, see Calt and Wardlow, *King of the Delta Blues*, 52; and F. Davis, *History of the Blues*, 3.

38. My transcription of the lyrics takes the recording as a copy-text but is also indebted to published transcriptions, including Calt and Wardlow, *King of the Delta Blues*, 324, and Spottswood, "Going Away," 57. Spoken interjections are rendered in italics throughout.

39. Papa Charlie Jackson, "All I Want Is a Spoonful," *Complete Recorded Works in Chronological Order*, vol. 1, *1924 to February 1926*, Document DOCD 5087, 1994.

40. Fahey, "Charley Reconsidered," 48.

41. These include Luke Jordan's "Cocaine Blues" (1927) and the Memphis Jug Band's "Cocaine Habit Blues" (1930). See Paul Oliver, *Blues Fell This Morning: Meaning in the Blues* (Cambridge: Cambridge University Press, 1990), 162–63.

42. Fahey, "Charley Reconsidered," 53.

43. See, for example, Jonathan Daigle, "Paul Laurence Dunbar and the Marshal Circle: Racial Representation from Blackface to Black Naturalism," *African American Review* 43, no. 4 (Winter 2009): 633–54; and Michel Fabre, *The World of Richard Wright* (Jackson: University Press of Mississippi, 1985), 56–76.

44. Although "Stovall" is a relatively common name in Mississippi, it is striking that this character in "That Evening Sun" bears the same name as a Coahoma County planter who hired the black Chatmon family musicians—associates of Patton—to serve as his "personal minstrels" (Calt and Wardlow, *King of the Delta Blues*, 144). Stovall's plantation would later become famous as the location of Muddy Waters's first recordings for the Library of Congress in the early 1940s.

45. William Faulkner, "That Evening Sun," in *Collected Stories of William Faulkner* (New York: Random House, 1950), 291.

46. Philip Momberger, "Faulkner's 'The Village' and 'That Evening Sun': The Tale in Context," *Southern Literary Journal* 11, no. 1 (Fall 1978): 30. See also Doreen Fowler, "Tracing Racial Assumptions: Teaching 'That Evening Sun,'" in *Teaching Faulkner:*

Approaches and Methods, ed. Stephen Hahn and Robert W. Hamblin (Westport, CT: Greenwood, 2001), 50. For a seminal analysis of Faulkner's mobilization of "Negro" as an abstract concept, see Thadious M. Davis, *Faulkner's "Negro": Art and the Southern Context* (Baton Rouge: Louisiana State University Press, 1983).

47. Faulkner, "That Evening Sun," 291; emphasis added.

48. For debates about Nancy's use of narcotics, see Jim Lee, "The Problem of Nancy in Faulkner's 'That Evening Sun,'" *South Central Bulletin* 21, no. 4 (Winter 1961): 49; and Laurence Perrine, "'That Evening Sun': A Skein of Uncertainties," *Studies in Short Fiction* 22, no. 3 (Summer 1985): 299.

49. Laurel Bollinger, "Narrating Racial Identity and Transgression in Faulkner's 'That Evening Sun,'" *College Literature* 39, no. 2 (Spring 2012): 59; Paula Sunderman, "Speech Act Theory and Faulkner's 'That Evening Sun,'" *Language and Style* 14, no. 4 (Fall 1981): 309.

50. William Faulkner, *Go Down, Moses*, rev. ed. (1942; New York: Vintage International, 1990), 149.

51. Sunderman, "Speech Act Theory," 309. As Gartner notes, one of the lines in Handy's "St. Louis Blues" derives from a traditional blues formula, "Ef de whiskey don't get you den de cocaine must." Ibid., 56.

52. Francis Ford Coppola, dir., *The Godfather* (Paramount, 1972).

53. Greil Marcus, *Mystery Train: Images of America in Rock 'n' Roll Music* (New York: E. P. Dutton, 1982), 96.

54. Faulkner, "That Evening Sun," 297, 298.

55. William Faulkner, *Light in August*, rev. ed. (1932; New York: Vintage International, 1990), 350.

56. For a survey of this racial trope's long and pervasive history, see Jean Michel Massing, "From Greek Proverb to Soap Advert: Washing the Ethiopian," *Journal of the Warburg and Courtauld Institutes* 58 (1995): 180–201.

57. My thanks to Seth Berner and Jay Watson for their astute comments and questions regarding my reading of this passage and for inspiring me to develop my interpretation further.

58. Faulkner, "That Evening Sun," 291.

59. Ibid., 293. See also ibid., 297, 309.

60. For a different reading of this element of the story, see Bollinger, "Narrating Racial Identity," 67. For critical debates about Nancy's fate, see John Gerlach, *Toward the End: Closure and Structure in the American Short Story* (Tuscaloosa: University of Alabama Press, 1985), 130–43; and Perrine, "'That Evening Sun,'" 295–307.

61. T. Davis, *Faulkner's "Negro,"* 246.

Narrative Leaps to Universal Appeal in McKay's *Banjo* and Faulkner's *A Fable*

DOTTY DYE

According to Walter Benjamin, there are two kinds of storytellers: the one "who has come from afar" and the one "who has stayed at home," the "trading seaman" and the "tiller of the soil."[1] In "The Storyteller," Benjamin tells us that we cannot begin to understand the import of storytelling if we do not consider the interaction of these two archaic storytelling types. Benjamin claims that the interconnection of the two "tribes" of storytellers was particularly effective in the Middle Ages as a result of trade structures that brought the "resident master craftsman and the traveling journeymen" together to work in the same rooms: "If peasants and seamen were past masters of storytelling, the artisan class was its university. In it was combined the lore of faraway places, such as a much-traveled man brings home, with the lore of the past, as it best reveals itself to natives of a place."[2] Although Benjamin's "reflections" principally lay out a genealogy of the material events that brought about the development and downfall of storytelling as a collective experience, most notably in the form of the novel, his analysis and imagery can also help us understand what a consideration of Claude McKay reveals about William Faulkner and vice versa.

Faulkner and McKay did not work together in the same workshops, so to speak, but an intertextual reading of the products of their labors suggests two masters of the craft of storytelling, artisans who traded on the currency of travel and native soil in order to explore the experience of life for the individual in the face of modernity. What separates the two writers may seem to create too great a distance to overcome; at first pass, one might hastily classify Faulkner's body of work as regional—he is the storyteller "who has stayed at home"—while the Jamaican-born McKay's fiction is generally marked by his self-described international-ism—he is quite literally the man "who has come from afar" to American letters.[3] However, his summary description does not reflect the way that, for Faulkner, travel, the foreign, and France function as imaginary layers in the shaping of Yoknapatawpha, placing local characters and ideas into foreign spaces and revealing fresh perspectives on southern problems. Nor does it convey the way McKay's vagabond fiction reaches back to his native Jamaica in order to formulate the moving signifier of home that floats among his diverse characters, pulling memories of warm waters and jungles into narratives that "wander and wonder" as they grapple with questions of race.[4]

I wish to posit these two writers as complementary opposites. Both play distinctively on the dialectic between the particular and the universal, where the particular expresses itself variously as the local, the native, the primitive, the national, or quite abstractly as "home," and where the universal is understood in different contexts as the international, the diasporic, the transnational or *ailleurs* (elsewhere). Both the Mississippi boy with his "postage stamp of native soil" and the self-proclaimed vagabond possess an international consciousness that operates in an oppositional manner against their "native" roots.[5] The textual and aesthetic interaction between the particular and the universal in each writer's work informs, in intersecting ways, their approaches to race, gender, class, and nationalism. In this essay, I will begin the work of exploring this vast range of intersections by focusing on the mapping of race and home that operates within them.

Claude McKay was born in Jamaica, and after the publication of his first book of poetry, he moved to America in 1912 at the age of twenty-two to attend university. Like Faulkner, however, McKay seemed to have little patience for formal higher education. He wrote in his autobiographical sketch *A Long Way from Home*, "My leisure was divided between the experiment of daily living and the experiment of essays in writing. If I would not graduate as a bachelor of arts or science, I would graduate as a poet."[6] To that end, he sought a way to make a living that would not hinder him from pursuing his writing. He spent several years as a railroad porter, then as a contributor to radical socialist publications in New York and London. In 1922 he embarked on a "magic pilgrimage" to Russia, receiving an enthusiastic welcome from the Soviet bureaucracy and the Russian people and addressing the Third Communist International in Moscow as an independent poet. McKay was keen on emphasizing his independent artistic point of view, claiming to be "merely a poet" and not an official delegate, and declaring that he "could never be a disciplined member of any Communist party, for [he] was born to be a poet."[7] His hope that Communism might be an effective political instrument for addressing problems of discrimination around the world was ultimately destroyed during his Russian trip, and rather than return to the United States, he moved to France and began an eleven-year, relatively nomadic existence, moving between Europe and North Africa. He eventually moved back to the United States but never returned to Jamaica.

Throughout his life, McKay seemed always to be the one coming from afar, but as his travels deepened his transnational consciousness, his aesthetics and politics also developed. In terms of aesthetics, the importance of "home" became more explicit, culminating in his later fiction, which focused primarily on that native land to which he had never returned. In terms of politics, he transitioned from socialism and Soviet-style Communism to black nationalism, a move that intertwined his notion of home and the native with an artistic primitivism. As McKay's crosscultural experiences developed and his sense of exile increased, he began to promote strategic essentialisms that would be foundational to black nationalist and black power movements. As Wayne Cooper demonstrates, he was one of the most influential early promoters of these ideas and had a particularly profound impact on the development of Négritude.[8] What I find particularly interesting and apropos to this essay is the way that McKay works to articulate a division between his political and literary selves while inscribing his work with the deep interconnectedness of those two aspects of human life. This is a personal political position (as opposed to the public political persona) that I find echoed in Faulkner's aesthetic approach to social and political realities.

Both Faulkner and McKay perform a mapping of the native and the foreign, creating imaginative layerings in their texts that connect their aesthetics of place and their interrogation of identity to their social contexts. For Faulkner, the interrogation of identity begins with the local and the oppressive weight of history on the individual. Joe Christmas, for example, struggles to locate his racial identity in the mire of his personal history and the history of the South, ultimately resulting in tragedy, and Quentin Compson resists a distinctively southern communal memory by insisting on a transnational memory, one that is manifest in the act of storytelling in which he and Shreve engage while constructing the narrative of Henry Sutpen and Charles Bon in *Absalom, Absalom!* The memory, constructed rather than lived, and often revealing more about its narrators than the subjects of their narrative, is transnational because the Canadian Shreve helps drive it. In spite of Quentin's often tacit participation in this construction of memory, however, he fails to escape the pull of his origins. Faulkner's reach toward the elsewhere provides a space in which to engage with issues endemic to the South—the history of slavery, segregation, miscegenation, and gendered violence—at a distance that allows his thoughts on those issues room to breathe.

In *Faulkner, Mississippi*, Édouard Glissant perhaps most beauti-
fully articulates the palimpsest of place that occurs in Faulkner's fiction.
Glissant highlights the "interconnected roots and plantings" that come
from the shifting and negotiating that occur as frontiers are challenged
and their contradictions destroyed and reformulated with different
borders and renewed exclusions.[9] "Faulkner's world is a frontier," Glissant writes, "an anonymous, various, scattered frontier."[10] For Faulkner,
place emanates from the particular but expands across a landscape of
meaning that "reaches far into the distance, not like an expanse of territory, but like a contagion, an infection of the imaginary."[11] Even in the
most Yoknapatawphan of novels, for example, France is pulled into the
territory through the experiences and identities of the characters: Darl
Bundren's World War I service (as well as Shreve McCannon's), the narrative jumps in *Flags in the Dust*, Caddy in the South of France in the
Compson appendix, and Temple in the Jardin du Luxembourg. But the
infection travels in both directions, even into stories that are set entirely
in France. The Great War tales in the "Waste Land" section of *Collected
Stories*, for example, include links back to Yoknapatawpha. There is a
correspondence, a calling and recalling that links the American South
with France in the interrogation of history, war, and the political and
social institutions of modernity. This correspondence opens up imaginative spaces in the foreign that Faulkner uses to interrogate the local.

In the latter part of his career, Faulkner further exploited the imaginary connection between the South and France in *A Fable*, his 1954
novel set somewhere on the French front in May 1918. On the surface, *A Fable* is the story of a mutiny and an attempted fraternization
between French and German soldiers, brutally quelled with a barrage of
fire from both sides and the execution of the corporal who is identified
as the leader of the mutiny. This central story line is complicated by a
vast range of characters, subplots, and storytellers that expand the reach
of the primary action, which is punctuated with allusions to the life of
Christ and chronologically organized around the Passion Week story.
Faulkner tells us that the source for *A Fable* was the idea to synthesize
the legend of the Unknown Soldier and the story of the Passion into "a
fable, an indictment of war perhaps."[12] As Glissant so eloquently puts it,
"When the county spreads out toward distant shores, its damnation goes
with it. . . . In *A Fable*, the ship of shadows is built on the run in the glow
of bombs and in the terror of the trenches of the First World War. The
curse of the European war is complete, continuous, renewed, and per-
fected in Jeffersonian fatality. The faraway echoes the county."[13] In other
words, the problems, concerns, and experiences of the locals orbiting
around Jefferson are given universal expression on the battlefields of the

Great War; the history of the Bundren family, linked to France through Darl's service, finds unexpected resonances in the poverty surrounding the French front, and issues of race exposed in Quentin's tellings and retellings of Sutpen's story echo against *A Fable*'s French and American narrative layers. In *A Fable,* the strategic placement of black characters in the narrative—particularly the American soldier Philip Manigault Beauchamp, a private from Mississippi, no doubt related to the unforgettable Lucas Beauchamp—provides a direct link to Yoknapatawpha and, as Theresa M. Towner has argued, racializes the narrative even when the discussion of race is not overt.[14]

In McKay's 1929 novel, *Banjo,* a kind of sequel to *Home to Harlem,* we follow the Haitian writer-intellectual Ray across the Atlantic to 1920s Marseilles, where McKay offers a portrait of a band of roving vagabonds in the Vieux Port, a popular red-light district. Many of the characters will eventually be given the official status of "Nationality Doubtful," thereby limiting their rights and access to the modes of transportation so critical in their vagabond lifestyle. In his article, "Traveling Harlem's Europe," Michael Chaney uses the history of slave narratives to contextualize modernist black vagabondage narratives, demonstrating the way that the motif turns the idea of the Grand Tour on its head, inverting signs, using Harlem, for example, "as a standard of comparison, a point of reference from which to survey Europe."[15] Blacks in Europe, at least American ones, reverse the poles of colonialism within their travel narratives, solidifying national identity by mapping Harlem onto Paris and other metropoles while also reinforcing a transnational identity. The search for a homeland is still present, however, in the transnational circulations of racial discourse. As Chaney points out, "Home is a symbolic construct as much as a geographical, historically 'locatable' landscape," and McKay's texts feature moving signifiers of home that circulate in contexts where terms of origins are read across categories of race and class (read primarily as economic resources) and where being denied claims to national citizenship is a real threat.[16] In American travel literature, the idea of home is often produced as a stable signifier that provides an anchor in self-discovery. For the vagabond, however, the terms of home are absent or blurred, resulting in the lack of a unified narrative to counteract the disorientation and fragmentation of perpetual movement.

The vagabond motifs in *Banjo* extend into the formal structure of the novel; the subtitle, "A Story without a Plot," points to a narrative progression that collapses into a polyphonic representation of experience "emphasizing tropes of movement, national identity, narrative fracture, and collaborative or embedded orality. Posing questions of racial identity alongside questions of nation and class, the vagabondage plot stages an encounter of identities decontextualized from native racializing frameworks."[17] The narrative instabilities mirror the wanderings of the vagabond characters, demonstrating "circularity and deploy[ing] structural disorientation and genre transformations to dislocate the reader and to charge those interstitial and liminal moments of fracture with 'potentializing energy.'"[18] The novel strings together a series of encounters, conversations, and narrative descriptions that does not provide a clear story line but that rather follows the main characters in their daily peregrinations, slowly expanding the reader's perspective as new experiences are added to the collection. We first encounter the title character, Banjo, from a slight distance, observing him observing his surroundings and the other characters he will soon encounter; then the narration keys to his thoughts, providing his background and how he came to the port, panning quickly back to note his sartorial style, and then abruptly switching to a dialogue that records his introduction to "the beach boys." The narrative then follows a rapid mapping of the boys' movements from street to street, quickly delimiting their sphere of circulation. The entire novel follows a similar pattern of unpurposeful movement and circumambulation that results in a slowly expanding sense of transnational black experience.

It is the foreign that operates as the site of identity for McKay's characters confronted with modernity—fragmented, restless, fluid, without boundary, and constantly in flux—and so McKay reaches to the imaginary of the native, mapping it onto the French port, providing the historical connections and contexts that give hope to the black man facing modernity. The novel thus lays the foundation for a Pan-African nationalism that capitalizes on the dialectic between the particular and the universal. The narrator, through the perspective of Ray, insists on the magic and "foamy fascination" of Marseilles, on the beauty of its "gorgeous bowl of blue water unrestingly agitated by the great commerce of all the continents."[19] But if the text insists on Ray's preference for this European city, the linguistic reaching toward images of home and the mapping of tropical places onto this French port betray the imaginative gymnastics that are required to arrive at such a fascination: "He loved the docks," the narrator claims, but this love is explained by alluding to "picturesque proletarians from far waters whose names were warm with romance" and to the "barrels, bags, boxes, bearing from land to land the primitive garner of man's hands. Sweat-dripping bodies of black men naked under the equatorial sun, threading a caravan way through the time-old jungles, carrying loads steadied and unsupported on kink-thick heads. . . . Barrels . . . bags . . . boxes. . . . Full of the wonderful things of life. . . . There was a barbarous international romance in the ways of

Marseilles that was vividly significant of the great modern movement of life."[20] The modern is expressed in terms of a primitive native that, in its evocation of the Caribbean, echoes of home for McKay and thus betrays a double consciousness grounded in a race-based experience of modernity, one that is implicit in the narration and that becomes explicit within the dialogue.

The plotless vagabondage of the *Banjo* narrative contrasts with *A Fable's* tightly constructed allegorical structure. The narration in *A Fable* layers episodes that illustrate, from various vantage points, the same story: that of the struggle between institutions and individuals. This episodic construction provides intersecting story lines with characters who become symbolic analogues and opposites of one another. The horse in the American tall-tale story is a more successful version of the corporal and perhaps the "true hero of the novel" because it, like Caddy Compson, is kept alive in the narratives of those dedicated to it. In another parallel, the runner can be seen as a more active and enduring version of the corporal (and of the individual). Rather than merely resisting the war as the corporal has done in refusing to attack, the runner aims to bring the two sides together to fraternize in no-man's-land. The runner represents a dark idealism that is willing to sacrifice others to a higher cause (though, admittedly, he also is willing to sacrifice himself). In his pursuit of the corporal and his "disciples" within the main plot, the runner mirrors the deputy in the American story who pursues the horse and its servants in the "pastoral analogue" of the war context.[21] The parallel pursuits of the deputy, motivated by a desire for truth, and the runner, motivated by a delirious pride and insistence on the primacy of the individual, complicate a dichotomized view of the institution and the individual in which the former is evil and the latter good.

The novel's oppositional spaces, represented in the French wartime setting and the American home-front setting of the racehorse tale, provide a dehistoricized symbolic depiction of place. In the logic of the text it is the characters, and not the external narrator, who emphasize this symbolic function of the setting.[22] "France," the corporal's sister, Madga, claims, is

a word a name a designation significant yet foundationless like the ones for grace or Tuesday or quarantine, esoteric and infrequent. . . . We . . . were . . . bound for . . . France as others might be for some distant and irrevocable state or condition like a nunnery or the top of Mount Everest . . . some peculiar and individual esoteric place to which no one really wants to go save in idle speculation yet which reflects a certain communal glory on the place which was host to the departure and witnessed the preparations.[23]

The specific place of departure to which the sister is referring is given little importance but becomes a symbol of origins, the place from which one comes, and though for the sister this place is the Balkans, her discussion pulls in echoes of the myriad places of departure associated with the many characters in the novel: the United States, Britain, France, Africa, the West Indies, Germany, the Middle East, China. These sites also provide a diverse cast of characters who lay the foundation for the undercurrent of ideas about race that, though never expressly discussed, haunt the text in its discussions of origins and nation.

While this unstated preoccupation with race connects A Fable to Faulkner's Yoknapatawpha fiction, it also connects A Fable to McKay's work in corresponding ways. The text repeatedly describes the Senegalese soldiers who guard the mutinous regiment, silent and ever present: "the Senegalese guarding them, lounging haughtily overhead," "the red eyes of the Senegalese sentries' cigarettes," "the gaudy uniforms and arms and jangling accoutrements and even the ebon faces too of the Senegalese regiment seemed to gleam."[24] This insistence on their mute presence recalls the more vocal presence of Senegalese and other blacks in McKay's Banjo, where the Senegalese (a classification, the text tells us, that is "the geographically inaccurate term generally used to designate all the Negroes from the different parts of French West Africa") participate in the storytelling and discussions that highlight the way that race and origins influence belonging.[25] Banjo vocalizes the intersections of race and nationality by assembling a diverse cast of characters from the United States, Britain, the West Indies, West Africa, North Africa, China, the Middle East, and all over Europe in bistros, cafés, and bars to argue over claims to represent the transnational experience of race. Given the French setting in both novels and the less than ten-year difference in historical setting, the characters in both narratives are confronting similar contextual concerns about nationality and race, and in this respect the French settings of each novel can be read as opposite sides of the same coin. A Fable deals with race symbolically, using language and color to stand in for nation and empire, as in the description of a second front enclosing the mutinous one:

> Another front, manned by all the troops in the three forces who cant speak the language belonging to the coat they came up from under the equator and half around the world to die in, in the cold and wet—Senegalese and Moroccans and Kurds and Chinese and Malays and Indians—Polynesian Melanesian Mongol and Negro who couldn't understand the password nor read the pass either: only to recognize perhaps by memorised rote that one cryptic hieroglyph. . . . Before, the faces behind the machine guns and the rifles at least

thought Caucasian thoughts even if they didn't speak English or French or American; now they dont even think Caucasian thoughts. They're alien.[26]

Here the impersonal institutional layers are highlighted in the image of an impersonal empire that can provide brute and unquestioning force to keep the masses in line, or to exterminate them. *Banjo*, on the other hand, deals with personal experiences of race in order to paint a contradictory picture of those experiences within the imperial institutions brought to the forefront in Faulkner's text. In this way, McKay's work seems to beckon to Faulkner's Yoknapatawpha in its preoccupation with the personal experience of living with racial barriers while connecting to his fictional French settings through the federated collections of characters with diverse national backgrounds who highlight the arbitrary and oppressive weight that national and racial classifications can carry. Indeed, the race consciousness present in both texts is connected to transnational consciousness. For Faulkner, the foreign, as imaginary extension of Yoknapatawpha in the ways I discussed above, provides the artistic space in which he feels most at liberty to play with questions of race because it removes the claims to southern distinctiveness that plague those efforts in his Yoknapatawpha fiction.

If *A Fable* provides episodic retellings of the individual's struggle against collectives, *Banjo* strings together a series of stories that the multilingual, multinational band of characters recounts, providing intersecting perspectives on race relations throughout Europe, Africa, and the Americas. As in *A Fable*, there is a great deal of dialogue, but rather than making long speeches that grapple with existential and political questions in seemingly universal ways, McKay's characters argue, debate, and tell stories about their lives. Individual experiences of home are layered onto one another in order to reveal a complex, contradictory, and nuanced international experience of blackness. The writer-intellectual Ray explains, "You see, Goosey, a good story, in spite of those who tell it and those who hear it, is like good ore that you might find in any soil in Europe, Asia, Africa or America. . . . I am writing for people who can stand a real story no matter where it comes from."[27] The narrator uses fragments of individual experiences to come to general conclusions about the "color problem." The stories and languages map onto one another so that experiences begin to connect in surprising ways. When a barkeeper in the African Bar reads items from the journal *La Race Negre* listing complaints against the British and French colonial governments, Ray maps the experiences onto the American South: "You know, when he was reading that paper it was just as if I was hearing about Texas and Georgia in French."[28] In this moment, Ray hears a translation of racist oppression that layers various "native" experiences into a universal perspective that is the basis for black nationalism.

Ultimately, the story that the plotless novel tells intersects with Faulkner's concern in *A Fable* about the machinations of modernity and their impact on the individual. There are moments toward the end of *Banjo* when the narrator sounds remote in a way that echoes *A Fable*:

> They did not know that the Radical government had fallen, that a National-Union government had come into power, and that the franc had been arrested in its spectacular fall and was being stabilized. They knew little about governments, and cared less. But they knew that suddenly francs were getting scarce in their world, meals were dearer in the eating-sheds and in the bistros, and more sous were necessary to obtain the desirable red wine and white, so indispensable to their existence.[29]

McKay's focus on particular stories strung together seemingly without plot ultimately serves his critique of nationalist tendencies that create adverse economic conditions while also restricting movement for those most impacted by those economic conditions, marginalizing and then cementing the marginalized into cycles of violence, crime, and incarceration. In a more universalist way, *A Fable* makes the same gesture, showing how the individual experience connects to collective action and institutional oppression. In *Banjo*, the narrative perspective slowly widens to demonstrate the way institutional power affects the lives of individuals through examples of direct contact between the beach boys and authorities who have the power to influence their lives directly (such as the police, the consulates, hospital administrators, and employers). By contrast, the machinations of institutions are foregrounded throughout *A Fable*, and the narrative perspective narrows only momentarily (though frequently) in allusions that reach back to the local, and specifically to Faulkner's Yoknapatawpha fictions, suggesting that the reader revisit those fictions with the broader perspective of *A Fable* in mind.

While the actual for McKay was an international restlessness upon which he imposed an imaginary "home," Faulkner's work was grounded in the native and expanded into an international imaginary. In 1982, the Faulkner and Yoknapatawpha Conference explored international perspectives on and of Faulkner. In a talk titled "From the World to Jefferson," Joseph Blotner pondered what accounts for Faulkner's appeal to other nations: "Although he was a writer firmly based in the particulars of his own region . . . he was nonetheless an artist concerned with the human condition."[30] Blotner further explains how this concern for the human condition manifests itself in international contexts in Faulkner's work. Locating Faulkner as a transnationalist in this way provides readers and scholars who focus on the regional and local in Faulkner's fiction with an opportunity to approach that specificity in a more expansive context that provides new links with writers, like McKay, whose work seems to call and respond to Faulkner's. If, as I have argued, Faulkner's work is spurred by an imaginary of the elsewhere mapped onto home, and McKay's work is generated by an imaginary of home that is mapped onto the foreign, then to what extent is the oppositional nature of this dialectic in their work a result of racial experience? It would be productive to consider the ways in which the dialectic between home and the foreign found in the texts of Faulkner and McKay might find expression among other modernist expatriates, Harlem Renaissance figures, and diasporic writers. Such investigations might lead to a reevaluation of the way transnationalism functions as a link between modernist and postcolonial literatures.

NOTES

1. Walter Benjamin, *Illuminations*, ed. Hannah Arendt, trans. Harry Zohn (New York: Harcourt, Brace & World, 1968), 85.

2. Ibid.

3. Many scholars have demonstrated that Faulkner's work extends beyond region both in content and in aesthetic function. Most notably, his French critics, from Sartre to François Pitavy and Michel Gresset, along with Édouard Glissant, who brought a decidedly postcolonial perspective to Faulkner's work, have expanded its critical reception.

4. Claude McKay, *A Long Way from Home* (New York: Arno Press, 1969), 9. For more on McKay's Caribbean identity as a factor in his fiction, see Leah Rosenberg's "Caribbean Models for Modernism in the Work of Claude McKay and Jean Rhys," *Modernism/Modernity* 11, no. 2 (2004): 219–38; Kotti Sree Ramesh and K. Nirupa Rani, *Claude McKay: The Literary Identity from Jamaica to Harlem and Beyond* (Jefferson, NC: McFarland, 2006); and Tyrone Tillery, *Claude McKay: A Black Poet's Struggle for Identity* (Amherst: University of Massachusetts Press, 1992).

5. William Faulkner, interview by Jean Stein (1956), in *Lion in the Garden: Interviews with William Faulkner, 1926–1962*, ed. James B. Meriwether and Michael Millgate (New York: Random House, 1968), 255.

6. McKay, *A Long Way*, 10.

7. Ibid., 136.

8. Wayne F. Cooper, *Claude McKay: Rebel Sojourner in the Harlem Renaissance* (Baton Rouge: Louisiana State University Press, 1987), 327.

9. Édouard Glissant, *Faulkner, Mississippi*, trans. Barbara Lewis and Thomas C. Spear (Chicago: University of Chicago Press, 2000), 227.

10. Ibid., 227, 229.

11. Ibid., 230.

12. William Faulkner, *Selected Letters of William Faulkner*, ed. Joseph Blotner (New York: Random House, 1977), 178.

13. Glissant, *Faulkner, Mississippi*, 235.

14. See Theresa M. Towner, *Faulkner on the Color Line* (Jackson: University Press of Mississippi, 2000); and Richard Godden, *William Faulkner: An Economy of Complex Words* (Princeton, NJ: Princeton University Press, 2007). Towner provides a convincing portrayal of the racial undercurrent in Faulkner's later fiction, arguing that "Faulkner took racial culpability as a given and became increasingly interested in scripting responses to it" (32). Godden also provides a provocative reading of *A Fable* that addresses issues of race through the twice-removed figure of the black Jew (157–78). His analysis is particularly interesting in light of my argument because of the causal link he establishes between economic structures and Faulkner's text.

15. Michael A. Chaney, "Traveling Harlem's Europe: Vagabondage from Slave Narratives to Gwendolyn Bennett's 'Wedding Day' and Claude McKay's *Banjo*," *Journal of Narrative Theory* 32, no. 1 (2002): 66.

16. Ibid., 60.

17. Ibid., 54.

18. Ibid., 55.

19. Claude McKay, *Banjo* (London: X Press, 2000), 55.

20. Ibid., 56–57.

21. François Pitavy, "The Two Orders in *A Fable*: A Reappraisal of Faulkner's 'Elephant,'" *Mississippi Quarterly* 62, no. 3–4 (July 2009): 416. Pitavy provides a helpful reading of the narrative layers in *A Fable* that demonstrates the way the novel functions as a decentered center of the Faulkner oeuvre.

22. Faulkner's use of place names also contributes to this symbolic depiction. As Pitavy notes, Faulkner only uses fictive names for the two central settings, Chaulnesmont and Vienne-la Pucelle. All other places, towns, and battles, such as Passchendaele, Chemin des Dames, and Verdun are real place-names that have passed into collective memory and stand as symbolic allusions to the horror of all wars.

23. William Faulkner, *A Fable*, rev. ed. (1954; New York: Vintage International, 2011), 322.

24. Ibid., 143, 405, 421.

25. McKay, *Banjo*, 38.

26. Faulkner, *A Fable*, 349.

27. McKay, *Banjo*, 98.

28. Ibid., 65.

29. Ibid., 192.

30. Joseph Blotner, "From the World to Jefferson," in *Faulkner, International Perspectives: Faulkner and Yoknapatawpha, 1982*, ed. Doreen Fowler and Ann J. Abadie (Jackson: University Press of Mississippi, 1984), 304.

Reconstructions:
Faulkner and Du Bois on the Civil War

T. Austin Graham

At the same time that he was writing *Absalom, Absalom!* and summoning the "garrulous outraged baffled ghosts" of the southern past, Faulkner was pursuing a more modest project, drawing on episodes from his family history and turning them into a series of short stories about a boy caught up in the Civil War.[1] They were the work of the Faulkner who could command thousand-dollar checks from popular magazines like the *Saturday Evening Post*, not the one who handed down respected but seldom-read novels of uncompromising modernism. The stories were considerably more welcoming than much of his previous output, and when they were collected in 1938 and published as a novel called *The Unvanquished*, Faulkner had produced the most accessible book of his career thus far.

The Unvanquished recounts the loosely connected adventures of Bayard Sartoris, an adolescent Mississippian who is too young to join the army. Bayard is on the home front, but his life is still full of crowd-pleasing incident and color: buried treasure, close shaves with Union troops, vigilante justice, a wartime mule racket run by his devious grandmother, and so on. The novel conforms obediently to various genre conventions, at once a memoir (narrated by an older, rather poetic Bayard), a bildungsroman (bringing its protagonist through a series of maturing experiences), and a historical novel (following the South's path from military resistance to Reconstruction). It is also one of Faulkner's most chronologically linear works, free of the disorienting flashbacks and extravagant counterfactuals that distinguish his earlier fiction. And within the larger context of Faulkner's career, it is the most focused and thorough study of the Civil War that he ever undertook.

Yet *The Unvanquished* is among the least loved and most neglected novels in the Faulknerian canon. Some of its readers have dismissed it as a cheap appeal to popular taste, echoing Faulkner's own descriptions of it as "a pulp series" and "trash" that he wrote to pay the bills.[2] Others have seen it as Faulkner's respite from the agony of writing more serious fiction, "a kind of safety-valve" for the regional nostalgia that he "simply could not and would not entertain" elsewhere.[3] Still others find it crudely reactionary and even "neo-Confederate" in its politics: after the heresies of his previous novels, the theory goes, Faulkner must have felt obliged to take an "extended bow toward southern pieties."[4] The novel has its admirers, though, and some have even hailed it as one of Faulkner's most progressive works, with Craig A. Warren praising it as nothing less than a groundbreaking effort "to restore race and race relations to the story of the Civil War."[5]

None of these interpretations is entirely satisfying, yet all are quite compelling, and one might even say that *The Unvanquished* actively invites contentious reading. Indeed, the disagreements elicited by it point to some of its greatest achievements: it is a novel that considers various historical approaches to the Civil War rather than chooses one, that suggests the overwhelming importance of race to the conflict even as it tries to overlook it, and that is successful insofar as it leads readers to widely differing conclusions about the conflict's ultimate meaning. Faulkner's slippery novel becomes yet more interesting when considered alongside other histories of the Civil War that appeared around the same time, for he wrote it during a moment of unprecedented scholarly disagreement about the war's stakes. There was a striking lack of consensus about the war in the 1930s, for a skeptical generation of "revisionist" historians was offering new, counterintuitive, frequently irreconcilable explanations for its causes and leaving many of the old ones behind, slavery in particular.[6] Appearing in the middle of this period and anticipating much of its debate, *The Unvanquished* did two remarkable things. First, it demonstrated Faulkner's range and ambition as a historian: it presented many sides of the increasingly complex Civil War debate rather than choosing one; it surveyed a historical field rather than staking out a part of it; and it staged a historical conversation rather than advancing a historical argument. Second, it aligned Faulkner with prescient yet marginalized historians like W. E. B. Du Bois, who continued to hold the then-unfashionable position that the Civil War had been a fight over slavery but who would have to wait many years for vindication by the larger academic community.

The Unvanquished is a difficult historical novel precisely because it appears not to be. At first glance, its reassuring simplicity seems to promise a straightforward account of the war, the people who experienced it, and their motives for fighting—history as it really was, not as it is imagined to be. Whereas *Absalom, Absalom!* announces its historical unreliability and deconstructs itself on nearly every page, *The Unvanquished* is the steady, poised testimony of a single narrator. And yet the novel is suffused with a dreamlike ambiguity, even as it offers a direct view upon the past. Its opening sentences set a mood of both historical particularity and historical elusiveness, with Bayard and his best friend introduced as they play war games in either 1862 or 1863[7]:

> Behind the smokehouse that summer, Ringo and I had a living map. Although Vicksburg was just a handful of chips from the woodpile and the River a trench scraped into the packed earth with the point of a hoe, it (river, city, and terrain) lived, possessing even in miniature that ponderable though passive recalcitrance of topography which outweighs artillery, against which the most brilliant of victories and the most tragic of defeats are but the loud noises of a moment.[8]

The scene functions as a kind of reverse Gettysburg Address, suggesting that the world will little note, nor long remember, what either boys or soldiers do upon it in the nineteenth century. Bayard and Ringo are representing the siege of Vicksburg in as much detail as they can, and yet the event has literally been minimized by their playacting and then subsumed by the land's "ponderable" totality. The unique character of a military engagement seems to blur and vanish upon examination: the informed reader knows that the Confederacy suffered a mortal wound at Vicksburg, but such a thing seems not to matter in the longer, geological conception of history being invoked here. From the very first page, then, Faulkner's war novel suggests that no war is especially significant, and that all wars are essentially interchangeable. Or as Bayard will put it later in the novel, they are "the same exploding powder when there was powder, the same thrust and parry of iron when there was not—one tale, one telling, the same as the next or the one before" (383).

But Faulkner does not allow his readers to linger in abstraction, for the boys' game is soon interrupted, and interrupted in such a way as to underscore the actual stakes of this singular war. One of the Sartoris family's slaves, a man named Loosh, appears seemingly out of nowhere and looms over the children, watching their game while his wife, Philadelphy, watches him.

> He stood there laughing, not loud, looking at the chips.
> "Come on here, Loosh," Philadelphy said from the woodpile. There was something curious in her voice too—urgent, perhaps frightened. "If you wants any supper, you better tote me some wood." But I didn't know which, urgency or fright; I didn't have time to wonder or speculate, because suddenly Loosh

stooped before Ringo or I could have moved, and with his hand he swept the chips flat.

"There's your Vicksburg," he said. (322)

An avenging angel of history and a bit of a bully, Loosh has foretold the fall of Vicksburg and the Confederacy's eventual defeat, which for him means that "hit's on the way"—that is to say, emancipation is coming for his race. Abruptly putting an end to a white boy's ahistorical reveries, a black slave reminds readers that the present moment is a vitally important one, and in so doing he stands as a figure of assertiveness, wisdom, and justice. It's a small moment, but it neatly encapsulates Faulkner's larger project in *The Unvanquished*, which is to ask whether any war is more historically significant than any other, and to suggest, without quite saying so explicitly, that the abolition of chattel slavery might have made the Civil War a uniquely righteous conflict. Drifting between dreamy abstraction and insistent reality, *The Unvanquished* at times contends and at times denies that racial issues motivated the war. Faulkner provides ammunition for both sides, and so too does he ambush them.

Faulkner most obscures the war's racial stakes by telling a sharply limited story, presenting the conflict from the perspective of a boy who almost never reflects on larger questions of politics, law, or justice. What is more, Bayard has a tendency toward universalization and is almost constitutively unable to see why the world he lives in should be subject to dispute. Consider his intense friendship with Ringo and his insistence that they are, in some hazy but fundamental way, brothers—an extraordinary claim given that Ringo is black and has always been the property of the Sartoris family. Bayard's mystical sense of selfhood, his determination not to acknowledge racial difference, and his inability to see the significance of bondage all cry out for analysis:

> Ringo and I had been born in the same month and had both fed at the same breast and had slept together and eaten together for so long that Ringo called Granny "Granny" just like I did, until maybe he wasn't a nigger anymore or maybe I wasn't a white boy anymore, the two of us neither, not even people any longer: the two supreme undefeated like two moths, two feathers riding above a hurricane. (323–24)

The novel's tone can be difficult to fix here, and the insistent, overdetermined quality of Bayard's words surely indicates that Faulkner did not want readers to accept them at face value. This might be a moment of childhood naïveté, or a sentimental recollection from an older adult, or a sad acknowledgement that the veil of race must inevitably separate two friends, or a dishonest refusal to face the realities of plantation life. Bayard may even be speaking more truth than he knows, for an earlier, 1933 Faulkner story about the Sartoris family, "There Was a Queen," had insinuated that Bayard's father had also fathered at least one of his slaves.[9]

If Bayard's thoughts about the relations between black and white are somewhat slippery, those of the Sartoris family slaves can seem positively inexplicable, for some of them fail to see the war as having any particular racial significance. Ringo, for example, appears to share his young master's exaggerated humanism, so absorbed in the heroic myth of the Confederacy that he acts in opposition to what virtually any modern reader would identify as his self-interest. He is a figure of disturbing contradictions, a slave who enjoys impersonating southern generals during war games, who remains loyal to his owners even though he has been legally emancipated, and who helps Bayard fire on a Union soldier who has approached the Sartoris homestead—"Shoot the bastud!" he cries (336). Again, is this young man motivated by naïveté, or by false consciousness, or by a loyalty that is somehow greater than race and politics? In these moments and elsewhere, Ringo thinks of identity and warfare in essentially abstract terms, but so too does Faulkner use him to suggest an important connection between abstract thinking and the persistence of material injustice. This young slave may be too expansive to value black over white or blue over gray, but his social and political future—and that of Loosh and of millions more—depends very much upon those distinctions.

In foregrounding this friendship between a master and his slave, Faulkner deployed a powerful and time-honored narrative trope, one that had important and rather uncomfortable implications for his larger treatment of the Civil War. Interracial affection had abounded in the sentimental "plantation fiction" of the postwar years, with authors from Thomas Nelson Page to Margaret Mitchell mourning the loss of an imagined southern Arcadia and its allegedly paternal social order. Faulkner disliked this school of writing and thought it described a world that "never existed anywhere," but his humanistic treatment of race in *The Unvanquished* often leaves the impression that the South had been enlightened and benevolent enough to have resolved the problem of slavery on its own, without the spur of war.[10] In one of the novel's most striking episodes, for example, Bayard, Ringo, and Granny Millard flee the advancing Union army, head for the town of Jefferson, and encounter Uncle Buck McCaslin, perhaps the most liberal plantation owner in all of American literature. McCaslin and his brother are slaveholders, but they have collapsed the old hierarchies by renouncing their manor house, allowing their black chattel to go free every night, and employing an interracial labor force. All of this grows out of a farsighted historical vision and sense of scale:

> Father said they were ahead of their time; he said they not only possessed, but put into practice, ideas about social relationship that maybe fifty years after they were both dead people would have a name for. These ideas were about land. They believed that land did not belong to people but that people belonged to land and that the earth would permit them to live on and out of it and use it only so long as they behaved and that if they did not behave right, it would shake them off just like a dog getting rid of fleas. (351)

There is an echo of Bayard's reveries here, with the McCaslins thinking in terms larger than the South, and perhaps larger than humanity itself. There may as yet be no name for their ideas, but the novel suggests that there could be one in the future, especially if Faulkner's young protagonists represent a rising, color-blind generation.

Faulkner's rosy, even Edenic view of race and labor in *The Unvanquished* has unsettled many of his readers, and his broad-minded slaveholders and unbounded slaves might appear at first to be the fanciful products of artistic license.[11] But it is important to note that a similar sense of humanism could also be found in some of the most respected works of Civil War history in the 1930s—works that claimed to have made rigorously empirical surveys of the antebellum South. The most noteworthy was Avery Craven's study, *The Repressible Conflict*, published a year after *The Unvanquished*. Craven's book was dedicated to the proposition that the war had been a mistake, and it based its argument on the assumption that slavery had not been worth fighting over. The "peculiar institution," according to Craven, had not been "peculiar" at all, for relations between masters and slaves had been no different from those between white employers and free black laborers in the same period. "Human nature was stronger than any artificial setup," Craven wrote, and "both Negro and Southerner had their share of that."[12] His scholarly picture of a typical plantation accorded remarkably well with Bayard's rather romantic one: it was a place where "blacks and whites living and working together tended to become individual human beings regardless of station."[13] Slavery, in Craven's view, was not a uniquely wicked system of labor, nor was it unique in any other way; problems arose only when it came to be viewed as such by overzealous northern reformers in the 1850s. Today, of course, Craven's book is profoundly outdated as a work of history. But it still stands as an object lesson in how easily humanistic impulses can be marshaled in the defense of deeply unjust social and political doctrines, and it demonstrates just how credible Faulkner's frequently dubious narrator could seem in his times.

There was at least one historian of the 1930s, however, who was determined not to let the war's racial stakes disappear: W. E. B. Du Bois, perhaps the most eminent African American writer of the early twentieth century. In 1935 he published his magnum opus, *Black Reconstruction*, one of the only works of the decade to put race at the center of the Civil War and to argue for the absolute justice of the conflict. Du Bois was primarily concerned with foregrounding the perspectives of slaves and black laborers, but so too was he determined to bring moral clarity to what he perceived as an increasingly and dangerously muddled scholarly field. Baffled by arguments that Americans had fought and died for generalities like "union and national power," Du Bois spent much of his book demanding that historians stop discussing the war in the "vague ways" that were then in vogue.[14] As Du Bois saw it, narratives of the conflict that failed to note the overriding importance of slavery in American life were positively dangerous, and histories that invoked economic forces, political principles, or abstract theorizations to explain the war left a "comfortable feeling that nothing right or wrong is involved" (714–15). Worse still, such works utterly misrepresented the nation's past: "Easily the most dramatic episode in American history was the sudden move to free four million black slaves in an effort to stop a great civil war, to end forty years of bitter controversy, and to appease the moral sense of civilization," he wrote (3). To say otherwise was to miss "the real plot of the story" (715).

Did Faulkner, who wrote much of *The Unvanquished* while Du Bois was finishing *Black Reconstruction*, see the war in this light? His novel leaves many indications that he might have, one of which is the emergence of Loosh as a figure of liberation and black agency. Once the Union army has penetrated deep enough into the South, Loosh claims his freedom and leaves his owners, ignoring Granny Millard's warnings that, without her family's support, he will face "misery and starvation" (370). Granny seems in some ways to have a persuasive argument, for Ringo chooses to remain in her service and Philadelphy only follows her husband begrudgingly. But Loosh has been possessed of a vision, looking "like he was asleep, like he didn't even see us or was seeing something we couldn't" (369). He is following "God's own angel," who has "proclamated me free and gonter general me to Jordan," but so too is he taking revenge: before he departs, he makes sure that his northern liberators know where the Sartoris family silver is hidden. Asked what right he has to impoverish the family, he defies his absent Confederate master with poetic conviction. "Where John Sartoris?" he demands. "Whyn't he come and ax me that? Let God ax John Sartoris who the man name that give me to him. Let the man that buried me in the black dark ax that of the man what dug me free" (369–70). With that, he leaves the Sartorises to curse the Union and their disloyal slave—"The bastuds! The bastuds!" (370)—and he disappears into the smoky dusk, "yellow and slow and turning coppercolored in the sunset."

Loosh's departure is more than just a plot point. As the historian Don H. Doyle has observed, Faulkner's decision even to include such a character in his novel is radical, given that freedmen were "mostly ignored" in war writing during the early twentieth century.[15] What is more, Loosh's self-determination (as well as his self-righteousness) fits the story of the Civil War that Du Bois had been almost alone in telling in 1935. As Du Bois saw it, the conflict was decided not by generals, industrial might, or diplomacy, but rather by "a general strike against slavery" on the part of southern blacks (57). The Confederate army obviously could not mount a resistance without being armed, clothed, and fed, and so laborers "held the key to the war" (63). The southern states contained nearly four million slaves, and the war effort hinged upon their continuing to work as usual. But a critical mass of slaves chose to abandon their masters when the opportunity presented itself, and the rest was history: the South was bereft of labor, the Union army enjoyed a surge of new recruits, and European nations grew less inclined to enter what had become a war of liberation. Crucially, all of this occurred not as a consequence of northern strategy, but in spite of it. Du Bois noted Lincoln's frequent denials that the Union fought for abolition, and he observed that northern laborers were often unsympathetic to the plight of southern blacks, but none of that mattered once slaves became masters of their destinies and turned the war to their own purposes. "When Northern armies entered the South they became armies of emancipation," Du Bois wrote, despite the fact that this was "the last thing they planned to be" (55).

For all that he distrusted abstraction in accounts of the war, Du Bois had a taste for lyrical, collectivizing language: at one point he described the general strike against slavery as "the great unbroken swell of the ocean before it dashes on the reefs" (65). And in some of its most memorable moments, *The Unvanquished* depicts the self-emancipation of slaves and describes their ascendance in similar terms, though Faulkner's reasons for doing so are much more elusive than Du Bois's. As he wanders war-torn Mississippi with Granny and Ringo, Bayard becomes aware that he is in the midst of a profound social upheaval: as Loosh had prophesized, southern blacks are taking to the road and following the Union army, their "blank eyes not looking at anything" as they move into the future (389).

We never did overtake them, just as you do not overtake a tide. You just keep moving, then suddenly you know that the set is about you, beneath you, overtaking you, as if the slow and ruthless power, become aware of your presence at last, had dropped back a tentacle, a feeler, to gather you in and sweep you remorselessly on. Singly, in couples, in groups and families they began to appear from the woods, ahead of us, alongside of us and behind; they covered and hid from sight the road exactly as an infiltration flood water would have. (388)

There is an undeniable power, even sublimity, in this image, with a rising people imagined as an inexorable force of nature. The war and the black response to it have made freedom irreversible, and Bayard has witnessed, perhaps more clearly than anywhere else in the novel, history in the making. And yet Bayard's ever-universalizing perspective can seem to rob these freed slaves of their agency even as it affords them a kind of majesty. They drift without words or apparent destination; they eddy about Union officers who beat them back with their sabres; and in a horrifying climax, a "mob" of them surges across a bridge that has been wired with explosives and is blown sky-high (391). Their forceful collectivity can also seem to be mindlessness, and Faulkner leaves the impression that these slaves have been swept up in history every bit as much as they have directed it, engaged in what one literary scholar has called an "inexplicable and futile pursuit of 'Jordan,' a non-existent promised land."[16] As the Civil War draws to its end, Faulkner seems to be depicting two very different events at the same time. This is America undergoing what Du Bois called an "upheaval of humanity like the Reformation and the French Revolution" (727), and yet Bayard is still dreaming just as he used to in his backyard, with the nineteenth century's battles and migrations and emancipations vanishing once more into the land's ponderable vastness.

The questions remain open: how momentous was the Civil War, what did it accomplish, and what did it mean when considered in the context of human history? If *The Unvanquished* remains uncertain to the very end, it is in part because it suggests, in the words of Ringo, that in America, "This War aint over. Hit just started good" (454). The novel's plot continues past the Confederacy's military defeat and into postwar Reconstruction, and while North and South no longer oppose one another on the battlefield, they continue to at the polls. The novel's penultimate section, "Skirmish at Sartoris," dramatizes a bloody suppression of the black vote in postwar Jefferson that Faulkner had previously alluded to in both *Flags in the Dust* and *Light in August*, and it foreshadows a coming century of African American disenfranchisement.

Carpetbaggers have traveled south to register the former slaves, and they represent "a new foe whose means we could not always fathom but whose aim we could always dread." Bayard's father, home from the war and incensed by a black candidate for town marshal, vows that "the election would never be held with Cash Benbow or any other nigger in it," and so on Election Day he kills two canvassers, seizes the ballot box, and ensures the continuation of white political dominance (456). As he and his fiancée, Drusilla, ride through town, they are saluted by the demobilized Confederate soldiers who once served in his troop:

> It came back high and thin and ragged and fierce, like when the Yankees used to hear it out of the smoke and the galloping:
> "Yaaaaay, Drusilla!" they hollered. "Yaaaaaay, John Sartoris! Yaaaaaaay!"
> (462)

The story comes to an end here, and it should go without saying that Cash Benbow has lost his campaign, by a unanimous vote.

This moment has struck many of Faulkner's readers as profoundly disappointing, whether aesthetically, politically, or historically. Faulkner's biographer finds it to be uncharacteristically hokey and triumphalist, and he suggests that the author "may have gagged as he closed the happy-ending story."[17] More racially attuned audiences, however, are likely to be most bothered by Faulkner's flirtation with white supremacy and the blasé manner with which he treats the murder of two civil rights workers. So too will they be concerned about the black characters who had once showed signs of escaping slavery, for at novel's end Ringo works for Bayard and is referred to as "my boy" rather than as a brother (464), while Loosh seems to have grown tired of pursuing Jordan and is now back working in the Sartoris family stable. Those inclined to defend Faulkner for this might say that he was, in a sense, obliged to advance such commentary. Because he was taking various historical approaches to the nineteenth century in the novel, and because it was common at the time for historians to describe Reconstruction as a "tragic era" for allegedly victimized southern whites, perhaps Faulkner could not have avoided including such a perspective.[18] Yet this does little to mitigate the uncomfortable qualities of the tale, which cast a pall over the final pages of *The Unvanquished* in much the same way that Tom Sawyer's reenslavement of Jim mars the ending of Mark Twain's *Adventures of Huckleberry Finn* for many readers.

It is also possible, however, that Faulkner intended this episode to mark the symbolic beginning of the Jim Crow South, which later historians would recognize, in Du Bois's words, as a "long step backward toward slavery" for American blacks (708). Seeing this requires attending to the story's tone rather than its plot and noting that there is something perfunctory and weary in Bayard's account of this latest Confederate victory. When Colonel Sartoris's soldiers assemble to cheer the suppression of the black vote, they are motivated by a combination of routine, boredom, and masculine shame that seems to have little to do with any political convictions:

> Maybe from the old habit of doing everything as one man; maybe when you have lived for four years in a world ordered completely by men's doings, even when it is danger and fighting, you dont want to quit that world: maybe the danger and the fighting are the reasons, because men have been pacifists for every reason under the sun except to avoid danger and fighting. And so now Father's troop and all the other men in Jefferson, and Aunt Louisa and Mrs Habersham and all the women in Jefferson were actually enemies for the reason that the men had given in and admitted that they belonged to the United States but the women had never surrendered. (446)

Moreover, when these men muster enough energy to raise the old rebel yell and celebrate Sartoris's strike against the North, the effect is anticlimactic:

> And then it was loud; I could hear them when they drew in their breath like when the Yankees used to hear it begin:
> "Yaaaaa—" But Father raised his hand and they stopped. Then you couldn't hear anything. (459–60)

And just as these men seem something less than wholehearted in "Skirmish at Sartoris," so too has Faulkner frequently been said to have written the story without any real energy or feeling. Perhaps the shoddiness that critics like Blotner and Doyle have found in it—"the cardboard characters and stilted dialogue that carries the thin story line"—was Faulkner's way of deflating the reactionary ideology he was giving space to.[19] Or perhaps, as the literary scholar Walter Taylor has intriguingly suggested, Faulkner's fuller depictions of black characters in the novel's earlier installments had made him realize that an entirely different, more radical story "was threatening to emerge from beneath the smug nostalgia of Bayard's narrative."[20] Better, then, to dispatch that more confrontational story in *The Unvanquished* as quickly as possible and treat it more thoroughly in *Absalom, Absalom!*, which Faulkner was writing at the same time.

    The Unvanquished is Faulkner's most sustained engagement with the Civil War, but in the final analysis it can seem frustratingly noncommittal and overly enamored with eternal recurrence. The war was singular, and it was like every other one; the war was about race, and it was about something much broader than that; the war existed in a particular moment, and it cycled on and on and on.[21] In creating these tensions and posing these contradictions, however, *The Unvanquished* captures not the past but rather the ongoing struggle of Americans to understand, interpret, and shape that past. And in Faulkner's 1930s, it truly was a struggle. Du Bois was a lonely voice when he published *Black Reconstruction*, but he hoped the historical profession would eventually face the truth about race in the nineteenth century. How disappointed he must have been, then, if he ever read Paul H. Buck's *The Road to Reunion*, a study of Reconstruction that won the Pulitzer Prize for History in 1938, pleased the author of *Gone with the Wind*, and introduced the old doctrines of black inferiority to yet another generation of readers. For Buck, the Civil War ended only after North and South accepted an eternal fact of national life and agreed upon the wisdom of racial segregation. "The unchanging elements of the race problem had become apparent to most observers and the old impatient yearning for an immediate and thorough solution had passed away," Buck noted approvingly.[22] "Once a people admits the fact that a major problem is basically insoluble they have taken the first step in learning how to live with it." More than seventy years after Appomattox, it would seem, the Confederacy still held the field.

The war went on in the histories, and the dust would not settle for years after Faulkner's death. Eventually, scholars came to recognize the evils of slavery, the righteousness of abolitionism, and the perseverance of freedmen. Historian Eric Foner wrote in 1988 that "no part of the American experience has . . . seen a broadly accepted point of view so completely overturned."[23] As for Faulkner's vividly elusive novel of the Civil War, part of its enduring value surely lies in its ability to so completely overturn itself.

NOTES

1. William Faulkner, *Absalom, Absalom!, Novels 1936–1940*, ed. Joseph Blotner and Noel Polk (New York: Library of America, 1990), 6.

2. William Faulkner, *Selected Letters of William Faulkner*, ed. Joseph Blotner (New York: Random House, 1977), 84.

3. Richard Gray, *The Life of William Faulkner: A Critical Biography* (Oxford: Blackwell, 1994), 227.

4. Daniel J. Singal, *William Faulkner: The Making of a Modernist* (Chapel Hill: University of North Carolina Press, 1997), 282, 224.

5. Craig A. Warren, *Scars to Prove It: The Civil War Soldier and American Fiction* (Kent, OH: Kent State University Press, 2009), 84.

6. For an excellent account of "revisionist" history and the Civil War, see Peter Novick, *That Noble Dream: The "Objectivity Question" and the American Historical Profession* (Cambridge: Cambridge University Press, 1988).

7. While most readers of the novel presume an 1863 setting, James Hinkle has made the case for its taking place the year before, when a "seldom-remembered year-too-soon rumor about the fall of Vicksburg" spread through the Confederacy. Wolfgang Hochbruck has also noted the haziness of Faulkner's Civil War time line and argues that the novel's historical inaccuracies anticipate, "by several score years," postmodern aesthetics of "self-reflexivity." See James Hinkle, "The Civil War in the Apocrypha according to William Faulkner," in *Faulkner and History*, ed. Javier Coy and Michel Gresset (Salamanca, Spain: Ediciones Universidad de Salamanca, 1986), 32; and Wolfgang Hochbruck, "Writing a Civil War in William Faulkner's *The Unvanquished*," in *Re-Visioning the Past: Historical Self-Reflexivity in American Short Fiction*, ed. Bernd Engler and Oliver Scheiding (Trier, Germany: Wissenschaftlicher, 1998), 228.

8. William Faulkner, *The Unvanquished, Novels 1936–1940*, ed. Joseph Blotner and Noel Polk (New York: Library of America, 1990), 321. Subsequent references to this edition will appear parenthetically in the text.

9. Faulkner was, of course, oblique about this matter: "There Was a Queen" begins by introducing a black woman and stating that Bayard "was her half-brother (though possibly but not probably neither of them knew it, including Bayard's father)." See William Faulkner, *Collected Stories of William Faulkner* (1950; repr., New York: Vintage International, 1995), 727.

10. William Faulkner, "An Introduction to *The Sound and the Fury*" (1973), in *The Sound and the Fury: An Authoritative Text, Backgrounds and Contexts, Criticism*, ed. David Minter, 2nd ed. (New York: Norton, 1994), 229.

11. Darwin T. Turner, "Faulkner and Slavery," in *The South and Faulkner's Yoknapatawpha: The Actual and the Apocryphal*, ed. Evans Harrington and Ann J. Abadie (Jackson: University Press of Mississippi, 1977), 73.

12. Avery Craven, *The Repressible Conflict, 1830–1861* (Baton Rouge: Louisiana State University Press, 1939), 55.

13. Ibid., 52–53.

14. W. E. Burghardt Du Bois, *Black Reconstruction: An Essay toward a History of the Part Which Black Folk Played in the Attempt to Reconstruct Democracy in America, 1860–1880* (Philadelphia: Albert Saifer, 1935), 15, 715. Subsequent references to this edition will appear parenthetically in the text.

15. Don H. Doyle, "Faulkner's Civil War in Fiction, History, and Memory," in *Faulkner and War: Faulkner and Yoknapatawpha, 2001*, ed. Noel Polk and Ann J. Abadie (Jackson: University Press of Mississippi, 2004), 5.

16. Gray, *Life of William Faulkner*, 231.

17. Joseph Blotner, *Faulkner: A Biography* (Jackson: University Press of Mississippi, 2005), 336.

18. See, for example, Claude G. Bowers's very influential and deeply racist work *The Tragic Era: The Revolution after Lincoln* (Cambridge, MA: Houghton Mifflin, 1929).

19. Don H. Doyle, "Faulkner's History: Sources and Interpretation," in *Faulkner in Cultural Context: Faulkner and Yoknapatawpha, 1995*, ed. Donald M. Kartiganer and Ann J. Abadie (Jackson: University Press of Mississippi, 1997), 26.

20. Walter Taylor, *Faulkner's Search for a South* (Urbana: University of Illinois Press, 1983), 97.

21. Indeed, a recent study of *The Unvanquished* has surveyed many of the same scenes and concluded that the novel is as much about the Great Depression as about the Civil War. See Ted Atkinson, *Faulkner and the Great Depression: Aesthetics, Ideology, and Cultural Politics* (Athens: University of Georgia Press, 2006), 221–36.

22. Paul H. Buck, *The Road to Reunion, 1865–1900* (Boston: Little, Brown, 1938), 297.

23. Eric Foner, *Reconstruction: America's Unfinished Revolution, 1863–1877* (New York: Harper & Row, 1988), xix.

"The President Has Asked Me": Faulkner, Ellison, and Public Intellectualism

Joseph Fruscione

I want to make the following case: Faulkner exercised an active and dynamic mode of influence on Ralph Ellison, both as a racially attuned novelist and as a publicly active critic refining his intellectual brand in the 1950s and 1960s. As such, I seek to deepen our understanding of how a key African American writer-intellectual of the twentieth century engaged with Faulkner's work and politics throughout the civil rights era. Ellison's connection with Faulkner was partly direct, partly indirect: there was some shared correspondence, at least two brief meetings, and a lot of reading and writing on Ellison's part. As such, I examine two related threads here: the authors' exchange of letters in 1956 and 1957 about the White House–sponsored People-to-People Program and Ellison's interest in Faulkner as literary model and racial critic. Throughout his career as novelist, essayist, and educator, Ellison "had accepted the challenge of William Faulkner's complex literary image of the South," in Albert Murray's words, as his essays, archival documents, and the media items he collected for forty-odd years indicate.[1]

In ways problematic yet somewhat admirable, Ellison turned his praise of canonical writers into something self-beneficial in becoming a novelist and critic of great moment. He mobilized intellectualism, aesthetics, and racial politics to navigate Faulkner's influence and broader issues of intellectual celebrity, as seen through selected correspondence, essays, and various drafted writings. As Lawrence P. Jackson has explored in *The Indignant Generation*, Ellison was operating within the tradition of black intellectuals with academic ties, such as Arna Bontemps at Fisk, Sterling A. Brown at Howard, and many others. These and other writer-educators had enjoyed "startling aesthetic, institutional, and commercial successes," though more individually than collectively.[2] Part of Ellison's public intellectualism entailed academic labor, such as university teaching, lectures, and commencement addresses at some forty (or more) universities from the 1950s through the early 1990s—including work at West Point seven years after Faulkner's visit.[3]

Ellison's aesthetic and racial engagement with Faulkner complements yet complicates his engagement with other mainstream American writers, such as Henry James, Herman Melville, Mark Twain, and Stephen Crane. The post–*Invisible Man* Ellison offers different modes of radical politics and public intellectualism compared to a Du Bois or a Wright, as well as a kind of double consciousness inflecting his professional self-conception.[4] Ellison's essay writing, lecturing, and university teaching after *Invisible Man* represent, in my view, a significant stage of his career spanning more than thirty years. In this case, I veer from Jackson's framing of Ellison's post–*Invisible Man* work:

> What Ellison did not know was that, in essence, his own career had come to a conclusion in the mid-1950s. He would produce at least two fascinating pieces of critical work after *Invisible Man*—"Change the Joke and Slip the Yoke" in 1958 and "The World and the Jug" in 1963 and 1964—but these were ripostes, not investigations, and they showed him as anxious and touchy. He censored his public career to omit the years between 1937 and 1947—the indignant leftist years—and to maintain this lacuna required an aching acrobatics of rhetoric that looked like something else.[5]

The narrative of Ellison's post–*Invisible Man* career—partly defined by his creative struggles with his second novel—also contained meaningful essays and work as a critic and educator, some of which I foreground here as key to understanding Ellison vis-à-vis Faulkner. This is not to say that Ellison's career in the 1960s and beyond was not arduous or conflicted, particularly in his tense relations with Amiri Baraka and other radical writers. Unquestionably, Ellison's reputation as a novelist suffered after *Invisible Man*, but his reputation as critic and canonical figure was strong for the rest of his career. Jackson is also correct about Ellison's later muting his leftist sensibility from the 1930s and 1940s, though my primary concern here is with the later Ellison's self-determined role as a black public intellectual embracing Faulkner and other majority authors. His active engagement with Faulkner and other literary "ancestors" helped him carve out a parallel role as a critic at a time when he was struggling creatively.

A key element of the Faulkner-Ellison dynamic, then, is considering how these two very race-conscious writers developed their respective forms of public activity and intellectual labor in the 1950s and 1960s. I want to continue asking how Ellison's engagement clarifies Faulkner's active influence—that is, how it is not simply a matter of absorption or mimesis but of active self-fashioning. Ellison's published and archival texts represent a nuanced association with Faulkner in which he located himself within literary tradition yet sought to enhance his professional ethos. As such, when Faulkner writes Ellison in October 1956, he begins strengthening a connection Ellison had already been making for over a decade.

Correspondence and Meetings

The dawn of Ellison's public life merged with the twilight of Faulkner's in the mid-to late 1950s. Their careers intersected most meaningfully in their short-lived correspondence about the People-to-People Program. This White House–sponsored initiative, launched to promote American culture abroad and to counter the spread of Communism, joined yet distinguished the writers, while also helping Ellison feel that he was entering the upper echelon of American literary culture. With this in mind, I want to consider how the public Faulkner helped expand the public Ellison, in large part through Ellison's own efforts and aggressive self-promotion.

Faulkner and the *New York Times Book Review* critic Harvey Breit first wrote Ellison and other writers on October 1, 1956, to gain support at the program's inception: "The President has asked me to organize American writers to see what we can do to give a true picture of our country to other people. . . . Will you join such an organization?"[6] Faulkner's signature and typewritten name conclude the letter. Faulkner and Breit outline some of the program's objectives regarding the Iron Curtain and anti-Communist actions the American government could take. Accompanying this letter—"in a more serious vein," Faulkner notes in the postscript—was a single-page overview of the program from the White House, almost literally giving the letter a presidential imprimatur. Faulkner and Breit sent a similar letter to Ellison and others on October 11, again trying to shepherd politically engaged writers into People-to-People. These October letters were sent on Random House letterhead, which would have looked familiar to Ellison since Random House had published *Invisible Man*, and as such offered a direct connection to Faulkner, whose work he greatly admired.

After a few meetings but little progress through the fall and winter of 1956, Faulkner and fellow committee chairs John Steinbeck and Donald Hall sent out more letters of invitation on January 2, 1957, then on the People-to-People letterhead. This one describes "a representative group of American writers led by William Faulkner" and gives a two-page overview of their involvement to date.[7] In enumerating the committee's goals and the "adequate government subsidy" they would require, the writers discuss freeing Ezra Pound as an objective: "While the Chairman of this Committee"—that is, Faulkner himself—"appointed by the President, was awarded a prize for literature by the Swedish Government and was given a decoration by the French Government, the American Government locks up one of its best poets." Despite Faulkner's somewhat tepid involvement with President Eisenhower's program, he draws on his public role as a decorated American writer and Nobel Laureate in this brief correspondence with Ellison, whose essays and university teaching reveal a similarly self-aware performance. At different points in their lives, Faulkner and Ellison had links to the White House—to Presidents Eisenhower and Johnson, respectively—that buttressed their public efforts as writer-intellectuals in the era of *Invisible Man*, *A Fable*, and other bold literary works. In the case of People-to-People, Faulkner as Nobel Laureate had the potential to persuade other writers to join, though the writers' segment of the program eventually dissolved not long after this January letter.

On February 22, Ellison respectfully declined the invitation, largely because his aesthetic and intellectualism were more nationally centered. Ellison supports some of the committee's proposals. He notes in the first paragraph, "I find myself very much in agreement with the first three of the committee's proposals and would be willing to do whatever I can to help make it effective," namely reducing visa requirements and sending American books and films to East Germany "at least to match what the Russians are doing."[8] Ellison sounds an almost nationalistic note in supporting the program's plan to bring groups of Communists to the United States, namely "to try to bring people from all over the world . . . to this country for a duration of at least two years to live a normal American life." Yet the sticking point was Ezra Pound: despite the plea from a writer he greatly admired, Ellison resists freeing the poet. He asks, "Isn't it a bit incongruous that the Pound question with its problems of hate and genocide should be connected with ou[r] efforts to help those who are trying to free themselves from that same type of evil, given the authority of the State, which Pound encourages?" Ever aware of the intersections between writing, race, and nation, Ellison takes a different tack from a group nominally headed by Faulkner while still maintaining a connection with him.

The People-to-People Program was for Faulkner a potentially significant but ultimately minor aspect of his public life in the 1950s. Although, as Blotner has it, Faulkner acted as chair of the writers' committee "out of duty rather than conviction," his activities on People-to-People's behalf enhanced his image in the era of his University of Virginia residency, travels to Asia, and other more robust public efforts. As Blotner, Jay Parini, and others have noted, the program enabled Faulkner—though somewhat lukewarmly—to engage with novelists, poets, and critics over various politically charged matters in arguably the most public phase of his career.[9] His work under the auspices of People-to-People suggests a degree of public intellectualism, writerly camaraderie, and awareness of Cold War politics—but not as deep, sustained, or self-constructed as Ellison's efforts.[10]

Although this is their only known correspondence, Faulkner and Ellison had met in New York in January 1953 during a reception at Random House for the National Book Award. In this brief encounter, Ellison complimented Faulkner on the many literary "children" he'd sired. In an April 1953 letter to Murray, Ellison recounts his conversation with Faulkner (calling him "the great man") regarding his wide-reaching influence:

> "Well, Mr. Faulkner, this really completes the day for me," I said.
>
> "Yes," he said, "I guess this really is a day for you."
>
> "Ralph's book is *Invisible Man*," Saxe [Commins] said.
>
> "Yes, I know," Faulkner said. "Albert [Erskine] sent me a copy almost a year ago."
>
> "You know," I said, "you have children all around now. You won't be proud of all of them, just the same they're around."
>
> "Yes," Faulkner said, "I was surprised to learn how many people like the stuff."
>
> "You shouldn't be at all surprised."[11]

That Faulkner mentions receiving—though not necessarily reading—*Invisible Man* suggests a kind of aloof respect for Ellison and his work. In the same letter, Ellison discusses seeing Faulkner at Columbia in early April 1953 "at a reception for a visiting Japanese intellectual." Both writers left early and without engaging in much conversation of substance, though Ellison suggests Faulkner's awareness of racial issues by asking Murray, "You thinks he's been hanging around with Mose?"[12] By and large, this rich (though too brief) link achieved through letters, People-to-People, and a pair of meetings telescopes the different ways Faulkner and Ellison sharpened the public facets of their careers in this decade. Ellison, though, was not done negotiating with Faulkner in his writing.

Ellison: Critic and Archivist

Direct correspondence aside, Ellison indirectly engaged with Faulkner at a key personal and national moment. The younger writer devoted significant essay space to refining his persona as a critic and novelist of consequence, virtually a continuous act in Ellison's public life. For Jackson, Ellison as writer-intellectual belonged to "a group who theoretically transformed their indignation at Jim Crow to manufacture a strata of artworks that secured and pronounced a new era of psychological freedom for African Americans."[13] After *Invisible Man*, he welcomed the brighter spotlight brought by interviews, lectures, essays, the National Book Award, and professorships at Bard (1958–1961); Chicago (1961); Rutgers (1962–1964); and most prestigiously, NYU (1970–1979.)[14] Many Ellison essays and lectures praise Faulkner's style, framing of black humanity, and "driving honesty and social responsibility."[15] Six essays and his National Book Award address from *Shadow and Act* (1964) reveal that Ellison's praise of Faulkner was sincere yet a touch self-serving, as if acknowledging ties to literary forebears in writing elevated his critical standing. Faulkner thus becomes a literary-racial touchstone and intellectual springboard for Ellison in this essay and many other works.[16]

Most famously in "The World and the Jug," Ellison articulated his multiracial canon and his own place in it through an embrace of literary "relatives" and, more so, "ancestors," particularly Dostoyevsky, Eliot, and Faulkner.[17] He posits throughout his critical oeuvre what Jackson has termed an "underlying shared American cultural history" between the black experience and his mainstream "ancestors" and contemporaries.[18] In his National Book Award address—rife with such cultural-historical sharing—Ellison singled out Faulkner as the only modern novelist who embraced Twain and his "responsibility for the condition of democracy"; Ellison also spoke of "the conflicts within the human heart," a clear borrowing from Faulkner's Nobel Prize address (a copy of which Ellison owned, as I discuss below).[19] Faulkner, for Ellison, was always the exception for any shortcomings he saw in modern American literature, setting up an important Twain-Faulkner-Ellison literary lineage.

"The Shadow and the Act," furthermore, opens with a discussion of the recent *Intruder in the Dust* film: "We see Chick recognize Lucas as the representative of those virtues of courage, pride, independence and patience that are usually attributed only to white men."[20] To Ellison's mind, the film—and likely the source novel—embodies "a process by which the role of Negroes in American life has been given what, for the movies, is a startling new definition." Ellison makes a dual argument about Faulkner's "metaphor" in *Intruder in the Dust*, namely concerning

Faulkner's superlative treatment of race and also his own critical acumen in unpacking it from a complex text.[21] *Intruder in the Dust*—particularly Lucas's refusal of Chick's money after rescuing him from the ice—is for Ellison "one of the most sharply amusing studies of Southern racial ethics to be seen anywhere."[22]

As *Shadow and Act* and, later, *Going to the Territory* (1986) reveal, Ellison avidly read Faulkner's novels, speeches, and other works and often extolled the nuanced black humanity in *Go Down, Moses*; *Intruder in the Dust*; and other texts. Ellison's use of Faulkner was twofold: he often wrote about and then almost obsessively collected materials on Faulkner to enhance his own intellectual acclaim, part of what Jackson describes more broadly as the writer-intellectual's "performance of his everyday life."[23] Virtually all of his writing on Faulkner was laudatory. His essays and unpublished notes and fragments extend what Jackson locates only in *Invisible Man* as "an affirmation of indigenous black American culture . . . with the idiom of high modernism."[24]

In conjunction with published texts, Ellison's archival material indicates further sustained, meaningful engagement with Faulkner's literary-racial example. He wrote and then saved numerous drafts, notes, and fragments for all major writing projects, in the process revealing the development of his critical sensibility and editorial obsessiveness. After *Shadow and Act*, Ellison wrote more fully on Faulkner's handling of black characters. An unfinished piece from 1968—which he may have geared toward the *New York Times Book Review*—highlights Faulkner as a southern writer particularly attuned to racial politics. Ellison never finished or published it, but the draft bears his typical compositional footprint: he kept multiple typed and handwritten sections, added marginal notes, and left occasional misspellings, many pencil corrections, and partly illegible words.

In the essay, he writes—and rewrites—about valuing Faulkner's novels, which unlike other modern white writers' work, "contained Negroes whom I could recognize as human, as people who though caught up in the [specific] circumstances of their regional, familial and racial histories were endowed with human passions[,] beliefs, ideals and failures in human measure."[25] Ellison notes elsewhere in the piece that "the fact that Fa[u]lkner could transform himself into that huge body of literature which today we identify as *Faulkner* still strikes many as something of a miracle—and certainly it is evidence of a major triumph of the artistic will."[26] These and other reflections show Ellison's characteristic triangulation of aesthetics, intellectualism, and racial politics, such as his praising Faulkner as writer and symbol ("*Faulkner*") for being "not only committed to the heroism of achieving fictional truth but in so involving himself he was freeing the Negro of the stereotypes and negative myths which had shackled him in much of Southern fiction." Ellison notes his critical qua racial awareness of how Faulkner "had brought the vision-quickening glamour of modern poetic and fictional technique and vision not only to the South from which my parents had sprung, but in doing so he pointed [to] a direction for getting the complex cultural and social reality of Negro Americans into literature."[27]

Several Ellison essays had foregrounded this "complex . . . reality" as a key rubric in examining how Melville, Twain, Hemingway, and others explored race in their fiction. This draft, in conjunction with published essays and the Ellison-Faulkner correspondence, shows him negotiating Faulkner's artistic and political influence, praising his great literary merit, and forwarding himself as a dominant writer-intellectual dialed in to the era's racial climate. These actions further underscored Ellison's role as an ambitious novelist and racial critic with a multiracial web of influence.

Shorter, though no less intriguing, is an undated note likely written in the late 1950s and not intended for publication. This one-page note discusses Ellison's two major Mississippi influences. Ellison praises Faulkner and, as usual, somewhat denigrates Wright.[28] For him, Wright's work had declined since *Uncle Tom's Children* (1940), whereas Faulkner's work continued to explore race relations and positive black humanity.

> Richard Wright + William Faulkner
> What would both think of Whats happening in Missi[ssi]ppi? Today Wright became an exile Faulkner, said he'd shoot Negro[e]s in the street? Where is the heroism now? Faulkner saw it *most* of the time; Wright seldom saw anything but the viscious [*sic*] of the whites but none of the heroism of the Negroes after *Uncle Tom's Children*.[29]

Ellison's attitudes of unreserved embrace and influence/anxiety toward Faulkner and Wright, respectively, indicate his continued thinking about black humanity and "heroism" in modern American fiction. Although this piece is essentially a note, it reveals his thinking of Faulkner as aware of racial matters in ways Ellison the critic valued. He seems to have known Faulkner's highly charged comment about "shooting Negroes in the street," though he contextualized it and continued to admire him.[30] He may have read Faulkner's "A Letter to the Leaders in the Negro Race." This piece advocates a civil rights position somewhat in line with Ellison's—that is, one of moderation, "flexibility," and working nonviolently within the system.[31] Such ties with consciously intellectual black writers such as Ellison enable us to read Faulkner as developing a newly cosmopolitan and intellectual engagement with race.

Other archived notes discuss Ellison's reading of Faulkner and T. S. Eliot and his own travels in the South. An undated fragment notes that he "couldn't have been more shocked by some of the things" in *Sanctuary*, *The Sound and the Fury*, and *Light in August* when he read them in the 1930s.[32] In the same undated fragment he notes, "Recently I made my first trip to Mississippi I'm even more certain that culturally, he had been . . . touched, as the old ph[r]ase had it, 'by the tar brush.'" This notion of Faulkner symbolically having black ancestry complements Ellison's linking of him to "Mose" in the 1953 letter to Murray quoted above and counterpoints Ellison's concern with literary ancestry in "The World and the Jug." What Ellison views as a positive representation of race and black characters accounts for his continued superlative treatment of Faulkner and his work. Ellison's rich nonfiction and archive of drafted material further advances critical sensibility and legitimacy, while continually exploring a claim he made about Faulkner as "the greatest artist the South has produced."[33]

Earlier, likely in April 1950, Ellison offered Peter Bunzel of the *New Yorker* a kind of model for reading Faulkner's work—namely, "carefully" and "in sequence." Ellison locates the most genuine Faulkner—"what he *is*"—in his fiction as he "seems to work out his conflicts in the process of his writings."[34] Most significantly, the arc of Faulkner's oeuvre shows an evolving treatment of blackness: "The Negro characters thus change from book to book, becoming more complex and thus more human, as Faulkner battles out the conflict between his Southern heritage of bigotry, as far as Negroes are concerned, and his deep feelings for mankind and his respect for his art."[35] This letter anticipates the kinds of analysis and praise Ellison would advance in various kinds of writing in later decades, such as the "new definition" of black humanity he felt *Intruder in the Dust* emblematized or Faulkner's inheriting Twain's sense of literary-racial responsibility. As Ellison the novelist wrote in similar ways about race, Ellison the critic foregrounded Faulkner's writing and literary sensibility.

While writing and drafting ideas about Faulkner, Ellison also treated him as he did other literary figures; namely, by collecting media material written by and about him. Ellison archived hundreds of magazines, newspaper clippings, and other materials from the 1940s through the 1980s, all of which are housed in the Manuscript Division of the Library of Congress.[36] In considering Ellison as collector of Faulkner-related material, we should consider a few questions: What did he collect? Why and when? How was collecting Faulkner-related matter meant to boost

his ethos and intellectual brand? A short list of the materials Ellison collected—always with an eye toward augmenting his own prominence—
reads as follows:

- Pieces about *Intruder in the Dust* from *Harper's Bazaar*, *Vogue*, and *Camera*
- Edmund Wilson's review of *Intruder in the Dust* (*New Yorker*, October 23,
  1948) and Eudora Welty's response to Wilson (*New Yorker*, January 1, 1949)
- A reprint of the Nobel Prize address (The Spiral Press, March 1951)
- A typed transcript of the National Book Award address for *A Fable* (January
  1955)
- Faulkner "Special Issues" of *Harvard Advocate* (November 1951) and *Per-
  spective* (Summer 1949 and Autumn 1950)
- Obituaries from *Life*, *Vogue*, and other publications
- A 1954 flyer from the Book-of-the-Month Club asking members whether *A
  Fable* should be chosen as an alternate selection[37]
- Complete magazine issues containing "Race at Morning" (*Saturday Evening
  Post*, March 1955), "An Innocent at Rinkside" (*Sports Illustrated*, January
  1955), "Mr. Acarius" (*Saturday Evening Post*, October 1965), and others
- Faulkner's letters to the editors of the *New Yorker* (November 25, 1950) and
  the *New York Times* (December 26, 1954), among others
- A *Vogue* piece on Faulkner's visit to West Point (July 1962)
- A flyer and registration form for the 1975 Faulkner and Yoknapatawpha
  conference
- A May 1989 review of Frederick Karl's biography of Faulkner by Michiko
  Kakutani in the *New York Times*.

This was a typical move for Ellison in his author-archivist capacity; he
saved comparable material on Wright, Baldwin, Hemingway, and other
contemporaries. Late in his life, he ensured that his papers would go to
the Library of Congress, seemingly to provide evidence of his national
literary importance.[38] Keeping originals of these media materials treats
both Faulkner and *Faulkner* as a kind of history or archive supporting
Ellison's intellectual credibility.

Taken together, Ellison's archival writings and holdings point toward
a dual literary performance: namely, a younger writer publicly, even
eagerly, locating himself within Faulkner's sphere of influence yet with
ambitions to match Faulkner's example. In his mind, *he* was the modern
black writer to undertake such a lofty task—not Baldwin, not Wright,
and not any younger writers. Although his high professional goals
impeded the structuring and editing of his never-finished second novel,[39]
they enhanced his role as a critic, academic, and intellectual, showing an
awareness of Faulkner and, in the Ellisonian parlance, other "ancestors."

There was always this duality with the public Ellison, in the civil rights era especially. Having left his more Du Bois- or Wright-like radicalism behind in the 1940s—and alienating black power and Black Arts writers in the process—Ellison pursued a more traditional, mainstream model of literary writing in his mature career while wrestling with American racial politics in ways he felt Faulkner did superlatively.[40]

Dignifying the South?

A typewritten note on a late page of Ellison's draft essay—though not necessarily the intended conclusion—captures ideas written at different times and indicates his constant self-editing. "We know now in 1968," he writes,

> that the failure to represent the minorities in our depiction of American society can lead to chronic problems of identity and to an aggravated sense of alienation. Faulkner by doing his job as a novelist and addressing himself to the riddle of the truth is not guilty in this omission and indeed even the most alienated might go to his fiction to gain an idea of what has been missing inmuch [*sic*] of American fiction during the twentieth century.[41]

As he had done in his National Book Award address thirteen years earlier, Ellison foregrounds what we can call Faulkner's racial avant-gardism in terms of his attunement to race relations and complex black characters. A short handwritten sentence beneath the above section encapsulates his view: "By staying at home he dignified the South, redeemed the more viable [a]spects of its myth[.]"[42] Though Ellison ultimately did not reach Faulkner's level of literary output, his published and archival writings trace a narrative of ambitiousness, intellectualism, and keen literary-qua-racial vision. Ellison's was ultimately a successful quest for a viable role as critic, educator, and intellectual, thanks in part to his leveraging of Faulkner, Twain, and other literary models in his writing. There was influence, but there was also active engagement, connection, and continuous rethinking. For Ellison, Faulkner inherited what he called elsewhere a "personal responsibility for the condition of society" from Twain—a meaningful link on Ellison's part, given how often he pointed to *Adventures of Huckleberry Finn* as an ur-text in American race relations.[43]

While tackling the "challenge" of Faulkner that Albert Murray has described, Ellison viewed his evolving intellectual work as essayist and critic as a means to becoming a major (black) man of letters, critical influence, and canonical writer. Seeing Ellison as viable public intellectual augments the presiding critical view of his self-cultivated and ambitious career aspirations. Eagerly following (yet veering from) Faulkner's example shows Ellison himself trying to compensate for certain gaps in postwar American writing. Writing to, writing about, meeting, and collecting a lot of material on Faulkner enabled Ellison to have it both ways: he could model himself in part on a major white novelist while creating a prominent role for himself as a—or perhaps *the*—modern African American writer and public figure.

NOTES

1. Albert Murray, preface, *Trading Twelves: The Selected Letters of Ralph Ellison and Albert Murray*, by Ralph Ellison, ed. Albert Murray and John C. Callahan (New York: Modern Library, 2000), xxii.

2. Lawrence P. Jackson, *The Indignant Generation: A Narrative History of African American Writers and Critics, 1934–1960* (Princeton, NJ: Princeton University Press, 2011), 3.

3. For a more thorough discussion of Ellison's academic labor, see Joseph Fruscione, "From *Invisible Man* to Visible Professor: Ralph Ellison as Educator and Public Intellectual," *EAPSU Online: A Journal of Critical and Creative Work* 9 (2012), http://www.eapsu.net/eapsu-online-archive.html.

4. I am most concerned with the post-1952 Ellison who had jettisoned his early radicalism and leftism. For a persuasive view of his earlier radicalism and leftist writing, see Barbara Foley, *Wrestling with the Left: The Making of Ralph Ellison's* Invisible Man (Durham, NC: Duke University Press, 2010), as well as Lawrence P. Jackson, *Ralph Ellison: Emergence of Genius* (New York: Wiley, 2002).

5. Jackson, *Indignant Generation*, 360–61.

6. William Faulkner to Ralph Ellison, October 1, 1956. For all Faulkner-Ellison letters discussed here, see Correspondence I:47, Folder 8 (1956–57), Ralph Ellison Papers, Manuscript Division, Library of Congress, Washington, DC. Hereafter Ellison Papers, LC. I am grateful to Ellison's literary executor, John Callahan, for generous permission to quote from this letter and other archival material. Blotner's edition of Faulkner's correspondence reprints the October 1 letter. See William Faulkner, *Selected Letters of William Faulkner*, ed. Joseph Blotner (New York: Random House, 1977), 404.

7. William Faulkner to Ralph Ellison, January 2, 1957, Correspondence I:47, Folder 8 (1956–1957), Ellison Papers, LC.

8. Ralph Ellison to William Faulkner, February 22, 1957, Correspondence I:47, Folder 8 (1956–1957), Ellison Papers, LC.

9. See, for instance, Jay Parini, *One Matchless Time: A Life of William Faulkner* (New York: HarperCollins, 2004), 386–87.

10. Joseph Blotner, *Faulkner: A Biography* (New York: Vintage, 1991), 627. On the writer's public personae, see esp. James G. Watson, *William Faulkner: Self-Presentation and Performance* (Austin: University of Texas Press, 2000); Timothy Parrish, *Ralph Ellison and the Genius of America* (Amherst: University of Massachusetts Press, 2012); and Alan Nadel, "The Integrated Literary Tradition," in *The Historical Guide to Ralph Ellison*, ed. Steven Tracy (New York: Oxford University Press, 2004).

11. Ralph Ellison to Albert Murray, April 9, 1953, in Ellison, *Trading Twelves*, 44–45.

12. Ibid., 45. In their correspondence, Ellison and Murray used "Mose" to refer to a black trickster figure wearing a subservient mask.

13. Jackson, *Indignant Generation*, 3.

14. Ellison taught Faulkner's work at Bard and elsewhere; earlier in his career, he also retyped work by Faulkner, Hemingway, Malraux, and others as a means to improve his own style by (literally) rewriting theirs. See Arnold Rampersad, *Ralph Ellison: A Biography* (New York: Vintage, 2008), 109.

15. Ralph Ellison, "Stephen Crane and the Mainstream of American Fiction," in *The Collected Essays of Ralph Ellison*, ed. John Callahan (New York: Random House, 1995), 127.

16. Ellison's unfinished novel, published first as *Juneteenth* (1999) and then unexpurgated as *Three Days before the Shooting . . .* (2010), echoes *Absalom, Absalom!*, "The Bear," and *Light in August* stylistically and thematically.

17. Ralph Ellison, "The World and the Jug," in *Collected Essays*, 185.

18. Jackson, *Indignant Generation*, 429.

19. Ralph Ellison, "Brave Words for a Startling Occasion," in *Collected Essays*, 152–53.

20. Ralph Ellison, "The Shadow and the Act," in *Collected Essays*, 303.

21. Ibid., 302.

22. Ibid.

23. Jackson, *Indignant Generation*, 429.

24. Ibid., 356.

25. Writings II:43, Folder 4, Ellison Papers, LC. This notion of Faulkner's black characters being human in part because of "failures" echoes Ellison's praise of Twain's handling of Jim in *Adventures of Huckleberry Finn*. See Ellison, *Collected Essays*, 82.

26. Writings II:43, Folder 4, Ellison Papers, LC.

27. Ibid.

28. Several scholars have written convincingly on the Ellison-Wright relationship, particularly Ellison's later downplaying of Wright's influence and support. See Joseph Skerrett, "The Wright Interpretation: Ralph Ellison and the Anxiety of Influence," in *Speaking for You: The Vision of Ralph Ellison*, ed. Kimberly Benston (Washington, DC: Howard University Press, 1990), 217–30. Jackson (*Ralph Ellison*), Rampersad, and Foley also discuss Ellison's handling of Wright thoroughly.

29. Writings II:43, Folder 4, Ellison Papers, LC.

30. Cf. Ellison to Harry Ford, January 1957, quoted in Rampersad, *Ralph Ellison*, 324.

31. Late in the article, Faulkner calls for "decency, dignity, moral and social responsibility," in a way echoing Ellison's *Invisible Man* with the "social responsibility" phrase. See William Faulkner, *Essays, Speeches, and Public Letters*, ed. James B. Meriwether (New York: Random House, 1965), 110. The essay was originally published as "If I Were a Negro" in the September 1956 issue of *Ebony* magazine (70–73). In the "Battle Royal" chapter of *Invisible Man*, the narrator is made to repeat his call for "social responsibility" by a drunken, racist audience.

32. Writings II:43, Folder 4, Ellison Papers, LC.

33. Ralph Ellison, "Twentieth-Century Fiction and the Black Mask of Humanity," in his *Collected Essays*, 97.

34. Writings II:43, Folder 4, Ellison Papers, LC. As this note indicates, Ellison had initially ended his list with *The Unvanquished* but crossed it out in favor of *Light in August*—an expected choice, given the latter text's deeper engagement with race.

35. Writings II:43, Folder 4, Ellison Papers, LC. For dating this letter from 1950, see Rampersad, *Ralph Ellison*, 248–49.

36. See Reference File I:185, Folders 4, 5, 6, Ellison Papers, LC.

37. For an image and fuller discussion of this text, see Joseph Fruscione, "Hail Faulkner?: *A Fable*, Competitive Modernism, and 'The Nobelist' in the 1950s," in *Fifty Years after Faulkner: Faulkner and Yoknapatawpha, 2012*, ed. Jay Watson and Ann J. Abadie (University Press of Mississippi, forthcoming).

38. Rampersad, *Ralph Ellison*, 551.

39. See Adam Bradley, *Ralph Ellison in Progress: From* Invisible Man *to* Three Days before the Shooting . . . (New Haven, CT: Yale University Press, 2010), and John C. Callahan and Adam Bradley, eds., *Three Days before the Shooting* . . . (New York: Random House, 2010) for a fuller view of Ellison's arduous labor on his never-completed second novel.

40. According to Jackson in *The Indignant Generation*, after *Invisible Man* "Ellison had an impossible time convincing fellow black writers of his political credentials, and he never stood as an impressive figure for the artists of the 1950s who invested heavily in heroic characterizations of black freedom fighters and describing political problems" (359).

41. Writings II:43, Folder 4, Ellison Papers, LC.

42. Ibid.

43. Ellison, "Twentieth-Century Fiction," 89.

Dangerous Quests: Transgressive Sexualities in William Faulkner's "The Wild Palms" and James Baldwin's *Another Country*

BEN ROBBINS

In Baldwin's "Autobiographical Notes," which prefaces his first essay collection from 1955, *Notes of a Native Son*, the author credits Faulkner as being one among a handful of writers who have begun to grapple with the question of black identity in America contextually, this "context being the history, traditions, customs, the moral assumptions and preoccupations of the country."[1] Baldwin names Faulkner alongside Robert Penn Warren and—most significantly for him among newly emerging writers—Ralph Ellison as the key literary figures making progress in this regard. Baldwin praises Faulkner for providing his generation of writers with a base from which it is possible to write about race in a way that encompasses its multiple contexts within American life and society. Revealing here is that Baldwin does not situate himself within a black writers' tradition, a northern black man instead seeing himself as the successor (along with Ellison) to two white southern writers. This demonstrates that the writer is a mobile subject, free to identify imaginatively across racial (and geographic) lines, gathering from the breadth of American literary tradition autonomously.[2] It is also a rhetorical gesture on Baldwin's part as we see him sidestepping his possible categorization as a successor to another Mississippi writer from Faulkner's generation, Richard Wright; as such, Baldwin refutes the essentialist notion of a black succession of literary heirs.

However, Baldwin's sense of debt to Faulkner does not preclude points of conflict in the literary relationship. In his essay "Faulkner and Desegregation," published in 1956, Baldwin attacks Faulkner's statement that the process of racial integration in the South should "go slow." Baldwin opens the essay with a challenge:

Any real change implies the breakup of the world as one has always known it, the loss of all that gave one an identity, the end of safety. And at such a moment, unable to see and not daring to imagine what the future will now bring forth, one clings to what one knew, or thought one knew; to what one possessed or dreamed that one possessed. Yet, it is only when a man is able, without bitterness or self-pity, to surrender a dream he has long cherished or a privilege he has long possessed that he is set free.[3]

Baldwin argues here that there are two possible responses to the dangerous processes of social reorganization—resistance and surrender—but only through the latter is one liberated. The passage reveals Baldwin's frustrations with Faulkner on the level of the social but also by implication on the level of the literary. Elsewhere, Baldwin credits Faulkner with the progressive—even courageous—exploration of race in his art through characters who wrangle with categories of identity; he comments in his 1972 memoir-cum-essay collection, *No Name in the Street*, that Faulkner's black characters are infused with "the torment of their creator."[4] In "Faulkner and Desegregation," though, Baldwin expresses his anger that Faulkner fails to carry that work into his public statements on race, clinging instead to retrograde demarcations. Faulkner appears across Baldwin's essays as a split self—alternately progressive and backward, forward-thinking and restrictively traditional, his voice vacillating between the private realm of literature and the public realm as self-appointed spokesman for the national consciousness. When Baldwin accuses Faulkner of lacking courage, he successfully highlights how Faulkner's novels explore forms of social change and development that the same author publically advocates retreating from.

I am conscious that this may seem like a one-sided verbal exchange between Baldwin and Faulkner. Aside from Baldwin's prominence as a public intellectual in the late 1950s, Faulkner would likely have been aware of Baldwin's "Faulkner and Desegregation" essay, which appeared in *Partisan Review* in the fall of 1956. The journal was influential from the late 1930s to the early 1960s, a period during which it served as home to some of Faulkner's fellow modernists, publishing two of T. S. Eliot's *Four Quartets* (1943) and Clement Greenberg's high-profile essay on the cultural divide, "Avant-Garde and Kitsch" (1939). Faulkner also had a copy of Baldwin's debut semiautobiographical novel, *Go Tell It on the Mountain* (1953), in his library at Rowan Oak.[5] Faulkner's was a first-edition copy, which raises the tantalizing possibility that he had read the novel by the time "Faulkner and Desegregation" was published in 1956.

It is within Faulkner's fiction that the older author lives up to Baldwin's charge to face "the loss of all that gave one an identity, an end of safety." In the two novels I will consider, Faulkner's *If I Forget Thee, Jerusalem* (1939) and Baldwin's *Another Country* (1962), both authors use sex and sexuality as the tool that motivates and effects this loss of stable selfhood in the formation of a new social order. Baldwin has been recognized as an important writer on issues of race and sexuality in the twentieth century, but critics have approached these two areas of study separately until relatively recently. Dwight A. McBride, in his introduction to a collection of essays on the author, *James Baldwin Now* (1999), charges that scholarship has tended to relegate Baldwin to one or the other of the identity categories to which he can be said to belong, but that at the beginning of the twenty-first century, it is time for reassessment, since with the insights afforded by cultural studies models of analysis, we need not locate Baldwin as "exclusively gay, black, expatriate, activist, or the like but as an intricately negotiated amalgam of all of those things, which had to be constantly tailored to fit the circumstances in which he was compelled to articulate himself."[6]

The ability of Baldwin's work to transcend borders of race, gender, and sexuality is a crucial aspect of his ideological project that I am keen to demonstrate as a point of common ground with Faulkner. Both authors utilize transgressive sex, in which alternative, challenging modes of sexuality disregard normative sociosexual practices to question—and even destroy—preexisting social boundaries. Baldwin's novel, *Another Country*, is set in New York in the late 1950s and focuses principally on a group of Greenwich Village and Harlem bohemians: musicians, artists, actors, and writers among them. It radically addresses many sexual taboos of the time: homosexuality and bisexuality, interracial couples, and extramarital affairs. Baldwin himself moved to the Village in 1944, initially staying with his artist friend Beauford Delaney, who introduced him to the art world, along with blues and jazz, new genres of music to him at the time. The novel studiously imagines all its central male characters within equivalent and plural erotic configurations, as the three principal protagonists all engage in both homosexual and heterosexual sexual affairs with both black and white partners, creating a complex web of transgressive alliances. These couplings critique the American ideal of sexuality that, for Baldwin, has created absurdly fixed polarities, leaving us with "cowboys and Indians, good guys and bad guys, punks and studs, tough guys and softies, butch and faggot, black and white," as he writes in his essay "Freaks and the American Ideal of Manhood," first published in *Playboy* magazine in 1985.[7]

To combat this, Baldwin gives us a vision of New York through the eyes of a mobile subject in search of sexual adventure. This motion is not simply a joyous surrender to new erotic possibilities, though; it is an often-painful flight from prescribed and imprisoning social identities. During the composition of *Another Country*, Baldwin himself was also engaged in a period of intense mobility; during the time he worked on the novel, between 1956 and 1961, he crossed the Atlantic by sea at least six times, traveling extensively within both Europe and North America. The novel was consequently written during the most transatlantic period in Baldwin's career up to that point. Baldwin had initially moved to Europe in 1948, urgently feeling the need to leave America in order to transcend the fatal social role he felt was thrust upon him as a black man in postwar New York; he felt he would have ultimately killed himself had he remained in the city, as his friend Eugene Worth did in the winter of 1946 by jumping from the George Washington Bridge.[8]

The pressures of the American metropolis that spurred Baldwin's restless movements are reflected in *Another Country*. We are presented with different phases of Baldwin's life story through two characters: a black jazz musician, Rufus, who stays in New York but is ultimately driven mad by the city and commits suicide, and Eric, a white gay southerner and actor, who leaves New York for Paris. Baldwin places these two characters in a sexual relationship before Rufus's suicide and Eric's journey to Europe, which results in a violent clash between alternate versions of the author. Eric senses that Rufus despises him as a southerner and has had sex with him to explore that hatred; comprehending this, Eric flees to Europe.[9] The consequences of their sexual relationship reveal how high the stakes are in the erotic landscape of Baldwin's novel: sex can be the catalyst for self-destruction or self-imposed exile. James A. Dievler demonstrates how Baldwin uses sex as a means to escape narrow identity categories in the sexual culture of the American postwar period, arguing that Baldwin is "advocating a postcategorical, poststructural concept of sexuality that we might call 'postsexuality.'"[10] He goes on to argue that Baldwin's emigration from America was necessary for his characters to express their own sense of being exiled, and as such the author prescribes this state "as an almost necessary way of coming to terms with an exclusive culture."[11] While I similarly explore the link between sex and motion in *Another Country*, I see exile as but one form of generative motion the novel explores. Particularly in the character of Eric, we see the threat of total disconnection from one's native culture that might result from exile; when Eric is offered a role in a Broadway play while still in France he faces a dilemma as he realizes that "to accept it was to bring his European sojourn to an end; not to accept it was to transform his sojourn into exile" (184). Eric does return to New York to take up the role, ultimately seeing exile as a poor solution to his troubled relationship with the country of his birth. Baldwin came to the same decision in 1957 when he returned to the United States to witness the growth of the civil rights movement firsthand. Baldwin's characters actively fight against disconnection and an attendant erosion of resistance by seeking points of contact with the Other. My focus is on productive and dangerous acts of transgression that critique the way power polices the boundaries of social division. Such acts find multiple avenues of expression, most prominently, for Baldwin and Faulkner, in sex and art.

Between the extreme options of death or exile, Baldwin, in an attempt to explode social demarcations, drives the novel's bohemian crowd frenetically between zones of the city in pursuit of sexual adventure: white men seek adventures with black women uptown and black men with white women downtown. This reflects the way geographic space can become racialized in Faulkner's work; in *Light in August* (1932), for example, Joe Christmas journeys north to become black, leaving his southern white upbringing behind him.[12] Baldwin explores the motivation of eroticized movement through the character of the young artist and working-class Italian American, Vivaldo—himself an admirer of Faulkner's craft and work ethic —who makes frequent journeys to Harlem to sleep with prostitutes:

> For several years it had been his fancy that he belonged in those dark streets uptown precisely because the history written in the color of his skin contested his right to be there. He enjoyed this, his right to *be* being everywhere contested; uptown, his alienation had been made visible, and therefore, almost bearable. It had been his fancy that danger, there, was more real, more open, than danger was downtown and he, having chosen to run these dangers, was snatching his manhood from the lukewarm waters of mediocrity and testing it in the fire. He had felt more alive in Harlem, for he had moved in a blaze of rage and self-congratulation and sexual excitement, with danger, like a promise, waiting for him everywhere. . . . His dangerous, overwhelming lust for life had failed to involve him in anything deeper than perhaps half a dozen extremely casual acquaintanceships in about as many bars. (135)

This passage demonstrates the manner in which characters seek out experiences loaded with perceived deviance. The sexual danger that Vivaldo explores in Harlem is double-edged: he relishes how his otherness in uptown New York contests his sense of belonging anywhere in the city as a stable subject, but his casual sexual encounters there are essentially superficial since the risks involved are low. Though charged with adventure, they are a mask for the deeper reorganization of self that is necessary; Vivaldo avoids confronting the "clash and tension of the adventure proceeding inexorably within" by "taking refuge in the outward adventure" (136), a subject adrift in the sexual territories of the modern metropolis. Baldwin makes us aware that a deeper engagement with the perceived Other and the geographical space in which one encounters otherness is required for personal and social progress.

On a similarly double-edged quest are the two central lovers of "The Wild Palms" sections of *If I Forget Thee, Jerusalem*. Faulkner once stated that Harry Wilbourne and Charlotte Rittenmeyer are looking in the novel "to escape from the world."[13] This need for escape takes them from New Orleans to Chicago, to a cabin in the Wisconsin woods, to a mining camp in Utah, on to Texas, back to New Orleans, and finally to the Gulf Coast. It is a utopian journey as the lovers attempt to craft an idealized union seemingly incommensurate with the world around them (and also wholly outside Yoknapatawpha). In the novel, the lovers' flight is presented as a joint attempt to liberate themselves from bourgeois constraints in New Orleans: Charlotte from her husband and children, Harry from his training to become a doctor. Charlotte's desire to escape from the orthodox configuration of the nuclear family is also a desire for constant motion in the pursuit of sexual intensity:

> [Charlotte] grasped [Harry's] hair again, hurting him again though now he knew she knew she was hurting him. "Listen: it's got to be all honeymoon, always. Forever and ever, until one of us dies. It cant be anything else. Either heaven, or hell: no comfortable safe peaceful purgatory between for you and me to wait in until good behavior or forbearance or shame or repentance overtakes us."[14]

Charlotte wants to put distance between herself and what she perceives as the static "purgatory" of marriage, the family unit, and the attendant framework of erotic inertia and control. She replaces these qualities with a new mode of sexual dialogue with Harry—hard, spontaneous, frank, and unchecked—which is the initial motor for their quest. Flight in both novels then is initially sexually motivated, as characters like Vivaldo and Charlotte seek a more productive, creative relationship to the Other, and to themselves, through erotic journeys fueled by a sense of transgressive (and potentially fatal) danger. Their attempts to forge alternative, challenging modes of sexuality result in flux and flight within and away from the inhospitable metropolis: New York for Baldwin, New Orleans and Chicago for Faulkner.

It is in this mobile state that these characters hope to fashion a new social identity through transgression against limiting demarcations of gender and race. Both Faulkner and Baldwin explore fears connected to this mode of being, but realize somewhat different conclusions. Baldwin shows how racial and gender antagonism can be confronted by engaging personally and intimately with all its points of contact, even when this inspires anxiety. In *Another Country*, Vivaldo enters into a deep and painful relationship with Ida, a black woman from Harlem, an affair far more challenging than any of his previous "casual acquaintanceships" in that part of the city. Baldwin is frank about the destructive emotions this interracial union provokes in both lovers: fear in Vivaldo and anger in Ida. Late into the novel, after his long affair with Ida, Vivaldo experiences an epiphany. The insight he gains into how far he has come from his days of running Harlem is provoked by his superficial assessment of the sexual availability of a blonde woman in the bar in which he is sitting: "Something in him was breaking; he was, briefly and horribly, in a region where there were no definitions of any kind, neither of color, nor of male and female. There was only the leap and the rending and the terror and the surrender" (297).

Vivaldo has shifted into another territory beyond unchallenging promiscuity, a space without clear sexual polarities. Ida struggles to separate her generalizations about white people from the particular reality of her love for Vivaldo, illustrated when she confesses that "if any *one* white person gets through to you, it kind of destroys your—single-mindedness. They say that love and hate are very close together. Well, that's a fact. . . . Wouldn't you hate all white people if they kept you in prison here?" (343–44) Through these lovers' difficulties in reconciling themselves to one another, Baldwin seeks to show how profound sexual engagement manifests, beyond mere sexual pleasure and the pursuit of orgasm, all of what he calls "the terrors of life and love" in his 1961 essay, "The Black Boy Looks at the White Boy."[15]

In "The Wild Palms," Charlotte's erotic life is spontaneous, unaffected, and productively linked to her creativity as an artist, but her androgyny and unselfconscious sexual desires result in her lover Harry's fear that he will be emasculated and engulfed by her. John Duvall names this dynamic a "counterhegemonic alliance" in which male dominance is subverted through its occupation of a passive position to the female.[16] Harry is a virgin when he enters the relationship with Charlotte, and he fears that her strength and relative sexual experience will unman him; he jokes, among many similar expressions, that Charlotte's courage makes her "a better man than I am" (586). The quip masks Harry's deeper anxiety about his disempowerment as a man within a union in which gendered roles have been subjected to flux. Metropolitan Chicago transforms under Harry's gaze into a feminine territory that threatens to consume him. In a Chicago department store in which Charlotte temporarily works, he observes a nightmare of "charwomen [who] appeared on their knees and pushing pails before them as though they were another species just crawled molelike from some tunnel or orifice leading from the foundations of the earth itself" (577). This image is part of the novel's critique of commerce and wage labor, in which, as Richard Godden argues, "Man appears just as an instrument of passage for the circulation of commodities," a world which the fugitive lovers attempt to escape in search of authentic experience.[17] However, Harry's view of commodity culture is clearly aligned with his sexual fears, what Anne Goodwyn Jones calls the novel's "patriarchal oxymoron" of masculine anxiety: Harry may place the twin specters of the feminine and commercial culture in a position of alterity, but the fear that accompanies this gesture undermines his relative position of patriarchal mastery.[18] In accord with his vision of the department store, Harry later describes his loss of virginity to Charlotte as the moment when you "feel all your life rush out of you into the pervading immemorial blind receptive matrix, the hot fluid blind foundation—grave-womb or womb-grave, it's all one" (589). Harry views the commercial metropolis through the same frame as his disproportionate and melodramatic response to a sexual act. The Chicago department store is conversely a world in which Charlotte feels at comparative ease; it is the market for her art objects, which she produces with an erotic charge. It would appear that Faulkner therefore wishes us to view Harry's emotional state critically as a consequence of his character's inability to manage his sexual relation to Charlotte productively. Where Charlotte's flight seems motivated by a search for increased sexual dynamism, Harry appears to run from the sight of his exaggerated fears. As such, Harry sabotages any possibility of purging the gender antagonism between them.

The aspect of the lovers' experience in "The Wild Palms" with which Faulkner most explicitly sympathizes is Charlotte's vital engagement with her art as an expression of sexual freedom. Charlotte produces a series of small, marionette-like sculptures that playfully depict compromised mock-heroic figures. Her work exhibits a deft blending of high and low imagery as she traverses categories of cultural distinction in a wild medley of visual referents not too dissimilar from the allusive practice of a high modernist work like *The Waste Land*:

> a Quixote with a gaunt mad dreamy uncoordinated face, a Falstaff with the worn face of a syphilitic barber and gross with meat (a single figure, yet when [Harry] looked at it he seemed to see two: the man and the gross flesh like a huge bear and its fragile consumptive keeper . . .), Roxane with spit curls and a wad of gum like the sheet music demonstrator in a ten cent store, Cyrano with the face of a low-comedy Jew in vaudeville. (556–57)

Charlotte ambitiously references the Spanish, English, and French literary canons in her work, producing a cubist Quixote, a Falstaff that evokes the popular entertainment form of the bear fight, a commercially framed Roxane and a vaudevillian Cyrano de Bergerac. The troubling racism of this last image can perhaps be explained by the influences Charlotte gathers into her practice. Her ailing Falstaff alludes to Harry's first job in Chicago as a laboratory assistant in a charity hospital "making routine tests for syphilis" (552). The anti-Semitism of her Cyrano may also have been gleaned from Harry's own racist comments about his patients' sexual health: he claims that he doesn't need a microscope or any other medical method to diagnose them, because "all you need is enough light to tell what race they belong to" (552). It should also be noted that our view of Charlotte's art is mainly focalized through Harry's consciousness, so he may bring his own xenophobic interpretations to bear on her work. Her high-low fusions do not signal dumbing down but rather her mastery of a breadth of seemingly antagonistic influences. Charlotte's art insistently flattens out and reformulates high/low distinctions, a divide frequently coded along gender lines, as argued most influentially by Andreas Huyssen, who demonstrates how mass culture has been insistently gendered as female within patriarchal structures, associated with the rise of first-wave feminism's mass movements, which challenged and threatened male-dominated culture.[19] Working through Huyssen's ideas in relation to Faulkner's fiction, Jones sees Charlotte as an exception to Faulkner's codification elsewhere in his work of popular culture as a promiscuous and threatening woman because Charlotte maintains her sexual autonomy and integrity within a novel that broods on modes of cultural distinction.[20] Additionally, though, for a female artist whose integrity in the face of the market is continually questioned to produce such artful modernist objects shows how a woman can transcend prescribed positions within cultural practice and shatter oppositions within hierarchies of cultural taste.

Another Country also shows how art has the potential to transcend cultural boundaries. Ida performs in a jazz bar in the East Village, which attracts an "unorthodox" (244) and racially diverse downtown crowd. Vivaldo worries about the power dynamic of "rank and color and authority" within which his role as audience member positions him in relation to the black jazz musicians (249). As if to counter Vivaldo's consciousness of hierarchical relations, Baldwin describes Ida's voice as having a quality that "involves a sense of the self so profound and so powerful that it does not so much leap barriers as reduce them to atoms . . . it transforms and lays waste and gives life, and kills" (250). Ida's voice violently overcomes the racial and class divisions of the audience as she merges with the audience's collective identity by generating affect and emotional identification. I should acknowledge here that Harry's melodramatic "voice" is also an affective mode designed to generate emotional identification. But Harry's overwrought emotional register distances him from the communities of the novel and alienates the reader; we anxiously watch Harry turn material realities into threatening spectacles resulting in crippling states of mind, an imaginative journey we may recognize but on which we do not wish to accompany him. The important factor is the "sense of self" that Ida's voice retains; by powerfully asserting themselves through their art, characters such as Ida and Charlotte are able to shatter cultural boundaries that divide along lines of gender and race.

Vivaldo and Ida's relationship concludes in the narrative with a moment of intense physical identification in which the boundaries of the body are exploded: "His heart began to beat with a newer, stonier anguish, which destroyed the distance called pity and placed him, very nearly, in her body, beside that table on the dirty floor. . . . He went to her, resigned and tender and helpless, her sobs seeming to make his belly sore" (416). Vivaldo shares Ida's physical and emotional pain and almost enters her body through the experience in a form of profound intimacy that is more metaphysical than sexual. This moment occurs simultaneous to Vivaldo's experience of intense feelings of anger, fear, and shame, stemming from Ida's confession that she has been having an affair with her manager. The experience as a whole, however, has a transformative effect on Vivaldo, leading him first to a moment of intense creative insight when a much-sought-after detail for his novel falls "neatly and vividly, like the tumblers of a lock, into place in his mind . . . [which] illuminated, justified, clarified everything" (417). In addition, he experiences a calm postracial epiphany, now perceiving that "not many things in the world were really black, not even the night. . . . And the light was not white, either, even the palest light held within itself some hint of its origins, in fire" (419–20). Finally, when Vivaldo weeps and Ida comforts him near the end of the passage, the text states that "she was stroking his innocence out of him" (420) as he realizes a new maturity. Collectively, these developments point to a remolding of Vivaldo's consciousness.

While their relationship is left unresolved in its enduring tension between the liberatory and the traumatic, Baldwin sees the productive potential of the transmutative processes of transgressive sex. Baldwin elsewhere writes of the central gay couple in the novel, Eric and Yves, that "each was, for the other, the dwelling place that each had despaired of finding" (184). Though more anguished in nature, Vivaldo and Ida experience a similar realization, moving toward inhabiting one another's bodies as they exit from the novel. It becomes apparent that the other "country" Baldwin alludes to in the novel's title is not geographical but corporeal—the body of a lover with whom one has transgressed against social constraints. For Baldwin, one can find a home in the other through a painful, yet ultimately necessary, explosion of the boundaries of the self. Such a process reveals Baldwin's fierce advocacy of utopian discoveries of identity in new, nonnormative, or taboo forms of sexual practice. The utopian effect is of course slippery as it expresses an imaginative investment in a perfect place or state of mind that may not actually exist. The impalpable nature of social utopia achieved through sex is reflected in the unintelligibility of Baldwin's prose; it is an "unnameable heat and tension . . . as close to hatred as it [is] to love" (420) that Vivaldo and Ida share in their final dramatic scene in the novel. Utopia gestures beyond the real; as Karl Mannheim argues, the utopian "state of mind" is "incongruous with the state of reality within which it occurs," and as such, in its orientation it aims to transcend reality.[21] Additionally, when such utopian orientations "pass over into conduct, [they] tend to shatter, either partially or wholly, the order of things prevailing at the time."[22] We recognize Baldwin looking toward what may lie beyond the borders of the individual body with a utopian mindset but finding it difficult to fully locate that idealized space of collective identity in the imagination as it transcends the real. Baldwin nevertheless forcefully asserts that attempting to locate such a space is of great social importance. As he argues at the close of his essay "Down at the Cross," an important milestone in the author's increasingly active and vocal engagement with the civil rights movement published just five months after *Another Country* in November 1962,

> If we—and now I mean the relatively conscious whites and the relatively conscious blacks, who must, *like lovers*, insist on, or create, the consciousness of the others—do not falter in our duty now, we may be able, handful that we are, to end the racial nightmare, and achieve our country, and change the history of the world.[23]

Vivaldo senses that he is "very nearly" in Ida's body, tantalizingly close, yet still at some indecipherable degree of remove. This nevertheless represents a necessary step within Baldwin's utopian vision: merging consciousness with the racial Other with whom one engages as a lover.

This ultimate dissolution of self is one that Faulkner's characters do not realize. Where Baldwin gives us a final metaphysical merging of identities, at the close of "The Wild Palms," Harry's distance from Charlotte's body is emphasized. After Charlotte's death by the botched abortion she demands that Harry perform on her, Harry is imprisoned. His state at the conclusion of the novel demonstrates his resistance to some

of the more drastic courses of action that Baldwin's characters pursue.
First, he refuses flight from America when Rittenmeyer, Charlotte's husband, offers him money to jump bail and run to Mexico or some other
faraway destination. Second, he rejects suicide as a way to end the pain
of his incarceration, taking the cyanide tablet Rittenmeyer gives him
after he rejects the money and crushing it against the bars of his cell window. Though Harry does thereby manage to refuse those paths of escape
that eradicate or defer fully confronting the self's relationship to a hostile
world in which social and sexual identity threaten to become warped, his
rejection of suicide or flight does not strike the reader as noble in the
same way as does Vivaldo and Ida's ongoing struggle with their identities and relation. In the end, Harry pays homage to a mere phantom,
his imagination resurrecting the memory of Charlotte, "remembering,
the body, the broad thighs and the hands that liked bitching and making things" (715). From his cell on the Gulf Coast, Harry attempts to
reanimate the sensual charge of Charlotte's body by masturbating. Harry
wishes to engage in erotically motivated productive grief, but the gesture
does not compensate for the fear that he had of Charlotte as a sexual
subject while she was alive. Harry idealization of the vitality of Charlotte's body and her creativity arrives too late to signal progression.

One may account historically for this discrepancy between the
two writers' visions of the social potential of aberrant sexual culture.
Faulkner wrote "The Wild Palms" in the late 1930s, at a time when the
gender and sexual revolutions of the 1920s had been curtailed by the
Great Depression. As John D'Emilio and Estelle B. Freedman argue,
although American society was moving toward sexual liberalism in the
1920s, during the Depression "the consumerism and commercialized
amusements that gave play to sexual adventure temporarily withered.
Sobriety and gloom replaced the buoyant exuberance of the previous
decade."[24] In a potentially ironic hangover from the Roaring Twenties,
Chicago, one of the cultural hubs of that excessive decade, proves in
the text to be particularly inhospitable to Harry and Charlotte's sexual
desires in the 1930s. Baldwin, however, published *Another Country* at
the dawn of the sexual revolution of the 1960s. This potentially allowed
him to see more clearly how the transgressive register of his fiction could
effect tangible social change in the near future, hence his relative opti-
mism. At the close of "Faulkner and Desegregation," Baldwin advocates
an urgent casting off of the constraints that society places on the individual, challenging the public Faulkner of the 1950s that "there is never
time in the future in which we will work out our salvation. The challenge
is in the moment, the time is always now."[25] Faulkner was able to channel
this spirit of urgency into the potentially fruitful, and socially disruptive,

erotic wanderings of Harry and Charlotte in "The Wild Palms," but it took Baldwin to visualize some two decades later what transcendent outcome such a traumatic sexual quest might produce.

NOTES

1. James Baldwin, "Autobiographical Notes," in his *Collected Essays* (New York: Library of America, 1998), 9.

2. Such identification with Faulkner is, however, not without its dangers. Baldwin later wrote in *No Name in the Street* (1972) that Faulkner's situation as a canonical author within the white patriarchal tradition of history renders his work problematic for the black subject. Baldwin advocates the discovery of an autonomous black identity unshackled from white history, a move that for the black writer may entail a new relationship to his own influences, potentially resulting in a temporary rejection of Faulkner (Baldwin, *Collected Essays*, 380–82).

3. James Baldwin, "Faulkner and Desegregation," in his *Collected Essays* (New York: Library of America, 1998), 209.

4. James Baldwin, *No Name in the Street*, in his *Collected Essays* (New York: Library of America, 1998), 381.

5. Joseph Blotner, *William Faulkner's Library: A Catalogue* (Charlottesville: University Press of Virginia, 1964), 16.

6. Dwight A. McBride, introduction to *James Baldwin Now*, ed. Dwight A. McBride (New York: New York University Press, 1999), 2. In addition to this collection of essays, D. Quentin Miller, ed., *Re-Viewing James Baldwin: Things Not Seen* (Philadelphia: Temple University Press, 2000), and Douglas Field, ed., *A Historical Guide to James Baldwin* (Oxford: Oxford University Press, 2009), have done much to foster critical engagement with Baldwin's work from the perspective of both race and sexuality.

7. James Baldwin, "Freaks and the American Ideal of Manhood," in his *Collected Essays* (New York: Library of America, 1998), 815.

8. Jordan Elgraby, "James Baldwin, The Art of Fiction No. 78," *Paris Review* 91 (Spring 1984), http://www.theparisreview.org/interviews/2994/the-art-of-fiction-no-78-james-baldwin.

9. James Baldwin, *Another Country* (1962; repr., London: Penguin, 2001), 53. Subsequent references to this edition will appear parenthetically in the text.

10. James A. Dievler, "Sexual Exiles: James Baldwin and *Another Country*," in *James Baldwin Now*, ed. Dwight A. McBride (New York: New York University Press, 1999), 163.

11. Ibid., 168.

12. William Faulkner, *Light in August*, in *Novels 1930–1935*, ed. Joseph Blotner and Noel Polk (New York: Library of America, 1985), 564–65.

13. Frederick L. Gwynn and Joseph L. Blotner, eds., *Faulkner in the University* (Charlottesville: University of Virginia Press, 1995), 178.

14. William Faulkner, *If I Forget Thee, Jerusalem*, in *Novels 1936–1940* (New York: Library of America, 1990), 551. Subsequent references to this edition will appear parenthetically in the text.

15. James Baldwin, "The Black Boy Looks at the White Boy," in *Collected Essays* (New York: Library of America, 1998), 277.

16. John N. Duvall, *Faulkner's Marginal Couple: Invisible, Outlaw, and Unspeakable Communities* (Austin: University of Texas Press, 1990), xiv.

17. Richard Godden, *Fictions of Labor: William Faulkner and the South's Long Revolution* (Cambridge: Cambridge University Press, 2007), 203.

18. Anne Goodwyn Jones, "'The Kotex Age': Women, Popular Culture, and *The Wild Palms*," in *Faulkner and Popular Culture: Faulkner and Yoknapatawpha, 1988*, ed. Doreen Fowler and Ann J. Abadie (Jackson: University Press of Mississippi, 1990), 146.

19. Andreas Huyssen, *After the Great Divide: Modernism, Mass Culture, Postmodernism* (Bloomington: Indiana University Press, 1986), 47.

20. Jones, "'Kotex Age,'" 145.

21. Karl Mannheim, *Ideology and Utopia: An Introduction to the Sociology of Knowledge* (1929), trans. Louis Wirth and Edward Shils (1936; repr., London: Routledge and Kegan Paul, 1949), 173.

22. Ibid.

23. James Baldwin, "Down at the Cross," in his *Collected Essays* (New York: Library of America, 1998), 346–47; emphasis added.

24. John D'Emilio and Estelle B. Freedman, *Intimate Matters: A History of Sexuality in America* (New York: Harper & Row, 1988), 241–42.

25. Baldwin, "Faulkner and Desegregation," 214.

From Yoknapatawpha County to St. Raphael Parish: Faulknerian Influence on the Works of Ernest J. Gaines

John Wharton Lowe

*Faulkner's oeuvre will be complete when it is revisited and made
vital by African Americans. Already this process has begun, Toni
Morrison being perhaps the first to do what I am trying to do here.*
                                                         —Édouard Glissant

When Édouard Glissant wrote these words in the 1990s,[1] he was offering his impression of trips he made to Faulkner's Mississippi and of his experience, as a black man from the Caribbean, of reading the great but often problematic works that that space and culture produced. He was right to claim the centrality of Morrison's work to any new understanding of Faulkner. Indeed, Morrison herself had already stated that "Faulkner wrote what I suppose could be called regional literature and had it published all over the world. It is good—and universal—because it is specifically about a particular world. That's what I wish to do."[2] However, even earlier, Ernest Gaines's novels, which were strongly influenced by Faulkner, had done this kind of work.

Gaines calls Louisiana his "back yard": "Joyce couldn't write about anything but Dublin or Faulkner about anything but Mississippi. . . . I'm still too close to Louisiana to write about anything else."[3] We might note the affinity here of the "back yard" to the space his characters inhabit in the plantation quarters, so akin to the public square. All of Gaines's work is set in the fictional parish of St. Raphael, just as most of Faulkner's is set in Yoknapatawpha County, and there are names, characters, and types that repeat from time to time in the respective works of both artists. Although I am unable to go into this in detail here, each writer's assembled books speak in a kind of dialogue with each other, creating an intertextuality that one finds in few other writers.

Ernest Gaines was born on Martin Luther King's fourth birthday, January 15, 1933, in Cherie Quarters, River Lake Plantation, near New Roads, Louisiana. His family had farmed the land for generations, and the family's life in the thirties and forties was not dissimilar to that of their enslaved ancestors. Gaines had to go into the fields as a child, and there was no black high school near him. His mother and stepfather escaped to a better life in California, leaving him and his siblings in the care of his Aunt Augusteen; although she was unable to walk, she gardened, cooked, disciplined the children, and occupied a central role in the community. A famous storyteller, she attracted people to her porch, where they exchanged jokes and tales before a rapt young Ernest, who echoed in this regard Zora Neale Hurston, who absorbed folk culture on the porch of Joe Clarke's store in Eatonville, Florida.

Fortuitously, Gaines's parents sent for him, and he was educated in a multicultural California; after serving in the army he attended San Francisco State University and then Stanford, where he studied with Wallace Stegner. Failing to create satisfying narratives set in California, Gaines became determined to write about Louisiana. He struggled for years to make ends meet, but as with Faulkner, his early novels and stories brought in little income. He hit pay dirt in 1971, however, when his third novel, *The Autobiography of Miss Jane Pittman*, was published to great acclaim and then made into an award-winning movie starring Cicely Tyson.

For years Gaines alternated between California and Louisiana, where he taught at the University of Southwestern Louisiana in Lafayette, but after he met and married Dianne Saulney, they built a lovely home on land purchased from his native plantation, just across the road from False River. In 2013 he received the National Medal of Arts from President Obama at the White House.

Gaines built his texts on the rich foundation of the oral black culture of Louisiana, which has always inspired and sustained him, particularly during his years of exile in California. Yet his academic training as a writer did not place him in contact with key African American writers, who at that time had not been "rediscovered." Although he had read Ralph Ellison, he was, and is, skeptical of that writer's perceptions of black southern culture. His chief literary influences, in fact, as he has often stated in various interviews, were the Russians: Tolstoy; Dostoyevsky; Gogol; and especially Turgenev, whose *Fathers and Sons* and *A Sportsman's Sketches*, with their country estates, serfs, and noblemen, provided telling parallels with the hierarchical agricultural society that he knew in Louisiana. Two US writers also played key roles in Gaines's artistic development: Ernest Hemingway and William Faulkner. These

Nobel Laureates appealed to him in different ways, however. As Wolfgang Lepschy has demonstrated, Hemingway was more important in terms of style, particularly in connection with dialogue and sparely constructed description.[4] Faulkner, on the other hand, profoundly shaped Gaines, in terms of both models and things to avoid, as the Louisianan struggled with modes for presenting the tragic racial history of the South while simultaneously seeking to go beyond the Mississippian's ultimately limited habit of too often presenting African Americans as victims or at moments when they are in conflict with dominant white culture. Further, as Gaines has recently stated, "Much of our history has not been told; our problems have been told as if we have no history."[5] On yet another occasion, he observed, "After [my first] two books had been published as well as the collection of stories, *Bloodline*, I realized that I was writing in a definite pattern. One, I was writing about a definite area; and, two, I was going farther and farther back into the past. I was trying to go back, back, back into our experiences in this country to find some kind of meaning to our present lives."[6] This was Faulkner's aim as well. We're all familiar with Faulkner's pronouncement that the past isn't dead, it isn't even past. Compare Gaines's remark: "I'm a southerner myself, and we all live in the goddamned past. We just can't get rid of it. We think of it all the time, and it haunts the living hell out of us. And all of a sudden, reality and the modern world catch up and break us."[7]

Gaines has commented at length on his debt to Faulkner, most recently in an interview he gave to Lillie Mae Brown. He told her that he and Faulkner write about the same kind of characters, people who

> hang around the storefronts, working in the fields. . . . Faulkner made me concentrate more on my characters. He showed me how similar they were, white or black characters in a field. . . . He's a master at capturing that southern dialogue, whether it's white or black. But it was a certain level of dialogue that Faulkner was interested in. He could get the most illiterate of black dialogue, but he was never interested in writing middle class black or upper class black dialogue. . . . He showed me how to describe the country stores, how people sat around on the porches. I knew that, but I didn't know how to do it on paper until I saw what he had done.[8]

Gaines was strongly influenced by the voices of *The Sound and the Fury*, the interplay of the monologues of the Compson brothers. He was also struck by Faulkner's extension of this method in *As I Lay Dying*. Gaines, who usually focuses on black folk culture, was also impressed by the strategies Faulkner created to attribute complexity to characters who had limited linguistic ability. The narrations in this novel offer a set of paradoxes. Two characters, for example, Jewel and Addie, have only one speech apiece, yet these two prove key to understanding the book. Other characters demonstrate a progression or deterioration of narrative voice, and in those cases a dialogics develops within their vocality and with their other utterances.[9]

Gaines employed similar methods in his fourth novel, *A Gathering of Old Men*. His narrators, however, speak much more for communal issues, and therefore their contributions to the book work together in a very different dialogic. Gaines also intertwines his narrative with a mystery-like plot, wherein we wonder who actually committed the murder that sparks the action. The novel opens with the old black man Mathu standing over the body of the Cajun sharecropper Beau Boutan, holding a shotgun. Candy Marshall, the young plantation mistress whom Mathu has helped raise, concocts a scheme whereby she and Mathu's elderly black friends will all claim responsibility for the murder in order to protect Mathu. The old men take up guns for another reason, for the sheriff, Mapes, may not be able to fend off an attack by Beau's vengeful kin and fellow Cajuns.

The novel employs fifteen narrators, which is interesting, in that Faulkner also has fifteen narrators in *As I Lay Dying*. In the latter text, however, there are fifty-nine sections, some of them quite short, as in Vardaman's notorious one-sentence chapter, which reads, "My mother is a fish."[10] Many of *Gathering*'s narratives are quite long and almost self-contained, detailing in several cases an entire biography, somewhat akin in fictional terms to Hamilton Holt's famous 1906 immigrant anthology, *The Life Stories of Undistinguished Americans*.[11] Here, as there, however, the composite picture offers a spectrum of experiences that together comprise ethnic/racial history. But *A Gathering* focuses on a single group in a single place with a distinct and resonant culture.

Unlike *As I Lay Dying*, Gaines's novel centrally addresses the tragic racial situation of the Deep South, skillfully employing Faulkner's narrative breakthroughs in breathtaking new ways. The developing figures of Candy, Mathu, and the journalist Lou Dimes give a sense of progression to the novel, but they also contrast with the old men, and the differentiation of the narrative voices into three distinct groups—southern whites, southern blacks, and Cajuns—evinces the cultural layering and conflict that is unique to Louisiana and provides another dimension that one does not find in Faulkner's masterwork. *A Gathering* was not Gaines's first attempt at multiple narration; his magnificent short story, "Just Like a Tree," the concluding piece in his collection *Bloodline*, employs ten narrators to tell the story of Aunt Fe and her refusal to move away from her home.[12] As with *A Gathering*'s Candy, the central female figure of

"Just Like a Tree" isn't given a section of her own; instead, she speaks within the narration of others, and this is the case with A *Gathering's* Mathu as well.

Like Faulkner, who included Italians, Native Americans, and many other ethnic characters in his work, Gaines goes beyond the notion of the biethnic South, especially in his detailed depictions of Cajuns, represented in A *Gathering* by the dead man's family, the Boutans. They are distinguished by their class hostility more than by racism, and Beau's brother Gil, the star running back on LSU's football team whose gridiron partner is black, has definitely learned racial lessons from his athletic exploits, so much so that his grief over his dead brother is tempered by his dread of the coming racial apocalypse of revenge. Gaines's modulation of Cajun speech is finely done, taking into account the effects that college has had on Gil as compared to his father and the other members of the Cajun clan. Still, there are risks to giving every character an independent voice; in a recently published interview, Gaines states that he was told by a reader, "'You gave life to the Ku Klux Klan. You made the Ku Klux Klan look good.' But that's something I would not have done. I just give them humanity."[13] Gaines, that is, lets his characters show why they think as they do, as Faulkner did with Jason Compson, say, in *The Sound and the Fury*.

The matter of voice is crucial in both novels, especially since Faulkner and Gaines were dealing with largely uneducated people who speak in vernacular. Faulkner solved the problem by presenting his figures largely through their consciousness. On the first level, they use the dialect of actual speech and report speech among themselves literally: "'It was her wish,' pa says. . . . 'She will rest quieter for knowing . . . that it was her own blood sawed out the boards and drove the nails'" (19). There is a heavy emphasis on sensation, rendered through dialect but with a limited vocabulary and much repetition. The style is realistic and highly colloquial. The second level, however, conscious thought, focuses on what is realized internally, often in a conventional way, but supplemented by a more ornate vocabulary, a groping for words, and an effort toward clarity and reason fraught with struggle. As a result, there is a loss of sensory detail from the first mode. Here we find an emphasis on the search for meaning but also on action. Vardaman observes, "The trees look like chickens when they ruffle out into the cool dust on hot days. I can feel where the fish was in the dust. It is cut up into pieces of not-fish now, not-blood on my hands and overalls" (53). The third level, unconscious or intuitive speech, has sensation and feeling restored by transcendent, poetic language that the characters would be incapable of employing in actual speech. Dewey Dell, for instance, says, "I feel like a wet seed wild in the hot blind earth" (64). There is no longer an attempt to analyze experience but instead more of an effort to feel it. Here Faulkner abandons all attempts to render thought realistically; instead we find a highly poetic, impressionistic, tactile, and deeply psychological mode of expression, along with a profound use of literary symbolism. This is the realm of intuition and contemplation and is preeminently expressed through the two single monologues of Addie and Jewel, each key in many ways, as I have suggested, to the entire narrative and frame of reference.

In this respect, we would do well to ponder the fact that the Bundren siblings have very little conversation among themselves with a few exceptions, most notably those exchanges between Darl and Cash, many reported in flashback. By contrast, the entire point of the Gaines novel is a kind of running collective dialogue, akin to public confession and communion. Bakhtin has stated that an element of response and anticipation penetrates deeply inside intensely dialogic discourse: "Such a discourse draws in, as it were, sucks in to itself the other's replies."[14] This, of course, suggests the profoundly African pattern of call and response, which is evident on virtually every page of Gaines's novel, unlike *As I Lay Dying*, where the Bundrens are isolated in their own private worlds of grief and silence.

Further, since Gaines's novel begins with a message taken to the old men by the boy Snookum, who will presumably be present when the men "testify," we have in the youth an avatar of the child Vardaman Bundren in his limited ability to understand significant events, but also in his representation of childhood as a scene of instruction. However, whereas one can speculate that Vardaman will be scarred by the events suffered by the Bundrens, Snookum will have absorbed the dialogics of the old men and the heroic lesson of their deeds as well. Again, Gaines has stated that the twin lessons of his novel are, first, the gathering itself, and, second, the internal victory of Charlie, who returns to face the consequences for killing Beau, thereby exonerating all the brave old men but also "standing" himself. It seems important to note that the alchemy of their dialogics represents the group's assumption of the courage and manhood that has always been Mathu's, who has tried, as Charlie's *parrain* (godfather), to instill it in him. Charlie proudly declares that the murder, done in self-defense, has finally made him a man; although he fled the scene, something was calling him back, and clearly, it was the heroism of Mathu and his compatriots, who have given Charlie the example he needs to "stand."

How does Gaines echo Faulkner, and how does he differ in his multivocal special effects? He chooses a method of presentation that tends to merge Faulkner's three levels of consciousness, but with only a taste of the poetic language that characterizes the third level of unconscious thought. In many of the sections, despite the fact of first-person narration, we move close to the effects of *personale Erzahlsituation*, a focalized narration, usually rendered in the third person but not that of the central character. For example, Johnny Paul poses a question, "How can a man beat a machine," that summons up memories of the classic story of John Henry.[15] But he answers his question by telling the tale of his brother: "With them two little mules, he beat that tractor to the derrick. . . . They pulled for him, sweating, slipping, falling . . . the bit cutting their lips, the slobber and blood mixing. . . . They pulled, pulled, pulled in all that mud for him. And yes, they did win. . . . But they wasn't supposed to win. How can flesh and blood and nigger win against white man and machine?"

In other passages Gaines, a master of dialect and dialogue, finds poetry in the vernacular. Johnny Paul says he killed Beau because of the tractor the Cajun was using to tear up the quarters:

> "Remember Jack and Red Rider hitting that field every morning with them two mules, Diamond and Job? . . . Thirty, forty of us going out in the field with cane knives, hoes, plows—name it. Sunup to sundown, hard, miserable work, but we managed to get it done. We stuck together, shared what little we had, and loved and respected each other.
>
> "But just look at things today. Where the people? Where the roses? Where the four-o'clocks? The palm-of-Christians? Where the people used to sing and pray in the church? . . . Under them trees. . . . And where they used to stay, the weeds got it now, just waiting for the tractor to come plow it up. . . . I did it for them . . . 'cause that tractor is getting closer and closer to that graveyard. . . . One day that tractor was go'n come in there and plow up them graves, getting rid of all proof that we ever was." (92–93)

This lyrical utterance magically merges cherished memories with current devastations to both the landscape and the people, through *lieux de memoires*, recalling a harmonious work group and a moral community, many of its members now in the graveyard threatened by the Cajun tractors.[16]

When the German director Volker Schlondorff created a cinematic version of the novel, he had to address the inherently static quality of the men gathered for a long period of time in a confined space before the porch stages of the quarters. Gaines objected to Schlondorff's solution, which was to show the old men doing other things like playing baseball or riding a bicycle. He had deliberately confined his literary narrative to the utterances and most deeply felt thoughts of the men in question, often restricting action to gestures expressive of these inner concerns and the crisis itself. Southern and African American narrative traditions lead naturally to this kind of "telling," as groups of men waiting for an event to happen will talk, tell tales. As such, the space before the cabins is a kind of public square, where a terrible kind of carnivalization is enacted. For here, as in carnival, everyone has a role to play in a public space. Their confessions of private pain and humiliation in the "square" of the quarters yard creates a dialogic of community that transforms their stories, which in the eyes of the white world are insignificant, into tales of torment; endurance (that profoundly Faulknerian term); and, ultimately, survival and resurrection.

In all his works, however, but particularly in *A Gathering*, Gaines goes beyond the basic pattern of "endurance" that Faulkner establishes for his black characters. As Craig Werner has noted, Gaines substitutes a "call and response" pattern for communal action.[17] The characters in *A Gathering* echo the prisoner in Gaines's powerful short story, "Three Men," who elects to stay in jail rather than be released into virtual slavery on a plantation: "By God I will be a man. For once in my life I will be a man."[18] As Herman Beavers has memorably stated, Miss Jane, the old men in *Gathering*, and other key characters become "articulate witnesses," using eloquent narration to create a symbolically free southern space.[19] In the world of *A Gathering*, unlike *As I Lay Dying*, people must come to know one another again, come into contact, and above all, talk. Bakhtin usually associates this type of activity with carnival; Gaines seems to see crisis as a kind of carnival in this respect. In a dialogic welling up from memory that becomes transformed by the alchemy of brotherly communion, the prospect of standing as men becomes a reality, one shaped by their voices as much as by their guns. In this mode of presentation, Gaines demonstrates an affinity with Dostoyevsky that Faulkner often shares as well. As Bakhtin notes, "In every voice [Dostoyevsky] could hear two contending voices, in every expression a crack, and the readiness to go over immediately to another contradictory expression; in every gesture he detected confidence and lack of confidence simultaneously," in "an eternal harmony of unmerged voices."[20] Gaines, more than Dostoyevsky and Faulkner, pushes his narrative toward real harmony, as African American culture has always privileged the communal. He understands that no man—and certainly no oppressed man—can find complete "fullness" alone.[21] As in Paschal ritual, out of death comes life; in this case, the death of Beau Boutan brings about a rebirth of the quarters community in the awakening manhood of the old men. The white "Queen" of the quarters, the latter-day "Big Missy," Candy, is uncrowned, as is her male counterpart, Sheriff Mapes.[22]

Gaines plants a seed of hope in us that the old men have been last-ingly changed, but is it likely they will be able to keep their newfound dignity intact as they leave the transformed space of the quarters yard and return to their individual struggles with "the man"? Gaines himself, however, is clearly interested in fomenting permanent change, and the emphasis is on renewal. In the novel (but not the film), the men joyfully shoot off their guns amid great laughter when the Cajun thug Luke Will attacks. As Coot reports,

> Me and Clatoo looked at each other and grinned, and reloaded. . . . Everybody was firing. I could tell Rooster's high-pitched voice, Dirty Red's dry hoarse voice—and Yank's voice. Yank didn't hoot like the rest of us. He hollered the way you holler at a rodeo when somebody's riding a bucking horse. "Ya-hoo," and shot. . . . All the way down the quarters they was hooting and shooting. I didn't know the last time I had felt so good. Not since I was a young man in the war. Lord, have mercy, Jesus. . . . They hooted and fired. You woulda thought you was listening to a bunch of Indians—Lord, have mercy. (Gaines, *A Gathering*, 198–99)

Gaines noted he paid a price for this insertion of humor at the climax of the book: "I have been criticized for the very last chapter of the book by those who think it's too much of a farce."[23] We might note here the ways in which *As I Lay Dying* constantly interbraids the comic and serious, often tragic thematics as well.

Moreover, Gaines, like Faulkner, sees that rural whites and blacks share common sources of humor; he loves Faulkner's story "Mule in the Yard" but notes that the same comic sequence of that story was echoed during his childhood, when he chopped down weeds that were keeping a mule inside a yard; everyone laughed at the owner who would "chase the mule, the mule would stop and eat. . . . Then he'd run off again. . . . Everybody in the South has seen this. . . . You don't have to be in Missis-sippi. . . . Let's say I had never lived in the South, had never seen anything like this. Then you could say I was imitating Faulkner."[24] Events like these mule antics become part of what Faulkner called "old tales and talking."[25] Similarly, in an October 1972 interview, Gaines described the "tremen-dous storytellers or liars or whatever you want to call them" in his own family and community. "The old people . . . would talk and talk and talk, and I listened to them. . . . Say there was a funeral today, or a wedding, the old people would sort of gather in a little room and they would talk about things, you know. They might start with the wedding, or they might start with that particular funeral, but by the time they end up, they've talked about everything that had happened in the last twenty years."[26]

Gaines's enduring 1971 masterwork, *The Autobiography of Miss Jane Pittman*, has often been admired as a meticulously crafted work of fiction that mimics the nonfictional form of autobiography. It has just as often been praised, however, as a valuable reflection, albeit fictional, of actual history, as it views a turbulent hundred years of our nation's past through the eyes of a 110-year-old black woman who has lived through slavery, Reconstruction, the Depression, and the civil rights movement. The novel's signal strength is the degree to which both the fictional stories and the retelling of history are enhanced and indeed made magnetic through the use of orality. Characters engage in conversation with Miss Jane and each other in a dazzling mix of Louisiana voices and cultures, from the inhabitants of the big house to the field hands, from the decorous Creole schoolmarm to the raucous Cajun roustabout. All of these voices summon up pungent, local forms of address and expression, and the common people depicted provide, through their richly figured speech, indelible portraits of folk culture. The opening section of the book portrays Yankee soldiers coming to Miss Jane's plantation. Her cruel mistress warns her, "You say anything about your master and the silver, I'll have you skinned."[27] Gaines thus evokes the thematics and specifics of Faulkner's Civil War novel, *The Unvanquished*, in which the slave Loosh divulges the location of the Sartoris family silver to Union army invaders.[28] In *Miss Jane*, however, the point of view is that of the slave, not that of the white plantation family. The mass movement of the newly emancipated people portrays them heroically, rather than as an undifferentiated mob, as Faulkner does.[29]

The voices in the book include those of field hands and educated blacks. But most of the people in the quarters speak in dialect, which is never used in a demeaning way. It is Gaines's great gift to make dialect emerge as creative, expressive, and sometimes eloquent, although he also embraces dialect's ability to amuse and subvert. He has stated that he learned much about the craft of dialect from Faulkner: "He has made me listen to dialects over again. I find that so many of my contemporary black writers probably don't listen well to dialects around them. . . . The dialects from the part of the country I come from are distinct. . . . Reading Faulkner just makes me pay more attention to dialect, to dialogue . . . but . . . you have to make it readable, you know, you just cannot stick too totally to the way people talk."[30] Faulkner helped in another way as well; Gaines once noted that Faulkner taught him how to leave things out: "You can say one word and if you say it right and build up to it and follow through, it can carry as much meaning as if you had used an entire sentence."[31]

When *The Autobiography of Miss Jane Pittman* appeared in 1971,

Newsweek reviewer Geoffrey Wolff asserted that Miss Jane could "stand beside William Faulkner's Dilsey in *The Sound and the Fury*. Miss Jane Pittman, like Dilsey, has 'endured,' has seen almost everything and foretold the rest."[32] Wolff, of course, intended this as a high compliment; but as Gaines once told me, it makes a big difference whether you're listening to Dilsey in the Compson kitchen or in her kitchen.[33] Miss Jane does get into the big house kitchen, but she never really steps outside her own culture the way Dilsey often does in her almost stereotypical posture as keeper of her "white children." But Miss Jane does indeed *stand*, as Wolff implies, and Gaines, who was raised by his Aunt Augusteen Jefferson, who could not walk, has praised her in similar terms in the dedication to *Miss Jane*: "to the memory of / My beloved aunt, *Miss Augusteen Jefferson*, / who did not walk a day in her life / but who taught me the importance of standing" (n.p.).

Gaines has stated that although Miss Jane is the center of the novel, it actually revolves around the story of four men in her life. Ned, her adopted son, leaves Louisiana for Kansas and an education but returns to teach and inspire the children; constantly under surveillance by whites, he is assassinated after giving an inspiring riverside sermon urging resistance. Jane's husband, Jim, breaks horses, a dangerous career that eventually kills him, but he escapes the plantation's grip for a time and takes Miss Jane with him to a freer space near Texas. Interestingly, Gaines includes a white figure, Tee Bob, the son of the plantation owner, who loves a near-white Creole teacher, Mary Agnes. When their love cannot be consummated, he kills himself, a narrative that daringly reverses the end of the traditional "tragic mulatta" story where the mixed-race woman usually dies. Fourth and finally, the quarters' chosen young man, Jimmy, is helped to get an education, which prepares him for his ultimately fatal leadership role during the civil rights movement. Miss Jane, somewhat like Melville's Ishmael, is more of a force in the first parts of the novel but retreats into narration toward the end. Throughout, however, she is a masterful historian, and we may remember that two of Faulkner's most prominent local historians were the elderly Miss Jenny Du Pre and Miss Rosa Coldfield.

Unlike those two prolix ladies, Miss Jane uses folk idiom to boil things down to their essence. Her summaries of historical events are always pungent, but also economical. The following passage offers a brilliant compression:

> The letter [from Ned] told how people was coming into Kansas by the boatload. At first how the white people in Kansas was helping them. How they collected money . . . [and] organized committees to go to Washington. . . . The

people at first was almost too nice. But that was the first letter. When I got the second letter things had changed already. . . . Now the white people didn't want them in town. . . . There was other States where they could go and find comfort. But the people had heard of Kansas first. Like sheeps they had to go where everybody else had gone. Now the riots. (79)

Gaines generates Miss Jane's voice here mainly through standard English, but with irregular verb usage, folk expressions ("boat-load"), much repetition, and spare but revealing imagery. The sheep image leads up to the slaughter of the riots. But other major historical events are handled in merely a few sentences. "He [Ned] stayed there [Kansas] till that war started in Cuba, then he joined the army. After the war he came back here. He wanted to teach at home now" (80). In two sentences, we learn about black participation in the Spanish American War and find a way to date the events of the book, since we know the date is 1898. (Miss Jane's oral narration is notably lacking in actual time markers.) We might note here that Faulkner similarly lets us know about Sartoris family participation in the Spanish American War by one brief reference to a wound suffered in that conflict.[34]

Gaines takes care to show differences between oral traditions among the folk community. When Miss Jane goes to the hoodoo woman Madame Eloise Gautier to keep Joe from being killed by a stallion, Gautier, a former rival of Marie Laveau in New Orleans, speaks in a different, Creole-inflected way as she predicts Joe's death: "Mon sha, mon sha, mon sha, mon sha. . . . I have told you the horse is just one. If not the horse, then the lion, if not the lion, then the woman, if not the woman, then the war, then the politic, then the whisky. Man must always search somewhere to prove himself. . . . This horse your Pittman will not break. Your Pittman . . . [n]ot the man he think he is'" (94–95).

By contrast, Albert Cluveau, the Cajun assassin who kills Ned, crosses over into black culture; for years he is Miss Jane's fishing companion on the river. Her description of him proves blunt and telling: "A short bowlegged Cajun. Face looked like somebody had been jobbing in it with an ice pick. Had that big patch of hair out the left side of his head, his head white where the hair had been. Sitting there telling me about the people he had killed" (102). Cluveau's warning to Jane is made in yet another new voice for the book: "They talk 'bout your boy there, Jane. They don't want him build that school there, no. . . . They want me stop him, Jane" (104–5). Gaines has told me that this character is based on an actual Cajun assassin who is still talked about around False River, which recalls how Faulkner similarly used the details of the Nelse Patton lynching in Oxford to configure *Light in August*.[35]

Local lore, however, in both Gaines and Faulkner, was shored up by careful historical research. Gaines has written about combing through slave narratives for materials he could use in the first quarter of *Miss Jane*. He was particularly taken by the commonality of name changes, moving away from the plantation, and the desire for literacy, elements identified by James Olney and several others as key to the genre of slave narrative.[36] We should not forget that among Gaines's chief sources for *Miss Jane* were the narratives gathered in the 1930s by the Works Progress Administration, all based on oral interviews with elderly former slaves. The setup of the novel more closely resembles these latter "texts" than the nineteenth-century narratives, in that the taped record is less amenable to change by the redactor or northern editor. We might parallel this with Faulkner's discovery of the Leak family plantation ledgers that, as Sally Wolff has shown us, strongly influenced virtually all of his books, particularly in terms of the presentation of slavery in *Go Down, Moses*.[37]

The wisdom in Miss Jane's oral culture still has much to tell us today as we deal with the aftermath of Katrina. Commenting succinctly on the Great Mississippi Flood of 1927, which she calls "the high water," Miss Jane remarks,

> The damage from that high water was caused by man, because man wanted to control the rivers, and you cannot control water. The old people, the Indians, used to worship the rivers till the white people came here and conquered them and tried to conquer the rivers, too. . . . I don't know when the first levee was built—probably in slavery time; but from what I heard from the old people the water destroyed the levee soon as it was put there. Now, if the white men had taken heed to what the river was trying to say to him then, it would have saved a lot of pain later. But instead of him listening—no, he built another levee. The river tored that one down just like the first one. Built another one; river tored that one down. . . . The river been running . . . taking little earth, maybe few trees, maybe a cabin here . . . but never, never a whole parish—till the white man came here and tried to conquer it." (147–49)

This magnificent passage is not about Miss Jane but about the wisdom of the Indians and the old people, wisdom infused with the sacral. We are reminded here how Tea Cake ignores the warnings of the Florida Indians when the hurricane is approaching in *Their Eyes Were Watching God*.[38] Miss Jane ends her observations with a prophecy that has tragically been fulfilled with Katrina: "Now he's built his concrete spillways to control the water. But one day the water will break down his spillways. . . . The water will never die. That same water the Indians used to believe in will run free again. You just wait and see" (150). We find similar folk reactions and commentaries on the Great Flood of 1927 in Faulkner's *Old Man*. Part of Gaines's planning for his novel consisted of conversations with the great black poet Alvin Aubert; they talked about how Gaines's Aunt Augusteen and her friends would have covered the great events of their time in their "porch talk." One of the subjects they speculated about was the 1927 flood, which was commemorated in varied registers of the folk consciousness.

When Miss Jane talks to Jules Reynard, Tee Bob's *parrain*, about the latter's suicide, they have a long discourse, white to black, black to white, meditating on the complex racial history that led to this tragedy. In many ways, it resembles the dialogue between Cass and Ike over the plantation ledgers in "The Bear," which we now know also reflects the conversations between Faulkner himself and Edgar Francisco Jr. over the Leak family ledgers in Holly Springs. Jules and Jane agree that they and the entire society created the tragedy by endorsing racial codes. "But ain't this specalatin?" Jane asks. "It would be specalatin if two white people was sitting here," Jules replies.

> "But it's us?" I said.
> "And that makes it gospel truth," he said. . .
> "He was bound to kill himself anyhow?"
> "One day. He had to. For our sins."
> "Poor Tee Bob."
> "No. Poor us," Jules Raynard said. (194–96)

The folk foundation of Gaines's novels and their setting in a mostly rural culture that the rest of the country only vaguely comprehends have given his oeuvre a distinctiveness and wholeness that is unusual in American letters; but at the same time, Gaines's "little postage stamp of native soil" is quite diverse, with Anglo, African, Cajun, Creole, Latino, and Asian cultures. All have been blended into a "cultural gumbo" that is unknown elsewhere in the nation, even in the South.

Faulkner's early masterworks received excellent reviews (particularly in Europe), but most of his books were out of print and his reputation was in decline when Malcolm Cowley jacked up Faulkner's literary standing with the publication of *The Portable Faulkner* in 1946. Similarly, while there has been a resurgence of interest in Gaines's work since Oprah Winfrey selected *A Lesson before Dying* for her book club, critical fashions have not been operating in his favor. Two powerful critics— one indirectly, another directly—have argued against the imperatives Gaines favors. Some years ago, Hazel Carby launched what amounted to an attack on Zora Neale Hurston, asking, in effect, what Hurston was doing writing about peasants in Florida while people were suffering in northern slums like Harlem. Why can't a Hurston, Carby in effect asked, write like a Richard Wright?[39] Gaines was indeed attacked on this basis during the civil rights movement, and that kind of argument has been raised again by Houston A. Baker Jr., who in a recent book attacks Ralph Ellison for a lack of militancy and names Gaines, Albert Murray, and James Alan McPherson (among others) as fellow slackers who create "blackface minstrel romps . . . for money."[40] Both Carby and Baker favor what I call "contact/struggle narratives," texts that concentrate on conflict between blacks and whites, over those that attempt a portrayal of what Thadious M. Davis calls "black space" in her profound study, *Southscapes*, which provides a detailed and revealing reading of Gaines's rural portraits.[41] Gaines himself has pointed to the fact that the culture he limned has been vanishing rapidly, as the people who used to live in the "quarters" have moved to Baton Rouge, or more recently to Houston or Atlanta, and Faulkner similarly felt a need to memorialize a vanishing culture and wilderness landscape, especially in *The Hamlet* and *Go Down, Moses*. However, Faulkner's "peasants" continue to draw the attention of both literary critics and general readers—witness Oprah's selection of three of the Mississippian's novels for her book club—and we can make the case that Gaines's characters and the folk he commemorates do indeed continue to speak to contemporary issues and to what Faulkner claimed was the proper concern of the writer, "the human heart in conflict with itself."[42] To his credit, Gaines has always seen this central struggle as one waged within and sometimes against the community, with the understanding that through reading the individual story the community learns, is strengthened, and is sustained.

In the concluding civil rights section of the novel (which richly contradicts Baker's portrait of Gaines), when Miss Jane decides to move out of the Samson house and into the quarters, she asks permission, causing a comic outburst on Robert Samson's part that is straight out of Faulkner: "You asking me? . . . I didn't know I was still running Samson. I thought you was. I thought it was up to you to tell me when you wanted to move and where. And it was my duty to go down there and clean up the place for you. To run a special pipe down there. . . . To run a special line of lectwicity. . . . I thought that was my duty at Samson. Is I done missed out on a duty?" (201–2). The speech, while amusing, actually serves Samson's purpose, for it points to the absurdity of a servant who hasn't done much work in a decade receiving all these favors from the patriarch of the plantation. But at the same time, the comic tirade endorses the old paternalistic fiction that a beloved servant is "like one of the family" and thereby fosters a benevolent, altruistic image of the employer-master. The exchange also offers evidence of a long-term joking relationship between master and servant, but one that is clearly not equal, for Jane has fewer options in their verbal duels because of her status. The white patriarch-employer, however, clearly enjoys the joking relationship in that it creates the illusion of the kinship that joking relationships always suggest; it clearly echoes Gavin Stevens's complaint about his duties to elderly blacks in the concluding story of *Go Down, Moses*.

Teachers play a crucial role in *Miss Jane*, including Ned, Mary Agnes, and (as a teacher of justice) Jimmy. But surely Miss Jane is the best teacher of all. Rambling, tangential, but always folksy and often comic, she deeply instructs her readers in the history of her people and the principles of communal involvement. In this aspect, her embrace of folk culture, tale-telling, and vernacular speech casts her in the role of the mythic Greek Silenus, the teacher of Bacchus, who had a rough exterior but uttered profound truths. Further, her narrative "uncrowns" those of the white plantation owners she serves as well as the Lost Cause historians and white writers like Margaret Mitchell who seemingly cornered the market on southern history as seen through fiction. Here too, Gaines follows Faulkner, who relished debunking Lost Cause hagiography, particularly in *The Unvanquished*.[43] Miss Jane and her fellow narrators encourage us to laugh at the pretentions of the white characters. Her humor creates an intimacy between her narration and the reader while simultaneously creating a democratic community, for as Bakhtin asserts, only equals may laugh.[44] Indeed, as many of Gaines's fictions demonstrate, white southerners did not permit their servants to laugh in front of them, as this would suggest disrespect and equality.

In his important study, *Neo-Slave Narratives*, Ashraf Rushdy acknowledges that *Miss Jane* was in many ways the first neoslave narrative but that it differed from later versions in specifically linking the struggle for emancipation with the civil rights movement.[45] Although he goes on later in his study to talk of the centrality of Gaines's text for those who followed him—particularly Sherley Anne Williams—Rushdy does not provide an extended analysis of *Miss Jane*, a curious lapse that has in fact been repeated by other commentators on the genre, possibly because Gaines does not, like most original slave narratives and their neocounterparts, concentrate solely on the line of struggle with white culture. Rushdy does, however, note the strong aspect of *intertextuality* in the genre, taking the term from Julia Kristeva's notion of how one text can rewrite another. Kristeva saw intertextuality as born of "an anticolonialist resistance to the concept of hegemonic influence," thereby focusing on social forces that radiate between texts.[46] This concept is strongly present in Edward P. Jones's novel, *The Known World*, which engages with many classics within the genre, both actual slave narratives and neoslave narratives. Like Gaines, Jones explores the world of work, mining its possibilities for cultural resistance and symbolic commentary.

Any discussion of Gaines's treatment of rural work must take into account his reiteration that he is writing about peasant culture, a perception that led him to rely on Russian writers for models: "I went into the Russians and I liked what they were doing with their stories on the peasantry; the peasants were real human beings, whereas in the fiction of American writers . . . they were caricatures."[47] On another occasion, he complained, "Northern liberals and radical whites were the only people who bought the works of Black writers, and they didn't care for tales about Black peasantry. I think they were much more concerned with the Black problem than with the Black character."[48]

Faulkner took great pains to limn the labor of workers, from the roofers in "Shingles for the Lord" to the carpentry of Cash Bundren or the kitchen chores of Dilsey Gibson. The hard life of farmers and their wives receives moving depictions in many of his stories and novels. Similarly, when Gaines talks about his relatives, he often refers to the work they did: "My maternal grandmother . . . used to work at this plantation where I come from. She was the cook at this place (unlike Dilsey, quite unlike Dilsey) . . . and she was the greatest cook probably that ever lived. She had mastered French Creole cooking. . . . She was very very strong and . . . sturdy. . . . No job was too hard, you know. And I think that's a characteristic of Miss Jane, too."[49] But he saves his most lavish praise for his crippled aunt who raised him: "She cooked for us. . . . She would lean over her little bench and put the wood into this little stove. . . . We had these old wash boards . . . and she'd just wash, wash, wash, with an old bar of soap. . . . She also patched our clothes, sewed our clothes, she baked cakes. . . . But that was not even enough for her. She would, in the evening, when work was over . . . crawl . . . out into the garden to work. It's that kind of spirit Miss Jane has."[50]

As is true of Faulkner, the dignity of work matters to Gaines. As he has stated, "Many of your white writers have written about black field workers who were clowns; they had strong backs, and they could pick a lot of cotton, and they could sing and be happy, but they did not have brains. . . . There are blacks in the city who are not pimps or pushers, who are not in jail and getting beaten up by white cops every day. There are people who work every day . . . people who struggle . . . for something. Those things are truly worth writing about."[51]

Craig Werner, writing about other black writers and Faulkner, speculates that many of them go beyond the repetition and revenge plot that John T. Irwin so memorably underlined in Faulkner's oeuvre.[52] One could argue that Gaines's interbraided story of two interracial love affairs, *Of Love and Dust*, demonstrates Werner's point. The central figure, Marcus, a black badman who accepts parole to a plantation owner as a virtual prisoner, seeks to spite the system by hitting on his Cajun overseer's black mistress; when she rejects him, he initiates a liaison with the overseer's love-starved wife, which leads to a deep but ultimately tragic love. Both affairs take Faulkner's tentative movement toward such relationships at the end of "Delta Autumn" into a new register, again revoicing and extending racial explorations that Faulkner did not, perhaps could not, imagine, while utilizing the revenge plot only to subvert it with unexpected—and powerful—accounts of sexual but also profoundly human love.

Although Gaines has never discussed this parallel, his perhaps least discussed novel, *In My Father's House*, strongly echoes the plot of *Absalom, Absalom!* Reverend Martin's respected role in the community is ruptured when Robert X, his son from an earlier relationship, appears demanding recognition. Martin's downfall and his son's death at the end of the novel are set against the backdrop of the civil rights movement, a fiery moment in American history that in black history parallels the earlier results of the Civil War and emancipation. In both Faulkner and Gaines, the return of the repressed in the form of the disavowed son proves traumatic. However, in another revoicing, the backward-looking despair of *Absalom* is counteracted in Gaines's novel as the chastened reverend learns from his guilt and seems on the road to spiritual and communal regeneration at novel's end.

Both Faulkner and Gaines understood the ways in which racial codes fenced in whites and blacks alike, and each of them created narratives that featured actual incarceration. Lee Goodwin, Popeye, Nancy Mannigoe, the Tall Convict, Harry Wilbourne, Rider, and Butch Beauchamp illustrate Faulkner's sense of both real and metaphysical cages. Southern racial codes dictated strict surveillance of boundaries, and as Michel Fabre observed of Gaines's Louisiana, "This world is enclosed by gates, barbed wire. Curtain of trees between kingdom-like plantations."[53] Then there are the actual prisons, most memorably in the great short story "Three Men" and more recently in Gaines's masterwork, *A Lesson before Dying*. In the latter work, the condemned prisoner Jefferson bears affinities to Butch Worsham Beauchamp in *Go Down, Moses*; in each case, elderly relatives seek either a dignified death (for Jefferson) or a respectful funeral (for Butch). Jefferson's aunt laments to Mr. Henri, the plantation owner whose help she seeks, "The law got him, Mr. Henri . . . and they go'n kill him. But let them kill a man."[54] "The law got him" registers one way with Henri and another with us as readers. It has the same effect as what old Mollie Beauchamp tells Gavin Stevens about her grandson Butch: "Pharaoh got him."[55]

Throughout *A Lesson*, the white gaze polices the plantation quarters, Grant's schoolroom, and the jail. Informants are used in all of these spaces, and indeed, Grant himself, a harsh and sometimes cruel instructor, uses them too. Eventually, as Grant and the community minister to Jefferson and inspire him to walk to his death as a man, they transform the space of the jail; meals are shared there, children come to talk with the prisoner, and a space specifically designed to strip away individuality instead bestows it, as it surrounds Jefferson with communal admiration and inspires him to register his newfound humanity in his diary.

Gaines's elevation of an uneducated, abused character into a Promethean figure whose example redeems Grant and inspires his students echoes Faulkner's similarly powerful use of the black prisoner Rider in "Pantaloon in Black." As Antonio Gramsci stated, "There is no human activity from which every form of intellectual participation can be excluded: *homo faber* cannot be separated from *homo sapiens*. Each man, finally . . . carries on some form of intellectual activity. . . . He has a conscious line of moral conduct, and therefore contributes to sustain a conception of the world, or to modify it."[56] In Faulkner's story, however, Rider's grief-ridden reflections and subsequent Samson-like actions are misunderstood by the white deputy and thus lead nowhere in the story proper. Gaines's great achievement in his novel is the complex set of interchanges and scenes of transfiguration that signal Jefferson's achievement for the reader, but more importantly, within the community itself, which now embraces him as a beacon of integrity and resistance. This powerful conclusion constitutes yet another revoicing by Gaines of issues raised but often truncated by liberal white writers like Faulkner.

Thadious M. Davis has mapped the black cultural geographies of Louisiana and Mississippi in *Southscapes*, and Gaines occupies pride of place in her discussion of the former. As she observes, Gaines has a "geographical imagination," so much so that the spatial imaginary in his work demands the examination of place she accords him.[57] In her study, place intersects with its history, but she notes Gaines's caution: "There is a difference between living in the past and trying to escape it. If you do nothing but worship the past you are quite dead. . . . But if you start running and trying to get away from the past, you will . . . eventually run yourself out of whatever it does to you. It will run you mad, or kill you in some way. . . . So you really don't get away. It's there, and you live it. That is especially true with the artist."[58] Since Gaines often cites Faulkner's

famous observations about the past, this comment offers a useful adden-
dum to and revoicing of the Mississippian's creed.

A coda: although I knew Faulkner had been a signal influence on Gaines's
art, I was startled when Gaines told me that his great-grandfather James,
whose middle name he bears, "looked just like Faulkner. In fact, someone saw [Faulkner's] picture in my house, and he said, 'Isn't that old man
Jimmy McVay?'" This startling visual legacy underlines the deep admiration that Gaines has for Faulkner's art but also his recognition that the
Mississippian ultimately could not see the world in the same way that
James McVay, his seeming double, did. Gaines's borrowings but also corrections of Faulkner's methods and concepts lead us to a greater appre-
ciations of both writers. Gaines's evocative landscapes of burning cane
fields, slow-moving bayous, and brooding skies offer a sentient backdrop
for his parables of the importance of standing, as his characters, toiling
on plantations, doing time in prison, or alternately, teaching and preaching, also create a rich and sustaining internal culture, one that helps us,
like them, to understand our own struggles to find moral moorings in a
troubled and dynamic world.

NOTES

1. Édouard Glissant, *Faulkner, Mississippi*, trans. Barbara Lewis and Thomas C. Spear
(New York: Farrar, Straus and Giroux, 1999), 55.

2. Thomas LeClair, "'The Language Must Not Sweat': A Conversation with Toni
Morrison," in *Conversations with Toni Morrison*, ed. Danille Taylor-Guthrie (Jackson:
University Press of Mississippi, 1994), 124.

3. Hollie I. West, "People Remember Miss Jane," *The Tuscaloosa News*, February 20,
1976.

4. See Wolfgang Lepschy, "Of Fathers and Sons: Generational Conflicts and Literary
Lineage—The Case of Ernest Hemingway and Ernest Gaines" (PhD dissertation,
Louisiana State University, 2003).

5. Lillie Mae Brown, "Movements in Dignity: A Critical Examination of Selected
Works by Ernest J. Gaines" (PhD dissertation, Florida State University, 2008), 123.

6. Ernest J. Gaines, "Miss Jane and I," in *Mozart and Leadbelly: Stories and Essays*,
ed. Marcia Gaudet and Reggie Young (New York: Knopf, 2005), 17.

7. Marcia Gaudet and Carl Wooten, eds. *Porch Talk with Ernest Gaines:
Conversations on the Writer's Craft* (Baton Rouge: Louisiana State University Press,
1999), 103.

8. Brown, "Movements in Dignity," 118–19.

9. Mikhail Bakhtin's concept of dialogics focuses on a continual dialogue of differing
"texts," a communication between different "authors"; all these utterances are dynamic
and relational. See Mikhail Bakhtin, *The Dialogic Imagination: Four Essays*, trans. Caryl
Emerson and Michael Holquist (Austin: University of Texas Press, 1981).

10. William Faulkner, *As I Lay Dying*, rev. ed. (1930; New York: Vintage International, 1990), 84. Subsequent references to this edition will be cited parenthetically in the text.

11. Hamilton Holt, *The Life Stories of Undistinguished Americans as Told by Themselves* (1906; repr., New York: Routledge, 1990).

12. Ernest J. Gaines, "Just Like a Tree," *Bloodline*, (1968; repr., New York: Vintage Contemporaries, 1997), 221–49.

13. Wolfgang Lepschy, "A *MELUS* Interview: Ernest J. Gaines," *MELUS* 24, no. 1 (1999): 202.

14. Mikhail Bakhtin, *Problems of Dostoevsky's Poetics* (1963), ed. and trans. Caryl Emerson (Minneapolis: University of Minnesota Press, 1984), 197.

15. Ernest J. Gaines, *A Gathering of Old Men* (1983; repr., New York: Vintage Contemporaries, 1984), 96. Subsequent references to this edition will appear parenthetically in the text.

16. Historian Pierre Nora defines *lieux de memoires* as sites "where memory crystallizes and secretes itself at a particular historical moment, a turning point where consciousness of a break with the past is bound up with the sense that memory has been torn—but torn in such a way as to pose the problem of the embodiment of memory in certain sites where a sense of historical continuity persists." See Pierre Nora, "Between Memory and History: *Les Lieux de Memoires*," in *History and Memory in African American Culture*, eds. Geneviève Fabre and Robert O'Meally (New York: Oxford University Press, 1994), 284.

17. Craig Werner, *Playing the Changes: From Afro-Modernism to the Jazz Impulse* (Urbana: University of Illinois Press, 1994), 40.

18. Gaines, "Three Men," *Bloodline*, 141.

19. Herman Beavers, *Wrestling Angels into Song: The Fiction of Ernest J. Gaines and James Alan McPherson* (Philadelphia: University of Pennsylvania Press, 1995), 131.

20. Bakhtin, *Problems*, 30.

21. For Bakhtin's sense of "fullness," see ibid., 177.

22. Bakhtin's concept of carnivalization includes the mock crowning and uncrowning of the event's king. More broadly, the upturning of social convention permits *"the pathos of shifts and changes, of death and renewal."* Ibid., 124.

23. Lepschy, "A *MELUS* Interview," 203.

24. Patricia Rickels, "An Interview with Ernest J. Gaines" (1978), in *Conversations with Ernest Gaines*, ed. John Lowe (Jackson: University Press of Mississippi, 1995), 133.

25. William Faulkner, *Absalom, Absalom!*, rev. ed. (1936; New York: Vintage International, 1990), 243.

26. Ruth Laney, "A Conversation with Ernest Gaines" (1973), in Lowe, ed., *Conversations*, 58.

27. Ernest J. Gaines, *The Autobiography of Miss Jane Pittman* (1971; repr., New York: Bantam, 1972), 6. Subsequent references to the reprint will appear parenthetically in the text.

28. William Faulkner, *The Unvanquished*, rev. ed. (1938; New York: Vintage International, 1991), 74.

29. Ibid., 102–4.

30. Laney, "A Conversation with Ernest Gaines," 66.

31. Fred Beauford, "A Conversation with Ernest J. Gaines" (1972), in Lowe, ed., *Conversations*, 19.

32. Geoffrey Wolff, "Talking to Trees," *Newsweek* (May 3, 1971), 103–4.

33. John Lowe, "An Interview with Ernest Gaines" (1994), in Lowe, ed., *Conversations*, 313.

34. William Faulkner, *Flags in the Dust*, rev. ed. (1973; New York: Vintage International, 2012), 87.

35. On the Patton lynching, see Joel Williamson, *William Faulkner and Southern History* (Chapel Hill: University of North Carolina Press, 1995), 162.

36. James Olney, "'I Was Born': Slave Narratives, Their Status as Autobiography and as Literature," in *The Slave's Narrative*, ed. Charles T. Davis and Henry Louis Gates Jr. (Oxford: Oxford University Press, 1995), 148–75.

37. Sally Wolff, *Ledgers of History: William Faulkner, an Almost Forgotten Friendship, and an Antebellum Plantation Diary* (Baton Rouge: Louisiana State University Press, 2010), passim.

38. Zora Neale Hurston, *Their Eyes Were Watching God* (1937; repr., New York: HarperPerennial, 1998), 156.

39. Hazel Carby, "The Politics of Fiction, Anthropology, and the Folk: Zora Neale Hurston," in *New Essays on* Their Eyes Were Watching God, ed. Michael Awkward (Cambridge: Cambridge University Press, 1991), 71–93.

40. Houston A. Baker Jr., *Critical Memory: Public Spheres, African American Writing, and Black Fathers and Sons in America* (Athens: University of Georgia Press, 2001), 37–38.

41. Thadious M. Davis, *Southscapes: Geographies of Race, Region, and Literature* (Chapel Hill: University of North Carolina Press, 2011), 79.

42. William Faulkner, Nobel Prize address (1950), in his *Essays, Speeches, and Public Letters*, ed. James Meriwether (1965; repr., London: Chatto, 1967), 119.

43. See John Lowe, "*The Unvanquished*: Faulkner's Nietzschean Skirmish with the Civil War," *Mississippi Quarterly* 46, no. 3 (1993): 407–36.

44. Mikhail Bakhtin, *Rabelais and His World* (1965), trans. Hélène Iswolsky (Bloomington: Indiana University Press, 1984), 92.

45. Asraf H. A. Rushdy, *Neo-Slave Narratives: Studies in the Social Logic of a Literary Form* (New York: Oxford University Press, 1999), 6.

46. Kristeva cited in ibid., 15.

47. John O'Brien, "Ernest J. Gaines" (1972), in Lowe, ed., *Conversations*, 28.

48. Tom Carter, "Ernest Gaines" (1975), in Lowe, ed., *Conversations*, 83.

49. Forrest Ingram and Barbara Steinberg, "On the Verge: An Interview with Ernest J. Gaines" (1973), in Lowe, ed., *Conversations*, 50.

50. Ibid., 51.

51. Jerome Tarshis, "The Other 300 Years: A Conversation with Ernest J. Gaines, Author of *The Autobiography of Miss Jane Pittman*" (1974), in Lowe, ed., *Conversations*, 74–75.

52. Werner, *Playing the Changes*, 41.

53. Michel Fabre, "Bayonne, or the Yoknapatawpha of Ernest Gaines," trans. Melvin Dixon and Didier Malaquin, *Callaloo* 1, no. 3 (1978): 112.

54. Ernest J. Gaines, *A Lesson before Dying*, rev. ed. (1993; New York: Vintage Contemporaries, 1994), 22.

55. William Faulkner, *Go Down, Moses*, rev. ed. (1942; New York: Vintage International, 1990), 361.

56. Antonio Gramsci, *The Prison Notebooks*, ed. and trans. Quintin Hoare and Geoffrey Nowell Smith (New York: International Publishers, 1971), 6.

57. Davis, *Southscapes*, 258.

58. Gaines quoted in ibid., 264.

"For Fear of a Scandal": Sexual Policing and the Preservation of Colonial Relations in William Faulkner and Marie Vieux-Chauvet

Jenna Sciuto

According to the Code Noir of 1685 applied throughout the French colonial empire, if a free man has children with a slave concubine, he is to be fined two thousand pounds of sugar, and if the woman is his own slave, she and her child are to be sent to work at the local hospital, remaining perpetual slaves.[1] If the offending father marries the slave within the rites of the church, however, she and her offspring are freed and the children become legitimate.[2] While the Code Noir was not always upheld, it was an attempt to regulate the social conditions of slavery, specifically detailing the status of slaves, the interactions between slaves and masters, and the punishments applied if either party should not act according to the Code. In particular, sexual control of the colonized in the French American colonies, such as Haiti, can be traced back to the Code Noir. In the words of Sander Gilman, the laws place "great emphasis on the control of the slave as a sexual object, both in terms of permitted and forbidden contact, as well as by requiring documentation as to the legal status of the offspring of slaves," thereby making control of that sexuality an official or national project.[3] Indeed, the Code Noir is an example of a colonial policy that relied on surveillance and the policing of sexuality in order to instate colonial hierarchies of race, gender, and class by regulating the interactions of individuals. A resurgence of support for such policies is characteristic of periods of historical transition in which adherence to colonial ideologies begins to break down. In this essay, I will analyze literary depictions of sexual policing from two such periods of transition—the late 1930s and early 1940s in Haiti and the US South—in the works of Marie Vieux-Chauvet and William Faulkner. In such periods of upheaval, communities worked to preserve colonial relations in the post-/neo-colonial era by controlling the sexuality of individuals.[4] I argue that the antebellum US South, in addition to

prerevolutionary Haiti, is a colonial society, making both postrevolutionary Haiti and the postbellum South post-/neo-colonial.

As in Haiti, control over sexuality was central to the plantation culture of the antebellum US South as a tool for policing the color line.
While the US South is sometimes framed as a homogenous entity dif-
ferentiated from the rest of the nation, the region is multiplicitous; each
southern state has a distinct history and is made up of both urban and
rural areas. Moreover, the history of colonialism in the South differs
from state to state, and consequently, racial categorization varies as well.
For instance, as a result of French and Spanish colonialism, Louisiana is
the area of the South whose racial situation is most comparable to that
in Haiti, where a third racial category distinct from both the black and
white races existed, known as the mulâtres-aristocrates.[5] Louisiana was
under the jurisdiction of the Code Noir after 1724 and in addition had a
threefold racial system, in which Creoles of color functioned as an elite
third racial group, similar to the mulâtres-aristocrates in Haiti.[6] Racial
categorization in Louisiana was at odds with the binary understanding
of race that resulted from the one-drop rule—which considered biracial
individuals to be black—predominant in other areas of the antebellum
US South, such as the more representative Mississippi. Even in regions
where different conceptions of race dominated, as in Haiti and Mississippi, communities worked to preserve colonial relations through policing sexuality and interracial sex into the 1940s, as reflected in literature
of and about the period.

The sexual policing, or the regulation of who sleeps with whom and
who marries whom in relation to race, gender, and class, was integral to
the era of the late 1930s and early 1940s depicted in William Faulkner's
Go Down, Moses (1942) and Requiem for a Nun (1951), as well as in
Marie Vieux-Chauvet's Love, Anger, Madness (1968). The policing of
sexuality portrayed in the novels allowed the beneficiaries of colonialism,
the plantocracy in the US South and the mulâtres-aristocrates in Haiti,
to control the intersection of race and sexuality and to uphold colonial
hierarchies and mentalities in post-/neo-colonial societies as adherence
to them began to wane.[7] For example, the periods of turmoil in the US
South when social roles and relations were most in flux, such as after
the Civil War or in the 1930s and 1940s, were also times in which the
maintenance of the color line became more important in an attempt to
preserve colonial ideologies and the status quo: hierarchical relations
among white men, white women, and former slaves.

The late 1930s and early 1940s was a period of transition in both
Haiti and Mississippi. Love, the first novella in the Love, Anger, Madness
trilogy, is primarily set in a small Haitian town in 1939, five years after

the conclusion of the almost twenty-year American military occupation of Haiti (1915–1934). In the novella, the black class, which had been historically subordinated by the mulâtres-aristocrates since the Haitian Revolution, has seized power.[8] The commander in control, Commandant Calédu, routinely persecutes all members of the community, from street beggars and starving artists to the former aristocracy. The novella's 1930s setting is meant to evoke another moment of transition in Haitian history: in 1967, the year *Love* was written, the dictatorship of François "Papa Doc" Duvalier and his son Jean-Claude (which lasted from 1957 to 1986) "was becoming more and more severe, enrolling the poor as henchmen and -women, killing them to reduce their number, and persecuting intellectuals for their ideas and artists for their creations."[9] By calling to mind both 1939 and 1967, Vieux-Chauvet uses the chronology of *Love* as a way to comment on the entrenched nature of colonial ideologies in Haitian society. The atmosphere of fear and turmoil evoked by the layered settings of Vieux-Chauvet's novella is the fertile bedrock in which a mania of surveillance and sexual control flourishes.

The policing of sexuality is also central to Faulkner's "Delta Autumn," set in the early 1940s in the rapidly shrinking wilderness of the Mississippi Delta. In the agricultural US South, the 1930s and 1940s were the final decades of the transition from the plantation economy to the modern capitalist system that had begun during Reconstruction with the spreading of modernity and consumerism to the South and the region's growing economic dependence on the North.[10] A tension is observable between the introduction of the modern capitalist system after Reconstruction and the survival of the South's plantation economy "through the second half of the nineteenth century and about a third of the twentieth century" as a result of the limited opportunities available to the black labor force.[11] This climate of transformation is essential to the setting of "Delta Autumn," which is riddled with comparisons between past and present eras: "The paths made by deer and bear became roads and then highways" and "land across which there came now no scream of panther but instead the long hooting of locomotives."[12] The modernization that happened in the South over Isaac McCaslin's lifetime displaced nature. In reaction to the upheaval that altered the rural South in the 1930s and 1940s, Isaac turns to the colonial hierarchies of an earlier era as a way to cling to the past, including its static, outmoded racial relations.

Although he positions himself as progressive—through distancing himself from the sexual crimes of his grandfather, Old Carothers McCaslin, and disavowing his plantation inheritance—Isaac is unable to accept interracial relationships in the 1940s. "Delta Autumn" depicts Isaac's distress at the discovery that the mistress of his cousin, Roth Edmonds, is biracial, which Isaac evidently finds more disconcerting than the fact that the two produced a child out of wedlock together (or even that the relationship was incestuous). Isaac discerns the unnamed woman's racial heritage after she mentions to him that her aunt took in washing to help support her large family.[13] For all of his seemingly progressive views on race and inheritance, Isaac McCaslin unwittingly becomes an agent of the sexual policing of the color line, telling Roth's mistress, "We will have to wait" (346).[14] Isaac gives the girl a "thick sheaf of banknotes" for Roth in place of the acknowledgement of their interracial child and their twofold familial connection (339). In a way, Isaac's action echoes Old Carothers's attempt to bequeath to his slave Thucydus ten acres of plantation land (or, later, the land's cash equivalent of $200) as compensation for violating and impregnating, first, Eunice, Thucydus's wife, and then Thomasina, the daughter whom McCaslin sires with Eunice. The substitution of money or property for affection or a rightful place in the family tree thus continues in the twentieth century, evidence of how slavery's disruption of intimate relations and familial connections lingered in the neocolonial US South due to the persistence of colonial ideologies.[15]

To explore in more detail what is threatened by this sexual activity, I turn to another case of sexual policing in "The Bear," an example culled from the period of transition that followed the Civil War. In this scene, Sophonsiba Beauchamp (Isaac's mother) polices the sexuality of her brother, Hubert. After Sophonsiba's marriage to Theophilus "Buck" McCaslin, Hubert takes on a biracial cook and implied lover, whose "nameless illicit hybrid female flesh" excites and disturbs young Isaac (289). Isaac remembers "his mother's tearful lamentations," his uncle's assertion that "They're free now! They're folks too just like we are!," and his mother's dramatic ejection of the cook from the family's home. Although Sophonsiba is agitated by the actions of her brother, not her husband, her hysterical reaction is comparable to the sexual jealousy experienced by many plantation mistresses.[16] Sophonsiba balks at the feeling that she has been replaced in her brother's home, and on a less personal level, she seems invested in the preservation of the family line and the upholding of colonial hierarchies in the immediate postbellum period.

Both Roth's and Hubert's affairs appear to be consensual interracial relationships, which through their egalitarian nature constitute an even greater threat to colonial relations in the South and the racial hierarchy upon which they rest. If both members of an interracial relationship have a say in their liaison, it diminishes the power and significance of racial differences. Racial differences were central to the hierarchical plantation system, as well as to colonialism more generally, as they helped the plantocracy justify the abuse of the black bodies they judged to be less than human, less vulnerable to suffering than white bodies. As such, the threat posed by consensual interracial relationships in their deemphasis of racial differences is also a threat to the colonial system in its entirety.

In the same way that Faulkner's neocolonial South inherited colonial mentalities from the slave system, postrevolutionary Haiti inherited colonial hierarchies and an emphasis on surveillance from the Code Noir of the French colonial period in distinct but still recognizable forms. As a result, postrevolutionary Haiti remained plagued by segregation between racial and class groups. Surveillance of the interactions between these groups was essential to maintaining the divisions. This legacy of surveillance can be seen during the two settings evoked by Marie Vieux-Chauvet's *Love*: the post–US occupation era and the era of the Duvalier regimes.[17] Ideologies of race, gender, and class within the French Empire were not constructed once and frozen in time but have been constructed and reconstructed continually over the centuries.[18] Nevertheless, the transmission of the surveillance central to the Code Noir to later periods shows the degree to which these ideologies were embedded in Haitian society during the colonial era and the far-reaching network of their effects.

The Code Noir's emphasis on surveillance and the policing of the interactions between slaves and masters may be seen as the historical precursor to the observation and regulation of others' behavior depicted in the multilayered setting of *Love*. As such, the policing of sexuality in Vieux-Chauvet's novella may be seen as a legacy of Haiti's colonial past. The actions of the novella's narrator, Claire Clamont, a dark-skinned member of the typically light-skinned mulâtres-aristocrates, are watched closely. Claire cannot visit her childhood friend Dora Soubiran, who has been ostracized after her torture-rape at the hands of the dictator figure, Commandant Calédu, without the rest of her town knowing it. Further, Claire herself spies on the interactions of others: she watches the uprising led by Jean Luze and Joël Marti from her window before she participates in it—arguably in one of her less lucid moments—by stabbing Calédu.[19]

Sexuality in particular is policed so severely in Claire's town that even sexless encounters are sexualized by the community. The quasi-paternal bond between Tonton Mathurin (a black man) and Agnès Grandupré (a young mulâtress-artistocrate) is sexualized both by Agnès's parents and by their neighbors. Claire's parents state that Claire is not to play with Agnès anymore because "she's a nasty little girl who goes to old Mathurin's house behind her parents' back" (89). Licentiousness is seen as transmittable by Claire's parents, who assert that Mathurin lives in sin and "sin is contagious."[20] As a result, they sexualize Claire's encounters with Agnès: "How many times have you seen her? What did she tell you?

What have you done together?" (90; emphasis added). Similarly, Father Paul interrogates Claire about whether there is anything "untoward" in her friendship with Jane Bavière, another woman shunned by the community as a result of her bearing a child out of wedlock (132). Father Paul tells Claire, "Life has denied you certain pleasures, my child; try not to seek them in sin." Although Father Paul insinuates otherwise, the friendship between Claire and Jane, like that between Old Mathurin and Agnès, does not have a sexual component. Nonetheless, in addition to interracial interactions, same-sex relations are also policed by the community. In the same way that consensual interracial relationships like Roth Edmonds's and Hubert Beauchamp's liaisons challenge colonial hierarchies, "queer egalitarianism," which includes both homosexual and homosocial relationships, "marks the limits of the plantation myth by presenting an image of interpersonal relations not distorted by any kind of power differential."[21] Therefore, consensual same-sex relationships like that between Claire and Jane are more of a threat to the colonial order, due their dismantling of hierarchical associations, than exploitative relations that reinforce such hierarchies, like Calédu's violent rape of Dora.

Given her longing for intimacy and a child—she envies the ostracized Jane and wishes to switch places with a prostitute whom she describes as young, beautiful, and free (38)—Claire may have made different sexual choices if not for the prying, damning eyes of her community. Along with racism toward blacks, she has internalized her community's rules concerning sexual conduct and appropriate pairing and admits, "For fear of a scandal, I have repressed an ocean of love within me" (25). This phrase, "fear of a scandal," is repeated elsewhere in the novella, highlighting its centrality not only for Claire but also for the community on which she reports to the reader. Claire notes that it was "for fear of scandal" that her sister Félicia agreed to reconcile with her other sister, Annette, and that if vivacious Madame Audier, a fellow mulâtress-artistocrate, settled solely for her husband, "it was only for fear of scandal" (56–57). The collective fear of scandal in Claire's community connects to the fear of the loss of colonial order among its former beneficiaries, the mulâtres-aristocrates. The private, public, and national are inextricably linked, as revealed by the rampant anxiety about keeping the private out of the public. Colonial values are dispersed among the community at large, which then tries to impose them in the private sphere in order to control the behavior of individuals.[22] As part of the mulâtre-aristocrate community, Claire adheres to the principles regulating sexuality purely for decorum's sake, resulting in her abstinence and to an extent in her alienation, her obsession with sexuality, and her at-times irrational behavior, which one scholar, Hellen Lee-Keller, has gone so far as to label her "madness."[23] As shown through the example of Claire's repressed sexuality, the regulation of the individual by the community through the fear of scandal helps to maintain colonial ideologies at the personal and the collective levels in the post-/neo-colonial period.

I will turn to an example from one of Faulkner's late novels, *Requiem for a Nun*, for a final illustration of the different forms sexual policing takes in the twentieth century. *Requiem for a Nun*, like Vieux-Chauvet's *Love*, is set in the late 1930s, although in Mississippi as opposed to Haiti.[24] Unlike Claire Clamont, however, Nancy Mannigoe does not operate out of the fear of a scandal. Indeed, her murder of Temple Drake and Gowan Stevens's infant daughter, for whom she acted as a nurse, causes just such a scandal in Jefferson, followed by a sensationalized court case. Nancy's behavior does not appear to be dictated by societal norms; her southern community does not have the same control over her actions that Claire's Haitian town holds over her. Unlike the other examples I've discussed, the sexual policing at work in *Requiem* occurs from the bottom of society upward as opposed to from the top down. Nancy is a poor black woman in the South, repeatedly characterized by Gowan and Temple as a "dope-fiend nigger whore."[25] She is not a beneficiary of colonial society; rather, her policing of sexuality seems to result from her desire to protect the child and preserve Temple's family unit, not from an investment in colonial hierarchies.

Nevertheless, like Sophonsiba Beauchamp before her (who succeeds in convincing her brother to fire his biracial cook and lover), Claire's Haitian community concurrent with her (which polices Claire's sexuality so effectively that, against her wishes, she remains a virgin at thirty-nine), and Isaac McCaslin after her (who cannot bear the thought of Roth Edmonds and his biracial lover and child living together as a family unit), Nancy functions as an agent of sexual policing. Her act of infanticide prevents Temple from leaving her husband for a sexual union with white, lower-class Pete. As a lower-class black woman who polices the sexuality of an upper-class white woman, Nancy thus reverses the typical racial and class dynamic at work in colonial surveillance and sexual discipline. Although she claims her deed is for the children more than for Temple and Gowan, her action ultimately reinscribes the family ties that hold Temple subordinate to her husband.[26] Though perhaps unintentionally, Nancy's act thus reifies colonial hierarchies of gender and class. Her example reverses colonial race and class dynamics while simultaneously reinforcing the hierarchical structures of colonialism, demonstrating the plurality of such structures in the neocolonial period. Nancy's act of sexual policing reveals the ways in which colonial relations spiral out through other hierarchical relationships, illustrating the enduring and viral power of colonial ideologies in the 1930s and 1940s.

Like the other examples examined here, Nancy's act of sexual policing calls attention to the damage done by colonial hierarchies. Similar to the sexual abuse of Dora Soubiran in *Love* or Eunice and Thomasina in *Go Down, Moses*, Nancy's physical and sexual abuse at the hands of a white man exposes the bodily trauma essential to the colonial system, which granted white men license over female and black bodies. Temple recounts how the white man "knocked [Nancy] across the pavement into the gutter and then ran after her, stomping and kicking at her face or anyway her voice, which was still saying, 'Where's my two dollars, white man?'"[27] Further, the violence of colonial relations informs the novel on another level as well; *Requiem* registers the long-term effects of Temple's own sexual abuse and abduction in the earlier *Sanctuary* plotline, implicitly linking these traumatic events with Temple's seeming inability to perform the role of a wife and mother. In this way, *Requiem* insists that Temple's decision to abandon her husband and children and run away with a criminal does not occur in a vacuum but is directly connected to her own sexual abuse as a white female in a neocolonial culture.

In this way, *Requiem for a Nun*, like *Go Down, Moses* and *Love*, demonstrates the abusive relations that result from continued adherence to colonial ideologies in the twentieth century. However, as discussed above, the novels also hint at other options, alternatives to the replication of destructive colonial hierarchies. For instance, the consensual interracial relationships depicted between Roth Edmonds and his unnamed biracial relative and between Hubert Beauchamp and his nameless biracial cook, as well as the same-sex friendships between Claire Clamont and Jane Bavière, Agnès Grandupré, and Dora Soubiran, respectively, have the potential to defy colonial hierarchies through the relatively egalitarian footing on which they are all are situated. Hidden within the threat these relationships pose to colonial society is a potential solution to the persistence of destructive colonial ideologies. Indeed, by including these examples of resistance, Faulkner and Vieux-Chauvet confront, rather than passively reinscribe, colonial relations in the post-/neo-colonial era.

NOTES

1. William Renwick Riddell, "Le Code Noir," *Journal of Negro History* 10, no. 3 (July 1925): 323.

2. Ibid.

3. Sander L. Gilman, "Black Bodies, White Bodies: Towards an Iconography of Female Sexuality in Late Nineteenth-Century Art, Medicine, Literature," *Critical Inquiry* 12, no. 1 (Autumn 1985): 231. I credit Nicole Aljoe with this observation.

4. I refer to the era following the colonial period as "post-/neo-colonial" to imply through the juxtaposition of "post" and "neo" that the postcolonial period becomes neocolonial as a result of the lingering effects of the colonial system.

5. Ramón Saldívar, "Looking for a Master Plan: Faulkner, Paredes, and the Colonial and Postcolonial Subject," in *The Cambridge Companion to William Faulkner*, ed. Philip M. Weinstein (Cambridge: Cambridge University Press, 1995), 104. Thadious M. Davis describes Louisiana as "a microcosm of multiculturalism within the southern region that was not allowed to become the nation's dominant societal model" (*Southscapes: Geographies of Race, Region, and Literature* [Chapel Hill: University of North Carolina Press, 2011], 20). Davis argues that Louisiana had the potential to develop an alternative to the nation's system of racial segregation and hierarchical relations (ibid., 8).

6. Ibid., 197. According to Davis, the Code Noir was "the first law regulating slavery in Louisiana" (ibid., 196). The Louisiana Code Noir was modified with *La Siete Partidas*, a combination of Spanish and Roman law, and the resulting law was upheld even after Louisiana was transferred back from Spanish to French possession in 1801 (ibid., 197–98).

7. As the group that benefited most from the racist internal colonialism of slavery, white southern men were particularly invested in reaffirming the color line in order to maintain the colonial hierarchies that granted them full authority over the slave population and white women. Although white men seem to have positioned themselves above the color line in the South (through their widespread sexual violation of black women), they adamantly prohibited sexual contact between white women and black or biracial men, since white women were assigned the role of maintaining the purity of family lines.

8. For most of Haitian history, the mulâtres-aristocrates have been able to "concentrate a great deal of the country's wealth and a disproportionate share of political power," but in *Love* this position is endangered by the rise of a movement based on black power. See Madison Smartt Bell, "Permanent Exile: On Marie Vieux-Chauvet," *Nation*, February 1, 2010, 30. This corresponds historically with the rise of the *noiriste* movement during the 1930s in Haiti, which "emphasized Haiti's African past" (David Nicholls, *From Dessalines to Duvalier: Race, Colour and National Independence in Haiti* [New Brunswick, NJ: Rutgers University Press, 1996], 167). Nevertheless, Bell notes that although Vieux-Chauvet sets the story in 1939, this power reversal "resembles nothing so much as the Duvalier regime" (Bell, "Permanent Exile," 31).

9. Edwidge Danticat, introduction to *Love, Anger, Madness: A Haitian Triptych*, by Marie Vieux-Chauvet, trans. Rose-Myriam Réjouis and Val Vinokur (New York: Modern Library, 2010), xi.

10. Jay R. Mandle, *Not Slave, Not Free: The African American Economic Experience since the Civil War* (Durham, NC: Duke University Press, 1992), 68–69.

11. Ibid., 66, 21. Although modernity—in the form of free market ideology and labor mobility—may have been introduced in the US South following the Civil War, it did not effectively supplant the plantation economy until the World War I period, which marked the beginning of the end of the plantation system (ibid., 68–69). While some scholars argue that the plantation economy ran counter to modernist sensibilities, Davis asserts that the South had begun the transition to modernity before emancipation; the South, he claims, "depended upon the spread of market capitalism, including the interstate traffic in slaves, as an expanding basis for accumulating wealth in new marketplaces, and that aggressive capitalism produced both the hierarchal social structure and the glaring economic and social inequities still apparent after the twentieth century" (*Southscapes*, 13).

12. William Faulkner, *Go Down, Moses*, rev. ed. (1942; New York: Vintage International, 1990), 324–25. All quotations refer to this edition, and subsequent page references will appear parenthetically in the text.

13. In Faulkner's Yoknapatawpha County, taking in washing is a profession historically relegated to black women. Describing the modernization of Jefferson in "That Evening Sun," Quentin Compson notes that "even the Negro women who still take in white people's washing after the old custom, fetch and deliver it in automobiles" (William Faulkner, *Collected Stories* [1950; repr., New York: Vintage, 1977], 289).

14. I find Isaac's choice of pronouns in this statement interesting. His use of "we" places himself and the girl in the same position in relation to interracial sex, although the issue is much more real and immediate for the girl than it ever was for Isaac. This reduces or demeans the immediacy of the girl's predicament, as well as the possibility that her situation could be resolved were Roth Edmonds to form a family unit with her and her son.

15. While slaves were technically freed from their subjugated status after the Civil War, new social and economic arrangements such as sharecropping, the convict lease system, the Black Codes, and the Jim Crow laws replicated the racist structures of slavery during the neocolonial era. Significant change did not come until the post–World War II period (Mandle, *Not Slave, Not Free*, 84).

16. Sophonsiba's reaction may be seen as standing in for that of Old Carothers's nameless wife. Mrs. McCaslin's response to her husband's infidelities is never described in the novel. As a woman, she would likely not have written entries into the plantation ledgers, the documents that endure for perusal by descendants such as her grandson, Isaac McCaslin, which may account for this silence. Her voice is notably absent from the excerpted passages written in her husband's hand described on pages 254 and 255. Indeed, *Go Down, Moses* contains no evidence that Mrs. McCaslin received a genealogical entry in the ledgers.

17. For instance, during the US occupation period, armed patrols enforced the "Marine-imposed curfew," confiscated arms from Haitians, and collected intelligence about where potential revolutionaries lived through surveillance (Mary A. Renda, *Taking Haiti: Military Culture and the Culture of US Imperialism, 1915–1940* [Chapel Hill: University of North Carolina Press, 2001], 83). Moreover, the suppression of any form of dissent was central to the reign of Duvalier generations later through his "ever-widening web of repression and terror" and the notion that he had eyes everywhere due to his Tonton Macoutes (Laurent Dubois, *Haiti: The Aftershocks of History* [New York: Metropolitan Books, 2012], 327–28).

18. I thank Laura Prieto for this insight.

19. Marie Vieux-Chauvet, *Love, Anger, Madness: A Haitian Triptych*, trans. Rose-Myriam Réjouis and Val Vinokur (New York: Modern Library, 2010), 155. Subsequent references to this edition will appear parenthetically in the text.

20. The term *contagious* recalls the fear of the contaminating qualities of black blood that originated in the colonial era. Although all blood is red, white racists believed in biological differences between the races, which may explain the fixation on blood.

21. Michael Bibler, *Cotton's Queer Relations: Same-Sex Intimacy and the Literature of the Southern Plantation, 1936–1968* (Charlottesville: University of Virginia Press, 2009), 4.

22. I credit Elizabeth Hopwood with these insights about the relation between the public and the private.

23. Hellen Lee-Keller, "Madness and the Mulâtre-Aristocrate: Haiti, Decolonization, and Women in Marie Chauvet's *Amour*," *Callaloo* 32, no. 4 (2009): 1267. While I am unconvinced that Claire is a "madwoman," as opposed to a woman who performs irrational acts or behaves eccentrically (as in her obsession with Jean Luze or her clandestine

devouring of romance novels and pornographic postcards), I agree with Lee-Keller that Claire experiences alienation and a fragmented subjectivity due to the contradictions between her race, color, and social position and the racism she internalizes.

24. These novels are set almost two decades after the Nineteenth Amendment was ratified in the United States in 1920, which can be seen as illustrating the partial breakdown of colonial hierarchies of gender. There is thus a link between this period and the post-Emancipation period in the US South, when the Thirteenth, Fourteenth, and Fifteenth Amendments challenged colonial hierarchies of race, a challenge met in turn by revived interest in the color line during the era of Radical Reconstruction.

25. William Faulkner, *Requiem for a Nun* (1951; repr., New York: Vintage, 1975), 55.

26. However, there is also a sense in which Nancy's actions recall the trope, common in earlier US southern and Caribbean literature, of the good slave who sacrifices herself—often for her white family. One of the first instances of this trope is found in "Friendly Advice to the Gentlemen-Planters of the East and West Indies" (1684), in Thomas W. Krise, ed., *Caribbeana: An Anthology of English Literature of the West Indies, 1657–1777* (Chicago: University of Chicago Press, 1999), 51–77. The trope of the good slave recurs in abolitionist literature throughout the eighteenth and nineteenth centuries and is perhaps most overt in Maria Edgeworth's "Grateful Negro" (1804; repr. Gloucester, UK: Dodo Press, 2008). I thank Nicole Aljoe for suggesting this connection.

27. Faulkner, *Requiem*, 96.

In the Book of the Dead, the Narrator Is the Self: Edwidge Danticat's *The Dew Breaker* as a Response to Faulkner's Haiti in *Absalom, Absalom!*

Sharron Eve Sarthou

"The Egyptians, they was like us."
                    —*Edward Danticat, The Dew Breaker*

William Faulkner's *Absalom, Absalom!* and Edwidge Danticat's *The Dew Breaker*[1] create worlds populated with peoples who bear the weight of history, guilt, consequence, and time. If the past is not even past, most certainly the trauma of history is with us always. Moreover, the often traumatic histories of the United States and Haiti are more interconnected than most citizens of the former would believe, or perhaps want to believe. Faulkner uses that peculiar relationship to effect in his early-twentieth-century novel. Edwidge Danticat's *The Dew Breaker* is set in a late-twentieth-century, post-Duvalier world, and of all the characters in her episodic novel, the barber and "dew breaker" (torturer) Bienaimé is perhaps the most evocative of Haiti's persistent public image and of the complicated and intertwined histories of the United States and Haiti. He represents the violent and even inhumane creations of multiple, often US-supported regimes of the past. He is also very human and very much a "civilized" and thinking man. When US southerner William Faulkner invokes a Haiti where slavery still exists when it should not, when he describes Sutpen's gang of "wild [Haitian] negroes" as hunting like dogs and more than capable of cannibalism, he is employing a body of imagery and ideas historically used to marginalize Haitians and rationalize US paternalism in Haiti.[2] However, when Danticat's eponymous dew breaker, M. Bienaimé, invokes the Egyptians, he is claiming a heritage that validates his own world and challenges those who continue to define Haiti as infantile, historyless, and even futureless.

As Marie Renda, John T. Matthews, and many other scholars have discussed at some length,[3] an invocation of Haiti can be read as paradigmatic of the paternalistic and colonial interconnectedness between the United States and the Caribbean as well as an extension of the webbed Caribbean that Srinivas Aravamudan describes so eloquently and that is implicit in Paul Gilroy's work.[4] J. Michael Dash, Maritza Stanchich, Barbara Ladd, and others have engaged with discussions of the political, moral, and cultural context of Faulkner's Haiti, the "little lost island . . . manured with black blood from two hundred years of oppression" (202) where Sutpen gets that gang of enslaved "wild negroes" (27) who bury themselves in the "absolute mud," live naked save for that mud, and speak a "sort of French."[5] With some few exceptions, the majority of these discussions situate themselves within a US-centric context, using Faulkner as an exemplar of the ways the United States looks at Haiti. Particularly useful within a modern discussion of the shared histories of Haiti and the United States are Sara Gerend's examination of Faulkner's Haiti in the context of US imperialism and paternalism and Marie Renda's concept of Haiti as a deliberate US construct—a "fatherless child" who craves recognition and needs outside paternalistic discipline.[6] At the same time, these discussions continue to situate Haiti and Haitians as objects of the US gaze. Gerend, for example, uses *Absalom* as the basis for an extended examination of US paternalistic perspectives, particularly but not exclusively with regard to Haiti.[7] At the very least, Faulkner's novel exhibits problematic attitudes regarding the historical relationship between the United States and Haiti. What is also true is that Faulkner could invoke Haiti quite specifically because he could have a reasonable expectation of his audience's peculiar image of Haiti and Haitians.

The idea of Haiti as an infantilized and demonized land has been prevalent in American society since the time of the Haitian Revolution, which, as Eugene Genovese and others have argued at length, was a terrifying event for US slaveholders, simultaneously proving slaves capable of organized resistance and offering US slaves a potential model for their own self-emancipation. Moreover, for eighteenth- and nineteenth-century readers, Haiti was the most black, most African, most Other of the Americas, and these readers, like contemporary readers, would believe anything of Haiti—cannibalism, zombies, barbarism, vodou, infant sacrifice, or satanism.[8] It is important to consider what is invested in such attitudes—what ignorance is revealed by this stereotype of a "little lost island" (lost to slaveowners, anyway, thanks to the Revolution), which Faulkner locates at

the halfway point between what we call the jungle and what we call civilization, halfway between the dark inscrutable continent from which the black
blood, the black bones and flesh and thinking and remembering and hopes and
desires, was ravished by violence, and . . . the civilised land and people.[9] (202)

Persistently troubling is that even today, authors and filmmakers can rely
on the majority of their audiences believing pretty much any mysterious
or blatantly exaggerated stereotype that offers what Edward Said calls
"bizarre jouissance."[10]

To summarize, in writing the history of the mythic and tragically
doomed Sutpen family, Faulkner makes use of an idea of Haiti that
presupposes an audience prepared to believe that Haiti and Haitians
are barbaric, more than uncivilized, and really not quite human. And
dangerous, for several reasons, not the least of which is their blurring
of racial lines. Soon after the start of the Haitian Revolution, people
in the United States began to be aware that in Haiti, race was often
relative. Refugees who called themselves French could just as easily be
persons of mixed race who had assumed a white identity. Especially after
the upheaval of the Revolution, Haiti was full of light-skinned persons,
jaunes, persons with mixed heritage who called themselves French.[11] As
John T. Matthews argues, Eulalia Bon's "French" father, as a wealthy
landowner at a time when whites were legally prohibited from owning
land in Haiti, would likely have assumed that Sutpen would know of
his mixed heritage and would think nothing of it.[12] The United States,
even in Faulkner's time, was terrified of hidden racial impurity—many
considered miscegenation an abomination—and Haiti represented
that persistent danger. At the same time, Haiti is only three hundred
nautical miles from the United States and has been a valuable resource
for US business interests throughout the nations' shared history. Poor
white men like Sutpen could and did make themselves fabulously rich
there. The island of Hispaniola was once the most valuable of Caribbean
colonies and by some estimates the source of more than 60 percent of
France's gross domestic product.[13] It was not just in the interests of US
and Caribbean slaveholders but in the interests of US business to maintain a belief in the idea of an incompetent and incapable Haitian Republic, a belief informed by narratives such as nineteenth-century British
diplomat Spenser St. John's disgracefully dismissive memoir,[14] in which
he describes a Haiti incapable of organizing itself and run by childlike
Africans performing what Faulkner will call "the tragic burlesque of the
sons of Ham" (*Absalom*, 160). It was this objectifying gaze and the possibility of exploitation that enticed the United States to extend the Monroe
Doctrine to Haiti. US investments in Haiti continued throughout the

nineteenth century. Well into the twenty-first century, narratives such as Faulkner's, sensational popular media depictions of Haiti, and equally sensationalized news coverage continue to define Haiti as "not like us," meaning not "civilized" and inhabited by less-than-human, historyless people. When Danticat's Bienaimé looks to the Egyptians to find a historical connection with his own people, he is perhaps doing so, and claiming a proud African heritage, as a response to an almost universal resistance to the idea of a proud Haitian history.

The persistent "problem" with Haiti is that it does not, never will, and cannot be made to fit into a neat idea of Eurocentric history. The very existence of Haiti remains a rebuke to anyone who ever justified the institution of slavery and/or the colonization of supposedly uncivilized and infantile Africans. Haiti is very much not historyless, although many have tried to make it so since even before 1805, both in the United States and in Europe. Susan Buck-Morss is not the first to note this particular effort to relegate Haiti to a permanent servile/objectified condition and to silence or hijack its history.[15] George Handley suggests that the anachronism of Sutpen's/Faulkner's Haitian slavery is an exemplar of the "empire's objectifying gaze that symbolically orders time and marginalizes people."[16] Furthermore, under President Jean Pierre Boyer (whose presidency lasted from 1818 to 1843), a kind of serfdom was established in Haiti, and throughout the nineteenth century there were repeated peasant uprisings such as Sutpen might have encountered in 1827. US businessmen were welcome, and a series of regimes conscripted peasants in a nation-building effort that included work on plantations and for other profitable business ventures. In the nineteenth century, the US intervened several times in Haiti's affairs on the pretext of protecting US interests[17] and with the understanding that Haiti was alternately what missionary Wilhelm Jordan described as a "wayward girl" or a minor needing guidance.[18] Eventually, shortly after the overthrow of Haitian president Vilbrun Guillaume Sam on July 28, 1915, US marines invaded Haiti at Port-au-Prince on July 28, 1915. It was the sixth time the United States had invaded Haiti; this occupation was to be the longest and harshest. Significantly, a number of these marines were handpicked southern troops, chosen, British diplomat R. S. F. Edwards suggested, with the rationalization that southerners understood how to "handle colored people."[19] Despite the efforts of many Americans to provide alternative narratives to the hopeless infantilized accounts of Jordan and others such as marine corps general Smedley Butler, the occupation was to cement already distorted views about Haiti in the United States and inform texts such as Faulkner's novel. In 1920, for example, James Weldon Johnson, field secretary of the NAACP, wrote a scathing denunciation of the US invasion, "Self-Determining Haiti," for the *Nation*.[20] As Renda has explored extensively, subsequent to this invasion, Haiti became the increased object of fascination and horror for American popular literature and sensational film. Tales of voodoo, devil worship, cannibalism, infanticide, zombies, and endless perversion became synonymous with Haiti and Haitians, and this trope continues into today.[21] Unfortunately, this distorted view continues to obscure the real problems Haiti faces and the complex history that has been both distorted by deliberate economic and political manipulation from outside and exploited by power-hungry people inside the culture. Danticat's fictional characters negotiate a very real world shaped by cycles of violence and perceived through a perverse lens.

Much recent scholarship positions the work of contemporary Caribbean women writers as an effort to regain control of representation and to offer alternatives to the master narrative of their region—in essence, to give rightful voice to colonial and postcolonial histories and to female voices silenced by patriarchal narratives. As Danticat suggests, "it's not always easy to tell who the rightful narrators should be," and for Haitians and Haitian Americans, her work offers an alternative narrative to that of the distorted, violent, and irredeemable Haiti of popular culture.[22] Carine Mardorossian argues that Danticat's work offers counternarratives to Eurocentric, patriarchal, hemispheric, and largely imperialistic narratives such as Faulkner's *Absalom*, and she suggests that recovering those narratives can help mediate the shared history of repeated trauma.[23] Furthermore, Martin Munro suggests that "writers from [Haiti] have often taken on the role of defenders of the nation and the black race in general."[24] Danticat herself defines the act of writing, of "creating dangerously," as a kind of revolt against the silence imposed by autocratic and violent governments and, by extension, against the imperialistic gaze of the US that persists in seeing Haiti as the Other of Others, Faulkner's "halfway point between . . . the jungle and what we call civilization" (*Absalom*, 202).

Regardless of their "civilized" or "uncivilized" nature, the Haitians and Haitian Americans who narrate the majority of chapters in Danticat's *Dew Breaker* are linked by a proud history but an undeniably violent and destructive present in which their people face dire poverty and too often become pawns of one or another corrupt power broker. The older generation represented by the torturer Bienaimé also connects them all and is both product of that corrupt and destructive world and a source of resistance to it. While the corruption in Haiti may be overwhelming and persistent, individuals continue to resist, and Danticat's people are linked to the United States and back to Haiti by invisible, unbreakable strands of culture and history—as are the histories of the US South and Haiti interconnected, not only through the shared history of slavery but through the commerce between Port-au-Prince and New Orleans, Charleston, Savannah, and other southern ports.[25] Historically, the United States has been an exploitive, intrusive presence in Haiti (although ostensibly in the name of benevolent paternalism). Danticat's Haitians have no energy to be concerned with that larger history, however, and are contending with their own personal and familial histories, in which the United States remains a sometimes problematic and elusive refuge from the economic and political violence of a homeland that is simultaneously breathtakingly beautiful and heartrendingly terrible. Faulkner's Haiti never did exist, except as a figment of US imagination. By contrast, Danticat's fictional Haiti is rooted in an undeniable, if equally damnable and cyclical reality.

One cannot learn from the past if one does not know it. This is an essential part of Quentin's purpose in passing on his history to Shreve, for by the time Faulkner writes *Absalom*, Ellen Coldfield Sutpen, Charles Bon, Henry and old man Sutpen, Judith, Miss Rosa Coldfield, and Quentin—the novel's supposed witnesses to history—are all dead. This past is most assuredly past yet still continues to act upon the present, which in turn demands witnesses to make the past accessible.[26] As Quentin thinks, *"Maybe nothing ever happens once and is finished. Maybe happen is never once but like ripples maybe on water . . . the ripples moving on, spreading, the pool attached . . . to the next pool which the first pool feeds, has fed, did feed"* (210). But the past only speaks to the present if someone remains to bear witness: someone like Quentin, or Danticat's Ka. How else can the dead (the slaver Sutpen, the colonizing American, the dew breaker barber) be defended and/or brought to justice?

Danticat's novel suggests that all actors share in the repeated history of trauma. Her characters are specifically and doubly part of Haiti's troubled history of torturer and tortured. It is through this dichotomy that I suggest Danticat's *Dew Breaker* challenges Faulkner's Haiti and Haitians. For Haiti and Haitians to mediate their past and redeem a future, first they must deal with an imagined past and future, one which defines them as irretrievably Other. Sutpen's negroes speak no recognizable language, sleep in the mud, hunt like a pack of dogs, and appear to expect the body of the French architect as a prize for finding him. Haiti and Haitians have often been imagined as barbaric and almost prehuman, and Faulkner is not the first employ these concepts. If the average person "knows" anything about Haiti, it is that it is a violent and chaotic place, an uncivilized place. To return to Danticat, torture is not civilized, and the torturer is also an uncivilized person. Yet his role is that of an enforcer, ostensibly a bringer of order, though his very existence creates disorder. In this way the image of Haiti, however rooted in "fact," perpetuates a disordered view of Haiti and Haitians that impedes their development. Yet Danticat's Haitians prosper in the United States; claim a historically situated culture; are aware of their own responsibilities to the past, the present, and maybe even the future; and often speak two or more languages (English, kreyol, and French), which places them most definitively within "civilized" peoples.

Moreover, these characters actively resist the dehumanizing forces of corruption and violence. When Anne Bienaimé's brother, the preacher, publicly challenges the administration, he does so knowing he will die if he refuses to recite the "national prayer, written by the president himself" ("our beast," the preacher said, an overt allusion to Jonah's whale and a covert reference to the president [186]), which reads in part,

> Our father who art in the national palace, hallowed be thy name. Thy will be done, in the capital, as it is in the provinces. Give us this day our new Haiti and forgive us our anti-patriotic thoughts, but do not forgive those anti-patriots who spit on our country and trespass against it. . . . And deliver them not from evil. (185)

Even the former dew breaker, barber Bienaimé, has his breaking point: when the preacher offers himself as a willing sacrifice for his people, the dew breaker decides to spare him. As we shall see, it all goes very wrong, but like so many of Danticat's characters, these two men are complicatedly human. Danticat's Bienaimé, like Faulkner's Sutpen, escapes poverty through violence. Not being a white man from the United States, however, he is poisoned in a Haiti that has been crippled internally and externally. He is seduced by power and becomes a *macoute*,[27] a member of the national militia and terrorist arm of the regime, and subsequently a dew breaker—an instrument of torture and terror for the US-backed Duvalier regimes. When he escapes to the United States, Bienaimé brings his history with him and lives with the fear of being discovered. More, he fears judgment. When his daughter, Ka, is sure she sees a Haitian "monster" at a Christmas Eve service, she does not know what her parents know—that she is with one of the monsters, the calm and patient man sitting next to her. In addition, I suggest that when Danticat's Bienaimé claims a heritage that predates the European, he both acknowledges regret and seeks forgiveness for his present. In the rituals of the Egyptian Book of the Dead, souls are judged for their earthly lives; Danticat's Bienaimé hopes for mercy mediated by his *bon ange*,

Ka, whose name means "soul." Whereas the people in Faulkner's Book of the Dead bear witness to an unforgivable past, the people in Danticat's Book of the Dead hope to be judged with compassion.

Although as a young man Bienaimé was drawn to the syncretic and pan-African religion of vodou (also a central tenet for Duvalier and his *macoutes*), his wife, Anne, clings to a belief in Christian miracles. After all, she explains, Bienaimé's life is a miracle. He was a torturer and has become a kind and patient man. Believing he can find no sympathy in the present, he looks back to Egyptian civilization. His African heritage offers him a context for his own experience and a faint hope for redemption, or at least for an end to the cycle of repetition and revenge. It is the US-supported Duvaliers' nightmare world that made him into a tool of terror. It is in this capacity that he encounters Anne's brother, a preacher who has chosen to offer himself as a sacrifice in the fight against despotism. Although the decision is made to release him (martyrs sometimes being more dangerous than victims), the preacher precipitates his death by attacking the master torturer—Bienaimé. Ironically, this sacrificial murder of Anne's brother releases Bienaimé from the role of dew breaker. Injured, in pain, and running from the prison, he encounters Anne, who aids him and falls in love with him. It is his need to seek absolution for his act that allows Bienaimé—in the United States—to become a patient and kind husband and father. Helen Scott suggests that this text "wants us to reject such simple formulae as 'hunter and prey' in favor of complexity and indeterminancy," for "*every* story can be told from more than one perspective" and "even torturers may be loving fathers."[28]

If Bienaimé expects compassion from his *bon ange*, his daughter, he doesn't get it. Instead, when he confesses his true identity to his daughter, she rejects him as a monster. She, who has always imagined him the victim, is horrified to find out he was a maker of victims. She begins to think of her father's bedtime reading selections for her—selections from the ancient Egyptian Book of the Dead such as "Driving Back Slaughters," which her father had read to her to "drive away [her] fear of imagined monsters" (32). What the reader and Ka learn is that Bienaimé's nightmares feature himself as the monster (23), but what she cannot see is that he is also the victim. Eventually, however, she begins to understand that her parents' loss of family and country was a complicated ordeal and that her father's obsession with the Egyptians is more than a simple desire to connect with an African past. "The Negative Confession" ritual with which Bienaimé is obsessed was intended to give the dead a chance to affirm the good they had done in their lifetime. "I am not a violent man," he had read. "I have made no one weep. I have never been angry without cause. I have never uttered any lies. I have never slain any men or women. I have done no evil" (23). Ka and the reader also learn why anonymity in "the unfamiliar [United States] might have been so comforting" for Bienaimé (34) and why Anne is always so timid. "I would never do these things now," Bienaimé tells Ka (24). But as she tells us, forgiveness was not possible, as "[her] father, if anyone could, must have already understood that confessions do not lighten living hearts" (33).

In another Danticat chapter, "Monkey Tails," the fall of the Duvaliers signals yet another cycle of violence—this time against anyone who had profited from, colluded with, or in any way seemed connected to the fallen regime, especially the national militia, the *macoutes*. The narrator, Michel, and his mother hide under their beds while violence rocks the capital. He tells the reader that "overnight our country had completely changed. We had fallen asleep under a dictatorship headed by a pudgy thirty-four-year-old man and his glamorous wife. . . . Now the population was going after those militiamen, those macoutes, with the determination of an army in the middle of its biggest battle to date" (140). Now the people were after the blood of people like Mr. Bienaimé, and the implication is that new dew breakers will take the place of the old—and the cycle of violence will continue.

Like many of Danticat's readers, Aline, the Haitian American aspiring journalist who narrates another chapter, "The Bridal Seamstress," is oblivious to the complicated and violent histories that have shaped her people. She cannot imagine the world in which people like Beatrice, the Haitian seamstress, existed, "men and women whose tremendous agonies filled every blank space in their lives. . . . Hundreds, even thousands, of people like this, men and women chasing fragments of themselves long lost to others" (137–38). Nor can she see that they all remain connected by history and blood to that place, even knowing that "in Haiti . . . people see everything, even things they're not supposed to see" (73), or not knowing, or maybe not caring or only forgetting that Haiti is also a place to which, as Faulkner writes,

> you were not supposed (your mother didn't intend to, anyway) to ever go back . . . which you were not supposed to know when and why you left but only that you had escaped, that whatever power had created the place for you to hate it had likewise got you away from the place . . . that you were to thank God you didn't remember anything about it yet at the same time you were not to, maybe dared not to, ever forget it. (239)

Unlike the suicide Quentin Compson, Danticat's Haitians cannot escape their own history, even if they wanted to—not even after death.

Ka's parents cannot go back to Haiti, but they remain trapped in a Haitian world—in the United States. Conversely, in Danticat's chapter "Night Talkers," the character Dany returns temporarily to Beau Jour to see his aunt, Estina Estème, and determine whether a barber he has encountered in New York (perhaps Bienaimé?) is the *macoute* who killed his parents. We never know, and by the end of Danticat's novel, the reader is as confused as Dany, and almost as confused as Beatrice the seamstress, for the identities of dew breakers appear to be amorphous and changing. While he most certainly was *a* dew breaker, Bienaimé was not even the most famous of dew breakers, and he may or may not be the dew breaker in question in the stories of other characters. Everyone in these stories is a victim of political, economic, and/or social violence, and in the end, theirs is a world of lost fathers. Who can cry murder with surety, and what is forgiveness, in a world where life has always been a "pendulum between regret and forgiveness" (242)?

When Faulkner's Henry Sutpen kills the half brother who is his sister's fiancé, he also kills his *bon ami* and sacrifices his family's and sister's whole life for that sin. Danticat's Bienaimé kills his wife's brother but spends his whole life trying to make amends, all the while believing himself unforgivable. Unlike Henry, Bienaimé does not retreat into a dark room. Instead, he saves Ka's mother, Anne, and together they flee to the United States and give life to Ka, whose very name means witness and whose father describes her as the "*bon ange*," the good angel, who with Michel and Aline can bear witness and offer hope for an end to the cycles of violence, revenge, marginalization, and retribution. His is a world haunted by guilt and responsibility—by the weight of history—although he does not surrender to it.

Danticat's Haitians and Haitian American survivors are trapped in a violent world and, unlike the supposedly civilized southern slaveholders and their descendants, these Haitians seek redemption and hope for reconciliation. Bienaimé is obsessed with the Egyptians, who were like Haitians, he explains to his daughter, because they "worshiped their gods in many forms, fought among themselves, and were often ruled by foreigners. The pharaohs were like the dictators . . . and their queens were . . . beautiful" (12). If Ka's youthful Saturdays were occupied by the "golden masks, the shawabtis, and the schist tablets" (13), that experience offers her another African heritage, one not bloodied in the present. While her mother clings to a hope for Christian redemption and a belief in miracles, her father hopes for understanding. When Anne tells Ka, "You and me, we save him" (25), she is claiming that Bienaimé is worth saving. And if Bienaimé cannot say, in the words of "The Negative Confession," "I am pure. I am pure. I am pure,"[29] he can say that he knows the depth of his sin and he regrets it.

Faulkner's Compsons and Sutpens are part of a flawed, violent, and traumatic history that has consistently denied agency to the marginalized and the colonized in Haiti and elsewhere. Faulkner's own representations of Haiti continue that process. We are a culture that loves even our hateful past. In that, we share much in common with Danticat's Haiti. Her Haitians and Haitian Americans are also marked—but not marginalized—by history and horrific violence. They will be heard and seen, not as baying hounds or zombies or children, but as humans.

NOTES

1. Edwidge Danticat, *The Dew Breaker* (New York: Knopf, 2004), 12. Subsequent references to this edition will appear parenthetically in the text.

2. William Faulkner, *Absalom, Absalom!*, rev. ed. (1936; New York: Vintage International, 1990), 27, 207. Subsequent references to this edition will appear parenthetically in the text. Richard King's analysis of Faulkner's Sutpen and Haiti is yet another instance in which this Haitian presence is depicted as a deliberate construct. King argues that Faulkner had a "real, if oblique, relationship to Haiti as a place whose tortured history helped shape the history of the US South." See Richard King, "From Haiti to Mississippi: Faulkner and the Making of the Southern Master-Class," *International Journal of Francophone Studies* 14, nos. 1–2 (2011): 93.

3. See Marie Renda, *Taking Haiti: Military Occupation and the Culture of U.S. Imperialism, 1915–1940* (Chapel Hill: University of North Carolina Press, 2001); John T. Matthews, "Recalling the West Indies: From Yoknapatawpha to Haiti and Back," *American Literary History* 16, no. 2 (2004): 238–62; Richard Godden, *Fictions of Labor: William Faulkner and the South's Long Revolution* (Cambridge: Cambridge University Press, 1997); and Alfred Hunt, *Haiti's Influence on Antebellum America: Slumbering Volcano in the Caribbean* (Baton Rouge: Louisiana State University Press, 1988).

4. Srinivas Aravamudan, *Tropicopolitans: Colonialism and Agency, 1688–1804* (Durham, NC: Duke University Press, 1999); Paul Gilroy, *The Black Atlantic: Modernity and Double Consciousness* (Cambridge, MA: Harvard University Press, 1993).

5. J. Michael Dash, *The Other America: Caribbean Literature in a New World Context* (Charlottesville: University of Virginia Press, 1981); Maritza Stanchich, "The Hidden Caribbean 'Other' in William Faulkner's *Absalom, Absalom!*," *Mississippi Quarterly* 49, no. 3 (1996): 603–17; Barbara Ladd, "The Direction of the Howling: Nationalism and the Color Line in *Absalom, Absalom!*," *American Literature* 66, no. 3 (1994): 525–51.

6. Sara Gerend, "'My Son, My Son!': Paternalism, Haiti, and Early Twentieth-Century American Imperialism in William Faulkner's *Absalom, Absalom!*," *Southern Literary Journal* 42, no. 1 (2009): 17–31.

7. See also Susan Buck-Morss, *Hegel, Haiti, and Universal History* (Pittsburgh: University of Pittsburgh Press, 2009); Édouard Glissant, *Caribbean Discourse: Selected Essays*, trans. J. Michael Dash (Charlottesville: University of Virginia Press, 1999); Godden, *Fictions*; and Dash, *Other America*.

8. When Pat Robertson pronounced that the 2007 earthquake was recompense for the demonic pact that Haiti supposedly made in exchange for its independence, one can only suppose that Robertson was thinking of the Haitian revolutionary Boukman, who was a vodun houngan (priest), and that Robertson believes that slavery was not evil. On January 18, 2010, a guest on *Focus on the Family* followed up by saying that Satan had "abso-

lutely free reign" in Haiti and "you could literally feel evil there." Focus on the Family Daily, January 18, 2010, http://listen.family.org/daily/A000002441.cfm. The site has since become inaccessible.

9. Discussing Frantz Fanon and identity, Homi K. Bhabha notes the "displacement of time and person" that results from being the object of the colonial gaze "fixed at the shifting boundaries between barbarism and civility." See Homi K. Bhabha, *The Location of Culture* (New York: Routledge, 1994), 41.

10. Edward Said, *Orientalism* (New York: Vintage, 1978), 103. Said employs the Lacanian concept of *jouissance* to imply a deliberate pleasure obtained through the objectification and exotification of the Orient. Bizarre jouissance is the understanding of a place that renders it inaccessibly exotic and the Orient a "living tableau of queerness." I would suggest the same principle applies to Haiti. Anthropologist William Seabrook's *The Magic Island* (1929), for instance, perpetuated the myths of cannibalism and mystic eroticism that Renda exposes in her discussion of early-twentieth-century sensationalism regarding Haiti. More recently, cinematic representations of an exotic, sentimentalized Haiti can be found in the James Bond film, *Live and Let Die* (1973), the horror movie, *The Serpent and the Rainbow* (1988), and episodes of the 1990s television series, *Lois and Clark*.

11. According to Joan Dayan, it was "impossible to verify how many light-skinned people . . . crossed over the 'racial' line and happily . . . took refuge in the United States during the Haitian Revolution." See Joan Dayan, *Haiti, History, and the Gods* (Berkeley: University of California Press, 1998), 324n125. Dayan offers an extensive discussion of the historical complexities of race, blood, and identity in French colonies.

12. Matthews also discusses the cultural and literary repercussions of the confusions between "French" and white in Haiti (253).

13. See C. L. R. James, *The Black Jacobins: Toussaint L'Ouverture and the San Domingo Revolution*, 2nd ed. (New York: Vintage, 1963), 50–51; and Jan Rogozinski, *A Brief History of the Caribbean: From the Arawak and Carib to the Present* (Madison, WI: Meridians, 1992), 164. For a discussion of the complicated philosophical issues regarding France, the importance of Haiti, and decisions to continue slavery in Haiti, see also Philippe R. Girard, "Napoléon Bonaparte and the Emancipation Issue in Saint-Domingue, 1799–1803," *French Historical Studies* 32, no. 4 (2009): 587–618.

14. Spenser St. John, *Hayti: The Black Republic* (London: Smith, Elder, 1884). See also Hesketh Prichard, *Where Black Rules White: A Journey across and about Hayti* (New York: Charles Scribner's Sons, 1900).

15. As Carole Sweeney argues, Danticat is giving "back . . . a disembodied history and people through the 'saying out loud' of history" (64). Carole Sweeney, "The Unmaking of the World: Haiti, History, and Writing in Édouard Glissant and Edwidge Danticat," *Atlantic Studies* 4, no. 1 (April 2007): 64. See also Buck-Morss, *Hegel*, 149; and Miriam J. A. Chancy, *Framing Silence: Revolutionary Novels by Haitian Women* (New Brunswick, NJ: Rutgers University Press, 1997), 15.

16. George Handley, *Postslavery Literatures in the Americas: Family Portraits in Black and White* (Charlottesville: University Press of Virginia, 2000), 137.

17. For in-depth discussion of economic and cultural interconnections between the southern United States and Haiti in the nineteenth century, see Hunt, *Haiti's Influence*, passim. For the twentieth century, see Renda, *Taking Haiti*, 10, 22–23, 32, 34, 47, 48–53, 98–100, 110–11, 114–16, 117–20, 128, 144, 215, 260, and 319. See also Charles Forsdick, "'Burst of Thunder, Stage Pitch Black': The Place of Haiti in U.S. Inter-War Cultural Production," *Contemporary French & Francophone Studies* 15, no. 1 (2011): 7–18.

18. Wilhelm F. Jordan, quoted in Renda, *Taking Haiti*, 3, 6. In addition, US Marine Corps general Smedley Butler wrote at length about Haiti and frequently used terminology of the orphan child in need of a firm parental hand. A highly decorated soldier, Butler

served in Haiti and supported the occupation; however, he later became disillusioned with US interventionist rationale and lectured widely on the subject. Of his time in Haiti, he was later to say, "I helped make Haiti and Cuba a decent place for the National City Bank boys to collect revenues." See Abigail Beardsley, "Smedley Darlington Butler," http://pabook.libraries.psu.edu/palitmap/bios/Butler_Smedley.html.

19. Paul Farmer, *The Uses of Haiti* (Monroe, ME: Common Courage, 2006), 85. For a more thorough discussion of the occupation, see Robert Heinl and Nancy Heinl, *Written in Blood* (Boston: Houghton Mifflin, 1978), 489. Farmer and the Heinls take issue with Edwards's account of the benevolence of the US occupation, a benevolence that is largely supported by various other contemporary accounts, including that of Colonel Waller and Captain John Houston Craige.

20. James Weldon Johnson, *Self-Determining Haiti* (1920), Project Gutenberg, http://projectgutenberg.org/etext/#35025 (accessed January 15, 2014).

21. As Farmer notes, it was almost a cliché that Haiti should become the mythical source of the HIV epidemic rather than a nation whose grinding poverty made it vulnerable to sexual tourism and other forms of exploitation by international visitors (226).

22. Edwidge Danticat, *Create Dangerously: The Immigrant Artist at Work* (Princeton, NJ: Princeton University Press, 2010), 102.

23. Carine Mardorossian, "Danticat and Caribbean Women Writers," in *Edwidge Danticat: A Reader's Guide*, ed. Martin Munro (Charlottesville: University of Virginia Press, 2010), 39–51.

24. Martin Munro, introduction in *Edwidge Danticat: A Reader's Guide*, ed. Martin Munro (Charlottesville: University of Virginia Press, 2010), 3.

25. See Hunt, *Haiti's Influence*, passim; Gerend, "'My Son, My Son!,'" 18–20; and Farmer, *Uses of Haiti*, 21–22 for comprehensive discussions of economic and cultural interconnections between the US South and Haiti.

26. Faulkner's novel suggests that time is fluid and nonlinear. Faulkner himself argued that "there is no such thing as *was*—only *is*." See James B. Meriwether and Michael Millgate, eds., *Lion in the Garden: Interviews with William Faulkner 1926–1962* (1968; repr. Lincoln: University of Nebraska Press, 1980), 255. David Watson has examined "the suspended time of the South" in Faulkner's work, "the aporia during which the South knows itself as the ghost of its own past." David Watson, "Southern Time: Transnational Temporalities in William Faulkner" (paper presented at the Annual Meeting of the Modern Language Association, Chicago, IL, December 27–30, 2007), 7.

27. *Macoute* translates literally as "bogeyman," and members of the Haitian militia were known as *tonton macoutes*, or *macoutes*.

28. Helen Scott, *Caribbean Women Writers and Globalization: Fictions of Independence* (Burlington, VT: Ashgate, 2006), 30.

29. E. A. Wallis Budge, *The Book of the Dead* (1895), Project Gutenberg, http://www.projectgutenberg.org/etext#7145, Book 9, 190–95, last modified December 1, 2004.

Contemporary Black Writing and Southern Social Belonging: Beyond the Faulknerian Shadow of Loss

LISA HINRICHSEN

The US South has long been thought of as a gothic region saturated in loss and haunted by a history that sets it apart from the progressive temporality of the nation at large.[1] While recent work has historicized such representation within the context of a national ideology wherein southern "backwardness" not only coexisted with but was a necessary component of the emerging identity of the United States as a liberal democracy, the region in many ways is still positioned problematically in the popular cultural imagination as a gothic space in which "the past is never dead. It's not even past."[2] As Teresa A. Goddu, Joan Dayan, and Harry Levin have noted, the gothic, as an elastic concept, is central to the development of American literary nationalism.[3] Yet in constructing and contesting national narratives, the gothic has also played a special role in representing the historically oppositional identity of "the benighted South," to use George Tindall's term, framing it as a dark other, a spatial repository for cultural contradictions that must be disavowed to enable a national mythology of innocence.[4]

From the tight family romance of "A Rose for Emily," with its studied appropriations of the British gothic tradition, to the growing narrative breadth of *The Sound and the Fury* and *Absalom, Absalom!*, Faulkner consistently deploys the gothic's emphasis on affect and defamiliarization to reveal the social and psychic dynamics that support southern life, parsing in the process his own ambivalent attachment to structuring social fantasies—ideologies of race, class, and gender—as they were beginning to be destabilized in modernity, thereby presenting the affective sensation of the unreality of this historical transition.[5] Faulkner's modernist engagement with the gothic mode, which peaks in the period from *The Sound and the Fury* (1929) to *The Hamlet* (1940), thus offers a complex formulation of individual psychology and collective identity. Consider his interest in *Soldiers' Pay* in isolation, failures of communication, self-destructive or sterile attempts to recapture a personal or cultural past—a vision of lost wholeness fundamental to his canon; *Mosquitoes'* emphasis on parental betrayal, incest, frustration, and the forging of identity; *The Sound and the Fury's* rendering of the family home as a haunted stage upon which the tragedy of patriarchal inheritance is dramatized in compulsive repetition, fantasy, obsession, and nostalgia; *Sanctuary's* sexualized coalescence of law, paternal order, communal life, and traumatic testimony left unheard because of socially mandated silences; the presentation in *Light in August* of Joe Christmas's occupation of a sphere of loss, separation, and abjection; and *Absalom, Absalom!'s* use of increment and recapitulation to reveal the disavowal and misrecognition that structure the ideologies of family and racial purity that leave Sutpen's dynastic design consumed, like the House of Usher, by its own originary violence. By exposing how dominant cultural currents circumscribe and inform individual psychology and by lending a narrative form to otherwise repressed or disavowed aspects of social and psychic existence, the gothic destabilizes the self-protective fictions that undergird traumatizing ideologies of communal belonging.

Reading Faulkner's use of the gothic in this manner takes it seriously as a mode of social critique and departs from a history of criticism in which critics have viewed the gothic's role in Faulkner's work in binary terms, seeing it as either an anachronistic, sensationalistic aesthetic mode to be dismissed (as when Cleanth Brooks defends *Absalom, Absalom!* against other critics who would reduce it to a mere "bottle of Gothic sauce") or as a form commensurate with a pathological reality, furthering the trope of the backward South, as a reviewer of *As I Lay Dying* did when he wrote that the rural Mississippi of the novel was "productive only of hatred, passion, and frustration."[6] Early responses to Faulkner's work, such as those by Henry Seidel Canby and Henry Nash Smith, called attention to his gothic obsession with decay and insanity and drew on the logic of the genre as a way, in Leigh Anne Duck's words, "to understand southern culture and to distance it . . . both spatially and temporally from national culture."[7] Offering up Faulkner's work as evidence, Ellen Glasgow's 1935 proclamation of a "Southern Gothic School" claimed that it dramatized "one vast disordered sensibility," a phrase that betrayed a belief in a collective "mind of the South," however disordered, with a set of shared affective energies and aesthetic visions.[8] Yet well aware of the way the romance of their work was understood as realistic, southern writers, Faulkner among them, spoke back to the ways in which national culture understood the southern gothic—the sense that it mirrored pathologies endemic to southern subjectivity—highlighting the intellectual provincialism of such views and reframing the function of the gothic and the grotesque in wry, ironic terms; think of Flannery O'Connor's observation that "anything that comes out of the South is going to be called grotesque by the Northern reader, unless it is grotesque, in which case it is going to be called realistic," and of Gavin Stevens's decrying of the northern "eagerness to believe anything about the South not even provided it be derogatory but merely bizarre enough and strange enough."[9]

While considering the stereotypes associated with the southern gothic and noting the way writers, including Faulkner, have resisted this label, more recent critics such as Elizabeth Margaret Kerr, Louis Palmer, Susan V. Donaldson, Eric J. Sundquist, and Duck have reinvigorated critical attention concerning the nuanced and vital role the gothic plays in Faulkner's work.[10] Emphasizing its role not only as an aesthetic mode but as a means of social critique, these critics have helped unfold the genre's function within the arc of Faulkner's fiction (Kerr), situating it alongside his interest in the pastoral and the sublime (Donaldson), unpacking its role in the imaginative construction of region and nation (Duck), and highlighting its relationship to the representation of race (Palmer, Sundquist). In contrast to a literary and cultural tradition that has historically understood the southern gothic in universalizing abstractions, Faulkner's version of the genre roots it in the specifics of space and place, less in "the South" (as imagined monolith) than *a* South, less in "the mind of the South" than in the mind in all its complexity. Rather than representing a monolithic cultural pathology, Faulkner draws on the gothic as a way to dramatize the nuances of individual experience that lie outside fantasies about social norms, pushing at the limits of psychoanalytic epistemologies in the process and destabilizing discourses of power and knowledge by demonstrating the reliance of modernity on excluded, denigrated, or superseded others.

Yet through the gothic, Faulkner's work cements a nexus of tropes about the region and its codes of racial and sexual life that comes to be both repeated and resisted by African American writers. Though blackness has functioned as an imaginative source for the production of the gothic, with its coded negotiations of racial discourses and oppression, as Harry Levin and Leslie Fielder have delineated, it has also historically been a mode for providing Anglo-American culture with a way of constructing racial, sexual, and gendered alterity. Especially in its American form, the gothic has historically stressed the black body's deviance; as Toni Morrison has argued, the realities of racism inform gothic romance, which is haunted by the "fabricated brew of darkness, otherness, alarm, and desire" that comprise American racial fantasies.[11]

Acutely aware of the variety of memory work in the South and the way in which, as Fitzhugh Brundage has noted, memory and commemorative practices provide "a genealogy of social identity" and "forge identity, justif[y] privilege, and sustai[n] cultural norms," African American southern writers in Faulkner's wake seek to contribute to the complexity of ideological beliefs, moral valuations, cultural mores, and symbolic boundaries of black belonging and to make visible and intelligible present-day black life where it has been obfuscated by white claims of past loss.[12] In confronting how conceptions—and popular misconceptions—of white loss might have been used to legitimize or excuse certain pervasive forms of exclusion, racism, and homogeneity and mobilized to found a community imaginatively and politically invested in nostalgic or memorialized pasts, these writers address the function of the gothic, as a genre of loss, in fostering a culture held in the grip of slavery but not of race. In reckoning with "Faulkner," and with narratives that have too often been read in ways that fetishize white (psychological) loss rather than acknowledge black (material) suffering, which give rise to what Michael Kreyling calls "the Quentin thesis," or "the promotion of Faulkner's Quentin Compson to the status of universally acknowledged spokesperson for the Southern psyche," contemporary black southern writers draw attention to the limitations of Faulkner's construction of racial identity and seek to inscribe nuanced representations of African American experience, dislodging in the process the equation of "southern" with whiteness.[13]

While there are a number of African American writers who write with a conscious yet ambivalent sense of indebtedness to Faulkner's configurations of the gothic while refiguring the genre to convey the particularities, complexities, terrors, and joys of African American experience—see Erna Brodber's fiction; Suzan-Lori Parks's work, especially *Getting Mother's Body*; Octavia Butler's recasting of the gender hierarchies of the gothic; and Toni Morrison's novels, especially her ghostly *Beloved* (1987)—I want to focus on Randall Kenan's queer appropriation of the gothic, which extends Faulkner's use of the genre as a form for signifying on dominant cultural fears and desires concerning race and sexuality. As George Hovis has argued, many of Faulkner's concerns—the myth of the South, the complex interplay of past and present, the significance of race, and the individual in relation to family and community—resonate within Kenan's work.[14] In this regard, as Brannon Costello claims, Kenan can be seen as a "gay Faulkner," drawing on established tropes and themes of canonical southern fiction while voicing the long-silenced realities of black queer life in the South.[15]

From short stories like "Tell Me, Tell Me," which explores the dilemma of white subjectivity moored in a past with which it refuses to come to terms, and "Let the Dead Bury Their Dead," to his novel, *A Visitation of Spirits*, Kenan challenges the mythic South—what we might call the South of "Faulkner"—by confronting the ghosts of southern history and memory, reworking stock stereotypes of the southern gothic and grotesque, and signifying on the power structures and the racial and sexual violence underlying everyday American life. By inscribing black queer identity into the South and emphasizing the ways "the South is always already queer," Kenan reacts against a monolithic conception of southern community—the type of supposedly "true community" "held together by manners and morals deriving from a commonly held view of reality" that critics such as Cleanth Brooks saw rendered in Faulkner's Yoknapatawpha.[16] In undermining the conventional notion of southern community as "organic," reacting against a notion of heteronormativity as the prerequisite for good citizenship and social belonging, Kenan calls into question the familiar orthodoxies of white Renascence fiction, drawing attention to the silenced bodies of the marginalized, reclaiming and reinscribing a multitude of voices made and silenced by normative discourse, and revising the gothic from a form of "backward glance" to a political force for present-day change.

Though gothic resolutions often assert heteronormative prerogatives, Kenan's queering of the genre problematizes monolithic constructions of African American identity by placing the often disparate discourses of black and queer subjectivity in conversation. In noting how the gothic is "coloured by the exoticism of transgressive sexual aggression" and experience, George Haggerty has demonstrated how, in queering reality through the aesthetics of defamiliarization and the fantastic, the gothic can foster an awareness of "otherness," reflecting anxieties about the patriarchal, heteronormative order of social relations allied to modern capital and yet threatened by it.[17] In mobilizing gothic tropes of haunting, ghosts, and the supernatural and reacting against an image of the South as "the mausoleum of all hope and desire,"[18] Kenan emphasizes how the marginalization of gay African American bodies has a disruptive, uncanny power that disturbs not only conceptions of monolithic southern community but also models of southern history and memory that demand the erasure of social, sexual, and racial difference. Aware of how the gothic has historically undergirded certain hegemonic versions of race, community, region, and nation, Kenan thus signifies on the regulatory implications of the genre, revealing how gothic effects are reimagined after an age of sexual and gender liberation while underscoring how this freedom is an unfinished project; in dramatizing the violent suicide of Horace Cross, queered by both color and desire, *A Visitation of Spirits* places the difficulty and the imperative of survival at its forefront. As both a figure of sympathy and a bearer of monstrosity, Horace, a child, is both a repository of the future and a force that threatens to destroy it, and his story emphasizes the difficult politics of life for queer black youth in the South, past and present.

A *Visitation of Spirits* narrates the events leading to and surrounding Horace's suicide. Set in the fictional town of Tims Creek, North Carolina, the novel recounts, via multiple perspectives and narrators, scenes from three noncontiguous days in 1985. The main story follows the final hours of Horace's life, narrating flashbacks of his experiences and describing the nightmarish adventures he undergoes on the night of his death, while alternating with his cousin (and preacher) James Malachai Green's narrative, which documents the impact his young cousin's death has had upon him. Realizing that his homosexuality dooms him in the eyes of his family—one of the founding families of Tims Creek—and the community in which they live, Horace "suddenly . . . became fully aware of his responsibilities as a man, and the possibilities of his being a homosexual frightened him beyond reason."[19] Thus "beyond reason," and driven by a desire "just to survive in some way. To live" (27), Horace turns to magic, desiring to cast a spell that will transform him into a bird, and signaling his wish for fluidity against the community's stringencies and inflexible "moral laws" (12). Through a gothic supernaturalism that recalls Faulkner's narrative experiments in *As I Lay Dying* with posthumous narration, queer knowledge, and magical thinking—all of which serve to expose the "real" as an arbitrary category, illuminating forms of queer knowledge at odds with the rationalizing and regulatory impulses of modernity—Kenan dramatizes Horace's desire for possibilities outside an imprisoning normative order shaped by the "rationality" of heterosexuality.[20] Magic works against traditions of sanctioned knowledge and practice and becomes, for Horace, an attempt at overcoming and negotiating his sense of lack and loss. Led by a wish to be "unfettered, unbound and free," he draws on the imaginative plasticity of magic in his search for political, social, and personal alternatives (Kenan, 13).[21]

Yet the spell, muddled because Horace finds himself unwilling to make the necessary sacrifice of a human infant, fails in its promises. Instead of offering a transformative freedom, the demon he invokes dramatizes his abjection, becoming "the very voice of pain and anguish and sorrow itself" (27), taking him on a nightmarish trip through his past. This journey reveals the contours of a world that has continuously assaulted him through its heteronormative demands, making him into "a tortured human" (12), "bound by human laws and human rules," and framing his identity as a "flawed" (188) "son of the community" marked by "a deviation." Within his family, there remains no place for those individuals who deviate: Horace's identity and sexuality will never be condoned by his church, family, or community: "Here was community. . . . It was from them he was running" (73). For Horace, survival means surviving "*into* threat."[22] As Kenan writes, "What does a young man replace the world with, when the world is denied him? True, the world was never his, but if the promise of the world, free of charge, is suddenly plopped in his lap and then revoked? If the rights and freedoms of patricians are handed to him and then snatched away? If he is given a taste of a shining city of no limits, and then told to go back to the woods?" (239).

Loss, as Haggerty has argued, functions in the gothic as a conspicuous mark of unrealized personhood, one which implicates normative culture in the undoing of queer desire. As a trope of excess, the gothic registers a failure of subjectivity brought on by a "cultural system that commodifies desire" at the same moment that it "renders it lurid and pathological."[23] This inscription of loss means that gothic novels reiterate (hetero)normative fictions—for instance, of the family—with a difference, calling attention to the disavowals and internal contradictions upon which the status quo depends. The gothic thus preserves what is lost "in a form that means it will be found—if ever it is found—with a specifically gothic mode of recognition."[24] With its aesthetics of estrangement, ambivalence, and affect, the gothic offers a means of defamiliarizing everyday order. As an ideologically contradictory and complex discourse system, it offers a "code" that is "not a simple one in which past is encoded in the present or vice versa, but dialectical, [with] past and present intertwined, each distorting each other."[25]

Like Quentin Compson, Horace finds himself unable to "grow sideways," to use Kathryn Bond Stockton's term, into his own queer belonging.[26] As Stockton notes, "'growing up' may be a short-sighted, limited rendering of human growth, one that oddly would imply an end to growth when full stature (or reproduction) is achieved."[27] Against the pressures of cultural tradition and mores, and the pressures of a family line that dictates behavior, Horace can only grow "up" into a self that is, in Quentin Compson's words, "shadowy paradoxical," and he ends up pushed out of time and space.[28] In a world that neither recognizes nor condones his desires, he comes to desire the fantasy of violent retribution. Thus possessed, exiled, and despairing, Horace takes his own life in the morning hours of April 30, 1984. Like Quentin, who speaks of "all I had done shadows . . . without relevance inherent themselves with the denial of the significance they should have affirmed,"[29] Horace's existence is lacking in affirmation and led by a driving desire for death: "Suddenly life beneath the ground had a certain appeal it had never had before. It was becoming attractive in a macabre way. No more, no more ghosts, no more sin, no more, no more" (Kenan, 231). Horace's vision of a South offers him "no future," only the linear temporalities of generational repetition that tortured Quentin.[30] Trapped in a community that seeks to negate his desires, rendering them "no more," Horace, like Quentin, is left melancholic, desperate, and depleted: like an "an empty hall echoing with sonorous defeated names," he, too, is "not a being, an entity," but "a commonwealth," bound to the imprisoning norms of his community.[31] Bound by the pressures of community, his psyche, like Quentin's, has no room of its own, "filled" as it is with the ghostly, gothic presence of the historical precedents that went into his making; each young man is "a barracks filled with stubborn back-looking ghosts still recovering . . . from the fever which had cured the disease."[32] Unable to grow up without being inhabited by ghosts they can neither comprehend nor exorcise, both Quentin and Horace are left with suicidal self-loathing that collapses individuality under the pressures of a family line that dictates behavior.

Yet in focusing on black queer subjectivity instead of melancholic white loss, Kenan swerves from a vision of history as inherently involving catastrophic self-dispossession without the possibilities of transcendence—a view that underlies white Lost Cause ideology, with its sense that the Civil War can never be transcended, that its past is never past, that progressive history is impossible. Instead, by exposing how dominant cultural currents circumscribe and inform individual psychology, and by lending a narrative form to otherwise repressed or disavowed aspects of social and psychic existence, the gothic, as Kenan uses it, provides a way of writing *past* trauma that destabilizes the self-protective fictions that undergird traumatizing racial and sexual ideologies. Though Horace kills himself, seeing suicide as the only way out of the demands of inheritance and patrimonial filiation that offer him "no future," Kenan's text extends beyond this viewpoint. As Maisha L. Wester has pointed out, Kenan "dismantles the genre's tropes of grotesque monstrosity and 'unspeakable' subjectivities to posit that the 'transgressive' bodies and behaviors themselves are not monstrous"; rather, "the social processes and institutions that define these bodies as aberrant monstrosities are the actual horrors."[33] As she argues, Horace's death establishes a haunting presence within the community that comes to change it.

Horace's death suggests a need to reconsider history and search its tombs for the bodies and voices of disruptive figures sacrificed for the sake of unity, foregrounding the necessity of altering the material conditions and circumstances on which queer futurity is predicated. At its conclusion, *A Visitation of Spirits* reminds us that without memory, there can be no future. The section describing Horace's death consequently concludes that in the case of his suicide, "Ifs and maybes and weres and perhapses are of no use. . . . The facts are enough, unless they too are subject to doubt" (Kenan, 254). The passages indicate that memory and history are subject to constant rewriting as we search for the voices, bodies, and elements that the "facts" missed, distorted, or suppressed. Against the impulse to remember the southern past as "'idyllic' and pastoral and perfect" (172), Kenan's work reminds us that "memories have a way of censoring themselves, calling up only the sweet, the pleasant, the joyful . . . rarely the pain or the hurt or the uncertainty." Kenan transcribes that loss and desire into the final pages of his narrative, which offer a corporealized—and queer—commentary on history, memory, and community. In his last recollected moments, Horace offers a form of testimony that juxtaposes the memory of the tastes and smells of home with the recollection of an erotic encounter: "I remember watching men, even as a little boy. . . . I remember thighs, the way they looked like mighty columns, steel bundles of fiber, covered with hair like down. I remember the way my neck would prickle and my breath would come shallow" (248). In mobilizing the friction between individual affect and fictive collectivity, echoing an ongoing tension within gay representation between "the unspeakability of desire . . . and group life,"[34] Kenan sets queer testimony ("I remember") side by side with communal memory ("Once upon a time") to change the structure of collective imagining.[35] In so doing, Kenan suggests that pleasure can be the grounds for a new version of the historical that draws on the collective, idealistic, and socially situated possibilities of sexual liberation and works against a community that has made a point of forgetting the joyous bodily experiences of queer belonging. As Charles E. Morris III suggests, a queer orientation to memory should "disrupt historiography as a regime of the normal by exploring queer historical imaginations" and complicate and question narratives of the past that minimize difference by solidifying national, cultural, and political identities.[36]

In this way, Horace's death initiates a communal rethinking of core ideologies, as the final lines of the novel indicate: "And it is good to remember that people were bound by this strange activity, . . . bound by the necessity, the responsibility, the humanity. It is good to remember, for too many forget" (257). In using the word "bound," Kenan's novel inscribes the history of enslavement against forgetting, mobilizing slavery as a source of historical haunting against a community's impulse to repeat structures of exile and subjection against its own members. By the end of his collection, Kenan posits that only through a confrontation with the space between remembering and history—a haunted, gothic space—can individuals alter the paradigms of identity. By drawing on the gothic while revising and appropriating a genre traditionally understood as Eurocentric, *A Visitation of Spirits* asks us to reconsider how we construct southern collective identity, challenging African American communities to become more inclusive. Like Quentin's untimely end, Horace's suicide requires us to confront silenced and sacrificed bodies in order to envision a different future for the presence of the southern past.

NOTES

1. See Leigh Anne Duck, *The Nation's Region: Southern Modernism, Segregation, and US Nationalism* (Athens: University of Georgia Press, 2006), esp. her chapter on "William Faulkner and the Haunted Plantation" (146–76); and Jennifer Rae Greeson, *Our South: Geographic Fantasy and the Rise of National Literature* (Cambridge, MA: Harvard University Press, 2010), esp. chapter 4, "The Enemy Within" (91–114).

2. William Faulkner, *Requiem for a Nun* (1951; New York: Vintage, 1975), 80.

3. See Joan Dayan, *Haiti, History, and the Gods* (Berkeley: University of California Press, 1995), chiefly chapter 4, "Gothic Americas" (187–268); Teresa A. Goddu, *Gothic America: Narrative, History, and Nature* (New York: Columbia University Press, 1997), esp. chapter 4, "The Ghost of Race: Edgar Allan Poe and the Southern Gothic" (73–93); and Harry Levin, *The Power of Blackness: Hawthorne, Poe, Melville* (New York: Knopf, 1958), esp. chapter 1, "The American Nightmare" (3–35).

4. See George B. Tindall, "The Benighted South: Origins of a Modern Image," *Virginia Quarterly Review* 40 (Spring 1964): 281–94.

5. See Lisa Hinrichsen, "Writing Past Trauma: Faulkner and the American Gothic," in *William Faulkner in Context*, ed. John T. Matthews (New York: Cambridge University Press, 2015), 219–27.

6. Cleanth Brooks, *William Faulkner: The Yoknapatawpha Country* (New Haven, CT: Yale University Press, 1963), 295; review qtd. in Thomas M. Inge, ed., *William Faulkner: The Contemporary Reviews* (Cambridge: Cambridge University Press, 1995), 49.

7. Duck, *Nation's Region*, 147.

8. Ellen Glasgow, "Heroes and Monsters," *Saturday Review of Literature* 12 (May 4, 1935): 3, 4.

9. See Flannery O'Connor, *Mystery and Manners: Occasional Prose* (New York: Farrar, Straus and Giroux, 1969), 40; and William Faulkner, *Intruder in the Dust* (New York: Random House, 1948), 153.

10. Elizabeth Margaret Kerr, *William Faulkner's Gothic Domain* (New York: Kennikat, 1979); Susan V. Donaldson, "Faulkner's Versions of Pastoral, Gothic, and Sublime," in *A Companion to William Faulkner*, ed. Richard C. Moreland (Malden, MA: Blackwell, 2007), 359–73; Louis Palmer, "Bourgeois Blues: Class, Whiteness, and Southern Gothic in Early Faulkner and Caldwell," *The Faulkner Journal* 22, nos. 1–2 (Fall 2006–Spring 2007), 120–39; Eric J. Sundquist, *Faulkner: The House Divided* (Baltimore: Johns Hopkins University Press, 1983), 44–60.

11. Toni Morrison, *Playing in the Dark: Whiteness and the Literary Imagination* (Cambridge, MA: Harvard University Press, 1992), 38.

12. W. Fitzhugh Brundage, *The Southern Past: A Clash of Race and Memory* (Cambridge, MA: Harvard University Press, 2005), 4.

13. Michael Kreyling, *Inventing Southern Literature* (Jackson: University Press of Mississippi, 1998), 100–125.

14. George Hovis, *Vale of Humility: Plain Folk in Contemporary North Carolina Fiction* (Columbia: University of South Carolina Press, 2007), 252.

15. Brannon Costello, "Randall Kenan beyond the Final Frontier: Science Fiction, Superheroes, and the South in *A Visitation of Spirits*," *Southern Literary Journal* 43, no. 1 (Fall 2010): 127.

16. E. Patrick Johnson, *Sweet Tea: Black Gay Men of the South* (Chapel Hill: University of North Carolina Press, 2008), 5; Brooks, *William Faulkner*, 339.

17. George E. Haggerty, *Queer Gothic* (Champaign: University of Illinois Press, 2006), 1.

18. William Faulkner, *The Sound and the Fury: An Authoritative Text, Backgrounds and Contexts, Criticism*, 2nd ed., ed. David Minter (New York: Norton, 1994), 48.

19. Randall Kenan, *A Visitation of Spirits* (New York: Vintage, 2000), 156. Subsequent references to this edition will be cited parenthetically in the text.

20. For Darl Bundren, for example, the intimate nature of knowing what another is feeling and thinking is caught up within a bodily erotics, and his transferential, telekinetic encounters involve transgressive crossclass, crossgender contact that questions the traditional grounds of gender and sexuality and queries the bonds that structure and suture individual and social identity. Numerous narrators characterize Darl as unnervingly "queer"; Cora declares that he is "the one that folks say is queer, lazy, pottering," and Tull notices his "queer eyes" that "makes folks talk." See William Faulkner, *As I Lay Dying*, rev. ed. (1930; New York: Vintage International, 1990), 24, 125. Darl's gaze, as Tull notes, unnerves and disturbs the usual borders of bodily integrity, psychic privacy, and social propriety, conjuring an uncanny intimacy that bends the bounds of inner and outer, private and public: "It's like he had got into the inside of you, someway. Like somehow you was looking at yourself and your doings outen his eyes" (125). As his "looking" registers what has been concealed from public knowledge, Darl's presence comes to resonate with the novel's other unsettling gothic elements: Addie's voice returning disembodied from the grave; Cash's invocation of "animal magnetism" (83); Jewel's telekinetic relationship with his prized horse; and the way the Bundren family repeatedly knows "without the words" (27), via what Faulkner describes as "a kind of telepathic agreement" (134). Darl's imaginative life, though mad, offers an alternative space for expression, self-definition, and fulfillment against the alienation and impoverishment of modern life that surrounds him. Against a world where "love" is "just a shape to fill a lack" (172), Darl thus "queers"— drawing on a sense of the word that exceeds sexuality to signal the antinormative—the culturally constructed boundaries of identity, threatening its foundational epistemological structures. For his queer thinking, Darl, of course, is exiled from the community and committed to an insane asylum. As such, Faulkner draws attention to the dynamics of familial and communal disavowal that protect the ideological edifices of normative social life. In resisting an adaptation to "reality," instead choosing a way of figuring radically different forms of knowledge and sociability, Darl stands against epistemological and communal norms and functions as a haunting figure of queer loss.

21. One thinks here of Faulkner's description of Joe Christmas at seventeen: "He felt like an eagle: hard, sufficient, potent, remorseless, strong. But that passed, though he did not then know that, like the eagle, his own flesh as well as all space was still a cage." William Faulkner, *Light in August*, rev. ed. (1932; New York: Vintage International, 1990), 160.

22. Eve Kosofsky Sedgwick, *Tendencies* (Durham, NC: Duke University Press, 1993), 3.

23. Haggerty, *Queer Gothic*, 10.

24. Ibid., 34.

25. David Punter, *The Literature of Terror: A History of Gothic Fiction from 1765 to the Present Day*, 2nd ed. (New York: Longman, 1996), 198.

26. Kathryn Bond Stockton, *The Queer Child, or Growing Sideways in the Twentieth Century* (Durham, NC: Duke University Press, 2009).

27. Ibid., 11.

28. Faulkner, *Sound and the Fury*, 108.

29. Ibid.

30. On the issue of queer futurity, see Lee Edelman, *No Future: Queer Theory and the Death Drive* (Durham, NC: Duke University Press, 2004).

31. William Faulkner, *Absalom, Absalom!*, rev. ed. (1936; New York: Vintage International, 1990), 7.

32. Ibid.

33. Maisha L. Wester, "Haunting and Haunted Queerness: Randall Kenan's Re-inscription of Difference in *A Visitation of Spirits*," *Callaloo* 30, no. 4 (2007): 1039.

34. Christopher Nealon, *Foundlings: Lesbian and Gay Historical Emotion before Stonewall* (Durham, NC: Duke University Press, 2001), 13.

35. See the penultimate section of the novel ("Horace Thomas Cross Confessions"), which is structured around the repetition of "I remember" (245–51). The temporality of "once upon a time" is invoked early in the novel ("Once, in this very North Carolina town, practically everyone with a piece of land kept a hog or two, at least" [6]) and returned to at the end: "You remember, though perhaps you don't, that once upon a time men harvested tobacco by hand" (254).

36. See Charles E. Morris III's essay, "My Old Kentucky Homo: Abraham Lincoln, Larry Kramer, and the Politics of Queer Memory," in Morris, ed., *Queering Public Address: Sexualities in American Historical Discourse* (Columbia: University of South Carolina Press, 2007), 111.

"It Was Enough That the Name Was Written": Ledger Narratives in Edward P. Jones's *The Known World* and Faulkner's *Go Down, Moses*

Matthew Dischinger

In this essay, I will examine the ways in which William Faulkner's 1942 novel, *Go Down, Moses*, and Edward P. Jones's 2003 novel, *The Known World*, deploy plantation ledgers. First, I will look closely at scenes in *Go Down, Moses* that seem to centralize both Isaac McCaslin's reading of his family's ledgers and the ledgers themselves, wondering whether the ledgers in *Go Down, Moses* might offer an ur-narrative for the surrounding novel. Questions about Faulkner's use of plantation ledgers have recently been addressed by placing his novels alongside actual plantation ledgers. Sally Wolff's study, *Ledgers of History* (2010), asserts that Faulkner studied the plantation ledgers of Francis Terry Leak when writing *The Sound and the Fury* (1929), *As I Lay Dying* (1932), *Absalom, Absalom!* (1936), *The Unvanquished* (1938), and of course, *Go Down, Moses*. By tracing names and settings from many of Faulkner's novels to the Leak ledgers, Wolff allows us to read into these linkages—however tenuous they might seem—and consider the possibility that Ike's experience with the McCaslin ledgers reformulates Faulkner's. With that discourse in mind, I will then compare Faulkner's ledgers to those found in *The Known World*, arguing that the latter work deploys varied modes of recording—census reports, judicial records, pamphlets, and most importantly for me here, plantation ledgers—to form an archival pastiche that throws the historical objectivity of any one of them into question, thereby pointing to the limitations of each medium through its accumulative mode.

I will examine the potential of reading *The Known World*'s use of plantation ledgers as a type of revision of the plantation ledgers in *Go Down, Moses* specifically, as well as plantation ledgers generically. I am curious whether *Go Down, Moses* allows for readings that also subvert the authority of the McCaslin ledgers, which Richard Godden and Noel

Polk rightly describe as "sacred documents"[1] to Ike but open to varied interpretations.[2] *The Known World*'s project may use strikingly different narrative techniques from those of *Go Down, Moses*—in fact, the thrust of my argument relies upon those narrative distinctions—but I want to trouble the notion that projects like Jones's should be read as discontinuous, abrupt shifts away from southern modernism. Thus, this essay begins to rethink the term *postsouthern*, a term that, broken into two parts, announces a hard historical break and reifies specific histories on either side of that break.

So while my essay locates discontinuities between the two novels, I will consider what the prefiguring of Jones in Faulkner does to our idea of so-called postsouthern texts. That is, if postsouthern parody affords writers the opportunity to deftly sidestep what Michael Kreyling calls "the presence of 'Faulkner' triumphant,"[3] perhaps Jones offers an alternative to this particularly southern anxiety of influence that avoids both parody and homage. Perhaps Jones troubles Martyn Bone's question posed about Richard Ford—"Neo-Faulknerian or Postsouthern?"[4]— asked in his seminal study of contemporary southern literature, *The Postsouthern Sense of Place in Contemporary Fiction* (2005). That is, if such a question relies on an established postsouthern praxis of dodging the Faulkner train entirely, then Jones, by at once extending and redirecting Faulkner's project, may provide an alternate route, emerging from the shadow of the Faulkner train with a set of tracks headed someplace new, albeit familiar.

I begin my discussion with *Go Down, Moses*, in which Ike learns of "his own nativity"[5] by reading his family's plantation ledgers. Part of the scene's apparent centrality to the surrounding novel might simply be a matter of location, as Ike's reading of the ledgers occurs in the middle of "The Bear," which is itself located near the novel's midpoint. The ledgers reveal that Ike's grandfather fathered a child with a slave, Eunice, and later fathered another child through committing incest with the resulting child, Tomasina. The scene takes on a biblical, mythic quality for Ike as he imagines the ledgers "being lifted down . . . and spread open . . . upon some apocryphal Bench or even Altar or perhaps before the Throne Itself for a last perusal and contemplation and refreshment of the Allknowledgeable" (250). For Ike, the story the ledgers impart feels both omnisciently divined and apocryphal—a Faulknerian dichotomy if there ever was one. The knowledge appears to offer Ike a chance for a pivotal turn. After reading the ledgers, Ike thinks that "the yellowed pages in their fading and implacable succession were . . . a part of his consciousness and would remain so forever" (259). In his argument with his cousin, Ike and McCaslin frequently gesture toward the ledgers.

These gestures help explain, through diegetic omission, the idea of the cursed land that Ike subsequently repudiates. He likens his decision to relinquish his patrimony to freeing himself from the curse that the ledgers appear to reveal.

Without getting into whether Ike's infamous repudiation offers any sort of practical method of social change, we should not miss the way the scene reifies the ledgers' authority. That is, rather than wondering about the legitimacy of the ledgers, this scene centralizes them by bringing into focus Ike's reaction to the ledgers rather than the story the ledgers briefly tell. The fact that the ledgers leave Ike in a state of Conradian horror gives the impression that they reveal more than they conceal.

Read against the backdrop of Wolff's *Ledgers of History*, Ike's experience with the ledgers might be read as a fictionalization of Faulkner's own experiences reading real plantation ledgers. These ledgers belonged to a friend in Holly Springs, Edgar Wiggin Francisco Jr. An interview Wolff conducted with Francisco's son, Edgar III, indicates that Faulkner seemed to arrive at a profound understanding of the plantation through his reading of the Leak Ledgers: "Will said the diary made him sad and angry about how things were and how they ended. Will said they bring back a lot of the raw unhappiness about the way things were. He bemoaned the fact that there was ever slavery."[6] Francisco even saw Faulkner "curse and yell at the diarist"[7] while taking notes.

Wolff's discovery might allow us to construct a narrative claiming that Faulkner uses *Go Down, Moses* expressly as a vehicle to carry the plantation ledger to his readers. If we consider Faulkner's experiences with the Leak ledgers, then, we may be tempted to map that profundity onto Ike and read his experience through Faulkner's reported experiences with plantation ledgers.[8] For Ike, and possibly Faulkner, one could argue the plantation ledger operates as a kind of foundational, consciousness-shifting text.

But while the ledgers might enable one narrative—Ike's realization of his place in history—they simultaneously obscure other narratives. The McCaslin ledger offers only this flat story of Eunice's life:

> *Eunice Bought by Father in New Orleans 1807 $650. dolars. Marrid to*
> *Thucydus 1809 Drownd in Crick Cristmas Day 1832 . . .*
> *June 21th 1833 Drownd herself . . .*
> *23 Jun 1833 Who in hell ever heard of a niger drownding him self . . .*
> *Aug 13th 1833 Drownd herself (255–56)*

The ledgers frame Eunice's life at the McCaslin Plantation in these four entries, starting with her acquisition by Old Carothers and ending with her suicide, stated as a fact of accounting. Other critics have examined the role early forms of accounting have played in creating the "modern fact."[9] For his part, Erik Dussere situates plantation-era bookkeeping forms in a long history of movement away from "Erasmian . . . *copia*" and toward writing that reflects the "literal, arranged, numbered, and abbreviated"—in short, the *accounted* for.[10] Dussere notes that the overtly stylized prose surrounding the ledgers in *Go Down, Moses* redirects the reader's attention from the cold calculus of bookkeeping and attempts "to get the violence and suffering of slavery off the pages of the ledger and into the foreground."[11] While this turn to style might seem to subvert the ledger narrative, even such a rebuttal has its limitations. Dussere is right in his association of Ike's language and "the cadences of the King James bible," which furthers the chapter's anxieties about history as told through "the dilemma[s] of a young white man."[12] The historical dilemma that the novel emphasizes, then, is Ike's. Leaning too heavily on Ike's reading of the ledgers covers up fuller narratives, such as that of Eunice's life and death, which are inaccessible to Ike or the reader through the novel's seemingly prescriptive hermeneutics as identified by Dussere. In other words, while the ledger offers *Ike* a sense of his family's history, the ledger's apparent historicity highlights a narrative bulwark: Eunice's abrupt presence in the ledger only emphasizes her narrative absence.

Where *Go Down, Moses* leaves the ledger's narrative gaps nearly unremarked upon, *The Known World* points to those gaps before filling them in. As Susan Donaldson points out, the novel often "hints at unrecognized, unacknowledged stories"[13] alongside *The Known World*'s primary story of Henry Townsend, slave turned master. In fact, the novel does more than hint in the case of Rita, one of Henry's caregivers, whose story might at first seem to be only a peripheral fragment early in the long, sprawling novel. Rita's brief appearance in the novel provides a useful case for thinking about its overarching interest in casting and recasting characters using different narrative media.

Rita is introduced after Henry's father, Augustus, first buys his freedom and then that of his wife, Mildred, from William Robbins, the owner of a plantation from which many of the novel's characters originate. The couple decides to leave young Henry under Rita's care. Robbins doesn't know Rita by name when he sees her with Henry; as the narrator notes, Robbins "would have called Rita by name but she had not distinguished herself enough in his life for him to remember the name he had given her at birth."[14] Rita's name was recorded in Robbins's ledger, of course: "It was enough that the name was written somewhere in his large book of births and deaths, the comings and goings of slaves.

'Noticeable mole on left cheek,' he had written five days after Rita's birth. 'Eyes gray'" (16–17). Had this been the novel's only description of Rita, it might be easier to miss the way the plantation ledger places the historical agency—the ability to control what is known and how it is known—in the hands of William Robbins, as his would be our only extant narrative of Rita's life. Robbins uses the space to describe Rita's body. It has a mole, and its eyes are gray. Rita is rendered as a specimen. As Sarah Mahurin notes, the ledger transforms people into "thingly humans," making "the elusive qualities that comprise 'humanity' fall away" in favor of human as object.[15] Where Mahurin argues that the novel's thingly humans are "buoyed by *love*,"[16] I want to suggest that the *narrative* surrounding the thingifying ledgers removes the latter's ability to turn people into things. Mahurin's analysis of that narrative examines the way love operates within it, but the presence of such a narrative represents a historical corrective—an alternative story to the sparse ledger narrative that undermines the latter's authority.

Let us contrast the ledger's description of Rita with others that the narrative space of the novel reveals. On the day that Henry joins his parents in freedom, leaving Rita at the Robbins plantation, Henry's parents load him onto their wagon. "The moment the wagon took off, [Rita] began to vomit" (45). Rita catches up with the wagon and pleads with Augustus and Mildred, "'Don't leave me here. Please don't leave me here.'" After Augustus and Mildred agree to help Rita, we read of her escape from the South à la Henry "Box" Brown in a box of walking sticks that Henry's father, Augustus, sends to New York: "When she was in it, with her head just an inch or so from the top and her feet with a little less than that from the bottom, he put wrapped walking sticks to either side of her. . . . Rita's people had always been people of more bones than meat and muscle, and at long last that was a blessing" (47–48). When she arrives in New York forty-one hours later, Rita hands the young boy opening her box a walking stick that Augustus made, hoping her offering will keep her new captors from sending her back to the Robbins plantation.

The scene ends, and it marks the last time Rita appears in the novel. Even this short narrative investigation, however, evokes a new Rita, one that the ledger narrative foreclosed through its brief, physical description. Her description in the ledgers limits Rita to two physical traits meant to highlight her so-called distinguishability *for Robbins*, but her narrative representation uncovers details about her relationship with Henry, her desire to escape the Robbins plantation, and even her ancestors. Donaldson notes that stories like Rita's emerge in *The Known World*'s "cacophony of competing stories" that problematize official histories "by unearthing discontinuities, anomalies, and multiple possibilities."[17] In short, the narrative space reconstructs Rita, and it does so by focusing on aspects of her life that the ledgers do not—and, possibly, *could* not—reveal. By contrasting ledger narratives with alternate narratives, particularly those that contradict the ledger narratives, Jones's historiographic novel makes the plantation-era South appear simultaneously more specific and less coherent. In Rita's case, the ledger narrative's objectivity is defined by "numeric representation and brevity"[18] and undone by the longer narrative of Rita's humanity.

As other critics have pointed out, *The Known World*'s critique of so-called official histories disauthenticates various media.[19] For instance, the narration includes details from three census reports, each of which offers flawed accounts of Manchester County. An alcoholic carried out the first census in 1830 (22), and issues with the 1840 census were likewise many. When tabulating the number of citizens in Manchester County by race, the 1840 census taker counted mixed-race free children as slaves based on their appearance. The narrator notes that "in the eyes of the law, they truly were" slaves, calling attention to the contrast between law and lived experience. Additionally, mountains in Manchester County "threw him off," making him "unable to take the measure of the land" and causing him to drastically underestimate the territory of the county (23). The 1860 census might be easiest to dismiss, as the census taker "argued with his wife the day he sent his report to Washington, D.C.," causing "all his arithmetic [to be] wrong because he had failed to carry a one" (7).

Even more contemporary accounts of Manchester County's history are shown to conceal their subjectivity as much as they reveal information. Most notably, a historian at the University of Virginia in 1979 describes in monograph form the era when one character served as the county sheriff as "a period of years and years of . . . 'peace and prosperity'" (43) before clarifying that "this meant, among other things, that not one slave escaped" (44). Perhaps the most interesting example is that of a pamphleteer from Canada, Anderson Frazier, whose series entitled *Curiosities and Oddities about Our Southern Neighbors* included a pamphlet in 1883 dedicated to "free Negroes who had owned other Negroes before the War between the states" (106). The twenty-seven-page pamphlet devoted seven pages to the story of Henry Townsend. In doing so, it attempts to offer a complete tale of Henry's journey from slave to master. In each of these official histories, Jones offers one sparse history before immediately subverting it with a fuller narrative. In the case of the pamphlet-as-history, we might read Jones's entire novel as a revision, since the story the pamphlet investigates for seven pages is the subject of Jones's 388-page novel.

The Known World, it should be said, trades in faux history. While many of the tropes it features have historical counterparts, Manchester County, like Yoknapatawpha, was Jones's creation. The historical documents under revision had to be made by Jones before his novel unmade them. The process of invention and revision makes the novel's conceit all the more notable, as it calls attention to the way so-called objective texts such as ledgers invented the plantation under the guise of documentation. Furthermore, the novel's introduction and subsequent disauthentication of historical documents might help us map a new trajectory for postsouthern literature.

Of the many critics cited here who examine *The Known World*'s historical reconstructions, Donaldson is the one most concerned with the novel's relationship to postmodernism. Casting the novel's critique of master narratives as set during "the crisis of Western mastery"[20] leading up to the Civil War, Donaldson emphasizes this postmodern critique as a part of a broad "cultural shift"[21] toward such historiographic metafiction that is most "concerned with the displacement of the modern white Western subject."[22] David Ikard's work on *The Known World* follows Donaldson's thread, reading the novel as a polemic against past and present ideologies of white supremacy, arguing that the novel's critique falls squarely on "normative white supremacy in the contemporary moment by resituating it within established historical narratives."[23] Katherine Clay Bassard, likewise, sees the novel "dismantling the 'known world'" of the historical record and "reconfiguring the ways in which we might (re)imagine other worlds."[24] Like Ikard, Bassard's critique extends to contemporary counterparts, noting that recent "black conservatism . . . has its root in the Henry Townsends of the world who see no difficulty in the full participation in a system bent on the oppression of their own people."[25]

Donaldson, Ikard, and Bassard, then, focus on the novel's continued suspicion of any single account of Manchester County—particularly those that place a white narrator at the center of the historical narrative. Their critiques move back and forth, but all tacitly rely upon the idea that postmodernism does represent a distinctive cultural shift away from history and toward histories.

Such a maneuver is commonplace in postmodernity. In southern literature, however, the move from modernism to postmodernism often uses the discourse of the postsouthern. Kreyling considers the potential of postsouthern artistic distance from the Southern Renascence, arguing that "the turn of southern literature into . . . postsouthernness" is either "an emergency" or "a relief,"[26] depending on one's investment in the whole. Kreyling builds on the work of Lewis P. Simpson, who introduced the postsouthern into critical dialect in 1980 by declaring the end of the journey toward southern self-consciousness and the beginning of the "quest for moral order amid the spiritual, political, and literary disorders of our age."[27] More recently, however, twenty-first-century southern texts like *The Known World* disturb the notion that postsouthern novels search for order amid literary disorder. Instead, *The Known World* seems to find potential in the very literary disorder that Simpson assigned postsouthern literature the task of pushing aside. That is, Jones's postsouthern plantation novel suggests that one needs a mixed-genre medium, a text that introduces and undermines espoused histories, to introduce and undermine the idea that a unified, spiritual, political order ever existed. Rather than merely calling this postmodern play, turning *The Known World* (and postsouthern texts more generally) into pacific, apolitical meditations on form, I read the novel as directly pointing at the representational politics of the plantation ledger.

Perhaps a volume examining Faulkner's African American interlocutors would seem an odd place to question the spectral presence of Faulkner in southern literature, but questions about the influence of southern modernism are essential to those attempting to establish a postsouthern poetics. As Patricia Yaeger points out, we have excellent reasons *not* to place Faulkner in a central position in southern literature. On the "Faulkner industry,"[28] Yaeger writes that Faulkner's "mystifications of oedipal angst and miscegenation have become bywords defining the ways in which race functions in America, making race-mixing the only game in town, *the* epic, underlying structure driving the whiteness of the American dream."[29] Yaeger is, of course, correct. We can no more say that Faulkner's investigation of race lies at the center of southern literature than we can that whiteness lies at the center of being southern. So rather than insisting upon the reality of Faulkner's South, let me instead insist upon the continued purview of Faulkner's South—a facet of postmodernism that Linda Hutcheon encourages us to read as the postmodern novel "openly [acknowledging] its own discursive, contingent identity."[30]

My essay has speculated that a twenty-first-century novel should be read as building on the tracks laid by Faulkner, specifically, to take southern literature to a new imaginative place. *The Known World* decenters various histories, including those mobilized by *Go Down, Moses*. However, Thadious M. Davis demonstrates that for all the ways in which *Go Down, Moses* might be said to centralize plantation economies, it also offers opportunities for readings that decentralize them. By focusing on the way the "liberatory and democratic" games played by Thomasina's son, Terrell, can subvert the "constrictive and arbitrary" nature of laws, Davis questions traditional readings of the novel that interpret the opening chapter "Was" as exclusively comedic and parodic.[31] And while Faulkner, unlike Jones, does not use a proliferation of embedded historical documents in his novel, he does account for and decentralize the ledgers in *Go Down, Moses* by showing Ike's reaction to the story they tell as one reaction among many. In other words, we could place Ike's reaction alongside Eunice's suicide, Tomey's Turl's escape attempts, or Lucas Beauchamp's sense of his own history. Or perhaps we could examine part one of the novel's title story, "Go Down, Moses," in which a census taker collects basic information from Samuel Worsham Beauchamp before his execution:

> "Samuel Worsham Beauchamp. Twenty-six. Born in the country near Jefferson, Mississippi. No family. No—"
>
> "Wait." The census-taker wrote rapidly. "That's not the name you were sen—lived under in Chicago."
>
> The other snapped the ash from the cigarette. "No. It was another guy killed the cop."
>
> "All right. Occupation—" (352)

The two-page scene offers the briefest of narratives for Samuel. He lived in Chicago under a different name; he was found guilty of killing a police officer; he was sentenced to death. But the section also opens a window for a fuller narrative by dramatizing how quickly the census taker shuts that window when he finishes the interview and "close[s] his portfolio" on Samuel with haunting finality. The scene shows the process of document production, the official narrative being constructed. The foreclosure at the end of part one is made more visible in part two, in which we see the information collected by the census taker reproduced in a "press association flimsy" (356) read by Wilmoth, the Jefferson newspaper's editor. The language of the press release should not surprise us: "*Mississippi negro . . . exposes alias by completing census questionnaire.*" For Wilmoth and Gavin Stevens, the news release reveals useful information, but we should read the revelation skeptically.

The Known World might have paused at the end of that scene before reconstructing Samuel's life in narrative. *Go Down, Moses* calls attention to the narrative erasure of Samuel's life begun by the census taker without going on to narrate Samuel's life directly. The novel's final section stages this very problem, casting it as an explicitly racialized one. When Gavin arrives at Belle Worsham's house to help explain Samuel's death to his family, Mollie cuts his explanation short, saying Roth Edmonds "'sold my Benjamin . . . Sold him in Egypt'" (362). Mollie, with choral accompaniment from Hamp Worsham and his wife, authors a counter-narrative to those collected by the census taker and circulated in the news release. This nonwhite narrative suffocates Gavin, who flees the room. This moment not only attempts to tell Samuel's story in a highly stylized manner but also shows the limitations of that attempt through Gavin's reaction. Samuel's narrative cannot be told in a way that Gavin can understand. By the end of the story, Mollie's desire for a full account of Samuel's death to be included in the newspaper's obituary baffles Wilmoth. In a gesture that might be read as a moment of hope, Gavin thinks, in light of Wilmoth's story, that he has misunderstood Mollie all along.[32] That the novel ends upon Gavin's mild epiphany suggests that such moments are fleeting: hardly recorded thoughts that remain unuttered, nearly incoherent, ending just as they begin.

Both texts, then, call attention to the way the novel form can both delimit and reimagine characters that were limited and restricted by genres such as ledgers. While Jones deftly installs these histories only to wipe them away, Faulkner points to the unknowable world these documents create. With this important similarity in mind, perhaps we should think about the postsouthern turn less as a turn away, an absolute shift, and more as something that had been long signaled by earlier literature generating similarly tenuous, contingent narratives of southern history.

One final example of Faulkner and Jones employing similar narrative techniques with divergent consequences is their use of the map. Both authors include maps that renarrativize their texts. Faulkner included his map of Yoknapatawpha County in the index of *Absalom, Absalom!* (1936). The map offers a visual retelling[33] of the novel's plot, with circles and lines indicating, for instance, the "CHURCH WHICH THOMAS SUTPEN RODE FAST TO."[34] It also includes census-like data, like the "2400 SQ. MI." area of the county and a population breakdown by race: "WHITES. 6298; NEGROES. 9313."[35] At the bottom of the map reads the inscription: "WILLIAM FAULKNER. SOLE OWNER & PROPRIETOR."[36]

If we compare Faulkner's map with Jones's, which we learn about in a letter printed in full near the end of *The Known World*, we can see important similarities and differences. Alice Night, an escaped slave who wandered Manchester County alone at night, constructs *The Known World*'s map with cloth, paint, and clay. Calvin Newman, the brother of Henry's wife, Caldonia, leaves Manchester County for Washington, DC, and stumbles upon Alice and her map in a hotel. Calvin calls it "a kind of map of the life of the County of Manchester, Virginia," before saying that "'map' is such a poor word for such a wondrous thing" (384). Calvin calls Alice's map "correct" (385) in its vision of Henry's plantation, saying that "it is what God sees when He looks down on Manchester" (384).

The perspective the map offers Calvin of Manchester County seems totalizing, divine, and "wondrous." As Bassard points out, Calvin's changed perspective on his familiar world offers a new type of knowledge, causing "the closest thing to an epiphany"[37] for one of the novel's black slaveowners. Calvin writes to Caldonia that he found memories he "did not know were there until [he] saw them on that wall," thinking others "would remember my history, that I, no matter what I had always said to the contrary, owned people of our Race" (386). Calvin's new perspective on personal, social, and racial histories is reconfigured upon his viewing of Alice's map, which like the larger novel, mixes various media. The combination of cloth, paint, and clay creates the illusion of a God's-eye view. The effect is an illusion, that is, because we know that Alice Night creates this *objet d'art*. Alice is the artist triumphant, possibly standing in here for the author of *The Known World*, a novel that surely "underscores its own provisional status by calling attention to its literary operations—that is, how it goes about representing the past."[38] While Donaldson stops short of extending this postmodern critique to Alice's map, we must remember that *The Known World* teaches us how to read. Alice's perspective is limited and contingent. Importantly, however, unlike plantation ledgers and census reports, Alice's map is signed and authored, highlighting its subjectivity and contingency. It does not attempt to offer a new master-narrative for Manchester County, an objective history that others can use to account for the county's history, offering instead an alternative to objective history, a concept the novel consistently disavows.

Faulkner's map would seem to offer a stark contrast. After all, Faulkner lists himself as the owner and proprietor of the county, an act that could be read as a self-deification. Perhaps this is another example of Faulkner evoking "the drama of whiteness" that according to Dussere privileges "white characters who can neither escape nor ameliorate their inherited and debt-laden pasts."[39] But we might also read Faulkner's map as an early iteration of what Jones's accomplishes. That is, if *The Known World* points to the artist as the only party capable of sorting through histories, stories of the past, and drawing them on the page, then both Faulkner and Jones situate the artist as offering a type of salvation.

The distinction between the novels is twofold. First, Jones embeds his map in the text, thereby giving at least some of his characters a fuller picture of their place in Manchester County. Faulkner, by contrast, doesn't make *Absalom*'s map available to his characters. By creating it, however, he seems to understand its narrative potential for readers. Thus, much as Ike fails to see the ledgers' concealment of narrative—their lack of objectivity—*Absalom*'s characters lack the means to fill in the space created by a narrative lack. Where *Absalom, Absalom!* and *Go Down, Moses* show white southerners trying, and failing, to free themselves from their pasts, *The Known World* persistently troubles that southern racial binary and, instead, identifies the ways in which the social order of Faulkner's South was never as cleanly ordered as it might have seemed. It was always dependent on the particular postage stamp of native soil—the particular known world—one inhabited.

NOTES

1. Richard Godden and Noel Polk, "Reading the Ledgers," *Mississippi Quarterly* 55, no. 3 (2002): 301.

2. Godden and Polk look closely at the ledger entries regarding Percival Brownlee, using those entries to establish a pattern of triangulation between Buck, Buddy, and Brownlee and thus to decentralize Ike's reading of the ledgers. While I will not discuss Godden and Polk's specific conclusions here, their methodology expertly identifies the way Ike's experience of the ledgers was a *reading* of a story that explodes with meanings.

3. Michael Kreyling, *Inventing Southern Literature* (Jackson: University Press of Mississippi, 1998), 161.

4. Martyn Bone, *The Postsouthern Sense of Place in Contemporary Fiction* (Baton Rouge: Louisiana State University Press, 2005), 75.

5. William Faulkner, *Go Down, Moses*, rev. ed. (1942; New York: Vintage International, 1990), 259. Subsequent references to this edition will be cited parenthetically in the text.

6. Sally Wolff, *Ledgers of History: William Faulkner, an Almost Forgotten Friendship, and an Antebellum Plantation Diary* (Baton Rouge: Louisiana State University Press, 2010), 106.

7. Ibid.

8. Edgar Wiggin Francisco III, in his interview with Sally Wolff, describes his reaction to hearing Faulkner read from the ledgers:

> EWF: He [Faulkner] was reading in the diary about one of the slave situations. He was upset by what he was reading in the diary. So that upset me, too, and I said to myself: "It's our fault. It's our family's fault." . . . Suddenly I realized that slavery had occurred in our family. I thought that slavery was our fault—my family's collective fault—that slavery had occurred so close at hand. I thought, "Yes, this has something to do with me."
> SW: You thought slavery was your fault, personally?
> EWF: Yes, I thought that it was my fault as much as the other members of my family. I remember also that day I bolted from the room. I went to my room and closed the door, and I didn't come out for a long time. (Ibid., 99–100)

9. Mary Poovey, *A History of the Modern Fact: Problems of Knowledge in the Sciences of Wealth and Society* (Chicago: University of Chicago Press, 1998), 31. Poovey's 1998 monograph, which expands on her work in "Accommodating Merchants: Accounting, Civility, and the Natural Laws of Gender" (*Differences: A Journal of Feminist Cultural*

Studies 8, no. 3 [1996]: 1–20) to emphasize accounting's role in fact-making, is germinal to Erik Dussere's analysis of the plantation ledger in *Balancing the Books: Faulkner, Morrison, and the Economics of Slavery* (New York: Routledge, 2003).

10. Dussere, *Balancing the Books*, 16.

11. Ibid., 20.

12. Ibid., 21, 23.

13. Susan Donaldson, "Telling Forgotten Stories of Slavery in the Postmodern South," *Southern Literary Journal* 40, no. 2 (2008): 272.

14. Edward P. Jones, *The Known World* (New York: Amistad, 2004), 16. Subsequent references to this edition will be cited parenthetically in the text.

15. Sarah Mahurin, "'Such a Poor Word for a Wondrous Thing': Thingness and the Recovery of the Human in *The Known World*," *Southern Literary Journal* 43, no. 2 (2011): 127.

16. Ibid., 129; emphasis added.

17. Donaldson, "Telling Forgotten Stories," 273, 270.

18. Dussere, *Balancing the Books*, 16.

19. Tim A. Ryan discusses an instance in which a character reflects on the limits of a photograph, stating that the novel wonders about "the world beyond the immediate frame" (Tim A Ryan, *Calls and Responses: The American Novel of Slavery since Gone with the Wind* [Baton Rouge: Louisiana State University Press, 2008], 196).

20. Donaldson, "Telling Forgotten Stories," 273.

21. Ibid., 270.

22. Ibid., 271.

23. David Ikard, "White Supremacy under Fire: The Unrewarded Perspective in Edward P. Jones's *The Known World*," *MELUS* 36, no. 3 (2011): 65.

24. Katherine Clay Bassard, "Imagining Other Worlds: Race, Gender, and the 'Power Line' in Edward P. Jones's *The Known World*," *African American Review* 42, nos. 3–4 (2008): 409.

25. Ibid., 418.

26. Kreyling, *Inventing Southern Literature*, 148.

27. Lewis P. Simpson, *The Brazen Face of History: Studies in the Literary Consciousness in America* (Baton Rouge: Louisiana State University Press, 1997), 268. Simpson is describing here Walter Sullivan's *Death by Melancholy: Essays on Modern Southern Fiction* (Baton Rouge: Louisiana State University Press, 1972), which he cites as a catalyst for the initiation of the postsouthern as he defines it.

28. Patricia Yaeger, *Dirt and Desire: Reconstructing Southern Women's Writing, 1930–1990* (Chicago: University of Chicago Press, 2000), xv.

29. Ibid., 97.

30. Linda Hutcheon, *A Poetics of Postmodernism: History, Theory, Fiction* (New York: Routledge, 1988), 24.

31. Thadious M. Davis, *Games of Property: Law, Race, Gender, and Faulkner's "Go Down, Moses"* (Durham, NC: Duke University Press, 2003), 9.

32. Gavin's reading of Mollie leaves much to be desired, but the moment of self-doubt might be read as a gesture toward rethinking his otherwise overtly racist descriptions of Mollie and Samuel.

33. Indeed, the map reembeds plots, creating a multivolume intertext. The map, in other words, suggests that the events of *Absalom, Absalom!* should be read in a framework that ultimately lies beyond the novel's frame. I will return to this gesture toward something we usually attribute to postmodernity—the simultaneous existence of multiple histories—at the end of this essay.

34. William Faulkner, *Absalom, Absalom!*, rev. ed. (1936; New York: Vintage International, 1990), endpapers after 313.

35. Ibid.

36. Ibid.

37. Bassard, "Imagining Other Worlds," 418.

38. Donaldson, "Telling Forgotten Stories," 270.

39. Dussere, *Balancing the Books*, 36.

Morrison's Return to Faulkner: *A Mercy* and *Absalom, Absalom!*

DOREEN FOWLER

> *In 1956 I spent a great deal of time thinking about Mr. Faulkner*
> *because he was the subject of a thesis that I wrote at Cornell. . . .*
> *I don't think that my response was any different from any other*
> *student at that time, inasmuch as there was in Faulkner this power*
> *and courage—the courage of a writer, a special kind of courage.*
> *My reasons, I think, for being interested and deeply moved by*
> *all his subjects had something to do with my desire to find out*
> *something about this country and that artistic articulation of its*
> *past that was not available in history, which is what art and fiction*
> *can do but sometimes history refuses to do.*
> —Toni Morrison, "Faulkner and Women," in Faulkner and
> Women: Faulkner and Yoknapatawpha, 1985

The fictional works of Toni Morrison and William Faulkner sometimes seem uncannily alike. I use the term *uncanny* here in the Freudian sense, that is, both alike and different. Unquestionably, the two Nobel Laureates, who are separated by both gender and race, are different. No one would ever confuse a novel of Morrison's with one of Faulkner's.[1] At the same time, however, readers of Morrison's fiction sometimes hear eerie echoes of Faulkner, and scholars have puzzled over the intertextual relationship between the two writers, one the great-grandson of a Confederate colonel and slaveholder, the other a descendant of southern sharecroppers and slaves. Some have suggested that Faulkner, who preceded Morrison by a generation, influences her writing; others have argued that Morrison corrects Faulkner.

Morrison's own comments about Faulkner have been remarkably ambivalent—even conflictual. On different occasions she has both owned to and disowned a relationship with Faulkner. On the one hand, Morrison has emphatically denied a Faulknerian influence: "I am not *like* Faulkner," she said forcefully in an interview with Nellie McKay.[2] On the other, in response to a question following a reading at the 1985 Faulkner and Yoknapatawpha Conference, she acknowledged that, as a reader, she was indebted to Faulkner: "There was for me not only an academic interest in Faulkner but in a very, very personal way, in a very personal way as a reader, William Faulkner had an enormous effect on me, an enormous effect."[3] As John Duvall notes of Morrison's contradictory statements about Faulkner, she seems to deny a literary influence and own to a "readerly" interest in Faulkner.[4] But can the one be separated from the other?

How, then, are we to read the recurring Faulknerian echoes in Morrison's fiction? In my view, Morrison is not Faulkner's disciple, nor is she critiquing or "correcting" his fiction. Rather, there is a complementary relationship between Faulkner and Morrison, and Morrison's novels influence our reading of Faulkner as much as Faulkner's affect our reading of Morrison. Alternatively stated, the two authors signify on one another. In particular, Morrison signifies on race in Faulkner's fiction. My position is that Morrison returns to racial motifs in Faulkner's fiction and uncovers a submerged perspective on race informing his novels. She teases out racial meanings in his texts that have eluded readers for whom black and white are discrete, dichotomous categories.

A novel of Faulkner's that Morrison returns to frequently is *Absalom, Absalom!*[5] The reason for this persistent interest is suggested in a comment that Morrison made about *Absalom* in a 1993 interview in the *Paris Review*, where she talked about the elusiveness of race in Faulkner's novel:

> Faulkner in *Absalom, Absalom!* spends the entire book tracing race, and you can't find it. No one can see it, even the character who *is* black can't see it. I did this lecture for my students that took me forever, which was tracking all the moments of withheld, partial or disinformation, when a racial fact or clue *sort* of comes out but doesn't quite arrive. I just wanted to chart it. I listed its appearance, disguise and disappearance on every page, I mean every phrase! . . . Do you know how hard it is to withhold that kind of information but hinting, pointing all of the time? . . . As a reader you have been forced to hunt for a drop of black blood that means everything and nothing. The insanity of racism. So the structure is the argument. . . . No one has done anything quite like that ever.[6]

If we compare Morrison's comments about race in *Absalom* in this 1993 interview with *Playing in the Dark*, her work of literary criticism that was published in the same year, we see a remarkable congruence. In *Playing in the Dark*, Morrison makes the case that a black presence is both "central to . . . our national literature" at the same time that it "hover[s] at the margins" of US literature.[7] When we turn to Morrison's comment about *Absalom*, she seems to be pointing to this same combination of racial centrality and marginalization: Faulkner "spends the entire book tracing race," but "no one can see it." In *Playing in the Dark*, Morrison attributes this hidden presence of Africanism in American literature to a "process of organizing American coherence through a distancing [of] Africanism," and she expresses her interest in "identify[ing] those moments when American literature was complicit in the fabrication of racism, but equally important, I wanted to see when literature exploded and undermined it."[8] Morrison returns repeatedly to Faulkner's novel *Absalom*, I would argue, because it belongs to this latter category: it "explode[s] and undermine[s]" racism.

In *Absalom*, as Morrison astutely observes, Faulkner focuses the reader's attention on the verbal exclusion of a black presence: "as a reader you have been forced to hunt for a drop of black blood that means everything and nothing." A reader familiar with *Absalom* will immediately recognize Morrison's allusion to Charles Bon's "drop of black blood," which, while central to the Sutpen story—it explains why Henry kills Charles and why Sutpen's "design" fails—is nonetheless withheld from the reader by the character-narrators until the last pages of the novel. As Morrison notes, Bon's racial heritage appears as "moments of withheld, partial or disinformation," and it is the revelation, at the novel's end, that Charles Bon is both Sutpen's son and black that exposes "the insanity of racism." Because white hegemony is threatened by racial intermixing, not only Thomas and Henry Sutpen but also the character-narrators, Miss Rosa, Mr. Compson, and for a time, Quentin Compson will not permit Sutpen's black son to signify in Sutpen's grand "design," and as a result, their narrations "dont explain."[9] Only when Quentin and Shreve finally replace the missing racial signifier do readers become aware that they have been reading a novel about the destructiveness of racism.

Absalom, Absalom!, then, exposes racial exclusion at the level of signification; that is, Faulkner exposes the way seemingly reflexively the white character-narrators withhold figuring a black presence as part of the Sutpen story. I propose that Morrison returns to Faulkner's novel to reclaim the racial meanings that have been disguised or covered over by what she calls "the dominant cultural body."[10] In revisiting Faulkner's text, Morrison shifts the focus from the dominant culture to the marginalized and explores the racial meaning that "*sort* of comes out but doesn't quite arrive" in Faulkner's novel. Let me be clear: it is my contention that both Faulkner and Morrison expose and critique racial marginalization,

but that Morrison writes from the other side, the side of the marginalized. Whereas Faulkner's great strength is to show the way whites use
language to socially exclude people of color, Morrison's is her ability to
channel the interiority of the marginalized, the ones she calls the forgotten ones.[11]

A number of scholars have already written about Morrison's re-seeing
of racial elements in *Absalom*: John Duvall, Roberta Rubenstein, Philip
Weinstein, and I have examined the intertextual resonances between
Charles Bon in *Absalom* and Golden Gray in *Jazz*, and Nancy Batty
has argued that Morrison's Circe in *Song of Solomon* "riffs on" Clytie
in *Absalom*. My project builds on these studies.[12] By reading Faulkner
through Morrison, I propose to analyze the intertextual relationship
between Morrison's 2008 novel, *A Mercy,* and *Absalom, Absalom!*

A Mercy reprises many of the central motifs of *Absalom, Absalom!*
While both the time period and the locale of the two novels differ—New
York in the 1690s and Mississippi in the Civil War period, respectively—
both novels focus on the drive of a lower-class white man to become
a powerful planter-patriarch. We can read Jacob Vaark in *A Mercy* as
an avatar of Thomas Sutpen in *Absalom*. Both men become obsessed
with building a house when they are summoned to the grand house of a
slaveholder. Both men identify the house with their posterity and their
identity: "What a man leaves behind is what a man is," Vaark says.[13] Both
men are dependent on women and slaves in ways they do not acknowledge; both men die without male heirs, and their houses eventually fall
into the hands of female slaves who are either literally or figuratively
their daughters. And both stories are told by the alternating voices of
character-narrators.

The significant differences between the two narratives can be traced
to the narrators in the two novels. Whereas the narrators of Faulkner's
Absalom, Absalom! are from the white upper class, in Morrison's novel,
the narrators include all the principal participants in the events—white,
black, Native American, free, and slave, and the central narrator is Florens, a young slave woman owned by Vaark. Because the difference in
narrative form makes all the difference, I want to begin by comparing
the discursive methods of the two novels, and to do so it is useful to turn
to Lacanian theory, which analyzes the power of the signifier over the
signified. The signified refers to natural existence in the world; the signifier is the term that Lacan uses for words that assign symbolic meanings
to people and things in the world. According to Lacan, these word signs
are arbitrary, empty, and artificial; nonetheless, because we know and
use a thing in the world by the name we call it, our word signs exert a terrible power over natural existence. Lacan refers to this power of cultural

signifiers as the domination of the signifier over the signified, and he even goes so far as to say that signified disappears under the signifier.[14]

Arguably, the purpose of *Absalom, Absalom!*'s nearly unreadable narrative form is to expose the domination of the signifier over the signified. In *Absalom*, language, the vehicle for meaning, is anything but transparent. Instead, language stands as a barrier between the reader and meaning. Faulkner's character-narrators tell the Sutpen story in seemingly endless sentences overburdened with qualifying phrases added to qualifying phrases and clauses heaped upon clauses. More maddening still, the character-narrators repeatedly turn to negative constructions[15] that seem to *not* tell the story, and that is exactly Faulkner's point: that the character-narrators are not telling "all of it" (214). Instead, with language, they try to make the signified, human existence in the natural world conform to an artificial, white-dominant, southern patriarchal "design." So Charles Bon and his drop of black blood disappear under the character-narrators' signifiers.

Morrison's novels approach the problem of language's power to marginalize from the other side, the side of the marginalized. Her novels revisit the precedence of the signifier over the signified and reverse it; that is, she attempts to re-presence the missing signified. Her language contrasts strikingly with the verbal circumlocutions characteristically used by Faulkner's white narrators. Morrison's densely metaphorical language is most closely aligned with nature poetry. She uses language in the service of the flesh and the material world in an attempt to create images and sounds with words. A number of scholars have pointed out that Morrison is an exemplar of what Hélène Cixous calls écriture feminine, writing that is characterized by a privileging of the body. According to Cixous, the practitioner of écriture feminine "physically materializes what she's thinking; she signifies it with her body."[16]

Because in both *Absalom* and *A Mercy* the form of the novel echoes the content (for both Faulkner and Morrison, form is meaning), the domination of the signified by the signifier is central thematically as well as structurally in texts. To compare the development of this theme in the two novels, I propose to explore parallels between two characters who at first glance would seem to have very little in common: Florens, the dark-skinned slave girl in *A Mercy*, and Charles Etienne de Saint-Valery Bon, the son of Charles Bon and his octoroon wife, a free man who could pass for white. The common denominator that links Bon and Florens is violence. As children, both Bon and Florens are described with the same word, *docile* (*Absalom*, 160; *A Mercy*, 171); some five years later, both have become homicidal. In *Absalom, Absalom!*, the character-narrators are mystified by Bon, a "slight" boy (164) "with womanish hands" (165) and "light bones" (162) who starts "trouble" (164) "for no reason," "noth-ing," lashing out against both white and black men and taking "blows and slashes which he . . . did not seem to feel" (164). Only a few pages in the novel are devoted to Charles Etienne Bon's short life; and, like Charles Bon and Clytie in *Absalom, Absalom!*, who are described by the white character-narrators as "impenetrable" (74) and "inscrutable" (126; emphases removed), Charles Bon's son is similarly written off as "incomprehensible" (167).

This central difference between the stories of Charles Etienne Bon and Florens is that Florens is central and Etienne is peripheral. In *A Mercy*, Vaark fades early from the narration—he dies from smallpox even as he is building his great house—and the novel quickly focuses on Florens, who is sent on a mission to save the life of her mistress, Rebekka, when she also contracts the pox. *Absalom*, on the other hand, is always the story of Thomas Sutpen, and Charles Bon's son is an eas-ily overlooked footnote to the Sutpen saga. Whereas Florens is given a voice, and we share her perspective, Charles Etienne Bon's story is distanced by layers of white narration. Indeed, he is both figuratively and literally buried in the text. His story is told in the Sutpen graveyard, where Quentin and his father, who are hunting quail, come across his headstone. I would note that Miss Rosa's narration is a model of the way Charles Etienne Bon is "buried" narratively. Rosa never once mentions Charles Bon's son by his racially mixed wife, whom Judith and Clytie raised at Sutpen's Hundred. Bon's son is absent from Miss Rosa's narra-tion even when she buries Judith in a grave next to him![17]

While the way we readers experience the two characters' stories is different, the stories, I maintain, are remarkably similar. Quite simply, both Florens and Charles Etienne Bon are refused signification in a white-dominant culture. Both stories dramatize a struggle to become interpellated into a culture that is inimical to black subjectivity. Because of this similarity-within-difference, reading Florens's story side by side with Charles Etienne Bon's can help us to interpret the recessed racial meanings in Faulkner's novel.

As Florens explains, she is "expel[led]" three times (160). She begins her life feeling that she is "the one to throw out" (161) when her mother, the abused slave of a wealthy tobacco planter, begs Vaark to take her daughter as payment for the debt her master owes him. Years later, Flor-ens experiences a second expulsion, which deepens the sense of a "dying inside" (167) that began with the first. This second trauma occurs after her mistress, Rebekka Vaark, falls ill with smallpox and Florens is sent to fetch the blacksmith, a free black man who has cured others of the pox. On her journey, she is stopped by white church members who, because her skin is dark, accuse her of being a demon. Refusing to touch her, they make her strip and examine her body. "Naked under their examination," Florens watches eyes "looking at me my body across distance without recognition. Swine look at me with more connection" (133). To mark herself as identifiable to them, she has to turn to a letter written by Rebekka that "vouches for the female person into whose hands it has been placed" and identifies Florens as "owned by me" (132; emphasis removed). A white woman's word is necessary to position Florens in the social order; it gives her a tie to the dominant community. But then the word, the letter, is taken away from Florens, and as she continues on her journey without her mistress's signifier, she experiences a profound interior loss, which she struggles to put into words: "I am losing something with every step I take. I can feel the drain. Something precious is leaving me. I am a thing apart. With the letter I belong and am lawful. Without it I am a weak calf abandon by the herd, a turtle without shell" (135). Florens senses that she is losing existence in what Lacan calls the symbolic order, the order of language and cultural exchange.

To register the effect on Florens of this second expulsion, Morrison turns to mirror imagery. That night Florens dreams that she looks into a beautiful blue lake but sees no self-reflection: "Where my face should be is nothing. . . . I put my mouth close enough to drink or kiss but I am not even a shadow there. Where is it hiding?" (162). To interpret Florens's dream image, we need to understand that, according to scholars of identity formation, identification with others "instantiates identity" as we locate a self-identity through the mirroring gaze of others.[18] Read this way, the point of the dream is clear: because others don't recognize her as a fellow human being, she feels as if she is "nothing."

The third time she is expelled is by the blacksmith, who is her lover. She looks to the blacksmith to validate her being in the world. His caressing touch on her body "is safe is belonging" (161); but when Florens hurts the little boy whom the blacksmith has adopted, he "knock[s] [her] away" from him and offers "no tender fingers to touch where [he] hurt [her]" (165).

The recurring motifs in Florens's narration—the signal importance of touching, of a mirroring reflection, and of cultural recognizability—all appear in the few pages in *Absalom* devoted to Charles Etienne Bon's life story. For both Faulkner and Morrison, the touch of flesh on flesh "cuts sharp" through culture's "decorous ordering" of "caste and color" (*Absalom* 111–12; emphases removed) and forges connection. Charles Bon longs for the touch of his father's hand: "he knew exactly what he wanted," "the physical touch even though in secret, hidden" (255). Similarly, the touch of Clytie's hand elicits from Miss Rosa the cry, "And you too, sister, sister?" (112–13; emphasis removed). But like Florens, whom the white church members refuse to touch and who by the novel's end is described as "untouchable" (179), Charles Etienne Bon learns early that his blackness is something to be erased and not touched. As a child, when Clytie washes him, she "scrub[s] at him with repressed fury as if she were trying to wash the smooth faint olive tinge from his skin" (161), and whenever Judith has to touch him, her hands "seemed at the moment of touching his body to lose all warmth and become imbued with cold implacable antipathy" (160).

Not only are Bon and Florens both denied self-affirming physical contact with others; they are also both culturally unrecognized. When Charles Etienne, a "white-colored man" (167), is brought to court for attacking a group of Negroes, the sentencing judge looks at the prisoner and says, "What are you?" (165; emphasis removed). The judge's question is striking. He asks not "who are you?" but "what are you?" The phrasing of the question tells us that, like Florens, who without her mistress's letter doesn't signify in culture, he too is something for which the dominant culture has no name, no signifier.[19]

Mirror imagery is another point of contact between the two narratives. In *Absalom*, in a sentence overburdened with clauses and interrupters, in a narration handed down to Quentin from his grandfather by way of his father, it is parenthetically noted that, when Charles Etienne is fourteen, Clytie or Judith finds hidden beneath his mattress a shard of broken mirror. No import is attached to the mirror, but if we read Bon's hidden mirror intertextually with Florens's missing reflection in a dream image, we can infer that the dominant culture's refusals to touch, see, or represent across artificial racial lines leave both Charles Etienne and Florens unmoored, with no coordinates to chart a self-identity. This reading aligns with the only words of Charles Etienne Bon that make their way to us through the filter of multiple white narrators. When asked who he is, he replies, "I dont know" (165).

At the end of *A Mercy*, when the blacksmith disowns Florens, she asks him, "Why are you killing me?," and he replies, "You are nothing but wilderness. No constraint. No mind" (166). Then, as he "shout[s] the word—mind, mind, mind—over and over and . . . laugh[s]" (166–67), Florens swings a hammer at the blacksmith's head. The contrast between "mind" and "wilderness" is the key to understanding the mindless violence that erupts in Florens and in Charles Etienne Bon. At one level, both Faulkner's and Morrison's novels are about the nature/culture dichotomy. Culture is produced by mind. It is a set of mental conceptualizations framed in word-symbols that a group in power assigns to material existence in the world. As we have seen, both Faulkner and Morrison are at pains to expose the power of culture's mentalizations over living people in the world. It is this determining power of culture's signifiers that a slave of Vaark's alludes to when she says, "We never shape the world. . . . The world shapes us" (83), and we see this domination of the word-sign at work in *Absalom* when Charles Etienne Bon is told "that he was, must be, a negro, who could neither have heard yet nor recognised the term 'nigger,' who even had no word for it in the tongue he knew" (161).

Underlying culture's symbolic meanings, the "mind" of which the blacksmith speaks is material existence in the world, what the blacksmith calls "wilderness." And, as he says, at the end of the novel Florens has become "wilderness." Told that she is culturally unmade, that she has "no consequence" (167) in the blacksmith's world of the mind's sym-bolizations, she feels that she is "living the dying inside" again even as within her "a darkness" (135) is growing. This "inside dark," she says, "is small, feathered and toothy," and when the blacksmith shouts the word "mind" over and over, she feels that "the only life" in her is a "clawy feathery thing" (136) that lifts its feathers, unfolds its wings, and attacks. The "clawy feathery thing" is Morrison's metaphor for material existence in the world that has been dismissed by culture. Feeling that it is being killed, this "dark matter . . . thick, unknowable, aching to be made into a world" (183), asserts its presence, its right to be in the world, through violence, the language of the body.[20]

In closing, I want to return to Charles Etienne Bon's compulsion to violence and the rationale offered for it by his white interpreters in *Absalom, Absalom!* We are told that the white community can see "no reason" (164) for this violence but that one man, Quentin's grandfather, "fumble[s], grope[s], grasp[s] the presence of that furious protest, that indictment of heaven's ordering, that gage flung into the face of what is." Grandfather is partially right. The violence is a "furious protest" that denotes a "presence." But Grandfather's elliptical, ambiguous language repeats the very insult that the "presence" protests. His language is typical of the discourse used by whites throughout the novel, which as Morrison points out, colludes in order not to see blackness. In assign-ing a cause for Bon's rage, Grandfather says that Bon protests "heaven's ordering" and "what is," leaving the reader to ask, "heaven's ordering" of what? and what is it that "is"? The "ordering" that Grandfather refers to is a social hierarchical ordering that enables white supremacy by the domination of people of color, but Grandfather's diction performs a kind of verbal sleight of hand. By calling this white-supremacist order "heav-en's ordering," he would make it divinely ordained. And by calling white domination "what is," he would, with words, make white suppression of blacks natural, innate, and fixed.

Both Faulkner and Morrison know well the power of language. In *Absalom, Absalom!*, Faulkner shows us that people of color are not only physically expelled from a white-dominant culture, they are also verbally expelled, and Morrison, who writes in *Beloved* that "definitions belong to the definers—not the defined," attempts in her novels to revisit verbal exclusion and undo it.[21] Above all, Morrison's texts trace back the signifier to its source in materiality. In *Beloved*, Sethe laments that she made the ink that schoolteacher uses to write his racist tract, and in *A Mercy*, at the end of the novel we learn that Florens has used a nail to carve her narration laboriously into the wooden walls and floors of Jacob Vaark's abandoned house. We can interpret this remarkable final image in multiple ways. At one level, Morrison means to make visible that the flesh and the material world are the substances that enable signification; but this image of the white man's house, the symbol of his legacy, now passed down to a black woman, may also carry another meaning. I suggest that we can read Florens, who is materially inscribing her story on the walls of the deceased patriarch's great house, as an avatar for Morrison herself, who carries on Faulkner's literary tradition by returning to black characters in his fiction, like Clytie, Charles Bon, and Bon's son, and continuing to tell their stories.[22]

NOTES

1. Some critics have argued that we should read Morrison's texts in relation to African American folk and oral tradition. See, for example, Denise Heinze, *The Dilemma of Double-Consciousness: Toni Morrison's Novels* (Athens: University of Georgia Press, 1993).

2. Interview with Nellie McKay in *Conversations with Toni Morrison*, ed. Danille Taylor-Guthrie (Jackson: University of Mississippi Press, 1994), 152.

3. Toni Morrison, "Faulkner and Women," in *Faulkner and Women: Faulkner and Yoknapatawpha, 1985*, ed. Doreen Fowler and Ann J. Abadie (Jackson: University Press of Mississippi, 1986), 296.

4. John N. Duvall, "Toni Morison and the Anxiety of Faulknerian Influence," in *Unflinching Gaze: Morrison and Faulkner Re-Envisioned*, ed. Carol A. Kolmerten, Stephen M. Ross, and Judith Bryant Wittenberg (Jackson: University of Mississippi Press, 1997), 8–9.

5. Morrison has talked about *Absalom* in interviews; she discusses *Absalom* in her *Playing in the Dark: Whiteness and the Literary Imagination* (New York: Vintage Books, 1993), 58. A sixteen-page chapter in her 1955 Cornell University master's thesis, "Virginia Woolf's and William Faulkner's Treatment of the Alienated," focuses primarily on Thomas Sutpen and Quentin Compson, and as scholars have noted, her character Golden Gray in *Jazz* seems to reinterpret *Absalom's* Charles Bon, and Circe in Morrison's *Song of Solomon* seems to revisit *Absalom's* Clytie.

6. Toni Morrison, "The Art of Fiction," interview with Elissa Schappell, *Paris Review* 129 (Fall 1993): 106.

7. Morrison, *Playing in the Dark*, 5.

8. Ibid., 8, 16.

9. William Faulkner, *Absalom, Absalom!*, rev. ed. (1936; New York: Vintage International, 1990), 80. All subsequent references to this work will be to this edition and will appear in the text.

10. Morrison, *Playing in the Dark*, 10.

11. In making this argument about the literary relationship of Faulkner and Morrison, I owe a debt to the work of a number of perceptive scholars. Carol A. Kolmerten, Stephen M. Ross, and Judith Bryant Wittenberg observe that "our reading of Faulkner has been—must be—profoundly changed by our reading of Morrison." See their "Introduction" to their edited work, *Unflinching Gaze: Morrison and Faulkner Re-Envisioned* (Jackson: University of Mississippi Press, 1997), xv. John Duvall points out that "placing Morrison against Faulkner is useful, not just for understanding Morrison, but for gaining a different critical purchase on Faulkner" (9). Patrick O'Donnell writes that "Morrison is committed in her novels to bringing black figures to the historical and narrative foreground." See Patrick O'Donnell, "Faulkner in Light of Morrison," in *Unflinching Gaze: Morrison and Faulkner Re-Envisioned*, ed. Carol A. Kolmerten, Stephen M. Ross, and Judith Bryant Wittenberg (Jackson: University of Mississippi Press, 1997), 227. Philip M. Weinstein has noted the "sparing representation" of black figures in Faulkner's novels. For example, he writes that Clytie in *Absalom, Absalom!* is "crucial to the articulation of a plot that never once articulates her." See Philip M. Weinstein, *What Else But Love? The Ordeal of Race in Faulkner and Morrison* (New York: Columbia University Press, 1996), 53.

12. See Duvall, "Toni Morrison," 13–15; Roberta Rubenstein, "History and Story, Sign and Design," in *Unflinching Gaze: Morrison and Faulkner Re-Envisioned*, ed. Carol A. Kolmerten, Stephen M. Ross, and Judith Bryant Wittenberg (Jackson: University of Mississippi Press, 1997), 167–80; Weinstein, *What Else But Love*, 147–53; Nancy Ellen Batty, "Riff, Refrain, Reframe: Toni Morrison's Song of Absalom," in *Unflinching Gaze: Morrison and Faulkner Re-Envisioned*, ed. Carol A. Kolmerten, Stephen M. Ross, and Judith Bryant Wittenberg (Jackson: University of Mississippi Press, 1997), 77–90; and Doreen Fowler, "Reading Faulkner through Morrison," in *Critical Insights: William Faulkner*, ed. Kathryn Stelmach Artuso (Ipswich, MA: Salem Press, 2013), 68–93.

13. Toni Morrison, *A Mercy* (New York: Vintage International, 2008), 104. All subsequent references to this work will be to this edition and will appear in the text.

14. Lacan writes, "Through the word—already a presence made of absence—absence itself gives itself a name. . . . And . . . there is born the world of meaning of a particular language in which the world of things will come to be arranged. . . . It is the world of words that creates the world of things." See Jacques Lacan, *Écrits: A Selection* (New York: Norton, 1977), 65.

15. See François Pitavy, "Some Remarks on Negation and Denegation in William Faulkner's *Absalom, Absalom!*," in *Faulkner's Discourse: An International Symposium*, ed. Lothar Honnighausen (Tubingen, Germany: Max Niemeyer Verlag, 1989), 25–32; Winfried Herget, "The Poetics of Negation in Faulkner's *Absalom, Absalom!*" in Honnighausen, ed., 33–37; and Jacques Pothier, "Negation in Faulkner: Saying No to Time and Creating One's Own Space," in Honnighausen, ed., 38–45.

16. Hélène Cixous, "The Laugh of the Medusa," in *New French Feminisms*, ed. Elaine Marks and Isabelle de Courtivron (Brighton, UK: Harvester, 1980), 251.

17. A flagrant example of her racial censorship is her refusal to see the picture of Bon's octoroon wife that Judith finds on Bon's dead body (*Absalom*, 286). In Miss Rosa's narration, Judith finds a photograph of herself on Bon's corpse (114).

18. Diana Fuss, *Identification Papers: Readings on Psychoanalysis, Sexuality and Culture* (New York: Routledge, 1995), 2.

19. In an essay that focuses on racial representation in Faulkner's *Light in August*, O'Donnell notes that Joe Christmas is similarly culturally excluded: "the abject, the non-figure, the non-identity" (222).

20. In Lacanian terms, what the blacksmith calls "wilderness" is the imaginary or pre-symbolic, a plane of existence that precedes conscious existence in the world. In the imaginary, the child is an uncognized, material, somatic existence. See Lacan, *Écrits*, 146–78. My essay, "Reading for the 'Other Side': *Beloved* and *Requiem for a Nun*," in *Unflinching Gaze: Morrison and Faulkner Re-Envisioned*, ed. Carol A. Kolmerten, Stephen M. Ross, and Judith Bryant Wittenberg (Jackson: University of Mississippi Press, 1997), 139–51, discusses similar violent eruptions of what Lacan calls the imaginary or the presymbolic in a different pair of novels by Morrison and Faulkner.

21. Toni Morrison, *Beloved* (New York: Vintage International, 1987), 225.

22. As support for my suggestion that the image is a veiled allusion to Morrison herself and Faulkner, I would point to a remark of Morrison's about Faulkner that seems to draw a parallel between herself and Faulkner as authors. In describing Faulkner, Morrison spoke of his peculiar and striking gaze: "He had a gaze that was different. It appeared, at that time, to be similar to a look, even a sort of staring, a refusal-to-look-away approach in his writing that I found admirable" ("Faulkner and Women," 297). What is remarkable about Morrison's description of Faulkner is that, consciously or unconsciously, this same image, "a refusal to look away," appears in the novel she was writing at the time of her appearance at Faulkner and Yoknapatawpha in 1985, *Beloved*, which describes Sethe as "the one who never looked away" (12). If we read Sethe (like Florens) as a persona for Morrison herself, then, at a latent level, Morrison may be pointing through her character to an authorial quality that she shares with Faulkner.

Natasha Trethewey's Joe Christmas and the Reconstruction of Mississippi Nativity

TED ATKINSON

In 2007, Natasha Trethewey, who serves as of this writing as both US Poet Laureate and Mississippi Poet Laureate, responded to a call by *Newsweek* magazine to list the five books that were most important to her. Trethewey ranked William Faulkner's *Light in August* second, alluding to a deeply personal investment in the novel when she explained that growing up biracial in Mississippi meant that the racially confused (and confusing) figure of Joe Christmas "spoke to identity issues I was dealing with."[1] This disclosure establishes an intriguing point of contact between two authors whose native ties to Mississippi are vital to their literary endeavors in general and to their probing explorations of race in particular. Trethewey's engagement with Faulkner is explicit in a poem titled "Miscegenation," which appears in her Pulitzer Prize–winning collection, *Native Guard*, published in 2006. The daughter of an African American mother and a white Canadian father who is also a poet, Trethewey signifies on Joe Christmas as part of a meditation on the traumatic effects of being born in Mississippi while antimiscegenation laws were still in effect. This work fits readily into a pattern in which Trethewey writes and speaks poignantly of a childhood shaped by rigidly constructed social mores and legal codes that defined her very person as taboo and illegal.

The reference to Joe Christmas in "Miscegenation" serves as a useful starting point for examining how *Native Guard* engages with *Light in August* through a series of shared themes and tropes that make for a complex and dynamic literary exchange between Trethewey and Faulkner. One of the most pronounced features of this intertextuality is the trope of nativity as embodied in the figure of the "Christmas child" through which Trethewey and Faulkner construct scenes of childhood trauma that show how the racial imperatives of the state intervene in the early stages of psychic development to make "legitimate" birth a condition of citizenship and social belonging. Both Trethewey and Faulkner expose how this process blurs the line culturally constructed to distinguish childhood from adulthood such that the two bleed into one another with serious consequences for those whose indeterminate or mixed-race identity produces not feelings of "legitimate" belonging but instead the longing to belong that comes with being labeled as "illegitimate." But Trethewey's take on the "Christmas child" accomplishes a productive reimagining of Faulkner as she returns to the scene of the "identity issues" that her initial reading of *Light in August* brought to the surface and enlists Joe Christmas in an endeavor to contend with the past as a means of reconstructing her Mississippi nativity so as to account for the pain of racial trauma and the desire to move beyond the debilitating effects it engenders. In so doing, Trethewey breaks the "tragic mulatto" mold that has formed around Faulkner's original and casts an alternative form suited to her confrontation with racial trauma in the process of redefining what it means to think of herself as a Mississippian. Natasha Trethewey's Joe Christmas is thus an integral component of a project of reclamation that involves literature, history, and memory and enables the poet to find a richly nuanced voice able to express the contradictory feelings and experiences of trauma and survival, of recollected exclusion and negotiated belonging, affecting what the poet has described as "the terrible beauty of my South—my Mississippi."[2]

In *Native Guard*, Trethewey merges the public sphere and the private domain to make legible and to monumentalize figures and events lost to the official record because of historical erasure or repressed memories of familial and individual trauma. Such figures range from the Louisiana Native Guard, an African American regiment of Union soldiers in the Civil War, to the poet's own mother, who was murdered by her former husband when Trethewey was nineteen. The poem "Miscegenation" appears in section III of the collection, which follows the deeply personal, sometimes confessional poems of section I and those in section II that stage vexed engagements with a history of racial oppression and strife within a wide scope encompassing Mississippi, the US South, the United States, and the Black Atlantic. The form is a variation on the ghazal—a type of poem composed of at least five couplets that are autonomous in terms of structure, theme, tone, and emotional content. The ghazal achieved prominence in thirteenth- and fourteenth-century Persia and evolved as a medium traditionally employed to express feelings of melancholy and longing that prompt metaphysical ruminations from the speaker. Seven couplets comprise Trethewey's poem, the fourteen-line structure indicating a meeting of East and West, a fusion of the ghazal and the sonnet constituting a miscegenated form that reinforces

the content announced in the title. This formal innovation yields a structure formidable enough to frame the troubled composite of emotions
that emerges from revisiting experiences of racial trauma shaped by the
social processes of racialization.

In the opening couplet, Trethewey establishes illegality as a frame of
reference for recounting the circumstances of her birth: "In 1965 my
parents broke two laws of Mississippi; / they went to Ohio to marry,
returned to Mississippi."[3] She further retraces the movements of her
parents in the United States from south to north and back to south,
then north again to her father's native Canada as they "followed a route
/ the same as slaves, the train slicing the white glaze of winter, leaving
Mississippi." In these lines, as is often the case in Trethewey's poetry, we
find mutually constitutive relations between space and time, place and
history, and "roots and routes," to borrow the phrase that Paul Gilroy
applies to the work of W. E. B. Du Bois and James Weldon Johnson.[4] Play
on language turns place names into signifiers of the societal condemna-
tion her parents drew by breaching laws and customs defining the racial
status quo in the Jim Crow South and the larger nation. Trethewey writes
that Cincinnati "begins with a sound like *sin*" and records "the sound of
wrong—*mis* in Mississippi." In this instance, she extends the pattern of
repetition established in the first two lines and continued throughout
the poem: stress placed on "Mississippi" and the phrase "in Mississippi"
in line endings. The formal element of end-placement thus functions
for Trethewey as a means of emplacement that reinforces the theme of
nativity. The poem charts familiar locales with subjective associations,
making the proper names signifiers of troubling personal memories. This
lyrical sound mapping segues into the engagement with Faulkner as the
first line of the next couplet invokes "Faulkner's Joe Christmas." In light
of the explicit reference, we might link the preceding description of the
journey undertaken by Trethewey's parents with Joe's travels after the
standoff with his stepfather, Simon McEachern, when Joe sets out on a
series of geographical border crossings fueled by the desire to test the
limits of the oppressive racial binary code that confines him and that he
repeatedly confounds through racially charged provocations.

In the second half of the poem, Trethewey makes the stress on nativity far more pronounced, adapting Christology to relate details of her life
to those of Joe Christmas's and thus to forge a comparative framework
that ultimately proves transformative for the poetic persona. Trethewey
explains that Joe Christmas "was born in winter, just like Jesus, given
his name / for the day he was left at the orphanage, his race unknown
in Mississippi." The phrase *race unknown* speaks to Joe's indeterminate
racial origins, according to the logic of the racial binary code, but it also

calls to mind the exclusionary practices of Jim Crow that define people with mixed-race identity as unworthy of being known, or recognized, as legitimate members of the community. While the arc of Joe Christmas's narrative from birth to death by lynching aligns with that of Jesus Christ from nativity to crucifixion, Trethewey's nativity story reverses the course and merges the coordinates. "I was born near Easter, 1966, in Mississippi," she recounts. The specific markers of time ("near Easter, 1966") and place ("in Mississippi") cast her nativity as a kind of crucifixion—the biracial child sacrificed to a birthplace whose laws and customs stipulate that being born "wrong" is her only birthright. The location of Trethewey's birthplace—definitively within the borders of Mississippi—places (in every sense of the word) her nativity story in contrast to that of Joe Christmas, whose birth and early years in the orphanage are clouded by an uncertainty about his exact whereabouts that underscores the racial ambiguity he comes to embody.[5] The turn from spatial to temporal orientation extends the crucifixion motif, as Trethewey recalls: "When I turned 33 my father said, *It's your Jesus year—you're the same / age he was when he died.*" The identical age and the enjambment—the first line of the couplet ends with *"you're the same"*—link Trethewey and Jesus, but the line also alludes to Joe Christmas, given that his arrival in Jefferson occurs in his Jesus year. These associations transform the poetic persona into a sort of trinity composed of Jesus-Joe-Natasha in which the elements of birth and death, nativity and crucifixion, converge to underscore the tragedy of imperiled being precluded from belonging.

What Trethewey hears in her Jesus year amounts to a death sentence from her father—an experience that further aligns the poetic persona with Jesus Christ and Joe Christmas. For Joe, the death sentence comes through the cultural transmission of ambiguous racial identity from father to son. Although this racial identity is uncertain, Joe inhabits a society that insists on defining race in no uncertain terms to maintain the hegemony of white supremacy. From this dominant ideological perspective, there must be a definitive answer to the question that Bobbie Allen succinctly puts to Joe: "What are you?"[6] The need to know Joe's racial identity sets the objectifying terms of her question and directs the gaze she fixes on him. This perception of Joe is far more acute in the case of his grandfather, Doc Hines, who maniacally believes that the Grand Father, God, grants him an answer to the question of Joe's racial essence through divine intervention. Hines orchestrates confirmation of this allegedly divine gift by projecting fantasies of shared racial knowing onto the white children in the orphanage. "They knowed," he says, implying that the white children who encounter the "black" Christmas child are innately capable of detecting racial essence (493).

What Hines believes he knows about Joe's racial makeup is what Joe begins to know in the orphanage as he becomes subject to racial marking as a product of miscegenation. This process starts with what Noel Polk defines as a primal scene involving surrogate parents—the intern who found him as an infant abandoned on the orphanage steps and the dietitian who feeds him.[7] Through careful manipulation, the grandfather influences the surrogate mother to speak on his behalf by articulating his racial fantasy. Revealing the secret of Joe's "blackness" to the orphanage matron, the dietitian says, "I think that children have a way of knowing things that grown people of your and my age dont see. Children, and old people like him, like that old man" (497). The matron's response— "We must place him. We must place him at once" (499)—expresses the immediate need to move Joe to an orphanage for black children, betraying a compulsion to assign a definitive racial category that connects the institutional operations of the orphanage to the racial prerogatives of the state. The scene exemplifies the process that Caroline F. Levander defines as "state and self intermingl[ing] through the child" to settle the question of belonging.[8] Levander claims that the child not only "represents the mythical racial purity of the nation-state or the often marginal civic status of racial others" but "more fundamentally constitutes the self as well as the state through representing racial identity as a constitutive element of each." This argument is readily applicable to Doc Hines's fantasy of detecting racial essence affirmed through the children on the playground and to the institutional directive to place Joe elsewhere because white supremacist ideology dictates that the discovery of his compromised whiteness requires recognition of his confirmed blackness.

Formative relations between the self and the state are integral to Trethewey's poetic meditations on what it means to be biracial in Mississippi and in the United States. The death sentence spoken by her father in "Miscegenation" suggests that the poet identifies with Joe's traumatic childhood experience of racial marking through a process that calls to mind Frantz Fanon's contention in *Black Skin, White Masks* that the family in Western societies functions as the nation in miniature when it comes to maintaining the regime of racial difference governed by white supremacy.[9] In poetry and interviews, Trethewey has expressed the pain she has felt as a consequence of her father's poem "Her Swing," in which he recollects watching his young daughter at play and writes that "I studied my crossbreed child."[10] This scene is eerily reminiscent of the descriptions of Doc Hines watching Joe Christmas on the orphanage playground with racially motivated curiosity. Trethewey has maintained that the most hurtful aspect of the line is her father's rendering of her as an object of racial fascination—the focus of the same kind of objectifying gaze applied to Joe Christmas, not just by Hines, but by all those compelled by the racial status quo to determine not *who* he is but *what* he is.[11]

In "South," a poem also collected in *Native Guard*, traces of the father's language are detectable in the mentality of the state as Trethewey recalls encountering Confederate iconography dotting the landscape upon her "return / to Mississippi, state that made a crime of me—mulatto, half-breed—native / in my native land, this place they'll bury me."[12] These lines reverberate with the trauma of Trethewey's criminalization at and by birth, but they simultaneously register as a bold redefinition of native status with all the complications of identification that it entails. The enjambment means that the terms *mulatto, half-breed* give way to *native*, which emphatically hangs at the end of the line. That Trethewey places herself "in my native land" and then envisions her burial in Mississippi stands in contrast to the racist placement of Joe Christmas through institutional measures and to Trethewey's own experience of having her birth framed in terms of criminalization by the legal codes of Jim Crow. This self-placement as a response to being placed suggests the poet's realization that coming to know who she is demands staging the titular "native guard" in large part on the grounds of Mississippi, where white supremacy once kept native status under close guard from her. Through the lines of "South," as Thadious M. Davis argues, "the poet restores her own physical self to the contemporary record and stakes claim to the very contradictions of her legal existence."[13] Renegotiating the terms of native status, Trethewey redefines and complicates the meaning of belonging as well, exploring a form of identification that accounts for the pain of exclusion and the desire for different emotional investments. In this regard, Trethewey attempts to contend with the melancholic effects of racial trauma that serve up a study in contradictions as they exert powerful and potentially debilitating influences on the racialized subject.

Anne Cheng offers a critical framework drawn from psychoanalytic theory that is useful for examining Trethewey's literary endeavor to confront racial trauma.[14] In *The Melancholy of Race*, Cheng points out the "still deep-seated, intangible, psychical complications for people living within a ruling episteme that privileges that which they can never be."[15] However, Cheng cautions against assuming that one with minority status cannot pursue "other relations to that injunctive ideal which can be self-affirming or sustaining." In a point readily applicable to Trethewey's engagement with Mississippi and the troubled past that it represents, Cheng argues that such a pursuit means that the minority subject must engage in "painful negotiation . . . with the demands of that social ideality, the reality of that always-insisted-on difference." Consequently, as Trethewey's project ably demonstrates, there is an urgent need for rethinking agency in the context of racial subjectivity to expand its meaning "beyond the assumption of a pure sovereign subject to other manifestations, forms, tonalities, and gradations of governance."[16] Only then, Cheng avers, can we comprehend "subjective agency as a convoluted, ongoing, generative, and at times self-contradicting negotiation with pain."

For Trethewey, the process of negotiation involves setting the desire for self-determination in the present and for the future against the conditions of history, society, and culture that determined her as tragically "illegitimate" in the past. In describing this dilemma, Trethewey has frequently repurposed terms with strong Faulknerian associations to explain the sense of responsibility that she feels to "tell about the South" in laying claim to it as a survivor, not just a victim, of racial trauma. The tall order of gaining sufficient perspective to account for the internal and external dimensions of this experience through the medium of poetry is apparent in Trethewey's observation that "what I have inherited to write is in my blood, in as much as my blood in the state of Mississippi was a problem, but that is a thing outside of me, not inside. That was law and custom, history and society."[17] This figurative rendering of blood as flowing internally to pump life into literary expression and constructed externally in keeping with the problem of the color line testifies to the agency that Trethewey exercises in confronting the legacies of discrimination.

The desire for such agency courses through *Native Guard*, not least in the closing lines of "Miscegenation," in which it animates a dramatic gesture toward empowered knowing and poetic emphasis. After the father's death sentence in the penultimate couplet—the marking of Trethewey's "*Jesus year*" as a season of death—the poem abruptly shifts course in the opposite seasonal direction through what might be called a life sentence. "It was spring, the hills green in Mississippi," Trethewey writes. At this point, the hybrid form of the poem becomes readily apparent as Trethewey combines the trademark Shakespearean delay of the *volta*, or turn, to the end of the sonnet with the conventional practice in the ghazal of citing the poet's name at the end. The opening of the final couplet thus becomes the poem's signature line, as it were. In the final couplet as a whole, Trethewey emphatically declares, "I know more than Joe Christmas did. Natasha is a Russian name— / though I'm not; it means *Christmas child*, even in Mississippi." Trethewey's claim to know more than Joe Christmas is crucial to the move beyond hopelessly tragic sensibility at the close of "Miscegenation." William Faulkner said of Joe Christmas that he didn't know what he was. He knew that he would never know what he was, and his only salvation in order to live with himself was to repudiate mankind, to live outside the human race. And he tried to do that but nobody would let him, the human race itself wouldn't let him. And I don't think he was bad, I think he was tragic. And his tragedy was that he didn't know what he was and would never know, and that to me is the most tragic condition that an individual can have—to not know who he was.[18]

Faulkner uses the objectifying terms found in Bobbie Allen's laconic query and in Doc Hines's racial fantasies until at the very end, when "what" suddenly gives way to "who" as he settles on not knowing as the crucial factor in Joe's doomed existence. Significantly, the epistemological advantage that Trethewey enjoys over Joe Christmas means that not only can she state her name for the record, but she can do so by tracing its origins, as well as what it means to her and for her as a strategy for avoiding merely rehearsing and stepping into the tragic role that Faulkner wrote for his doomed literary creation.

The turn in the poem where Trethewey writes of spring yields offspring in keeping with the trope of nativity; in effect, Trethewey gives herself new birth by assuming the persona of the "*Christmas child*" and redefining the nature of her kinship with Joe Christmas established when she first encountered him as a young reader. In terms of theme and imagery, this ending, figured as a surreal new beginning, alludes to the death and apparent afterlife of Joe Christmas at the end of chapter 19 in *Light in August*. On the floor of Hightower's kitchen, Joe is bleeding to death after Percy Grimm has castrated him and stepped back to join his cohorts in beholding the spectacle. The narrative focus shifts to Joe, who looks up at Grimm and the others "with peaceful and unfathomable and unbearable eyes" (742). Faulkner writes in language of biblical proportions that

> from out the slashed garments about his hips and loins the pent black blood seemed to rush like a released breath. It seemed to rush out of his pale body like the rush of sparks from a rising rocket; upon that black blast the man seemed to rise soaring into their memories forever and ever. They are not to lose it, in whatever peaceful valleys, beside whatever placid and reassuring streams of old age, in mirroring faces of whatever children they will contemplate old disasters and newer hopes. It will be there, musing, quiet, steadfast, not fading and not particularly threatful, but of itself alone, serene and triumphant. (743)

In a coauthored essay, Grace Elizabeth Hale and Robert Jackson note the symbolism of Christ's resurrection at work in this passage, adding that "the supposedly black Christmas takes on this identity not simply by dying, but by claiming a new life and presence" through the memories of Grimm and his cohorts.[19] Hale and Jackson further contend that, "in yoking Christmas's horrifying death to the racist white community's experience of the Christian mystery and redemption, Faulkner invokes blackness—indeed, a particularly stoic or long-suffering model of blackness—as a key resource upon which the redemption of the whites depends." These points are well made, but it is also important to allow for the expansive capabilities of the mythic Christmas, like the mythic Christ, to have an afterlife capable of transcending the bounds of the original narrative—in this case, the frame of memory calibrated to produce white redemption that Faulkner's text establishes. In this regard, the "Christmas child" that Trethewey fashions as her poetic persona in "Miscegenation" might be read as refusing to answer the call to serve as one of those "mirroring faces" that reflect tranquil, long-suffering silence that is "triumphant" only insofar as it enables reassuring feelings of white redemption. Instead, Trethewey draws on her experience of rereading *Light in August* to enlist Joe Christmas in a rewriting that envisions a way to "contemplate old disasters and new hopes" beyond the confines of the white redemption narrative or the tale of the tragic mulatto.

Confronting the past, Trethewey resists the model of trauma as hopelessly unknowable that formulates the victim as hopelessly tragic. She resists what Dominick LaCapra terms "acting out," a process by which "one is haunted or possessed by the past and performatively caught up in the compulsive repetition of traumatic scenes—scenes in which the past returns and the future is blocked or fatalistically caught up in a melancholic feedback loop."[20] Working through Joe Christmas, in part, Trethewey expresses the desire to "work through" trauma in the manner described by LaCapra as "an articulatory practice." In this mode, "one is able to distinguish between past and present and to recall in memory that something happened to one (or one's people) back then while realizing that one is living here and now with openings to the future."[21] The Faulknerian inheritance is profitable for Trethewey in this regard, as she thoroughly refigures her initial investment in Joe Christmas and applies it to a project of revisionary identification. The profit from this endeavor is not a utopian windfall of postracial triumph that underwrites white redemption and provides full compensation for the past and the pain that Trethewey has felt. But it does contribute to a hard-won purchase on native ground, with its "violent history" and "terrible beauty," that enables the poet to call Mississippi "my place in this world."[22] The poem "Miscegenation," like the racial category to which its title refers, speaks to "what" Natasha Trethewey once was according to the racist ideology of Jim Crow, but it also powerfully testifies to what she has come to know now, which is "more than Joe Christmas did": that the painful negotiation involved in discovering who she is opens up space for thinking through new forms of belonging, even in Mississippi.

NOTES

1. Natasha Trethewey, "My Five Most Important Books," *Newsweek*, August 6, 2007, 15.

2. Lisa DeVries, "Because of Blood: Natasha Trethewey's Historical Memory—Interview," *The Common Reader* 26, no. 6 (2008), http://www.ecu.edu/english/tcr/26-6/trethewayinterview.html.

3. Natasha Trethewey, "Miscegenation," in *Native Guard* (New York: Houghton-Mifflin, 2006), 36. All subsequent references to the poem are from this edition.

4. Paul Gilroy, *The Black Atlantic: Modernity and Double Consciousness* (Cambridge, MA: Harvard University Press, 1993), 133.

5. I wish to credit Jay Watson for pointing out the significance of this contrast. The fact that Trethewey can specifically locate her origins in Mississippi brings the matter of uncertainty with regard to Joe's native status into focus. After all, it is difficult to know whether Joe is born in rural Mississippi or Tennessee or Arkansas or to pinpoint the location of the orphanage. The blurring of the border between states thus serves as a spatial metaphor for Joe's impending trouble with the color line. In addition, this difference in spatial orientation signals the knowledge deficit that Trethewey uses to punctuate the comparison between herself and Joe near the end of "Miscegenation."

6. William Faulkner, *Light in August, Novels, 1930–1935*, ed. Joseph Blotner and Noel Polk (New York: Library of America, 1985), 543. Subsequent references to this edition will be cited parenthetically in the text.

7. Noel Polk, *Children of the Dark House: Text and Context in Faulkner* (Jackson: University Press of Mississippi, 1998), 84.

8. Caroline F. Levander, *Cradle of Liberty: Race, the Child, and National Belonging from Thomas Jefferson to W. E. B. Du Bois* (Durham, NC: Duke University Press, 2006), 6.

9. Frantz Fanon, *Black Skin, White Masks*, trans. Richard Philcox (New York: Grove Press, 2008), 127. Fanon describes the white family as "the guardian of a certain structure. Society is the sum of all families. The family is an institution: i.e., the social group or the nation" (127).

10. Eric Trethewey, "Her Swing," *Prairie Schooner* 54, no. 3 (1980): 48.

11. Trethewey has spoken in interviews about the damaging effects of her father's line. The line appears verbatim and in italics in Natasha Trethewey, "Knowledge," in her *Thrall* (New York: Houghton-Mifflin, 2012), 30.

12. Natasha Trethewey, "South," in her *Native Guard*, 46.

13. Thadious M. Davis, *Southscapes: Geographies of Race, Region, and Literature* (Chapel Hill: University of North Carolina Press, 2011), 76.

14. The use of psychoanalytic theory to explore constructions of race and the painful experiences of those marked by racial difference has been controversial, to say the least. Many scholars working in African American literature have been reluctant to apply this model out of concern that emphasis on individual racial subjectivity diminishes the far more important social factors that contribute to racial oppression. Moreover, there is serious concern that concentrating on the dysfunctional elements of the family romance runs the risk of perpetuating conceptions of blackness as a pathological condition. Finally, the

Eurocentric perspective of psychoanalysis leads many scholars to question its efficacy as a model for examining black experience. However, in Claudia Tate's *Psychoanalysis and Black Novels: Desire and the Protocols of Race* (New York: Oxford University Press, 1998), we find a compelling justification for the psychoanalytic approach. Tate notes the controversy and acknowledges the concerns of detractors, but she insists on the psychoanalytic approach as a valid and productive endeavor. Viewing a black text as "partly self-conscious fantasy," Tate argues, "facilitates our speculating about the author's inscription of pleasure and pain in the text" (17). Tate calls attention to repetition in discourses of literary analysis and psychoanalysis as a serious critical problem: "Repeating the popular racial story calcifies our roles in the prescriptive racial plots; and referring to familiar psychoanalytic models does the same thing." For Tate, object-relations theory offers a solution by opening up a "'transitional space' between past circumstances and future possibility" (20) to establish "a dialectic between desire and the cultural/material effects of racial difference" (21). This critical perspective has heavily influenced my thinking about the ambivalence of Trethewey's take on Mississippi in poetry and interviews, particularly the elements of pleasure and pain involved in her understanding of native status. I am grateful to Lisa Hinrichsen for suggesting this line of critical inquiry.

15. Anne Cheng, *The Melancholy of Race* (New York: Oxford University Press, 2000), 7.

16. Ibid., 15.

17. See DeVries, "Because of Blood." In this interview, Trethewey credits the poet Philip Levine with prompting her to think about the predicament of having to write about what one is given. Interestingly, she distinguishes her conception of blood from that of August Wilson—specifically, his notion of "blood memory"—and thus walks back earlier statements about blood that might be construed as essentialist. See, for instance, John Calvasina and Laura Brun, "Writing on the Knife's Edge: An Interview with Natasha Trethewey," *Hot Metal Bridge* (Fall 2012), http://hotmetalbridge.org/conflict-confluence/writing-on-the-knifes-edge-an-interview-with-natasha-trethewey.

18. Frederick Landis Gwynn and Joseph Leo Blotner, eds., *Faulkner in the University* (Charlottesville: University of Virginia Press, 1995), 118.

19. Grace Elizabeth Hale and Robert Jackson, "'We're Trying Hard as Hell to Free Ourselves': Southern History and Race in the Making of William Faulkner's Literary Terrain," in *A Companion to William Faulkner*, ed. Richard C. Moreland (Malden, MA: Blackwell, 2007), 37.

20. Dominick LaCapra, *Writing History, Writing Trauma* (Baltimore: Johns Hopkins University Press, 2001), 21.

21. Ibid., 21–22.

22. DeVries, "Because of Blood."

Contributors

Ted Atkinson is associate professor of English at Mississippi State University and author of *Faulkner and the Great Depression: Aesthetics, Ideology, and Cultural Politics* (2006). He currently serves as editor of *Mississippi Quarterly*.

Thadious M. Davis is Geraldine R. Segal Professor of American Social Thought and Professor of English at the University of Pennsylvania. She is the author of *Games of Property: Law, Race, Gender, and Faulkner's "Go Down, Moses"* and *Southscapes: Geographies of Race, Region, and Literature*.

Matthew Dischinger is a postdoctoral fellow in the Department of English at Louisiana State University. He is completing a book, "South of the Twenty-First Century: The Place of Melancholia in Twenty-First Century Fiction."

Dotty Dye is a PhD candidate in English literature at Arizona State University. She is at work on her dissertation, "Intersecting Anglo Transnationalisms: Marginal Modernists in France."

Chiyuma Elliott is an assistant professor of African American studies at the University of California, Berkeley. Elliott received her MFA in creative writing from Warren Wilson College and her PhD in American studies from the University of Texas at Austin. A former Stegner Fellow, Elliott's poems have appeared in the *African American Review*, *Callaloo*, the *Notre Dame Review*, the *PN Review*, and other journals. She has received fellowships from the American Philosophical Society, the James Irvine Foundation, and the Vermont Studio Center. Elliott's first book of poems, *California Winter League*, will be published in 2015 by Unicorn Press.

Doreen Fowler, professor of English at the University of Kansas, is the author of *Faulkner: The Return of the Repressed* (1997), *Drawing* *the Line: The Father Reimagined in Faulkner, Wright, O'Connor, and Morrison* (2013), and the coeditor of eleven volumes of the proceedings of the annual Faulkner and Yoknapatawpha Conference.

Joseph Fruscione is the author of *Faulkner and Hemingway: Biography of a Literary Rivalry* and is currently editing *Teaching Hemingway and Modernism.* He taught college English and First-Year Writing for nearly fifteen years in Washington, DC, where he continues to teach classes on various American authors at the Politics & Prose bookstore and works as a freelance editor and writing consultant. He is a regular writer for the *Chronicle of Higher Education, Inside Higher Ed*, and *Hybrid Pedagogy* and has twice appeared on *PBS NewsHour's* "Making Sense" segment (March 2013, February 2014) to talk about how adjunct issues are affecting higher education.

T. Austin Graham is assistant professor of English and comparative literature at Columbia University. He is the author of *The Great American Songbooks: Musical Texts, Modernism, and the Value of Popular Culture* (2013) and at work on a study of American historical fiction in the twentieth century.

Rachel Eliza Griffiths is a poet and photographer. Her visual and literary work has been widely published. She is the recipient of numerous awards, including fellowships from the Provincetown Fine Arts Work Center, the Cave Canem Foundation, the Vermont Studio Center, the New York State Summer Writers Institute, Soul Mountain, and the Millay Residency. Her fourth book, *Lighting the Shadow*, was published in April 2015 by Four Way Books. Griffiths teaches creative writing at Sarah Lawrence College and lives in Brooklyn, New York.

Derrick Harriell is an assistant professor of English and African American studies at the University of Mississippi and teaches community writing workshops. He has worked as assistant poetry editor for *Third World Press* and the *Cream City Review.* He received his PhD in English from the University of Wisconsin, Milwaukee, and an MFA in creative writing from Chicago State University. A two-time Pushcart nominee, Harriell's poems have appeared in various literary journals and anthologies. His second collection of poems, *Ropes*, won the 2014 Mississippi Institute of Arts and Letters Poetry Award.

Lisa Hinrichsen earned her PhD from Boston University and is an assistant professor at the University of Arkansas. She has contributed essays to the *Southern Literary Journal, Journal of Modern Literature,* and *African American Review*, among other publications. Her book, *Possessing the Past: Trauma, Imagination, and Memory in Post-Plantation Southern Literature*, was published by Louisiana State University Press in 2015.

Randall Horton is the recipient of the Gwendolyn Brooks Poetry Award, the Bea Gonzalez Poetry Award, and a National Endowment of the Arts Fellowship in Literature. Horton is a Cave Canem Fellow, a member of the Affrilachian Poets, and a member of The Symphony: The House that Etheridge Built. Horton is assistant professor of English at the University of New Haven. An excerpt from his memoir, *Roxbury*, has been published by Kattywompus Press. Triquarterly / Northwestern University Press published his latest poetry collection, *Pitch Dark Anarchy*, in 2013.

George Hutchinson is professor of English and the Newton C. Farr Professor of American Culture at Cornell University. He is currently writing a book on American literature and culture in the 1940s, for which he won a Guggenheim Fellowship in 2011–2012.

Andrew Leiter is an associate professor of English at Lycoming College and the author of *In the Shadow of the Black Beast: African American Masculinity in the Harlem and Southern Renaissances* (2010).

John Wharton Lowe is Barbara Methvin Distinguished Professor at the University of Georgia. He is the author or editor of seven books, including the forthcoming *Calypso Magnolia: The Caribbean Side of the South,* and is currently writing the authorized biography of Ernest J. Gaines.

Jamaal May was born in Detroit, Michigan, where he later taught poetry in public schools and worked as a freelance audio engineer. His first book, *Hum* (Alice James Books), received the American Library Association's Notable Book Award, *Foreword Reviews'* Book of the Year Silver Medal, and an NAACP Image Award nomination. Additional recent honors include the Spirit of Detroit Award, the J. Howard and Barbara M. J. Wood Prize from *Poetry*, and fellowships from Rose O'Neil Literary House, Lannan Foundation, and the Civitella Ranieri Foundation in Italy. May is currently a *Kenyon Review* fellow and codirects Organic Weapon Arts with Tarfia Faizullah.

Ben Robbins is a Postdoctoral Honors Fellow at the John F. Kennedy Institute for North American Studies of the Freie Universität in Berlin. His doctoral thesis, which he is currently developing into a monograph, was titled "Gender, Film, and Culture in the Novels and Screenwriting of William Faulkner."

Tim A. Ryan is associate professor of English at Northern Illinois University and author of *Calls and Responses: The American Novel of Slavery since "Gone with the Wind"* (2008) and *Yoknapatawpha Blues: Faulkner's Fiction and Southern Roots Music* (2015).

Sharron Eve Sarthou is assistant professor of English and English coordinator at Rust College. She is currently researching a book manuscript on the blans in Haiti, "Risible, Responsible, and Invisible: We, Too, Are Haiti."

Jenna Sciuto is an assistant professor of English at the Massachusetts College of Liberal Arts. Her research analyzes depictions of racism, sexual violence, and colonial inheritance in a range of novels from Rwanda, Haiti, and the United States.

James Smethurst is professor of Afro-American studies at the University of Massachusetts at Amherst. He is the author of *The African American Roots of Modernism: From Reconstruction to the Harlem Renaissance* (2011).

Index

CPSIA information can be obtained
at www.ICGtesting.com
Printed in the USA
BVHW07s0601060618
518318BV00001B/4/P